MOVING A MOUNTAIN

Moving a Mountain

Transforming the Role of Contingent Faculty in Composition Studies and Higher Education

Edited by

EILEEN E. SCHELL
Syracuse University

PATRICIA LAMBERT STOCK
Michigan State University

National Council of Teachers of English
1111 W. Kenyon Road, Urbana, Illinois 61801-1096

Staff Editor: Rita D. Disroe
Interior Design: Jenny Jensen Greenleaf
Cover Design: Carlton Bruett

NCTE Stock Number: 55081-3050

It is the policy of NCTE in its journals and other publications to provide a
forum for the open discussion of ideas concerning the content and the teaching of English and the language arts. Publicity accorded to any particular
point of view does not imply endorsement by the Executive Committee, the
Board of Directors, or the membership at large, except in announcements
of policy, where such endorsement is clearly specified.

Library of Congress Cataloging-in-Publication Data

Moving a mountain: transforming the role of contingent faculty in
composition studies and higher education/edited by Eileen E. Schell,
Patricia Lambert Stock.
        p. cm.
    Includes bibliographical references and index.
    ISBN 0-8141-5508-1
        1. College teachers, Part-time—United States. 2. College teachers—
Tenure—United States. I. Schell, Eileen E. II. Stock, Patricia L.
III. National Council of Teachers of English.
    LB2331.72 .M69 2000
    378.1'21—dc21

                                                    00-064067

From Eileen Schell—
For Connie Hale,
my first-year composition teacher,
whose intellectual guidance and inspirational pedagogy
changed my life

From Patti Stock—
For Vernon Robert Lambert,
an exploited worker,
and
Vernon Robert Lambert Jr.,
a gifted teacher and union leader

CONTENTS

ACKNOWLEDGMENTS xi

INTRODUCTION: WORKING CONTINGENT FACULTY IN[TO] HIGHER
EDUCATION
Eileen E. Schell and Patricia Lambert Stock 1

I Transforming the Cultural and Material Conditions
of Contingent Writing Faculty: The Personal and
the Institutional

1 *Shadows of the Mountain*
Chris M. Anson and Richard Jewell 47

2 *Non-Tenure-Track Instructors at UALR:*
Breaking Rules, Splitting Departments
Barry M. Maid 76

3 *The Best of Times, the Worst of Times:*
One Version of the "Humane" Lectureship
Eva Brumberger 91

4 *The Material and the Cultural as Interconnected Texts:*
Revising Material Conditions for Part-Time Faculty
at Syracuse University
Carol Lipson and Molly Voorheis. 107

5 *Trafficking in Freeway Flyers: (Re)Viewing Literacy,*
Working Conditions, and Quality Instruction
Helen O'Grady 132

II Collectivity and Change in Non-Tenure-Track
Employment: Collective Bargaining, Coalition
Building, and Community Organizing

6 *The Real Scandal in Higher Education*
Walter Jacobsohn 159

7 *Faculty at the Crossroads: Making the Part-Time Problem a Full-Time Focus*
Karen Thompson 185

8 *How Did We Get in This Fix? A Personal Account of the Shift to a Part-Time Faculty in a Leading Two-Year College District*
John C. Lovas 196

9 *A Place to Stand: The Role of Unions in the Development of Writing Programs*
Nicholas Tingle and Judy Kirscht 218

10 *Same Struggle, Same Fight: A Case Study of University Students and Faculty United in Labor Activism*
Elana Peled, Diana Hines, Michael John Martin, Anne Stafford, Brian Strang, Mary Winegarden, and Melanie Wise 233

11 *Climbing a Mountain: An Adjunct Steering Committee Brings Change to Bowling Green State University's English Department*
Debra A. Benko 245

III **Rethinking Non-Tenure-Track Faculty Roles and Rewards**

12 *Distance Education: Political and Professional Agency for Adjunct and Part-Time Faculty, and GTAs*
Danielle DeVoss, Dawn Hayden, Cynthia L. Selfe, and Richard J. Selfe Jr. 261

13 *The Scholarship of Teaching: Contributions from Contingent Faculty*
Patricia Lambert Stock, Amanda Brown, David Franke, and John Starkweather 287

14 *What's the Bottom-Line? Literacy and Quality Education in the Twenty-First Century*
Eileen E. Schell 324

SELECT BIBLIOGRAPHY: CONTINGENT LABOR ISSUES IN COMPOSITION STUDIES AND HIGHER EDUCATION (CURRENT TO 1998)
Margaret M. Cunniffe and Eileen E. Schell 341

Contents

INDEX 383

EDITORS 395

CONTRIBUTORS 397

ACKNOWLEDGMENTS

L ike all intellectual projects, ours is indebted to a number of people, and we wish to thank them.

From Eileen: My debts to others begin in graduate school when I first began writing about the issue of contingent employment. I thank my mentors at the University of Wisconsin–Milwaukee— Lynn Worsham, Alice Gillam, and Chuck Schuster—who encouraged me to speak my mind, to challenge my thinking, and to find ways to create ethical, pedagogically sound employment practices in composition.

I also thank three faculty activists who have shaped my thinking about contingent employment: Linda Pratt, from the University of Nebraska at Lincoln; Karen Thompson, from Rutgers University; and Sharon Crowley, from Arizona State University. Working from different vantage points, they have kept the issue of part-time labor at the forefront of academic conferences and publications. I thank Anthony Scott from the University of Louisville for his help with the bibliography.

Closer to home I thank Robert Jensen, dean of the College of Arts and Sciences at Syracuse University, for granting me a research leave that allowed me to complete this project; Keith Gilyard and Louise Phelps for helping to make the leave possible and for encouraging and inspiring my work. I also thank the professional writing instructors at Syracuse University who continually challenge me to think in more complicated ways about the issue of part-time employment and who daily challenge and inspire me to be a better writing teacher.

The true debt in this book is always to my mother, Neva D. Schell, and my late father, Robert E. Schell, M.S. As a child growing up on a family farm in eastern Washington state, I was frequently privy to my parent's mealtime debates over the labor

problems they were experiencing on the farm. From those discussions, I learned a great deal about sound, ethical employment
practices.

Profound thanks to Connie Hale, my first-year composition
teacher at the University of Washington in 1983, to whom I dedi-
cate this book. Last but not least, my greatest thanks goes to my
husband, Thomas C. Kerr, Ph.D., who took part-time positions
from 1993 to 1998 and followed my career until he was recently
appointed to a faculty role at Long Island University–Brooklyn.

From Patti: Of the many people to whom I am indebted for what
and how I think about teaching, learning, scholarship, fair employment practices, and their relationships to one another, I thank,
particularly, talented part-time and adjunct faculty and principled
academic administrators with whom I have had the privilege of
working at Michigan State University, the University of Michigan, Syracuse University, and the National Council of Teachers
of English. And I thank, especially, Michigan State University,
for a research leave that allowed me to complete this book project.

For what I understand more fully because of our conversations about issues surrounding the work of part-time and adjunct faculty, I thank Ann Austin, Louise Wetherbee Phelps, Janet
Swenson, Sharon Thomas, and Elaine Yakura.

For supporting my work and encouraging me to act on my
best visions of it, I thank several academic leaders with whom it
has been my privilege to work on projects important to our profession: Robert F. Banks, John W. Eadie, Daniel Fader, Miles
Myers, Louise Wetherbee Phelps, Jay L. Robinson, Lou Anna
Kimsey Simon, Barbara C. Steidle, and Donald Straney.

For excellent research assistance and wonderful good humor,
I thank Margaret Cunniffe and Sara Cole.

For years of inspiring conversations about education, I thank
you, Richard.

And, one more time, Heidi and Andrew, "I lucky to you."

From Eileen and Patti: Working together on this book has been a
gift to us. We have learned so much from one another; enjoyed
one another's company so much. We thank one another for good,
hard work that we believe in.

Working Contingent Faculty in[to] Higher Education

EILEEN E. SCHELL
Syracuse University, Syracuse, New York

PATRICIA LAMBERT STOCK
Michigan State University, East Lansing

In the utopian novel, Moving the Mountain, *feminist Charlotte Perkins Gilman imagines a society based on gender equity in times when gender equity was not yet realizable. In* Moving a Mountain: Transforming the Role of Contingent Faculty in Composition Studies and Higher Education, *we imagine a university where contingent faculty are recognized and rewarded equitably in our own time.*

During the last thirty years, the number of part-time and adjunct faculty in American higher education has grown dramatically. Problems associated with shifting enrollments, changing student populations, and funding cuts for higher education have led the academy to turn to contingent faculty to fulfill its mission. The result is that now, at the beginning of the twenty-first century, a system of higher education caught between fiscal constraints and the need to provide growing numbers of diverse students diverse course offerings has turned what it undertook as a temporary hiring strategy into a permanent one.[1]

To better understand this phenomenon, various research communities have studied contingent faculty—that is, their characteristics, the nature and quality of their work, the reasons why their numbers are growing, their working conditions, and the potential long-term consequences for postsecondary education of growing numbers of part-time and adjunct faculty and declining numbers of full-time faculty and tenure-track faculty. During the 1970s and 1980s, social scientists with particular interests in higher education as well as researchers in disciplines with substantial numbers of contingent faculty developed a body of empirical and phenomenological knowledge about contingent faculty. This research led academic policymakers, administrators, and professional associations in the late 1980s and the 1990s to develop guiding principles and position statements designed to influence hiring practices and working conditions affecting these faculty. The 1990s saw all concerned looking again, carefully, at issues surrounding the work of contingent faculty in the light of broader discussions aimed at reconsidering the work of all postsecondary faculty and reforming the shape of higher education in the United States. Not the least of reasons for this renewed attention is concern that academics are too little invested in undergraduate education.

The Academy Turns to Contingent Labor

Three factors are generally acknowledged to account for higher education's turn to contingent faculty to accomplish its mission, particularly to fulfill the teaching of lower-division courses: flexible staffing, responsiveness to needs arising in particular specializations and curricular areas, and fiscal constraints.

Between 1970 and 1985, demographers predicted a decline in student enrollments that did not materialize. Part-time faculty who were hired to meet what had been deemed a temporary need became a fixed labor force when enrollments remained stable. Policies and programs developed in the late 1960s and the 1970s brought underserved populations into the academy in substantial numbers, maintaining—even increasing—the number of students enrolled in higher education. Universities and colleges also began to hire contingent faculty to do more than supplement their existing faculties and accommodate shifts in student interests and career demands (Schuster, 1997, pp. 4–5). The academy turned to part-time and adjunct faculty to staff lower-division undergraduate courses such as first-year composition and introductory math, courses that full-time, tenure-track faculty at many institutions prefer not to teach.

This staffing strategy worked for a number of reasons, not the least of which is the fact that the last thirty years have been a "buyer's market" in the academy. Growth of the "research paradigm" and graduate education (to which tenure-track faculty increasingly devoted their energies as growing numbers of contingent faculty began to teach lower-division courses) led to increased production of doctoral and master's degree candidates who were prepared to become a next generation of full-time, tenure-track faculty. Their degree work completed, most of these candidates found that the only faculty roles available to them were part-time or non-tenure-track appointments (Abel, 1984, p. 2).

Given a workforce with unanticipated and constrained options, the academy was easily able to hire qualified faculty to fill contingent positions. In so doing, it was also able to save money in instructional budgets and to bypass skyrocketing fringe benefits costs at a time when government funding for education declined dramatically and the economy moved into recession. While 62 percent of all part-time faculty are on short-term contracts (Gappa & Leslie, 1997, p. 12), only 17 percent get medical benefits from the institutions in which they work; only 20 percent earn retirement benefits; and only 9 percent receive tuition benefits (Gappa, 1997, p. 18). The cost savings realized by institutions that do not provide benefits to contingent faculty are clear and dramatic.[2]

Landmark studies of higher education in the United States over the past thirty years document not only the reasons why the academy turned to contingent faculty but also the problematic working conditions in which these faculty labor. Judith Gappa and David Leslie call attention to these conditions in the introduction to their important book, *The Invisible Faculty*, when they reproduce a part-time faculty member's claim that she was dropped from her university's faculty because she "publicly criticized the school's treatment of its adjunct faculty" (1993, p. xi). Describing her working conditions in a local newspaper, the faculty member, a nominee for the National Book Award, outlines what numerous studies conducted during the 1970s and 1980s demonstrated to be an all-too-common situation:

> because I am . . . an adjunct faculty [member], I am denied access to the support and encouragement that full-time faculty are entitled to . . . . [We] receive no benefits, no health insurance, no pension, no paid vacation, no office space, no telephone, and no sabbatical. (p. xi)

With reference to working conditions like these, Gappa and Leslie give voice to an obvious question: "How can institutions expect people of talent to contribute to quality educational programs when those same people are victims of medieval employment conditions" (Gappa & Leslie, p. xi).

The working conditions of contingent faculty in higher education create widespread ill effects for all concerned. Although studies published since Gappa and Leslie's have not discounted these ill effects, they have focused more centrally on the proliferation of part-time and non-tenure-track roles in the academy and on the potential long-term consequences of the turn to contingent faculty for higher education as we know it. In "Reconfiguring the Professoriat: The Part-Timer Phenomenon and Implications for the Academic Profession" (1997), for example, Jack H. Schuster, drawing his data from the National Survey of Post-Secondary Faculty, reports that in fall 1992, part-time faculty comprised 41.6 percent of all "instructional faculty and staff" (p. 2). Projecting a hiring trend apparent since the mid-1970s, in 1997, Schuster estimated that "the number likely [had] reached 43 or 44 percent" (p. 2). In a paper he prepared for a 1997 *Conference on the Growing Use of Part-Time and Adjunct Faculty*, Ernst Benjamin, Secretary of the American Association of University Professors, confirms Schuster's observations: From 1975 to 1993, the growth of part-time faculty positions far outstripped the growth of full-time tenure-track positions. Benjamin notes, "[P]art-time faculty have grown four-times (97%) more than full-time (25%). While the number of non-tenure-track faculty has increased by 88%, the number of probationary faculty has actually declined by 9%" (Benjamin, Table 1). To state the case another way: Faculty who work off the tenure-track comprise over half of all teaching faculty in American colleges and universities. This figure does not account for the 202,819 graduate students who also teach (Benjamin, Table 2).

These employment statistics tell a story of a system of higher education transforming itself from a bifurcated faculty of full-time faculty supplemented by part-time faculty to a trifurcated faculty of "the 'core' (tenured/tenure-track faculty), the off-track full-time faculty, and the part-time/adjunct faculty" (Schuster, 1997, p. 9). Patterns indicate that we have entered an era of contingent employment in higher education that parallels a trend in the corporate, industrial, and service sectors of both the national and the global economy. It appears to be ironic, but true, that as higher education has become increasingly democratic, admitting and educating "millions of minorities, women, older students, low-income persons, the handicapped, and other non-traditional students" (Bowen & Schuster, 1986, p. 6), academic hiring practices have become increasingly undemocratic.

The turn to contingent faculty in the academy confronts us with challenges and consequences that call for responsible and ethical solutions. In the 1990s, we developed deeper understandings of the characteristics and the work of contingent faculty based on empirical studies, statistical summaries, and analyses of trends and issues conducted by researchers of higher education as well as personal narratives, case studies, and polemical and position statements of part-time and adjunct faculty and their subject matter organizations.

Developing conversations among policymakers and administrators of higher education in their professional communities (e.g., the American Association of Higher Education's *Faculty Role and Rewards* and *New Pathways* projects) and among discipline-based faculty in the *Coalition on the Academic Workforce* (CAW, a collaboration of ten of these faculty's professional organizations formed in 1997),[3] offer promise for the construction of a discourse capable of addressing the problems in ways that are just as practical and forward-looking as they are immediately expedient. In our view, unless and until there is a confluence of discussion among the parties invested in the issues arising from the use and abuse of contingent faculty in the academy, problems will increase rather than decrease. For example, current trends will go unchecked, the generative insights and promising practices being developed in one disciplinary community or another, in one professional community or another, in one locality or another, will go generally unrecognized, and all of us invested in higher education—students, tenure-track faculty, contingent faculty, academic administrators, and the publics the academy serves—will lose.

The growing reliance on contingent employment is not unrelated to what many predict will be the erosion of the tenure and faculty governance system of higher education, the virtual absence of tenure-line faculty in lower-division teaching, and the transformation of a system of higher education that is generally regarded as the finest in the world into one in which the long-term benefits of quality education will have been sacrificed for short-term economic gains.

We do not intend in this volume to advocate a dogmatic or single-minded agenda for improving non-tenure-track faculty's working—and teaching—conditions. The problems are far too complex to be addressed with uniform solutions. Rather, our aim is modest and twofold. First, we aim to present for the information and review of the field of composition studies (and for others in higher education who will recognize in this field employment practices and working conditions that are developing in their own) precursors of things to come in an academy that is establishing a part-time and adjunct faculty workforce to carry it into the twenty-first century. Composition studies may well be viewed as a canary in an academic mine in which contingent faculty have worked (at risk, underground, out of sight) to support others' more visible, more attractive labor. Second, we aim to draw attention to the work of a variety of faculty and academic administrators who are striving to effect productive and ethical change in the working conditions of non-tenure-track faculty at diverse institutions. We invite discussion of the various forms their work is taking as a means of grounding policy discussions in practical matters. In so doing, we encourage the development of the kind of discourse we believe must be constructed if those of us with vested interests are to shape policies and practices that ensure quality education.

Our own involvement in these issues is the result of both personal experience and professional concern. Schell began her career as a part-time writing instructor at a community college where she learned firsthand about the problematic working conditions of adjunct writing faculty. In graduate school, she began to write and speak about the connection between writing faculty's working conditions and students' learning conditions. As a feminist, she also began to investigate the gendering of part-time work. Hired directly out of graduate school into an assistant professorship with administrative responsibilities, she went from researching and writing about adjunct issues to working with part- and full-time writing faculty to create a viable teaching culture. She continues to work on a local level at Syracuse University and on a national level within the Conference on College Composition and Communication to bring the issue of employment equity and quality education together.

Stock began her career in higher education as a lecturer with the English Composition Board at the University of Michigan while enrolled in the Ph.D. Program in English and Education. After completing her degree work, Stock accepted an invitation to become associate professor of English and writing and associate director of the Writing Program at Syracuse University, where, among other things, she worked with professional writing instructors to develop policies and practices for part-time and adjunct faculty's self-definition of standards for and peer review of their work. On leave from her role as professor of English and director of the Writing Center in Michigan State University, Stock worked from 1995 to 1997 as the first associate director of the National Council of Teachers of English with special responsibilities for higher education. One of the projects to which she committed herself in that role was the improvement of the working conditions of part-time and adjunct faculty in composition studies.

Composition studies is a particularly fitting vantage point from which to study the academy's turn toward contingent employment as it has long been an instructional area staffed by non-tenure-track faculty. Most colleges and universities require first-year students to take one or two introductory composition courses, which are often staffed by non-tenure-track faculty and graduate teaching assistants. As early as the latter half of the nineteenth century (Connors, 1990), non-tenure-track faculty served as the main teaching force in required first-year composition courses. In spite of the growth of Ph.D. programs in rhetoric and composition, increasing job opportunities for composition specialists and rhetorical theorists, and the expansion of university presses and journals that regularly publish scholarship on writing and rhetoric, the majority of teachers of first-year composition continue to be teaching assistants and contingent faculty. As scholars in rhetoric and composition have pointed out, we have developed a promising new research field, but we have been less successful in changing exploitative working conditions for non-tenure-track faculty members (Crowley, 1991; Dasenbrock, 1993; Trimbur, 1996).

Reading the Discourse on Part-Time Faculty

We offer four reasons why we introduce this book with a critical reading of the literature that has emerged from studies of part-time and adjunct faculty during the past thirty years. The first is to introduce parts of the literature about contingent faculty to colleagues for whom this information may be new. Working, as we have, at the nexus of research communities and bodies of knowledge, we have been surprised again and again when we have mentioned studies conducted in one domain to scholars in another only to find that the research we have cited is unknown outside the community in which it was conducted. The second reason is to examine the discourse that has shaped the ways in which we currently talk and think about part-time and adjunct faculty in composition studies and beyond and to ask what kind of a discourse we must develop if we are to talk and think generatively and to move productively to solve the problems we have created with the use and overuse of contingent faculty. The third is to encourage the development of the kind of conversations and the kind of discourse for which we are arguing, conversations and discourse with some potential to help us toward fair and reasonable solutions to the problems at hand. And the fourth is to provide a context for the essays collected here, essays that document work currently under way to address the problems we face and directions in which we are moving.

From Composite Portraits to Disaggregated Profiles: Learning about Contingent Faculty

During the 1970s, an emerging body of social science literature documented the increasing numbers and problematic working conditions of part-time faculty in higher education in the United States. In publications directed primarily to an audience of postsecondary faculty, academic administrators and policymakers, demographers, economists, educationists, and sociologists published statistical surveys and analyses of the phenomenon of part-time academic labor: As their analyses described patterns and trends in student populations and academic hiring practices, they constructed composite profiles of part-time faculty. In one influential study of the time, two members of the Center for the Study of Education and Tax Policy, Howard P. Tuckman, an economist, and William D. Vogler, noted:

> The market for part-time faculty has been growing. For example, in the 1968–69 academic year, the first for which data on part-time faculty are available for American junior colleges, there were 36,420 part-time faculty or one for every 2.6 full-time faculty members. (American Association of Junior Colleges, The 1970 Junior College Directory, Washington, DC, 1970) By the 1975–76 academic year the number of part-timers had tripled to 110,976. This increase reduced the ratio to 1.8 full-time faculty for every part-timer. (American Association of Junior Colleges, The 1977 Community, Junior, and Technical College Directory, Washington, DC, 1977)
>
> Annual data are not available for the four-year colleges and universities, but an idea of the substantial growth in the part-time population can be gained from two studies conducted by the National Center for Educational Statistics (NCES) during the 1972–73 and the 1976–77 academic years. The ratios of full- to part-timers were 3.6 and 4.5 respectively. (1978, p. 70)

In addition to providing baseline statistical data, studies such as Tuckman and Vogler's revealed a set of generally held assumptions about why the academy was hiring part-time faculty and about their preparation and qualifications for and the quality of their work. For example, drawing conclusions from the survey data they studied, Tuckman and Vogler spoke about the pros and cons of hiring part-time employees:

> The growth in the number of part-timers employed in academe may be due in substantial part to the advantages they offer. Part-timers often teach at a per course rate less than that paid to full-time faculty. They receive fewer fringe benefits than their full-time counterparts, especially if they teach less than half time, require less office space, and can be employed only when needed. However, part-timers are often not as well-credentialed as full-timers, sometimes are not as abreast of the literature in their field, and almost always have less awareness of the policies and directions of the departments that hire them than their full-time colleagues. They also offer comparatively few services to students beyond those provided during the classroom period, and they contribute little to the national reputation of their department. (1978, p. 72)

Howard Bowen and Jack Schuster reinforce these ambivalent attitudes about the abilities, qualifications, and contributions of part-time faculty in their important book *American Professors: A National Resource Imperiled*:

> Everyone concedes that many of them are highly capable and add to the quality and diversity of available talent. Some of the most brilliant and capable physicians, lawyers, scientists, and public figures in the nation may be counted among them. On the other hand, many are of mediocre talent and training. The range of ability among part-timers is undoubtedly wider than among full-timers. One suspects that the average ability level among them is lower than that for full-timers, though there is no hard evidence on this matter. Part-timers have the disadvantage also that they usually do not become part of the academic community. They are not available to bear their share of student advising or participation in educational policy-making and of the intellectual discourse of the campus. By their not participating fully, the burden of maintaining the institutions falls increasingly on the full-time resident staff. (1986, pp. 64–65)

Although the existence of "no hard evidence" leads Bowen and Schuster to qualify Tuckman and Vogler's earlier claim that part-time faculty are less qualified than full-time faculty, when they claim that among part-timers whose abilities are "wider than among full-timers" are "[s]ome of the most brilliant and capable physicians, lawyers, scientists, and public figures in the nation," they communicate an unspoken message: Those part-time faculty who teach what Berlow and Collos (1974) have called the basic "gut" courses figure among the less-able members of this faculty corps. The implication is that professionals who are inclined to limit their work in the academy are more able than professionals whose limited participation in the academy has been determined by lack of opportunity, not by choice.

Even as scholars working in the social sciences in the early 1970s and 1980s pointed to financial pressures and the need for flexible hiring practices as a rationale for the growth in part-time positions, their discussions assumed that part-time faculty were neither as well prepared nor as well qualified to teach as full-time, tenure-accruing faculty. These scholars also assumed that part-time faculty met students only in class, that they did not confer with or advise students or contribute to educational programs beyond the classrooms in which they taught. In subsequent studies, assumptions such as these became objects of inquiry beginning a dialectic between generalization and differentiation in the literature on part-time employment—a dialectic that continues to this day. Yet, as David Leslie, Samuel Kellams, and Manny Gunne point out in *Part-Time Faculty in American Higher Education,* a report on interviews and surveys of faculty and administrators in eighteen institutions,

> the use of part-time faculty is a highly localized phenomenon . . . disaggregation, rather than generalization, is essential to its understanding. One must look at an individual department to account for how part-time faculty fit into the logic of academic staffing. (1982, p. vi)

Although some current literature continues to construct part-time faculty in composite terms, a substantial body of research supports Leslie, Kellams, and Gunne's claim that part-time faculty are a diverse group of professionals. In her role as provost at Wesleyan University in Connecticut, Sheila Tobias and Margaret

Rumberger distinguished three types of part-time faculty from one another: moonlighters who worked full-time in other roles; sunlighters who were committed to teaching part-time; and twilighters who, although employed primarily as college teachers, were not eligible for full faculty status (Tobias & Rumberger, 1974). Howard Tuckman developed another taxonomy, which included the semiretired, students, those wishing to become full time (Hopeful Full-Timers), those with full-time jobs (Full-Mooners), those with responsibilities in the home (Homeworkers), those with other part-time jobs (Part-Mooners), and all others (Part-Unknowers) (1978, p. 307). Gappa and Leslie "broadened Tuckman's typology into four loose categories: career enders, specialists, experts, and professionals; aspiring academics, and freelancers" (1993, p. 47).

In addition to these taxonomies, multiple articles and research studies published in the 1980s and 1990s explored the impact of the job market "crash" on new Ph.D.'s and labor force dynamics that have contributed to women's involvement in non-tenure-track employment. Emily Abel's sociological study (1984), based on interviews with recent Ph.D.'s who were unable to secure tenure-track work or who were denied tenure, drew attention to the shifting economic conditions that led a generation of bright young academics into contingent faculty roles. Abel's study also presented bargaining policies, legal action, and other forms of redress that were being developed as aspiring scholars turned into contingent faculty began to protest their problematic working conditions.

Other studies drew attention to the different reasons that men and women engaged in part-time teaching and to their differential commitments to the work. In a discussion of a survey she conducted in Santa Monica Community College, Abel observed differences between men and women working as part-time faculty. She noted that women, in greater numbers than the men, identified themselves primarily as teachers, relied on teaching for half or more of their income, had prior teaching experience and credentials, and invested more time in their teaching preparation (1976, pp. 41–42). A study of part-time hiring practices in Ohio colleges conducted by Shu Yang and Michele Zak (1981) supported Abel's findings. Howard Tuckman and Barbara Tuckman's (1980, 1981) reexamination of Ford Foundation data gathered in the 1970s also contributed to the developing base of knowledge about gender patterns in the employment of part-time faculty. In "Women as Part-Time Faculty Members," Tuckman and Tuckman identified several reasons why more women than men were "tracked" into part-time positions: Women lacked geographic mobility, frequently were not offered full-time jobs, and worked in lower-paying fields such as the arts and humanities that have been identified as "female" fields (1981, pp. 172–75).

Studies of the numbers of ethnic minorities who hold part-time and adjunct positions have been few and far between. The need for such studies is especially important in the face of broadly held impressions that affirmative action policies and programs have redressed, even reversed, hiring practices that have discriminated against ethnic minorities. In his essay, "The Myth of Reverse Discrimination in Higher Education" (Winter 1995–96), John K. Wilson, author of *The Myth of Political Correctness: The Conservative Attack on Higher Education* (1995), draws attention to a disparity between the number of whites and blacks who fill tenure-track positions (assistant professors) and non-tenure-track posts (instructors and lecturers). Writing in the *Journal of Blacks in Higher Education,* Wilson notes:

> In the fall of 1992, at all institutions, white men were 47.5 percent of all assistant professors but only 44.1 percent of instructors and 29.6 percent of lecturers. By contrast, blacks were only 5.8 percent of assistant professors but 6.9 percent of instructors and 6.3 percent of lecturers. (p. 89)

While some argue that because substantial numbers of African Americans have only recently become credentialed in areas that enable them to enter the ranks of the professoriate, these statistics are not particularly telling. Jacqueline Jones Royster and Jean C. Williams question such dismissals. In their article "History in the Spaces Left: African American Presence and Narratives of Composition" (1999), Royster and Williams remind us of data that W.E.B. Du Bois reported in 1903 in *The Souls of Black Folk*:

35 years after the end of chattel slavery, approximately 2000
African Americans had received college degrees from 34 historically African American colleges . . . 400 African Americans . . .
received bachelor's degrees from historically white northern colleges and universities such as Harvard, Yale, and Oberlin. These
data were for the turn of the century—that is, sixty plus years
before the era of open admissions and the emergence of people
of color as substantive entities in mainstream composition narratives. (1961, p. 582)

These data, like those Wilson reports, call out for study and discussion.

Studies published in the 1980s drew attention to discipline-
specific features of part-time and adjunct work. Faculty in the
disciplines, particularly disciplines in the general education curriculum, contributed complex and detailed portraits of the increased use of part-time and adjunct faculty in the teaching of
lower-division courses. Elizabeth Wallace's edited collection *Part-
Time Academic Employment in the Humanities* points to the
professional commitment of part-time faculty in the humanities.
Wallace distinguishes these faculty from "moonlighting" part-
timers who hold lucrative jobs apart from the academy:

Part-timers in the humanities, however, are more academically
oriented; they spend much more time outside class preparing lectures, reading, researching, and, particularly if they teach composition, grading essays and holding conferences with individual
students. (1984, p. xiv)

To address employment inequities and inadequate recognition of
the central role that part-timers play in the teaching of the humanities, contributors to Wallace's collection offered narratives
of policies and practices designed to improve part-time faculty
working conditions (p. xvi). Wallace also acknowledged an activist agenda, one that emerged in a variety of settings across the
1980s among part-time/adjunct teachers.

In the 1980s, another autobiographical body of literature
about part-time and adjunct faculty began to appear. In this literature, growing numbers of contingent faculty who had been
defined and categorized by others for purposes of discussion began to speak for themselves and to expose their unreasonable

working conditions and unjust wages. The seeds of this literature were sown a decade earlier in Lawrence H. Berlow and Alana L. Collos's article "Part-Time Employment: We Teach; Therefore, We Are" (1974).

Reflecting on survey information gathered by the Association of Departments of English (ADE) of the Modern Language Association (MLA), Berlow and Collos, adjunct faculty in English at the Bronx Community College of the City University of New York, speak as insiders about issues facing part-timers. While Berlow and Collos agreed that the academy hire contingent faculty to save money and to secure a transitional workforce, they did not recognize themselves as less qualified, less prepared, less committed to their teaching than their tenure-accruing counterparts; they did not recognize themselves in most of the profiles of part-timers and their work that had been published at the time. Arguing that adjunct faculty were often as well qualified for their work as their tenure-accruing counterparts, they spoke of themselves and their colleagues as "invisible," a descriptive term that gained currency thereafter throughout the literature published about contingent faculty. They also observed that part-time/adjunct faculty were often neither *part-time* nor *adjunct* in the true sense of those words but were, in fact, central to the teaching mission of the academy because they were hired in large numbers to teach the majority of the academy's "basic 'gut' courses" as well as "highly specialized courses for which they [had] unique talents" (1974, p. 9):

> A virtually invisible group known as part-time or adjunct faculty composes a large segment of the teaching staff of many colleges and universities. In the teaching profession, these people inhabit a twilight world. Many have higher degrees (M.A.'s or Ph.D.'s) or are active in the nonacademic worlds of business, culture, or government. But because they teach part-time, whether out of necessity or inclination, they are treated as second-class citizens of the academic community. This is ironic since adjuncts usually teach either the basic 'gut' courses or highly specialized courses for which they have unique talents. (pp. 9–11)

Summarizing colleagues' responses to survey questions, Berlow and Collos described part-time/adjunct faculty as "second-class" citizens for whom a "slowing down of the university growth industry in the 1970s" had led into "dead-end" jobs with "no career ladder" (p. 9). The contingent faculty for whom Berlow and Collos spoke saw themselves not as a flexible workforce but as underpaid, disrespected professionals cheated by a system that was also cheating their students.

> The students who are our major responsibility, are also being cheated by the system. Office space is frequently unavailable to adjuncts, so the only place to hold a conference might be the local "Joe's Lunch." When new introductory courses are prepared or syllabus revisions made for old introductory courses, adjuncts, who usually teach most of these courses, are closed out of formal considerations. If adjuncts want funding for a special project, such as a method of team-teaching or a multimedia approach to coursework, they are likely to find themselves cut off from the institution's support for research money. The adjunct is also cut off from much professional information. If he or she wants to travel to a convention or a professional meeting to keep up with his or her field, take part in a panel, or present a paper, he or she is likely to be refused access to travel funds. Information normally distributed through departmental mail frequently doesn't reach the adjunct; notices of library acquisitions, important new school resources, or statements of policy may be considered to be "for full-timers only." (p. 10)

Speaking for contingent faculty in the 1970s, Berlow and Collos discuss themes to be found in the writing of those who speak about these faculty. But the picture of their colleagues that Berlow and Collos paint is different from the one found in the social science literature of the time. They depict a corps of well-prepared, well-qualified faculty in higher education whose personal circumstances and professional development are constrained by the conditions of their work. Speaking for their colleagues, they turned readers' attention from themselves to the students with whom they work. From Berlow and Collos's perspective, part-time and adjunct faculty's working conditions were as counterproductive to students' learning as they were to teaching. By now, Berlow and Collos's criticism of hiring practices and working conditions that frustrate, rather than support, the learning of postsecondary students is commonplace.

In disciplines where contingent faculty staff a large proportion of introductory courses, a number of their personal narratives have shaded and textured the portrait that Berlow and Collos
outlined earlier. In "Memoirs and Confessions of a Part-Timer,"
for example, Cara Chell narrates a typical day in her life as an
adjunct writing instructor employed as a "freeway flier":

> Three mornings a week, I rise at six a.m., hit the road by seven
> and drive an hour. I teach an eight a.m. sophomore literature
> class, grade papers and prepare class plans until noon, teach a
> noon first-year composition class, dash back to my office (the
> pronoun is deceptive since the office actually also belongs to two
> other instructors, but I've never seen them: one is Tuesday/Thurs-
> day and the other is nights), pack up my books and papers and
> drive for another hour across town to another local university. I
> arrive there at two p.m., prepare, grade papers and hold office
> hours, then teach a 4:15 advanced composition class. On Tues-
> days, Thursdays, and Saturdays I write my dissertation. On Sun-
> days I do marathon grading and take out my hostilities on my
> husband.
>
> I am a part-time lecturer. I teach the youth of our nation
> those fundamental skills that slick magazines print indignant ar-
> ticles about. I do it for about $1,000 a section and no benefits
> except the use of the library of one of the universities, a privilege
> which I gather we part-timers only recently received for which
> we are suitably thankful. (1982, p. 35)

As personal testimonies such as Chell's began to accumulate
and cross-reference one another in conferences and in print, contingent faculty and their colleagues in tenure-accruing positions
charged their professional associations with the task of publicizing and protesting their working conditions. These calls led to a
series of statements addressing the employment conditions of part-
time and non-tenure-track faculty, among them American Association of University Professors (AAUP) "Status of Part-Time
Faculty" (1981), the AAUP "Report on the Status of Non-Tenure Track Faculty" (1993), the Association of Departments of
English "Statement on the Use of Part-Time and Full-Time Adjunct Faculty"(1983, 1987), the CCCC "Statement of Principles
and Standards for the Postsecondary Teaching of Writing" (1989),
the MLA "Statement on the Use of Part-Time and Full-Time

Non-Tenure Track Faculty" (1994), and the recent statement issued by a conference held in Washington, DC, in 1997 of ten professional associations including the AAUP, CCCC, MLA, and NCTE, the "Statement from the Conference on the Growing Use of Part-Time and Adjunct Faculty" (1997).

Although the particular recommendations advanced in these various statements differ, all of these statements predict that the overuse of part-time and adjunct faculty will erode tenure and compromise academic freedom, collegiality, and the quality of undergraduate education. Recommending that colleges and universities hire full-time, tenured or tenurable faculty, the statements encourage institutions employing large numbers of part-time and non-tenure-accruing faculty to create a regular class of "continuing" instructors, to ensure these instructors' reasonable salaries, appropriate fringe benefits, and professional development opportunities (e.g., CCCC Executive Committee, 1989, 332–35; AAUP Committee G, 1993, 45–46; MLA Executive Council, 1994, p. 59).

In the field of composition studies—the field in which contributors to this volume practice—the call that led most directly to the development of the Conference on College Composition and Communication's "Statement of Principles and Standards for the Postsecondary Teaching of Writing" (1989) was what is known as the Wyoming Resolution (see Figure 1). Approved in March 1987, at the annual meeting of the CCCC of the National Council of Teachers of English, the Wyoming Resolution was drafted jointly by contingent and tenure-accruing faculty during the summer of 1986 at the Wyoming Conference in English Studies.

In addition to outlining what might be called fair employment practices, statements such as the 1989 CCCC "Statement of Principles and Standards for Postsecondary Teaching of Writing" have provoked discussion and debate of political questions such as this one: Should professional organizations recommend the conversion of nontenure positions into tenure-accruing ones or should they urge improvements in the working conditions of existing contingent faculty? These debates have been especially energetic in the field of composition studies, giving voice to the competing professional and personal priorities of a large and diverse group of specialists who teach, study, and administer writ-

WHEREAS the salaries and working conditions of postsecondary
teachers with primary responsibility for the teaching of writing are
fundamentally unfair as judged by any reasonable professional
standards (e.g., unfair in excessive teaching loads, unreasonably
large class sizes, salary inequities, lack of benefits and professional
status, and barriers to professional advancement);
AND WHEREAS, as a consequence of these unreasonable working
conditions, highly dedicated teachers are often frustrated in their
desire to provide students the time and attention which students
both deserve and need;
THEREFORE, BE IT RESOLVED that the Executive Committee of
the Conference on Composition and Communication be charged
with the following:

To formulate after appropriate consultations with postsecondary
teachers of writing, professional standards and expectations for
salary levels and working conditions of postsecondary teachers of
writing.

To establish a procedure for hearing grievances brought by
postsecondary teachers of writing, either singly or collectively,
against apparent institutional noncompliance with these standards
and expectations.

To establish a procedure for acting upon a finding of noncompliance; specifically, to issue a letter of censure to an individual
institution's administration, board of regents or trustees, state
legislators (where pertinent), and to publicize the find to the public
at large, the educational community in general, and to our membership. (Robertson, Crowley, Lentricchia, 1989)

FIGURE 1. *The Wyoming Conference Resolution.*

ing programs. They have also highlighted issues of concern in the
larger academic community, issues that are framed in questions
such as these: What should be the shape and the work of the
second oldest institution in western society as we enter the twenty-
first century? What roles should contemporary faculty fulfill in
the academy, and how should they be rewarded for the various
parts of their work How can the academy's reward system encourage faculty investment in teaching and service as successfully as it has encouraged faculty investment in research and
personal expertise? How can adequate funding be secured to sup-

port the multiple functions the public expects of the academy? How should current levels of funding be allocated across the range of the academy's current responsibilities? How can an academy put into practice the democratic ideals it teaches in the curriculum?

During the 1990s, discussions and debates about the work of contingent faculty have been influenced by questions like these, questions emerging from calls within and beyond the academy for reformation of postsecondary education to meet the demands of a multicultural society in a global economy. At the same time, they have been grounded in the base of knowledge about contingent faculty that has emerged in the social sciences, the writings of faculty in various academic disciplines, the case studies, narratives, and polemical statements of contingent faculty themselves, and the position statements of professional associations.

Unions, Coalitions, and Globalization

Perhaps the most frequently cited study of part-time and adjunct faculty is Judith Gappa and David Leslie's *The Invisible Faculty*. Building on earlier, descriptive studies they conducted, Gappa and Leslie joined forces in 1990–91 to interview 467 administrators, department chairs, tenure-track faculty, and part-time faculty in eighteen colleges and universities that are representative of the range of educational institutions. Of those they interviewed, 243 were part-time faculty members. In *The Invisible Faculty*, Gappa and Leslie extended their own and others' earlier studies, demonstrating to the satisfaction of all interested parties that contingent faculty are a diverse group of academics who teach part time for a variety of reasons, within highly localized terms and conditions of employment, what they described as "a wildly random collection of institutional and departmental practices" (1993, p. xiii). Convinced that fiscal challenges as well as the desirability of flexible staffing, special expertise, and different work options for faculty would lead to increasing, not decreasing, use of part-time faculty, Gappa and Leslie urged institutions to value and support part-time faculty work. In a set of recommendations for proactive as opposed to reactive employment practices, they proposed a comprehensive set of policies and practices higher education might use to integrate part-timers into the academic community (pp. 6, 180).

While Gappa and Leslie approached staffing practices from the perspective of academic administrators facing constrained economic resources that did not look to improve in the foresee-able future, faculty activists working in the humanities—such as Michael Bérubé, Cary Nelson, and Linda Ray Pratt—approached the issues in the context of discipline-based scholarship and their work with professional associations. In *Higher Education under Fire: Politics, Economics, and the Crisis of the Humanities* (1995), editors Bérubé and Nelson question the "corporatization" of the university and urge colleagues to work actively against the over-use of contingent faculty. Describing their faculty colleagues as dangerously ignorant of how their institutions work, they go on to argue that faculty have not communicated successfully to their publics the meaning and value of their work. Together with con-tributors to this collection of essays, Bérubé and Nelson call for faculty and graduate students to become active citizens, to be-come "knowledgeable about the institutions in which they work and about the larger social and political formations in which those institutions are embedded," to "build relationships with relevant constituencies" (1995, p. 25).

Although Nelson is primarily interested in employment is-sues of concern to full-time, tenure-track faculty and graduate students, he draws attention to part-time employment issues as they contribute to the shape of academic policies and practices such as the following: the dwindling ranks of full-time faculty; the over-enrollment and graduation of Ph.D.'s in the humanities, where available jobs are few; the exploitation of graduate stu-dent teaching assistants. In "What Is to Be Done? A Twelve-Step Program for Academia," a chapter of his single-authored book *Manifesto of a Tenured Radical,* Nelson outlines a dozen means of redressing the interrelated problems he defines. Among his proposals are these: developing a bill of rights for fair salaries, better contracts, benefits, grievance procedures; unionization of teaching assistants and part-time faculty; challenging professional organizations to better address employment issues, the future of graduate education, and faculty careers; and closing down mar-ginal doctoral programs (1997, pp. 179–85). Urging an activist agenda aimed at social justice, Nelson openly confronts what he and Bérubé call the "idiot savant" stance of tenure-accruing faculty who have ignored employment issues in the academic ranks.

While serving as president of the American Association of University Professors, Linda Ray Pratt drew attention to how public funding for higher education (and the lack of it) contributes to the use, overuse, and abuse of part-time faculty. Furthermore, she warned that the problems associated with the overuse of contingent faculty will be here to stay as "long as institutions need the savings and want the management implications derived from a large number of underemployed faculty" (1997, p. 274). One argument Pratt offers for the preservation of funding for higher education is based on what it takes to provide quality education; another is based on the need to reduce the academy's reliance on part-time over full-time positions. When Pratt calls on faculty to urge their administrator colleagues to "put more money" into full-time faculty positions and "more stability behind" them, in effect, she calls for "two conditions that negate the attractiveness of part-time over full-time positions" (p. 273).

Like their tenure-eligible counterparts, contingent faculty have become increasingly outspoken advocates for improvement of their working conditions and for recognition of their achievements as teachers and scholars. As a result, they have challenged the popular notion that adjuncts are victims who are powerless or helpless to change their working conditions. Adjunct faculty such as P. D. Lesko, founder of the National Adjunct Faculty Guild and *The Adjunct Advocate*, the only national publication devoted solely to adjunct issues; Chris McVay, publisher of the radical newsletter *pro-fess-ing* at Kent State University; and Karen Thompson, president of the Part-Time Chapter of the Rutgers AAUP, have become active participants and agitators for reform of contingent faculty's working conditions. Thompson, chair of Committee G of the AAUP, regularly publishes articles on adjunct issues.

Three organizing principles of Thompson's activist agenda are also themes in her writing: Academics must become a unified, not a bifurcated faculty; they must work together with other university employees and students to build alliances with constituencies off campus; and they must take their issues to the public, demonstrating that redress of their complaints is in the public interest (A22–24). ✓

Discussion of contingent faculty issues in the 1990s was also influenced by public complaints and criticisms of the quality of higher education that emerged during the decade before. From muckraking attacks on the professoriate such as Charles Sykes' *ProfScam* (1988) to more measured academic criticism such as that found in Schuster and Bowen's "The Faculty at Risk" (1985), the word was out: The professoriate is neither interested in nor investing itself in teaching undergraduate students. Taken together the dissatisfactions with higher education voiced inside and outside the academy paved the way for proposals published in the 1990s aimed at redefining faculty work.

In what is perhaps the best known of the proposals, *Scholarship Reconsidered: Priorities of the Professoriate* (1990), Ernest Boyer, former president of the Carnegie Foundation for the Advancement of Teaching, challenges faculty to move beyond the counterproductive teaching versus research debate to reconsider scholarship in terms of four overlapping forms of academic work: the scholarship of discovery (work that adds to human knowledge and to the intellectual life of the academy), the scholarship of integration (work that makes connections between and among knowledge developed within disciplinary communities and that places disciplinary knowledge in broader contexts), the scholarship of application (work that emerges when academics' theories and the demands of practice interanimate each other), and the scholarship of teaching (work that transmits, transforms, and extends knowledge to others, some of whom may themselves become scholars).

In the *Forum on Faculty Roles and Rewards*, sponsored by the American Association of Higher Education (AAHE), faculty leaders, senior academic administrators, trustees, legislators, and other interested parties who were persuaded by ideas like those in Boyer's proposal initiated discussions aimed at refocusing faculty priorities and addressing pressing institutional and societal needs. Looking toward the future, participants in these conversations used lessons from the past to call current practices into question. In his essay "The Academic Profession in Transition: Toward a New Social Fiction," R. Eugene Rice, professor of

Sociology and director of AAHE, the *Forum on Faculty Roles and Rewards*, claims that the following complex of assumptions about academic work established during higher education's affluence and expansion between the 1950s and the 1970s constitute a "social fiction":

1. Research is the central professional endeavor and the focus of academic life.

2. Quality in the profession is maintained by peer review and professional autonomy.

3. Knowledge is pursued for its own sake.

4. The pursuit of knowledge is best organized according to discipline (i.e., according to discipline based departments).

5. Reputations are established through national and international professional associations.

6. The distinctive task of the academic professional is the pursuit of cognitive truth (or cognitive rationality).

7. Professional rewards and mobility accrue to those who persistently accentuate their specializations. (1986, p. 14)

Arguing that a once-applicable, now-problematic, set of assumptions have resulted in a "one-dimensional view of the academic career, a view that continues to be normative for the majority of faculty regardless of the type of institution in which they work" (1986, p. 15), Rice calls for a "new conception of the academic professional, one that is more appropriate, more authentic, and more adaptive for both our institutions and ourselves" (p. 12).

Statistical data support Rice's claim that current assumptions about academic life are no more accurate than they are appropriate. A 1989 survey of the Carnegie Foundation for the Advancement of Teaching reveals that 70 percent of all postsecondary faculty—93 percent of faculty at two-year colleges, 55 percent at doctoral-granting institutions, and 33 percent at research universities—identify teaching as their primary interest. Contrary to the generally held belief that faculty devote most or all of their time to their research interests, 34 percent of the faculty were not working on a scholarly project at the time of the survey; 56 percent had not published a book or monograph alone or with a co-author/editor; 59 percent had published five articles or fewer in professional publications; 26 percent had published nothing at all. Only 20 percent of faculty were frequent or high volume publishers (Bérubé & Nelson, 1995, pp. 3–4). K. Patricia Cross, professor of Higher Education at the University of California (Berkeley) complicates understandings of faculty work and values even further when she observes that although faculty claim a high interest in teaching, they fail to reward it (1993, p. 290).

Calls such as Rice's, together with empirical studies of faculty work, have inspired projects designed to restructure faculty roles, rewards, and career paths. In the context of the *Forum on Faculty Roles and Rewards*, a project entitled *New Pathways: Faculty Careers and Employment for the 21st Century* has engaged faculty, researchers, academic administrators, and policymakers in rethinking faculty work in the light of a renewed emphasis on undergraduate teaching, scholarship reconsidered, and concern for the quality of faculty lives across their academic careers. Among the themes emerging in these discussions are several that have particular relevance to contingent faculty. For example, many faculty hired into tenure-accruing roles in the academy find that expectations for publication during the early years of their careers work against investment in their teaching and development of healthy family lives. Academic timetables— third-year and tenure reviews and the productivity on which favorable reviews depend—recommend that faculty invest their time and energy in research that will be published and valued by peers in their disciplines or fields rather than investing their efforts into their teaching and their departmental, collegiate, and university programs. Many of these newcomers to the academy think that fairly compensated and stable part-time academic work during the early years of their careers might enable them to become good teachers, productive researchers, collegial university citizens, and responsible family members in ways that the demands of full-time, tenure-accruing academic work currently does not (Gappa & MacDermid, 1997).

Although AAHE's stance toward restructuring faculty roles, rewards, and career paths has raised questions among some advocates of academic freedom and tenure, a series of working papers, models, and prototypes emerging from the *Forum on Faculty*

Roles and Rewards and the *New Pathways* projects are contributing significantly to systematic change that is needed if undergraduate learning and teaching are to be improved and if faculty roles and rewards are to be realigned to accomplish these ends. Furthermore, because scholars working in the *New Pathways* project share Boyer's conviction that higher education must find ways to reward faculty who devote the majority of their professional energy to teaching and because at least two, Judith Gappa and David Leslie, are serious students of the work and contributions of part-time faculty in higher education, the project holds promise that the work of contingent faculty will figure significantly in discussions that are shaping visions of the twenty-first-century academy.

Another set of conversations that are reconsidering the work of contingent faculty are now taking place among representatives of the ten discipline-based organizations, including the American Association of University Professors. These and future conversations this group plans highlight a coalition-building movement that has developed in the 1990s to counter the ill effects of the overuse and abuse of contingent faculty. Coalitions are now sowing the seeds of activism in ground tilled in the preparation of position statements that concerned organizations composed and published in the 1990s. For example, in his 1998 outgoing AAUP President's Lecture, James Perley urged all college educators—part-time and full-time faculty—to unite around their common goals and declared policy statements and act to end the exploitation of part-time and adjunct faculty:

> This situation has arisen because we who are full-time faculty members have allowed it to develop. We have not been vocal enough in protesting the employment abuse of our colleagues. We need to come to see the problems of part-time faculty as our own. And we need to start talking about the value of education, saying with full voice that education is at least as worthy of support as is prison construction. (p. 56)

Perley goes on to argue for coalition building, not only among all ranks of faculty but also with accrediting agencies, governing boards, and legislative bodies:

We can insist that accrediting bodies be more than agents hired to certify that institutions are fiscally sound and do what their mission statements say they intend to do. We can insist that institutions meet minimal standards for certification. . . . [We can consult] with institutions and faculties, state governments and boards. [We can urge] funding disincentives or caps to discourage over-reliance on part-time faculty for undergraduate instruction. (1998, pp. 57–58)

Arguing for similar coalition-building goals, Linda Ray Pratt has offered her colleagues case-study models of faculty members and activists at three institutions who conducted public relations campaigns to ensure adequate funding for education. And Karen Thompson has pointed to the need for student support in the effort to ensure quality education and fair employment practices:

[S]tudents need to know who's in front of the classroom: they need to know how we're treated, how much we're paid, how insecure we are. They need to see where their money is going, or not going; how their issues are connected to our issues. It's not just tuition versus salaries. Restrictions in course offerings, reductions in enrollment, cuts in student aid are all part of the contraction of higher education, which includes downsizing faculty and rising administrative spending. It's the university as corporation where profit takes precedence over education. Student-faculty alliance can more effectively convince administrators to put quality education first by working together. A strong coalition of full-time faculty, part-timers, teaching assistants, support staff, and students would be the best vehicle to achieve success. (A23)

Plans for coalition-building and conversations among interested parties were topics that propelled eleven professional organizations to issue the "Statement on Growing Use of Part-Time and Adjunct Faculty" (1997), to establish the Coalition on the Academic Workforce (CAW). Members of CAW are currently using the "Statement on the Growing Use of Part-Time and Adjunct Faculty" as a starting point for conversations with accrediting associations, academic administrators, and policymakers aimed at improving the working conditions of part-time and adjunct faculty.

Over the past three decades, various parties have developed bodies of knowledge that have led to increasingly sophisticated and increasingly sensitive discussions of the conditions in which contingent faculty work. Although the various parties have not engaged one another in sustained conversations aimed at solving their common problems and they have not conducted collaborative research into the issues that concern them, contingent faculty, policymakers, academic administrators, researchers of higher education, and critics who are calling for academic reform share a number of understandings: the academy has come to rely too heavily on contingent faculty, particularly to teach the core curriculum to undergraduates; the working conditions of contingent faculty are, almost without exception, substandard; and contingent faculty often resemble tenure-accruing faculty in their talents, preparedness, and in the contributions they make to the larger educational enterprise.

It is with these common understandings that our collection of essays begins. What it contributes to the conversation are local narratives designed to speak to and encourage the development of national conversations with some promise to solve pressing problems. What all contributors share is a view that the quality of education that teachers are able to provide students depends on the integrally related conditions in which teachers are asked to work and students are asked to learn. Because all contributors are committed to quality education, they are necessarily committed to fair employment practices and quality instruction.

Reading Case Studies

Most of the literature on non-tenure-track employment published during the last thirty years has been "documentary," mapping the extent, scope, and demographics of contingent employment; "speculative," telling readers what they can do to improve working conditions in highly generalized ways; or "polemical," indicating the problematic politics of contingent employment but failing to address how local conditions figure into larger patterns. An essential foundation on which to build, this literature calls for another body of literature that documents enactments of reform. In this volume, we address how change can and has taken place within what Richard Miller calls a "social," as opposed to a pure "ideational," world (1998, p. 14). As Miller says in *As If Learning Mattered,* implementing educational reform involves understanding and acknowledging "the constraining forces that shape local labor practices" (p. 9). It means coming to terms with limits,

> anticipating and responding to, among other things, the reigning discourses of fiscal crisis, the expressed needs and abilities of resident student and faculty populations, mandated controls over class size and course load, and the physical plant's available facilities. (p. 9)

It also means having the courage to imagine change *within/inside* local, site-specific bureaucratic structures: programs, departments, colleges, universities.

Moving a Mountain: Transforming the Work of Contingent Faculty in Composition Studies was inspired by a challenge issued to the profession by the CCCC Committee on Professional Standards "to compose a series of case studies that may serve as guidelines for improved working conditions (CCCC Committee on Professional Standards, 1991). Contributors to *Moving the Mountain* offer case studies that describe strategies for transforming non-tenure-track faculty's hiring procedures, contractual arrangements, salaries and benefits, work orientation, teaching evaluation procedures, and professional development opportunities. They also examine the role professional organizations, collective bargaining units, and community organizing efforts have played in improving working conditions.

The authors in this volume range from non-tenure-track faculty, full-time tenure-accruing faculty, academic administrators, to policymakers. They represent different groups struggling with local constraints at two-year colleges, four-year colleges, regional, and research universities, in many parts of the country. In spite of their different local contexts and various narratives, contributors share a commitment to what Judith Gappa and David Leslie have described as a *proactive* rather than a *reactive* stance toward the employment of non-tenure-track faculty in higher education. All make the assumption that teaching writing is an important enterprise and that teachers of writing—no matter what rank—need working conditions that enable them to provide their students quality literacy instruction. The authors see better working conditions and professional development opportunities as crucial to the integrity of faculty work and the quality of undergraduate education. At the same time, contributors recognize the potential to exploit already overworked and underpaid non-tenure-track faculty when departments and colleges "up the ante" for professional development without improving salaries or contracts. They also recognize that efforts must be made to hire full-time tenure-track faculty and limit the number of temporary employees entering the profession.

Extending and updating a project that M. Elizabeth Wallace began with the publication of *Part-Time Academic Employment in the Humanities* (1984), *Moving a Mountain* presents case studies and narratives that offer complex, multilayered, multivocal accounts of efforts to reform the working conditions of part-time and adjunct faculty. Even as they document the work of nontenure and tenure-track faculty in composition studies to create working conditions within which teachers can teach effectively and students can learn successfully, essays in this collection reveal much about the state of our profession. They inform compositionists about working conditions in our field, and they provide writing program administrators, department chairs, deans, and provosts evaluative discussions of practices they may consider as they address the challenges of improving the working conditions of non-tenure-track faculty and the quality of undergraduate instruction, and they do something else as well. Taken together, they offer us a set of lenses through which we may look at the academy as it enters the twenty-first century, an academy in which teaching faculty is frustrated more often than not in spite of all the messages to the contrary. The volume shows us that non-tenure-eligible faculty are part of a wave of change washing over higher education. We see academics who are moving increasingly to unionize, an academy turning to its least secure faculty to lead the way in innovative teaching with new technologies, and marginalized academics who are inventing a scholarship of teaching for which higher education's leaders are calling.

The essays collected here are arranged into three sections. In Part I, "Reforming and Transforming the Culture and Material Conditions of Contingent Writing Faculty: The Personal and the Institutional," authors intertwine their personal and institutional histories. Individuals tell personal stories as they play out in particular institutional settings and against the backdrop of larger disciplinary and intellectual questions. They spotlight writing program administrators, tenure-track faculty, and non-tenure-track faculty working to construct professional writing programs and quality learning conditions for students. As authors in this section describe programs and settings, they present various cases for improving working conditions of non-tenure-track faculty. In their dialogic piece, Richard Jewell and Chris Anson narrate their individual work histories against the backdrop of the institutions in which they have worked. In so doing, they tell one story of the overuse and exploitation of non-tenure-track faculty in composition studies. Jewell reviews his work history as a non-tenure-track faculty member at community colleges and state universities in Minnesota. His story speaks for his tenacity, his love of teaching, and his ability to adapt to different teaching environments and political climates. Anson—a tenured professor, a writing program administrator, and a published composition scholar—tells a different professional story, one punctuated by his concern about employment issues and his efforts in local and national settings to limit the proliferation of non-tenure-track positions such as the one Jewell occupies. While Anson and Jewell agree that non-tenure-track faculty should be granted professional working conditions, they disagree about what the nature of the working conditions should be. As a writing program administrator in the University of Minnesota, Anson opposed creation of positions like the one Jewell now occupies in that institution.

In the next three essays, Barry Maid, Eva Brumberger, and Carol Lipson and Molly Voorheis describe how professionalized non-tenure-track instructorships with renewable contracts, better salaries, benefits, and opportunities for continued professional development were created in three different institutions. Speaking from different vantage points, Maid, Brumberger, and Lipson and Voorheis—like Anson and Jewell—reach different conclusions about the benefits and costs of such positions. Maid, a former writing program administrator and department chair, describes the political fallout that accompanied the professionalization and expansion of writing instructors' roles and rights in the English department of the University of Arkansas at Little Rock (UALR). Analyzing changes that took place, Maid reveals how different cultures, values, and work assignments of writing and literature faculty led the UALR Writing Program to leave the English department in 1993 to become the Rhetoric and Writing department. He also contends that such splits may be necessary at institutions where there is historical tension and conflict between literature and writing faculty. When he argues that the emergence of independent writing programs, may signal "the emergence of a new applied discipline," Maid names a theme echoed in essays in the third section of this collection in which the scholarship of teaching developed by non-tenure-track instructors is explored.

Like Maid, Eva Brumberger reflects on the problem of stratification between English faculty and writing faculty. A lecturer from the University of Wyoming currently on leave to pursue a Ph.D. at another institution, Brumberger discusses the development of "probationary to extended term academic professional lecturer" positions (know as the P/ET APL) at the University of Wyoming. Her essay assesses the costs and benefits of professionalized lectureships and ways to improve P/ET APL positions in light of suggestions made in evaluation of the practice by a consultant-evaluator from the National Council on Writing Program Administrators. Brumberger argues that "[c]reating a separate track of instructors to teach primarily writing courses in many ways makes the struggle more difficult rather than less so. As our education system has already amply demonstrated there is no such thing as separate but equal."

In their essay, Carol Lipson, a tenured faculty member, and Molly Voorheis, a professional writing instructor in the Syracuse University Writing Program, describe the costs and benefits of professionalized writing instructorships, positions that were created in Syracuse in 1986 when the Writing Program was established apart from the English department. Lipson and Voorheis describe the challenges and satisfactions of professional writing instructors (PWIs) experienced as they took on responsibility for developing a teaching culture, a merit tier system, and peer evaluation of their work. While they recommend the development of such instructorships at other colleges and universities, Lipson and Voorheis remind readers that contexts differ and furthermore that it is far from perfect.

Maid, Brumberger, and Lipson and Voorheis do not offer unqualified success narratives but partial ones that struggle to come to terms with how professionalized instructorships do and do not address inequities in professional status and working conditions. While a step toward achieving better working conditions, professionalized writing instructorships do not adequately address more fundamental questions about the weight and value assigned to undergraduate literacy instruction in the faculty reward system. Such positions may exacerbate the stratification that already exists between full and part-time faculty in traditional English departments (Brumberger, Maid). In fact, the authors in this section argue that improvements in working conditions often fall short of addressing more complex and troubling questions about the role of part-time and non-tenure-track writing faculty in writing programs and in departmental and university life.

In the last article in this opening section of the book, Helen O'Grady, a self-labeled "interinstitutional" teacher and graduate student, writes about the mismatch between institutional mission statements that boast of low faculty-to-student ratios and the realities of interinstitutional teaching faced by many writing instructors employed in these institutions. In her discussion, O'Grady goes on to demonstrate how critical literacy discourse, like institutional mission statements, subscribes "to the notion that teaching is primarily performed by privileged tenure-track or tenured full-time faculty." According to O'Grady, "Both discourses elide the material conditions under which many part-time and non-tenure-track writing teachers work." Drawing attention to the problematic working conditions of interinstitutional teachers, O'Grady reminds readers that they are as problematic for students as they are for writing instructors who are constrained in their ability to provide effective writing instruction. Such instruction, she notes, "depends on teachers having sufficient time and energy to prepare classes, to respond usefully to students' writing and to conduct writing conferences with students outside class during office hours." Interinstitutional teachers find those conditions a luxury, not a norm. O'Grady's essay, like Jewell's, reminds us of the continuing class of temporary part-time faculty who piece together work at multiple institutions. It also highlights how the full-time instructorships described by Maid, Brumberger, and Lipson and Voorheis, while still imperfect compromises, are improvements over the temporary positions and problematic conditions that O'Grady and Jewell describe.

Together the essays in the first section of this collection outline a variety of working conditions and contractual arrangements within which part-time and non-tenure-eligible writing faculty work. In so doing, they confirm earlier observations that policy and practice surrounding the work of part-time faculty is local, and, in some cases, haphazard and short-sighted, and they call attention to what remains to be done to improve the working conditions of contingent faculty in composition and to ensure that the nation's students receive quality writing instruction. Work reported in the second section of this book suggests that the snapshots of policies and practices revealed in these essays are part of a larger family album, one that contingent faculty have assembled, one whose images are leading them to join together to address their professional concerns.

In *Moving a Mountain*'s second section, "Collectivity and Change in Non-Tenure-Track Employment: Collective Bargaining, Coalition Building, and Community Organizing," authors document part-time and adjunct faculty's turn to collective bargaining and collective action in an effort to improve their working conditions. Contributors to this section discuss both the possibilities and problems of collective bargaining in part-time units and of bargaining jointly in full-time/part-time units. In addition, they discuss how professional organizations and community-organizing efforts can assist them in improving working conditions. In "Are Unions Good for Professors" Stanley Aronowitz points out that K–12 teachers, with 80 percent of their profession organized, "have the highest union density in the entire labor movement" (1998, p. 14). Aronowitz also argues that unionization is the "untold story" of higher education in the 1970s and 1980s. Contrary to popular opinion, white-collar professionals comprise a growing number of union membership, and professors, graduate students, and other higher-education professionals comprise a growing segment of the unionized workforce: "Until the rise of unions among health-care professionals in the 1980s and 1990s, the main leader in this trend was the professoriate" (p. 15). About one-quarter of full-time faculty or 130,000 professors and other higher education professionals currently work with union contracts" (p. 16). To give a sense of the significance of these numbers, this is a "higher percentage of union density than found in the labor force as a whole" (p. 16).

Walter Jacobsohn, a full-time instructor and former union officer, opens this section with a compelling account of why contingent faculty are organizing. His essay is an impassioned argument for non-tenure-track and tenure-track faculty alike to identify the social and poltical forces that have impeded organizing around adjunct faculty issues and to move past them. Jacobsohn identifies the tendency for adjuncts to wish to "pass" as "respected professionals" as one of the most serious impediments to their organization. Passing, Jacobsohn contends, "serves to make the working conditions of adjunct faculty almost impossible to change." While Jacobsohn draws attention to the impediments to adjunct organizing, in her essay Karen Thompson provides an agenda and catalogue of strategies for coalition building and collective change efforts.

Thompson, a part-time writing instructor, president of the Part-Time Faculty Chapter of the AAUP at Rutgers University, and chair of Committee G on Non-Tenure-Track Faculty issues for AAUP, urges part-time and full-time faculty alike to look to the 1997 United Parcel Services strike as an organizing plan for what must be done in higher education to stem the exploitation of contingent faculty. Arguing that the UPS strikers' "combination of high participation by part-timers in the strike and the full-timers' willingness to fight for part-time workers' concerns was key to the strikers' victory," Thompson claims that a model of "external" and "internal" collegiality must be used if change in higher education is to be accomplished.

The next three essays in this section are case studies, responses to the growth of contingent faculty across California's system of higher education. John Lovas, a former dean, assistant chair, and president of the American Federation of Teachers local chapter at Foothills–De Anza Community College, offers a "thick description" of the historical development of the community college system in his area, including an account of the increased use of part-time and adjunct faculty from the 1960s to the end of the century. Examining the interaction between legislative action and higher education development, funding, and strategic planning, Lovas discusses how Proposition 13 as well as AB1714 (a bill mandating California's community colleges to reach a 75 percent/25 percent ratio of full-time to part-time teaching hours) have affected funding and staffing in California's community colleges. Arguing that quality of education issues, not economic expediency, must drive discussions of faculty issues, Lovas insists: "Governors, legislators and trustees must be made aware of the significant threats to quality in this massive shift to part-time teachers. Campaigns must be mounted among students, parents and business leaders to support significant new funding to improve the quality of undergraduate teaching. As part of those efforts to improve teaching, full-time jobs and sound accountability measures must be the cornerstones of the new funding."

The next two essays suggest that the unionization of lecturers in the state of California has yielded important improvements in lecturers' working conditions and students' learning conditions. Judith Kirscht and Nick Tingle, lecturers in composition at the University of California–Santa Barbara (UCSB) trace the rise of instructorships in the University of California system, the growth of the UCSB Writing Program as an independent unit, and the move of faculty in the program to unionize to combat unfair labor practices. Elana Peled, Diana Hines, Michael Martin, Anne Stafford, Brian Strang, Mary Winegarden, and Melanie Wise describe a coalition-building effort that took place surrounding the announced "lay-off" of fourteen lecturers in ESL and composition in San Francisco State University. As a direct result of their efforts to mobilize the local chapter of the California Faculty Association (including full-time faculty), representatives of student government, the media, and undergraduate students (who would have access to fewer sections of required writing as a result of the lay-offs), the lecturers were reinstated. Coalition building succeeded. As Peled, Hines, Martin, Stafford, Strang, Winegarden, and Wise put it, undergraduate students participated in the protest because "[t]o support us [the lecturers] was to fight for themselves, for their education, for the justice they rarely receive but so deserve."

In the last essay in the section, Debra Benko describes one group of non-tenure-track writing faculty's efforts to improve their working conditions when they had no union to turn to. Benko analyzes how part-time and full-time lecturers established a Full-Time Temporary/Part-Time Steering Committee to improve working conditions for non-tenure-track faculty in the English department at Bowling Green State University. Even as Benko demonstrates what an interdepartmental committee did to help adjunct faculty, she reveals how success in coalition building can produce problems. Coalitions can and often do dissolve once short-term goals are met, leaving larger problems in place. Benko emphasizes the need to maintain and continually renew a "committee membership that will work toward long-term goals in improving working conditions even as short-term goals are met." Echoing a theme found in other essays in the section, Benko names unionization of contingent faculty as one long-term goal to be pursued.

In Part III, "Rethinking Non-Tenure-Track Faculty Roles and Rewards," contributors speak of significant ways in which non-tenure-track faculty are participating in the major shifts currently underway in higher education: the use of new technologies to extend access to higher education and the movement to make the scholarship of teaching visible in an academy engaged in reconsidering work across the academic mission. In the introductory essay, Danielle DeVoss, Dawn Hayden, Cynthia L. Selfe, and Richard J. Selfe Jr., experts in and critics of the uses of digital technology, observe that disproportionate numbers of non-tenure-track faculty in composition studies are asked to teach distance education offerings that the academy is currently developing. Speculating on reasons for the academy's turn once again to contingent faculty to meet a developing instructional need, the authors note that contingent faculty often have more technical expertise than conventionally-educated tenure-track faculty in English studies. They also note that contingent faculty's precarious working conditions often make them more willing to update their repertoire of teaching practices, more willing to experiment with promising innovations in teaching, and more willing to take on risky assignments—such as distance-education teaching—than are their more secure colleagues. Arguing for strategies that can improve conditions for contingent faculty and graduate-student teaching assistants who find themselves teaching in distance-education literacy programs, Hayden, DeVoss, Selfe, and Selfe speak from the perspective of the various stakeholders (graduate student teaching assistants, nontenure and tenure-track faculty, and academic administrators) who must work together imaginatively and justly if distance education is to realize its potential to make higher education more accessible to more diverse students in more diverse settings.

To date, few researchers have spoken out about where and how the work of part-time and adjunct faculty with teaching-intensive roles figures as scholarship, and those who tend to focus on how the scholarship figures as "local knowledge." In an essay composed to demonstrate that the scholarship of teaching being developed by contingent faculty has much to offer higher education as the academy reconsiders scholarship, Patricia Lambert Stock, David Franke, Amanda Brown, and John Starkweather present and discuss substantial chunks of two writing instructors' teaching portfolios. In the process, they argue that contingent faculty joined in a common teaching project not only represent their teaching and their research into teaching and learning to one another for peer review and community use but they also argue that the scholarship of teaching is a holistic scholarship of discovery, integration, application, and teaching all at once, all together.

In the last essay in the book, Eileen Schell circles back to the place we began, with an analysis of the discourse that has constructed images of and roles available to contingent faculty in higher education. With an eye toward a more equitable future history of future faculty, Schell asks us to abandon the "rhetoric of lack" in which part-time and adjunct faculty have been the blamed victims for education's failure to provide all students quality education. She urges us instead to take up the issues of contingent faculty's compensation, contracts, conditions of work, and coalition building within a "rhetoric of responsibility"—responsibility of institutions to faculty and students, faculty to students and institutions, students to learning. To do so, Schell argues will benefit not only contingent faculty and their colleagues but students and society as well.

A Last Word

When this collection of essays takes its place in the beginning of the twenty-first century among publications about the work of contingent faculty in higher education, we hope that reviews will note a shift in emphasis in the study just as we noted shifts in emphases between the 1970s and 1980s studies (that documented both the numbers and characteristics of contingent faculty and the nature and quality of their work) and the 1980s and 1990s studies (that documented contingent faculty's working conditions and growing numbers, in light of the declining numbers of full-time and tenure-track faculty in the academy, even as it speculated on the consequences of these phenomena). We hope reviewers will note that as contingent faculty assumed responsibility not just for their work but also for their working conditions, they did so for their students' as well as their own benefit.

Part-time and adjunct faculty have defined the issues surrounding their work in the academy differently from researchers of higher education, policymakers, and academic administrators who have understood the turn to contingent faculty in light of the academy's needs to respond to shifting demographics and curricular pressures and to address fiscal constraints. Beginning with Berlow and Collos (1974), contingent faculty have insisted that discussions of short-term needs—flexible staffing and budget reductions—be put in perspective by discussions of the long-term benefits of quality teaching and learning conditions. Aligning themselves with political figures who remind us that we are living in an informational era, a service society, and a global economy, contingent faculty have insisted that our nation's greatest resource is an educated citizenry that depends on a talented and secure corps of teacher-scholars. One by one, group by group, coalition by coalition, union by union, contingent faculty are moving toward realizing this vision.

The academy can move with them, behind them, or ahead of them. The academy cannot, however, stand still.

Notes

1. For a substantive discussion of shifts in student enrollments and in funding (both federal and state) from 1970 to 1990, see Margaret Gordon's "The Economy and Higher Education" (1993). For an account of economic, political, and social forces that brought us to our current use of part-time faculty, especially in writing instruction, see Eileen Schell's *Gypsy Academics and Motherteachers: Gender, Contingent Labor, and Writing Instruction* (1998).

2. What is less obvious are the hidden costs of employing part-time faculty on the short-term contracts: part-time faculty "must be hired, oriented, supervised, and evaluated to a greater extent" than full-timers; furthermore, they do "not always stay long enough to accumulate valuable experience. For all these reasons, the direct dollar savings per course are not as dramatic as they appear when the only variable being examined is the actual salary paid per course" (Gappa, 1997, 15).

3. The *Coalition on the Academic Workforce* (CAW) is one of the outgrowths of the 1997 *Conference on the Growing Use of Part-Time and Adjunct Faculty* that these organizations held in Washington, DC, to discuss their common concerns and to develop an action plan.

Works Cited

AAUP Committee A on Academic Freedom and Tenure. (1981, February–March). The status of part-time faculty. *Academe, 67(1),* 29–39.

AAUP Committee G Report on Part-Time and Non-Tenure Track Appointments. (1993, July–August). Report: the status of non-tenure track faculty. *Academe, 79(4)*, 39–48.

Abel, E. (1976). *Invisible and indispensable: Part-time teachers in California community colleges.* Santa Monica, CA: Santa Monica College. (ERIC Document Reproduction Service No. ED 132984)

Abel, E. (1984). *Terminal degrees: The job crisis in higher education.* New York: Praeger.

Aronowitz, S. (1998, November–December). Are unions good for professors? *Academe 84(6)*, 12–17.

Association of Departments of English. (1992, December). Statement on the use of part-time and full-time adjunct faculty. http://www.ade.org./policy/index.htm

Benjamin, E. (1997). Faculty appointments: An overview of the data. Paper presented at the Conference on the Growing Use of Part-Time and Adjunct Faculty in Higher Education, Washington, DC.

Berlow, L. H., & Collos, A. L. (1974, November). Part-time employment: We teach; therefore, we are. *ADE Bulletin, 43*, 9–11.

Bérubé, M., & Nelson, C. (Eds.). (1995). *Higher education under fire: Politics, economics, and the crisis of the humanities.* New York: Routledge.

Bowen, H. R., & Schuster, J. H. (1986). *American professors: A national resource imperiled.* New York: Oxford University Press.

Boyer, E. (1990). *Scholarship reconsidered: Priorities of the professoriate.* Princeton, NJ: Carnegie Foundation for the Advancement of Teaching.

CCCC Executive Committee. (1989, October). Statement of principles and standards for the postsecondary teaching of writing. *College Composition and Communication, 40(3)*, 329–336.

Chell, C. (1982, January). Memoirs and confessions of a part-time lecturer. *College English, 44(1)*, 35–40.

Connors, R. (1990, Fall). Overwork/underpay: Labor and status of composition teachers since 1880. *Rhetoric Review, 9(1)*, 108–126.

Cross, K. P. (1993). Improving the quality of instruction. In A. Levine (Ed.), *Higher learning in America* (pp. 287–308). Baltimore: The Johns Hopkins University Press.

Crowley, S. (1991, Fall/Winter). A personal essay on freshman English. *Pre/Text, 12(3–4),* 156–176.

Dasenbrock, R. W. (1993, September). Review: What is English anyway? *College English, 55(5),* 541–547.

Gappa, J. M. (1997). Off the tenure track: Six models for full-time, nontenurable appointments. *New pathways: Faculty career and employment for the 21st century working paper series.* Washington, DC: American Association for Higher Education.

Gappa, J. M., & Leslie, D. W. (1993). *The invisible faculty: Improving the status of part-timers in higher education.* San Francisco: Jossey-Bass.

Gappa, J. M., & Leslie, D. W. (1997). Two faculties or one? The conundrum of part-timers in a bifurcated work force. *New pathways: Faculty career and employment for the 21st century working paper series.* Washington, DC: American Association for Higher Education.

Gappa, J. M., & MacDermid, S. M. (1997). Work, family, and the faculty career. *New pathways: Faculty career and employment for the 21st century working paper series.* Washington, DC: American Association for Higher Education.

Gordon, M. (1993). The economy and higher education. In A. Levine, (Ed.), *Higher learning in America* (pp. 20–35). Baltimore: The Johns Hopkins University Press.

Leslie, D. W., Kellams, S. E., & Gunne, G. M. (1982). *Part-time faculty in American higher education.* New York: Praeger.

Miller, R. E. (1998). *As if learning mattered: Reforming higher education.* Ithaca, NY: Cornell University Press.

Modern Language Association Executive Council. (1994). Statement on the use of part-time and full-time adjunct faculty. In *A career guide for PhDs and PhD candidates in English and foreign languages.* Revised by Elaine Showalter. New York: Modern Language Association.

Nelson, C. (1997). What is to be done? A twelve-step program for academia. In C. Nelson (Ed.), *Manifesto of a tenured radical* (pp. 171–193). New York: New York University Press.

Perley, J. E. (1998, November–December). Educational excellence: Presidential address 1998 AAUP annual meeting. *Academe, 84(6),* 54–57.

Pratt, L. R. (1997). Disposable faculty: Part-time exploitation as management strategy. In C. Nelson (Ed.), *Will teach for food: Academic labor in crisis* (pp. 264–277). Minneapolis: University of Minnesota Press.

Rice, E. R. (1986, January). The academic profession in transition: Toward a new social fiction. *Teaching Sociology, 14(1),* 12–23.

Robertson, L. R., Crowley, S., & Lentricchia, F. (1989, March). Opinion: The Wyoming Conference resolution: Opposing unfair salaries and working conditions for postsecondary teachers of writing. *College English, 49(8),* 274–280.

Royster, J. J., & Williams, J. C. (1999, June). History in the spaces left: African American presence and narratives of composition. *College Composition and Communication, 50(4),* 563–584.

Schell, E. E. (1998). *Gypsy academics and mother-teachers: Gender, contingent labor, and writing instruction.* Portsmouth, NH: Boynton/Cook.

Schuster, J. H. (1997). *Reconfiguring the professoriat: The part-timer phenomenon and implications for the academic profession.* Unpublished paper presented at the Conference on the Growing Use of Part-Time and Adjunct Faculty in Higher Education, Washington, DC.

Schuster, J. H., & Bowen, H. R. (1985, September/October). The faculty at risk. *Change, 17(4),* 13–21.

Slevin, J. F. (1987, Fall). A note on the Wyoming resolution and ADE. *ADE Bulletin, 87,* 50.

Statement from the Conference on the Growing Use of Part-Time and Adjunct Faculty. (1998, Spring). *ADE Bulletin, 119,* 19–26.

Sykes, C. (1988). *ProfScam: Professors and the demise of higher education.* Washington, DC: Regnery Gateway.

Thompson, K. (1998, February). The ultimate working condition: Knowing whether you have a job or not. Forum, Newsletter of the Non-Tenure-Track Faculty Special Interest Group. *College Composition and Communication, 49(1),* A19–24.

Tobias, S., & Rumberger, M. (1974). Full-status part-time faculty. In W. T. Furniss and P. A. Graham (Eds.), *Women in higher education* (pp. 128–137). Washington, DC: American Council on Education.

Trimbur, J. (1996). Writing instruction and the politics of profession-alization. In L. Z. Bloom, D. Daiker, and E. White (Eds.), *Composition in the twenty-first century: Crisis and change* (pp. 133–145). Carbondale: Southern Illinois University Press.

Tuckman, H. P. (1978, December). Who is part-time in academe? *AAUP Bulletin, 64(4)*, 305–315.

Tuckman, B. H., & Tuckman, H. P. (1980). Part-timers, sex discrimination, and career choice at two-year institutions: Further findings from the AAUP survey. *Academe* (March), 71–76.

Tuckman, B. H., & Tuckman, H. P. (1981, March). Women as part-time faculty members. *Higher Education, 10(2)*, 169–179.

Tuckman, H. P., & Vogler, W. D. (1978, May). The 'part' in part-time wages. *AAUP Bulletin, 64(2)*, 70–77.

Wallace, M. E. (Ed.). (1984). *Part-time academic employment in the humanities*. New York: Modern Language Association.

Wilson, J. K. (1995). *The myth of political correctness: The conservative attack on higher education*. Durham, NC: Duke University Press.

Wilson, J. K. (1995–96, Winter). The myth of reverse discrimination in higher education. *Journal of Blacks in Higher Education, 10*, 88–93.

Yang, S., & Zak, M. W. (1981). *Part-time faculty employment in Ohio: A statewide study*. (ERIC No. ED 205 140). Ohio: Kent State University.140.

I

Transforming the Cultural and Material Conditions of Contingent Writing Faculty: The Personal and the Institutional

CHAPTER ONE

Shadows of the Mountain

CHRIS M. ANSON
North Carolina State University, Raleigh

RICHARD JEWELL
University of Minnesota, Minneapolis

Prologue

A Chinese tale in a children's picture book by Arnold Lobel describes the quandary of Ming Lo and his wife, who live in the shadow of a huge mountain. Their house is dark and wet, rocks tumble from the mountain and make holes in their roof, and nothing grows in their garden. In frustration, they consult a sage who offers them various suggestions for moving the mountain: push at it with a huge felled tree; scare it away by banging on pots and pans; cajole it with fresh cakes and baskets of bread. To the dismay of the couple, all of these methods fail. The mountain doesn't budge. Desperate, Ming Lo once again consults the wise man. After deep thought, the wise man tells Ming Lo and his wife to dismantle their home stick by stick, pack it into bundles, carry these bundles in their arms and on their heads, close their eyes, and perform an odd, backward-stepping dance. Following his instructions at home, they load themselves with their belongings and, eyes closed, step to the dance of the moving mountain. After several hours, they open their eyes to behold that the mountain has moved far away. Elated, they reassemble their house and live out their years in sunshine and bliss.

As the title of our essay and this volume suggest, the problem of working conditions for many teachers of writing has cast a dark shadow across the landscape of higher education. Looming above the field of composition itself, the subject of staffing and employment remains one of the most politically charged and educationally debated of all the issues in the huge industry of writing instruction. And with good reason: in record numbers, colleges and universities around the country are hiring itinerant workers to teach writing on the cheap, assigning them by the term to many sections of composition, without benefits, without training, and without material support for their work. Yet these lamentable practices go on in what may be the university's most important instructional domain: the development of written literacy.

Early proposals for improving employment practices in composition assumed that the problem could be pushed, threatened, or persuaded away. But the problem itself turned out to be much less monolithic for some members of the field than for others. People's opinions about working conditions are influenced by their own positions, experiences, and aspirations. An "exploited" part-timer may like the conditions of his job—a job free from the heavy committee work, student advising, and publication requirements that besiege many a tenured professor. Or a "boss compositionist," to use James Sledd's disparaging term, may fight constantly with her own higher administration to provide benefits and job security to her nontenured employees. Claims about the relationship between working conditions and quality of instruction may be equally specious: stunningly strong pedagogy daily graces the classrooms of badly paid part-time teachers, while some students must endure the dronings of uninspired tenured faculty who boast high salaries and excellent benefits.

This essay is our attempt to recognize the perceptual complexity that has characterized discussions about employment in the teaching of writing. In it, we aim to show how our job histories, and the broader personal and institutional dimensions of our work, have influenced our perception of employment standards and practices in composition. When we teamed up to write this piece, we were barely professional acquaintances. We had taught in the same department and knew its curriculum but had never worked together closely. Richard is currently an education specialist in the composition program at the University of Minnesota, a position in which he teaches multiple sections of writing classes on a yearly renewable appointment. He made a full-time job of working part-time for eleven years at St. Cloud State

University and in various community colleges, proprietary colleges, and community education programs. Chris was hired at the University of Minnesota in 1984 as a new assistant professor right out of graduate school, having never held a temporary or part-time teaching job except as a TA. He earned promotion and tenure in four years and became a full professor in 1996. He directed the Program in Composition from 1988 to 1996.

When the occasion for this piece arose, we decided to avoid the ordinary sense of collaboration and to collaborate in a different sense. We felt it important for each of us to first tell our own story about employment in composition and then to respond to each other's narratives about the issues they raised for us. As a result, our narratives became the context for a kind of response dialogue, whose pieces are interwoven throughout our stories.

In deciding on this structure for our essay, we were interested in mirroring the discursive practices that we believe should mediate our field's continued concerns about employment practices: attending to and respecting individual voices; responding to those voices in the spirit of negotiation and reform; and engaging in dialogues in which all stakeholders can participate openly, informing each other in ways that both reveal the complexity of the issues and move toward local and national consensus. In blending narrative and analysis, monologue and dialogue, the public and the private, we hope to suggest ways that discussion about crucial matters of employment can and should take place in many venues and through many kinds of discourse: conferences and coalitions; personal conversations; official and unofficial committees; and both sponsored and grassroots discussion groups and forums.

Adjunct Mountain Passes
Richard Jewell

Recently I was hired, along with eleven others, as an education specialist in the University of Minnesota English department's undergraduate writing program. Most of us teach five to six semester sections per year of first- and third-year composition and fulfill committee responsibilities. Most of us also have terminal degrees or are ABD. I have three master's degrees.

I started teaching composition part-time thirteen years ago at Minnesota's largest state university, St. Cloud State, which has about fifteen thousand students. The English department hired me immediately after I graduated summa cum laude from its master's degree program. Before starting my degree program at St. Cloud, I had been a free-lance writer earning four times the average free-lancer's income but still only enough to make half a living. I began teaching to increase my income, and during my first few years at St. Cloud, as a teaching assistant and then as a part-timer, I was content with my role: my children and I were eating, and I loved my work. The single father of three very young children, a happy innocent, little did I know of tenure wars or the insidious lines that separate the work of tenure- and non-tenure-accruing faculty.

My innocence continued longer than is normal for others, perhaps because I wanted to teach part-time, perhaps because the chair of the English department in which I worked was un-usually supportive of me. I did not know then that the chair fre-quently called one or two full-timers who were flexible, told them he had a single-parent part-timer who needed a later class, and asked if they would be willing to exchange for my earlier one. I did not learn until much later that when this chair allowed me to teach a 300-level research writing class fifty miles off campus that no one else wanted to teach, some members of the depart-ment were upset because, at that time, no part-timer was allowed to teach advanced writing courses. Neither did I understand why when the chair allowed me—an instructor with more published short stories than all but one person in the department—to teach a 300-level creative writing class forty miles off campus that no one else wanted, a committee was appointed to examine my cre-dentials before I was allowed to accept the chair's assignment.

Anson: There's an interesting complexity in your early history at St. Cloud State. You clearly had a supportive chair who saw, and valued, your preparation, your energy, and your talents. He of-fered you opportunities (if the unwanted "dregs" of the depart-ment can be considered opportunities) against the protests of the department. In a way, he was using his authority to resist the hierarchies that defined what was "allowed"—and for you, that was fortuitous. But the principle of a chair doing things in an unsanctioned way can be just as damaging to employment practices as reforming of them. It would be nice to think that the entire department could have collectively recognized the problems in their hiring practices and created more equitable positions for you and others with suitable preparation and strong evaluations. It's only in that collective process, to my mind, that we will ever reform current employment practices.

* * *

Jewell: Agreed. As I gradually realized how autocratic my first chair was, I became less comfortable with being a beneficiary. At my next school, an autocratic chair was very damaging to me. I also have seen highly democratic, functional departments: as a rule they seem to make an effort to support and treat their part-timers well.

Over time, I grew tired of formulating magazine articles, my principal source of free-lance income, and took increasing pleasure in teaching. Deciding to teach full time, I added to my university assignments additional part-time work teaching English, writing, and humanities at a nearby business college and in noncredit community courses. To my surprise, I was also almost hired by St. Cloud's English department, after a national search for what was called an NTTR—non-tenure-track renewable—position: a full-time, indefinitely renewable job.[1]

Anson: A recent report from the Modern Language Association argues that "freeway fliers" (non-tenure-track and part-time instructors who teach at several institutions in order to make a living) often worsen the quality of undergraduate education because, among other things, "they cannot give [students] the kind of outside-the-classroom guidance that has traditionally been considered good pedagogical practice" (MLA Report on Professional Employment, 9). How were you able to balance your commitment to good teaching against the obvious time constraints of teaching at several institutions (as well as keeping up with your freelance work)?

* * *

Jewell: I'm a quick study. I've been able to adapt to different institutions' needs. And I kept my courses at several schools as alike as was reasonably possible. Many of the schools for which I worked also had strict requirements about my being present for students at least an hour per week per class, and I've always given students my home phone number. Unfortunately, at times there was no way to develop syllabuses creatively. In addition, in my one-course or "freeway" schools, I regularly lamented the fact that I was not able to interact with students to the extent that I think necessary for quality education. I do believe that freeway-flier teaching is as effective as the teaching tenured faculty do in extension courses at distant locations. That said, the best student services are provided by on-campus teachers to on-campus students. My experience suggests that such services are provided well both by tenured faculty and by part-timers who are given sufficient and steady work and pay to remain at one school for several years.

Unfortunately for me, the chair of the St. Cloud English department retired, and three others took his place in quick succession. My work schedule changed: I was assigned early morning classes or none; I encountered greater resistance when I wanted to teach anything other than what I had taught, and I was less protected from the hothouse politics of academia at the departmental level. At one point, when the mass communications department asked me to teach a 400/500-level course, *Writing for Magazines*, a few English faculty objected to my teaching a graduate course. I had no doctorate. However, mass communications was willing to employ me because it still maintained a two-track system (professional and academic), a system that, in retrospect, I consider excellent. Over the years, I have discovered that hiring based exclusively on a certificate of intellectual knowledge is as shortsighted in terms of gaining excellent teachers as is hiring based exclusively on race, gender, or class. In this particular situation, I found it was not only a few English faculty who were upset. A part-time colleague in English with training in journalism, who had applied for part-time work in mass communications and had been refused, tore down posters about the course that mass communications hired me to teach and asked me to display. This taught me another lesson: part-timers competing for the same work often do not support one another.

Anson: It's clear that when competition increases for scarce resources, members of otherwise supportive, networked communities begin to distance themselves from one another. I've seen this happen regularly among the tenured professoriate, who can, in a bad climate, become jealous, competitive, wary, secretive, and calculating even while presumably working for the common good of their own department. How can administrators establish a supportive community among instructors at all levels? Hierarchies don't help. Marginalized groups can as easily prey on each other as those at the center prey on them. Including members of all employment categories in matters of departmental governance can help.

* * *

Jewell: Access to open governance is of great importance, but it isn't the only solution. At one of my schools, my department gave all part-timers full voting rights (by percentage of workload with absentee balloting allowed), and full representation on working committees, and at one time moved many of its part-timers into full-time, tenured positions. However, the school's higher administration found these practices counterproductive to their purposes. They stopped hiring part-timers to full-time positions almost entirely and cut part-time workloads. My experience has been that functional and democratic departments left to their own devices will attempt to support part-timers, but this support is easily thwarted from outside the departments when pay and guarantees of workload and permanence are at stake.

During my years teaching at St. Cloud, I participated in a state university conference and in a Midwest Modern Language Association conference. Activities such as these were acknowledged and praised by my departmental evaluating committee. Although I would like to have presented my work at other conferences, the administration did not provide money for part-timers to travel. Like most of my part-time colleagues, I limited my presentations to settings I could reach in round-trip car travel in one day. For economic reasons, with few exceptions, I was also unable to take advantage of opportunities for professional development. These opportunities were for teachers with extra money to spend in the summers or on sabbaticals, not typically for part-time faculty.

Professional development opportunities were not the only ones unavailable to part-time faculty. I received retirement but no medical benefits unless I had worked three-fourths time for three quarters. Often I would work full time in one quarter, two-thirds in the next, and be assigned just one course in the third quarter—keeping me just shy of benefits. No information about tracking such benefits was given to me, and the first time I qualified, no medical benefits were paid, even though they should have been, automatically. Later when I discovered the oversight, I requested replacement benefits and was refused. The administrator with whom I spoke offered me compensation for my medical costs during the previous quarter. I had none: like other long-term part-timers, I delayed all "yearly" medical checkups for my family for a quarter when I might qualify for compensation. When I asked my union representative about this problem, he said I could grieve it, but almost assuredly nothing would come of it. In addition, he said, my grievance might hurt part-timers by making the administration work even harder to cut their benefits and by making the union work harder to get rid of part-time positions.

Part-time salaries at St. Cloud when I was there, though better than wages for hand labor, were low. Part-timers were all on the instructor level of a union-bargained pay scale that fortunately did contain increases for up to ten years and slightly higher pay for those with doctorates. Our pay probably would have been worse had it not been for the union. After I left, salaries for English part-timers improved (a little more than $500 per quarter credit for a four-credit course, the equivalent of $750 per semester credit). However, in another part of the contract that set the higher pay rates, it was stipulated that if a part-timer did not teach more than three or four courses per year, pay would stay at the basic rate and contain no significant increases for years of service or for education. The union, I learned, had decided to give up some part-time rights in order to bargain successfully for a larger percentage of tenure-stream positions. As part of this new policy, NTTR (non-tenure-track renewable) jobs throughout the state were bargained away: existing NTTRs have kept their protected status and are even able to rise to associate professor status, but no new NTTRs or replacements can be hired.

After I left St. Cloud State, the part-time program was largely dismantled. Tenure lines were better protected throughout the state by union contract—a wise move in light of the decrease of tenured positions as a percentage of all faculty positions nationally. However, part-timers were sacrificed to achieve this protection. Part-timers in the Minnesota state universities could no longer earn the protected positions that earlier part-time colleagues had gained. At this time, the St. Cloud State English department began to register, hire, and train as teaching assistants an increasingly larger contingent of graduate students—up to twenty per year. In my TA group seven years earlier, there had been three, and only one in the year before that. This increase in TAs was a boon to many tenured department members, who never enjoyed teaching Composition I and could now hand that responsibility to the students who filled the graduate courses they loved to teach. It was, however, unfortunate for these graduate students that the number of applicants for an advertised English position in community colleges in Minnesota—the only colleges in which a master's degree is sufficient for tenure-track teaching in English—increased to as many as three hundred.

When the union abandoned part-timers in the state university system, it established a new degree qualification for postsecondary teaching. Previously the line drawn between those with master's degrees and those with terminal degrees had been blurred. Many departments at St. Cloud State had older teachers and occasionally (as in mass communications) younger ones with the master's who were tenured, as well as non-tenure-track teachers (e.g., NTTRs) with either the master's or a doctorate who had tenure-like job security. In the new hiring environment, only those with terminal degrees could aspire to tenure; those without such degrees could expect no tenure, even though they were needed.

I did not stay long enough at St. Cloud State to see these new policies take effect. My soon-to-be wife had a tenured position at a community college in Minneapolis, one hundred miles away, and so I, the untenured one, moved. During the next six years I taught part-time at two suburban community colleges. For the first four of those years, I was essentially a full-time, untenured teacher with a contract renewed quarter by quarter. In spite of the heavy workloads, I liked the community college system. Part-timers in it had many of the same rights and opportunities as tenured faculty in Minnesota. I participated fully in faculty development training projects both on campus and in state meetings, received a full travel allowance that helped me to present at several state and regional conferences and at the Conference on College Composition and Communication, and I was on the highest step of the pay scale, equivalent to that of a person with a doctorate. (In fact, at one time the community colleges had a short-lived, union-bargained system in which after two years, part-timers with enough courses were automatically given part-time tenure. With additional courses, they were able to gain full-time tenure.) I received full benefits in a system in which deans, not department chairs, hire, fire, and often choose courses for part-timers. I grew substantially as a teacher with the support of deans who helped and sometimes even encouraged me to teach new courses in philosophy, religion, and the humanities (my other two master's degrees).

Unfortunately, I was not a good fit in my first community college English department. The department emphasized the teaching of composition as writing about literature. Unaware of the national struggles among composition pedagogies, I was trained—and preferred—to teach writing as an interdisciplinary study. In addition, the chair and several members of the department, supportive neither of my training and preferences nor of part-timers in general, felt special displeasure when an assistant dean created a peer-tutor writing center and hired me as its first part-time director. I made other political mistakes too, in a department that I gradually discovered was rich with intrigue. I had supporters, however, none among those who held power in the department. Two years after I was appointed director of the writing center, I was asked to leave. Neither my supporters nor the dean who had hired me could protect me. I learned a lesson familiar to non-tenure-track faculty: contingent faculty must always have the support of the powerful factions in their departments to survive, and sometimes being as invisible as possible is the best way to avoid difficulties.

Anson: I find this part of your story especially unsettling. Because of your status, you were denied certain intellectual rights that tenured faculty don't even think twice about. Your choice was either to submit to curricular mandates and teaching methods to which you were theoretically opposed, based on current work in the field, or to risk your position by doing what you thought was best. Without a way to argue your perspective, you were held hostage by the system.

* * *

Jewell: I had a very tough three years at that school. In all fairness, I must say that I was caught between the dean who hired me and liked my pedagogical approaches and members of the department who did not. The department should have had the opportunity to choose or reject me initially. On reflection, I wish that I had kept very quiet—and left as quickly as possible. The reality was that for a part-timer, I had become too emboldened by my growth as a teacher at St. Cloud.

I moved on to another community college more in tune with my training and preferences. I was embraced fully by this new department, and my new assistant dean was highly supportive. After one year, though, the dean left, and members of the department made it very clear to me that though they supported me, the college's administration—which often has the final word in hiring in this system—did not like to move part-timers into full-time positions. The system experienced money problems, enrollments dropped, and my college lost a tenth of its funding. Part-timers at our college lost about half our work and in some cases two-thirds of our income. In Minnesota community colleges, part-timers who teach only one course per quarter are removed from the normal salary scale (calculated as a percentage of what a tenured, full-time teacher earns), and receive instead a lower salary (at that time, $350 per quarter credit, little better than the minimum wage at the time). Experienced teachers, those who cost too much, were given smaller loads. The courses they normally taught were assigned to new teachers, who cost less.

Anson: We badly need to examine the economics of higher education to ferret out discrepancies across different departments and disciplines. I think we would find, for example, that composition is among the worst areas for this kind of exploitation. At many institutions, low-cost part-time teachers are used to staff composition sections in order to generate profit for the university, which then channels its earnings into other areas. Achieving a better state of equilibrium between revenue and expenses in composition would go a long way toward pay equity, even if it didn't entirely eliminate the hiring of part-time instructors.

* * *

Jewell: As we seek this equilibrium, a realistic and even laudable goal is not to eliminate part-timers, but rather to give them per-credit pay equal to that of full-timers. In fact, concessions in part-time pay negotiated by two unions in Minnesota have led to fuller hiring of part-timers: once pay on a per-credit basis became more equitable, part-timers were more likely to receive larger work oads and even full-time work.

I found additional work teaching nights in a proprietary business college where full-time liberal arts teachers were required to have a master's degree, expected to teach six to eight courses per quarter for forty-eight weeks per year, and paid about $20,000 per year. At this business college I learned to grade quickly, to avoid innovation, and to spend a minimal amount of time with students individually. During these two busy years when I might have been teaching in as many as five different locations in a given week, I was one of the lucky ones among part-timers: few were as able as I to find sufficient work in teaching. I watched many excellent teachers leave college teaching, either temporarily or for good. During these lean times, I witnessed even more mistreatment of part-timers than I saw at other times, abuses no tenured faculty member ever suffered.[2]

In 1996, in the midst of these lean times, the University of Minnesota's English department advertised twelve "education specialist" positions. Reluctant to apply at first because of the relatively low pay ($28,500), I finally did and was hired. Although raises of those in my position approximate the rate of inflation, there is nothing like tenure. However, we do have health benefits and can begin to earn retirement benefits after three years. And, after three years, we are eligible to compete for term-length research projects (the equivalent of sabbatical leaves). We have no power in the English department, for we are not faculty members; however, compared to other adjunct positions at the local and national levels, our working conditions are good.

Anson: My own story explains why in this same program (which is now newly controlled by the English department) I resisted hiring non-tenure-track and part-time instructors. Across the spectrum of your many experiences, this position looks good: you can focus your energies in a single department, your remuneration and benefits are reasonable, and there is some opportunity for advancement. However, having been a member of this department for fifteen years, I am convinced that many of the inequities you described in other settings will continue, albeit on different scales—inequities the worst of which is the fact that no matter how hard you work, no matter how stunning your record, your position is always at risk should the department or the university decide to change directions, whether for financial, curricular, or structural reasons. And your burdens are greater than perhaps among any other employed class in the department. Whereas you must meticulously account for your activities annually, teaching assistants with little or no experience in the classroom are not evaluated formally at all, and are guaranteed reappointment for six years of graduate school. In some ways, you are less protected than a first-year graduate student who may know almost nothing about the highly complex and demanding job of teaching undergraduates how to become more effective writers. These and other inequities and discrepancies in status kept me from opening the door to new classes of employees, even while I recognized that keeping the door closed meant fewer (if exploitative) positions for people like you.

* * *

Jewell: I can understand your reasoning and agree with you on most points. I do think, however, that we, as a profession, have a tendency to try to solve the part-time problem simply by replacing part-time teachers with as many full-time, tenured positions as possible. This solution concerns me deeply. First, the reality is that part-time workers always will exist. Second, and much more important, when we focus so much energy on replacing part-time teachers with full-time positions, ongoing injustices are overlooked time and again. Part-timers are misused and underpaid. If justice is our goal, the reality is that more equal per-credit pay for part-timers and a ladder system allowing part-timers to rise to full-time and to tenured positions are at least as necessary as converting to more full-time, tenured positions. I might add that in my experience, equal pay and a ladder system also appear to contribute to collegiality in a department, just as collegiality often is improved when a respected faculty member—rather than an outsider—becomes an administrator in a department or college.

Over my years of work as a non-tenure-track teacher, I have experienced a mix of emotions. I have become cynical about the status and living conditions of part-timers; at the same time, I have become confident of my abilities. The unfairness with which part-time faculty live makes me cynical. Tenure-like systems and pay raises for part-time and other adjunct faculty are needed—now. Unfortunately, unions, faculty, and administrations are more often contrary opponents than collegial decision-makers in the current environment in which administrators are being asked to operate their units like efficient businesses. Nevertheless, I still love teaching in my discipline. My current role at the University of Minnesota is about the best one can do and not have tenure. I consider my job an acknowledgment of my skills, my record, and my willingness to keep trying. My students, my profession, and my work with my colleagues give me pleasure. If I had tenure or a similar guarantee and reasonable salary increases, I would be content to teach where I am permanently in spite of the low pay I receive.

Can Climbing the Mountain Move It?
Chris Anson

From 1988 until August of 1996, I directed one of the largest composition programs in the country, a budgetarily and administratively autonomous unit housed in the College of Liberal Arts at the University of Minnesota. In that capacity, I oversaw all personnel issues affecting the program, including the hiring, training, and supervision of its teachers and staff. Before that time, I had not given much thought to the principles of employment in the field of composition, except for the ones that directly affected my own livelihood. Then, in 1988, I had to face quite regularly decisions that reflected the ethos of the program and my own beliefs about employment in composition. It was a tough call.

The program I inherited had never employed part- or full-time untenured teachers except in evening courses. Every regular section of composition was taught by TAs, over one hundred of them, who were enrolled in graduate programs. The position paid a typical TA stipend and came with tuition benefits and some short-term health insurance. A dozen part-time instructors taught evening courses in our extension division, and most of them held permanent, full-time jobs at community colleges or in business and industry. Elsewhere, I have shown how the professionalization of graduate students (who freely opt into advanced degree programs) is enhanced by teaching classes and becoming involved in administration or teacher development (Anson & Rutz). Therefore, I have not viewed TA employment in quite the same way as I view the employment of adjunct instructors, although I know all too well how often TAs are also exploited for the financial gain of a department or institution.

Toward the end of my directorship, beginning in about 1994, the dean's office began urging me to hire full-time untenured instructors at high section loads. The reasons were purely financial: TAs incurred extra costs to the university, including health insurance and free tuition, but taught a limited number of classes. Full-time nontenured adjuncts, on the other hand, could teach nine or more sections of composition a year. The pay differences between the two groups seemed very small, but calculated over hundreds of sections of composition, they added up to several thousand dollars, a bottom line that did not escape the fiscally sharp eyes of our administration. In spite of the dean's urgings, I resisted opening the door to non-tenure-track instructors.

Jewell: I can't entirely agree with your initial resistance to hiring full-time adjuncts, however excellent your motives. I have observed resistance similar to yours in the two separate teachers' unions in Minnesota's state university and community college systems. In the 1980s, the state university union gave up a non-tenure-track-renewable position that virtually guaranteed indefinite renewal in order to bargain for more tenured positions. So did the Minnesota community college system in the early 1990s. In both situations, adjuncts did not significantly decrease in numbers but rather suffered more.

My experience suggests that individuals often choose part-time work purposefully as I did. Many teachers just out of graduate school take adjunct positions as a means of working their way into permanent teaching positions. My two years' experience, as one of a dozen full-time, annually renewable teachers in English at the University of Minnesota, has convinced me that full- and part-time adjuncts can provide a department greater quality and consistency in teaching, administration, and teacher training, than can TAs alone. In addition, excellent systems do exist to reward adjuncts with tenure-track positions. I saw one in the Minnesota community college system.

Unfortunately, there is a strong tendency in academia to assume that the grass is greener elsewhere; unknown teachers from other colleges are more attractive candidates for positions than a college's own known adjuncts, even when newcomers have no better credentials. Arguably, teachers whose excellence has been observed for several years and who are committed to local academic and civic communities are better-qualified candidates for positions than those who are found in national searches.

* * *

Anson: In response to what many perceive to be a "crisis" in faculty employment, especially in English departments and writing programs, we are seeing more arguments in favor of hiring tenure-track faculty and cutting back on our over-reliance on part-time and adjunct faculty. Now that you bring it up, I think that part of my resistance to hiring non-tenure-track adjuncts or part-timers may have come from my having argued year after year for new faculty positions in composition—exactly what you say led to the elimination of some adjunct positions in the state university system. If a college or university wants to hire well-prepared, committed faculty, it should try to hire them as permanent faculty. If the pay, benefits, and other conditions of work are roughly the same for an adjunct faculty member as for a tenure-track faculty member, there seems to be little reason not to hire the latter except for purposes of "flexibility" in times of financial distress. Nationally, if we don't keep urging for full-time tenure-track positions, the abundant candidates in that pool will be forced to take part-time and non-tenure-track jobs, which only exacerbates the problem.

My colleagues and I were also mindful that, without a contractual system in place that would guarantee pay levels, benefits, representation, and the like, our ambitions to treat adjunct faculty well could be thwarted later by our college administration. Not creating another class of potentially exploitable employees to begin with meant we would not be pressured to increase the number of such employees for the sake of generating institutional profit that could be used elsewhere (as it almost always is).

Although the dean's office never actually demanded that we hire non-tenure-track instructors, from their persistence I knew that they did not fully understand why I resisted the idea. After all, it was no more difficult administratively to assign adjunct instructors to composition courses than TAs, and might have even reduced the need for instructional development. Each year, we received half a dozen or more unsolicited résumés or letters of inquiry from seemingly well-qualified teachers in our metropolitan area, sent in the hope of teaching even one course in our curriculum. Everyone knew the market could provide us with a substantial number of teachers—why not exploit the labor potential? As my colleagues and I grappled with this question, I found myself exploring my own work history for answers. Did my background give me enough experience to help me understand the issues well? Did my position—a tenured professor with all the political and material amenities that title assumes—blind me to the problems of differential status among instructors of the same courses? Or did it not matter—was hiring adjuncts simply a matter of filling sections and putting people on a payroll?

Nothing in my graduate experience predicted that I would find objectionable the hiring of many nontenured instructors. In my early graduate studies (an M.A. program in English at Syracuse University), I worked for a while as a part-time administrative assistant in the offices of an instructional-development project on campus. A semester later, I was hired as a TA in Syracuse's composition program, and after teaching for a year, I finished my M.A. degree by assisting the director of that program and teaching a reduced load. My work as a composition TA and assistant to the director of composition continued for the next five years at Indiana University as I completed my second M.A. and Ph.D. During summers, I picked up extra, mostly academic work, and was never without a job. My wife, a medical technologist, worked full-time during almost all of my graduate education, and her salary, though modest, provided the bulk of our income. Although we struggled financially, we were really broke only once, for a month or two, but managed to get by with borrowed funds.

During this time, I looked ahead to the job market with great trepidation. I knew that finding a good academic position would be very hard, and each year my senior graduate student colleagues made that fact plainer to me as they reported on their own job searches. I knew that my own area of composition studies was burgeoning, and that there would be more jobs for me than for my peers in highly competitive literary areas. Still, I began to seek any way I could to enhance my credentials, driving hours to give papers at small, regional conferences; teaching and tutoring in every venue I could find; writing and rewriting essays for publication in regional and national journals; seeking any and every opportunity I could to be involved in something related to my field. What I hoped for eventually was a job. Tenure was not foremost in my mind early in my graduate program, but my advisors soon convinced me that I should seek only tenure-track positions. In such a position, with hard work, I could secure lifelong employment.

My job search in the last year of my doctoral program yielded over two dozen interviews and several strong offers. I accepted an entry-level, tenure-track position as a composition specialist at the University of Minnesota, my first and, at this writing, only job after completing my Ph.D. Although I was involved immediately in the administration of the composition program, issues of employment did not really concern me until after I simultaneously earned early tenure and became director of composition in 1988. My confidence describing and defending my philosophy of employment to the dean and associate deans of my college came in part from the tenure system. They could think me a poor administrator, or force me to go against my own beliefs in my hiring practices, or even replace me with another writing program administrator who would enact their wishes, but they could not fire me for my views. Ironically, this protection was one reason why I was opposed to hiring full-time adjuncts: I knew that it would create inequities of involvement, speech, and representation between groups of people who were expected to teach the same courses equally well.

When the suggestion to hire adjuncts first arose, I had served as a member and then as co-chair of the CCCC Committee on Professional Standards for the Teaching of Writing. This committee, with strong representation from part-time teachers, was continuing to grapple with employment issues on the heels of the "Statement," the CCCC document outlining principles and standards for the postsecondary teaching of writing. I had read much of the literature surrounding this document, and had talked to many administrators as well as to part-time, adjunct, and nontenured teachers of writing. What struck me most about the arguments in the field was the relationship between the desire for disciplinary respect and the desperation I sensed in the lives of many part-time and nontenured teachers. The more composition leaders urged the "elimination" of itinerant workers for the sake of establishing disciplinary legitimacy and "cleaning up" the teaching of writing, the more worried some part-timers became. At the same time, many composition directors knew that no matter how hard they tried to eliminate part-time and adjunct instruction on their campuses, their administrations would win the day. Leaders of coalitions representing part-time and nontenured instructors, in contrast, critiqued not their own existence but their lack of fair treatment.

My colleagues in composition understood the problem well. Literature professors I consulted at Minnesota, however, often saw the issue in terms of economic models of supply and demand, or even framed it in the ideology of social Darwinism. If there were qualified candidates willing, eager, even desperate to accept nontenured jobs, why not take advantage of them? This argument troubled me. I knew of half a dozen highly qualified people who would be happy for such a position. For most of them, work, any work, was better than nothing. Shut doors represented a more chilling fear than even the lousiest of teaching jobs.

Jewell: I'm as troubled as you are by these supply-and-demand and social Darwinism arguments that many administrators and tenured faculty members use to justify the poor working conditions of adjunct faculty. I find such arguments about as valid as when they are used by third-world police states to justify the economic enslavement of children, women, and the poor, and when such arguments are used to justify no limits for the sale of drugs, sex, weapons of war, or for that matter, human beings. Our social contract in this country requires not just economic worth, but also ethical fairness.

But even if we use arguments of supply and demand or social evolution, how is economic and social worth really to be calculated? I know of one excellent part-timer who, during an economic crunch at his college, couldn't pick up enough part-time work to survive, so he became a prison guard to feed his family; another who, after winning a coveted best-teacher award given by the student body of a college and praise from a majority of people in his department, was forced out of his college by an insistent tenured teacher who disliked him. He turned to work in construction. I know yet another teacher who, when she followed the suggestion of an administrator to develop a new advanced course, so upset the more traditional members of her department that she was given the choice in the following year of teaching developmental courses or none at all. The pay of another teacher I knew was so low that in the summers he received unemployment compensation.

How are these teachers and thousands like them serving our country's best interests economically when they do not have the protections, pay, or benefits granted to the great majority of people in business and the academic world who have similar or less education and skills? In fact, my experience and observation of part-time workers in academia has shown me that on average, part-timers who are regularly rehired generally work as hard and long per class, offer as many teaching innovations, and create results as good as do tenured teachers.

* * *

Anson: When faculty argue the supply-and-demand view of academic labor, they open the door to precisely the sorts of inequities you describe. How is it possible for a tenured faculty member to get a hard-working adjunct instructor fired? Such stories are common, of course, even within groups of tenured and tenure-track faculty, but it's much more difficult for a single person to wreak political or personal vengeance when there is equal status within the group. Part-timers who need to moonlight as prison guards are not being given the sort of regular appointments, adequate pay, and job security, in one institution, that I believe teaching in higher education requires. It's because tenured faculty and administrators exploit the desperation of some un(der)-employed teachers that you and I have heard so many unsettling stories. Just because there exists a ready-made labor force of writing instructors doesn't mean they should be exploited, especially if that exploitation is designed to advantage those in power by lessening their own responsibilities.

Part of my resistance also owes, I think, to various experiences I had in my high school and college years in which I either witnessed or directly experienced the atrocious treatment of workers in factories and on construction sites where I often held temporary positions. My resentment of exploitative employers and supervisors had a profound effect on the development of my attitudes toward fair treatment on the job. Forms of oppression and exploitation exist in all work situations, at all levels, across all professions. When the means are possible for a business or institution to improve the working conditions of its employees, there are few excuses for not doing so. Not many administrators in higher education will admit to violating OSSHA standards, discriminating against minority employees, or riding herd on workers to the point of destroying their morale. But more subtle inequities can be found in dozens of college and university literacy programs across the country—inequities of course assignments, scheduling, and sensitivity to personal situations; inequities of representation in decisions about class size or workload; pay inequities between people doing the same jobs with the same expectations; inequities in access to equipment, phones, office space, lounges, computer labs, and libraries; inequities in performance assessment; inequities in the advanced scheduling of course assignments; and inequities in curricular and pedagogical freedom. Any employer—in a warehouse, a manufacturing firm, a country club, or a composition program—has a responsibility to treat employees fairly and equally.

As the pressure to hire nontenured teachers increased at Minnesota, I knew we were fighting a losing battle. The foreign languages had, from the dean's perspective, successfully hired dozens of "teaching specialists" (a euphemism for full-time, nontenured instructors assigned by the term or year to many courses). Resistance had now become futile.

I realized that once we had made the first hire of an adjunct, we would be opening a door we might never be able to close. The practice of hiring particular classes of employees does not change easily, but the specific treatment of the class might vary considerably over the years. How could we avoid exploiting teachers by hiring them at low pay and expecting them to teach brilliantly in multiple sections of composition day after day? How could we bring them into the management of our program in ways that would help them to feel part of our enterprise when so much was at risk for them? What would stop us from hiring and firing such teachers by the term just because they gave us a new kind of flexibility in course scheduling? How could we avoid a system in which adjuncts were more "accountable," in terms of performance assessment, than TAs, whose transgressions were almost always understood developmentally and excused?

In the spring of 1996, I decided to work out a plan for exploring the adjunct question on a "pilot" basis. My plan allowed for the hiring of two full-time, nontenured instructors who would be assigned the equivalent of eight sections of composition per year on the quarter system. But at least two of these sections would be released in exchange for collaborative involvement in administration and the training of TAs. There would also be a

special fund set up exclusively for the continued professionalization of the two adjuncts. They would have access to (and be
strongly encouraged to use) money to give papers at regional or
national conferences. They would receive an entire year's teaching schedule all at once, highly responsive to their preferences,
before the fall quarter. They would be eligible for the program's
teaching award, which I had established several years before. They
would have full, year-round medical and dental benefits with
university-supported extensions to their families. They would have
special office space and access to phones, faxes, copy machines,
and other supplies. They would be given full representation on
our core staff, the administrative governing unit within the program. They would receive a contract for at least three years, pref-
erably five, subject to a standard year-end assessment of their
accomplishments and teaching. And finally, they would have
quarterly meetings with me to discuss their work and their
progress toward a permanent, tenure-track position at another
institution (my department hadn't hired any tenure-track faculty
in composition in almost a decade, a fact that persists even now,
after the recent loss of two of four faculty who claim composition as a specialty). While we knew that in this model, we would
be investing a lot of time and expense in people we were only
helping to move into better jobs, it was the only really responsible way I could imagine to do what we were being asked.

Jewell: The plan you developed for the hiring of full-time adjuncts
is admirable, and some of it (not all) has come to pass. Unfortunately, as you note, you didn't have the chance to enact it. After
the shift in leadership in 1996, twelve full-time, annually renewable specialists were hired. At this writing eight new part-time
specialists and lecturers also have been hired on quarterly contracts, and all eight of them have been told (five of them only after
they started their jobs) that there would be no work for them next
year. I don't blame the current administrator, who is making every effort to give annual contracts to all adjuncts who request
them; rather, I do blame a system of higher education in which
people's lives are so little valued.

Security exists only as long as does my job. How long will I
last? How innovative or political dare I be? And why must I re-

ceive such a low salary with increases amounting to no more than adjustments for inflation each year, no matter how wonderful a teacher I may be, how much I contribute to my profession in publication and presentation, or how much credit I bring to my university? For too many years when I was on quarter-to-quarter contracts, I felt panic every three months, wondering if I would have enough work to survive a bit longer as a teacher. About once a year on average some administrator at one of my part-time locations would make a mistake that would significantly change my income by forgetting to complete paperwork for it, or worst of all, forgetting to tell me of a canceled assignment in time for me to find a replacement for it somewhere else. Apologies, much less replacement work, were rare.

Now that I have an annually renewable contract and am married to a tenured teacher, I feel almost expansive in my relative security. But I see my old panic, fear, courage, and will to teach reflected in the faces of part-timers and friends around me who still live a hand-to-mouth existence. All of us are impoverished by the demeaning manner in which we treat these fellow teachers. Solutions to these problems exist. How many more decades must we wait before they are adopted?

* * *

Anson: I was dismayed when the new composition administration, populated by literary scholars in the English department, hired a dozen education specialists and then, on their heels, eight individuals in an even more vulnerable category of instructors (teaching specialists and lecturers) who are being hired and fired by the term. While you don't blame the current administrator (your boss), he is no more at the mercy of the higher administration than I was—and is willing to enact and tolerate what it suggests. You and the other education specialists are more involved in running the program than any faculty in the English department, and you do this alongside heavy teaching loads. In a way, that involvement has given you a special sense of responsibility, and has built a community from your ranks, that makes your overall employment at the University seem bearable, perhaps even desirable. But your uneasy security comes from a system in which the tenured literature faculty deliberately abrogate their responsibility to the program by giving you the administrative and training work that they ought to be doing. In so doing, they also shift some of the accountability from themselves and place you at greater risk than if you were only teaching classes.

This "distancing" of the tenured administrators from the inner workings of the program represents, for me, an especially dangerous move. Good writing programs not only treat all their employees with fairness and respect but also create a climate in which people of all ranks and employment categories work together in a spirit of cooperation and collaboration, sensitive to each other's needs and working for each other's good, for the good of the program, and for the good of the students it serves.

For me, the unresolved tension in our stories comes from knowing that you have found a position in which you feel some degree of security, but also knowing that had I continued as director, you might not be working for us at all. Thanks to the hiring concessions of the English department, you now have what you consider to be as decent a position as you've found in the last two decades. The faculty administrators who hired you also have the knowledge that, during a budget squeeze, you are expendable so that they can be guaranteed lifelong employment yet never teach more courses per year than they can count on one hand.

The merger of our once-independent composition program into the English department led to many changes in employment practices, not the least of which was the sudden hiring of many contingent faculty in at least two new ranks. The department also chose to keep me as uninvolved as possible in its new composition wing, a move that at first affected me strongly in light of what I considered to be a host of questionable practices in employment, teacher development and assessment, and curricular management. The experience, however, has left me realizing that reform will not occur if we rely on individuals to do the right thing in writing programs. In the past two or three years, several writing programs around the country have experienced administrative takeovers, political coups, and unprincipled mergers resulting in steps backward in the struggle for better working conditions for writing teachers. The writing program administrators on these campuses, even with the backing of many colleagues, were not able to prevent the worst from happening to, or in, their own programs. New technologies that support distance education and telecommuting also pose a major threat to the status and legitimacy of composition instruction as a whole, as I have argued elsewhere ("Distant Voices"). Much of this cost-saving technologizing of writing instruction is being urged and sponsored by higher administrations, potentially turning the industry of composition into a kind of piecework enterprise with a labor force of exploited reader-responders paid by the hour.

I now believe that moving the mountain will require major organizational intervention. In a contribution to a published symposium on the 1991 "Progress Report from the CCCC Committee on Professional Standards," Greta Gaard and I argued that reform in composition employment should ideally begin locally; "most major reforms in higher education," we wrote, "succeed contingently, directed in diverse ways at different institutions where they are put into motion" (172). We ended our essay on a note of optimism: "At Minnesota, where the [CCCC] Committee's involvement may be our next step, our hopes are high" (175).

Today, my hopes are still high for reform; but my convictions about local, grassroots efforts have given way to skepticism from seeing the efforts of principled but vulnerable units get thwarted by powerful institutional structures and hierarchies. Political and economic realities in higher education—cutting costs, taking a "free enterprise" approach to the labor force, and creating two- or multi-tiered instructional staffs based on missions of teaching and scholarship—will no doubt continue to loom above the field of composition. However, if many major organizations can join forces and collectively create and endorse strong positions on the principles of part-time and nontenured employees, administrations would be more likely to avoid the publicity and scandal that major deviations from these positions might yield. Accrediting boards and agencies, for their part, could begin by endorsing such principles as reflecting conditions of programmatic, departmental, or collegiate strength.

I am not alone in my belief that employment reform will best be accomplished through strong, national-level lobbying, the involvement of major national organizations, and perhaps even the threat of institutional censure. In the "Statement from the Conference on the Growing Use of Part-Time and Adjunct Faculty," published in the January–February issue of *Academe*, representatives of ten major higher-education organizations propose that a coalition be formed to include universities and professional, scholarly, and higher-education associations. Among almost a dozen suggested actions, that coalition should formulate statements of good employment practices that could be endorsed and acted upon by high-level government bodies; define the appropriate ratio between full- and part-time faculty appointments; "and collaborate with accrediting associations to secure the implementation of good practices regarding the use of part-time and adjunct faculty appointments *and the exercise of enforcement mechanisms where such practices do not occur*" (59; emphasis added). Far from being draconian measures insensitive to our local contexts, these mechanisms will pressure administrators and faculty leaders to find solutions to financial, curricular, and pedagogical problems that lead them to take advantage of teachers for whom the urgency of employment makes them easy targets for exploitation and oppression.

Jewell: It is said that a society can be judged by how it treats the least of its members. Nontenured teachers are the least in the higher education community. Ultimately the use of tenure or similar job security is the only way that administrations, unions, and tenure-accruing faculty will accept their non-tenure-track colleagues as equal, valued, and empowered. Tenuring the untenured—creating a system of steps leading to virtual or real tenure for all teachers who serve their students, colleagues, and schools responsibly and intelligently—would work in the best interests of teaching and learning. It would also serve as an example of ethical responsibility toward individuals from which other professions might learn. We should, in short, find specific methods of moving those who have earned it from the shadow of the teaching profession into the sunlight.

* * *

Anson: The system of tenure itself almost daily endures greater public scrutiny and uninformed criticism from those who believe no job should come with a guarantee of lifelong employment. In this milieu, the increasing replacement of tenured professors with part-time and contingent faculty will continue to undermine all of higher education. Providing a system of guaranteed employment for the latter (based, as is tenure, on proven excellence in teaching

---

and service to the institution), and ensuring them equality in pay, benefits, representation, and material support, will go a long way toward reversing what has become a dangerous trend.

That trend has its origins, however, in practices that have led to an overabundance of qualified individuals who encourage institutions to profit from their eagerness for employment. Just as we work toward equity for all teachers, we also need to be more responsible stewards of our graduate programs, producing new faculty in proportion to the opportunities and need for them as tenure-track hires. While there will always be teachers who do not want full-time employment, and while such teachers can provide excellent instruction and valuable support to the institutions that hire them, the quality of our colleges and universities depends crucially on full-time, tenure-track faculty whose time, commitment, involvement, and expertise are focused on their single place of work. At the same time, public respect for tenure, and for the faculty it supports, must be earned. Across higher education, we need to place much greater emphasis on excellence in teaching, perhaps even establishing programs that certify faculty as teachers (thereby ridding ourselves of the great irony that, unlike pilots, surgeons, attorneys, or tax consultants, professors need no certification or even prior experience to do what they are mostly hired to do: teach students). This stronger emphasis on teaching, especially in research institutions, will most certainly result in a rebalancing of work priorities, but the result will be a less easy division between scholarship and pedagogy, the latter now too often relegated to teachers who live and work in the shadows of our colleges and universities.

Notes

1. NTTRs were created in Minnesota in the 1970s and 1980s, when the state university teachers' union developed a strong protective system for non-tenure-track teachers. NTTRs have permanent, annually renewable positions. Although the positions are usually full-time, they carry a guarantee of at least three-fourths time and full benefits. NTTRs, most of whom do not have doctorates, may rise, after a requisite number of years and some publication, from instructor to assistant and associate professor status, and they may be granted sabbaticals. In times of cutbacks, NTTRs are released before tenure-track teachers; otherwise, they enjoy the full benefits of tenure.

2. In the 1980s, the union negotiated successfully a simple but powerful series of stepping-stones that charted a path from part-time temporary to part-time tenured, to full-time positions. Unfortunately for part-timers, the state community college system dismantled much of this structure. Since then, part-timers' job security and to some extent their pay have been determined by individual colleges. The union has been supportive of part-timers but unable to offer them a complete umbrella of protection.

Works Cited

Anson, C. M. (1999, January). Distant voices: Teaching and writing in a culture of technology. *College English, 61(3)*, 261–280.

Anson, C. M., & Gaard, G. (1992, May). Acting on the 'Statement': The all-campus model of reform. College Composition and Communication, 43(2), 171–75.

Anson, C. M., & Rutz, C. (1997). Graduate students, writing programs, and consensus-based management: Collaboration in the face of disciplinary ideology. *WPA, 21(1)*, 106–20.

Lobel, A. (1982). *Ming Lo moves the mountain.* New York: Greenwillow Books.

Modern Language Association Committee on Professional Employment. (1997, December). *Final Report.* New York: Modern Language Association.

Statement from the Conference on the Growing Use of Part-Time and Adjunct Faculty. (1998, January/February). *Academe, 84(1)*, 54–60.

Non-Tenure-Track Instructors at UALR: Breaking Rules, Splitting Departments

Barry M. Maid

Arizona State University East

L ike many institutions, the University of Arkansas at Little Rock (UALR) treated the problem of not having enough ten-ure-track English faculty to staff first-year composition as an aberration to be rectified in the future with additional tenure lines. The solution was to hire temporary part-time lecturers to staff the sections. Then in the mid- to late- 1980s, the English department realized those seemingly necessary tenure lines would never be forthcoming. As a result, the department went through the process of creating non-tenure-track, but permanent, full-time teaching positions in order to staff first-year composition. Though no one realized it at the time (1990), the creation of these new positions played an integral role in the creation of the Depart-ment of Rhetoric and Writing at UALR in 1993.

The story I tell here is a schism narrative that relates the ways in which it was not possible to "integrate" the two cultures of the Writing Program and the English department at the UALR. I speak here as an administrator who directed the Writing Pro-gram and chaired the English department. While this narrative is inevitably local—about one English department, one Writing Program—the story I tell has wider historical and political impli-cations. Two overarching questions guide my analysis: Should writing programs exist in English departments? Is the nature of the work done by the two groups in English—often non-tenure-track faculty teaching writing and full-time, tenure-track faculty teaching literature—so different that it is unproductive for them to be housed in the same unit? How is an academic department going to function successfully when it has faculty who have different professional records, different professional goals, and different teaching assignments?

Institutional and Departmental Overview

The University of Arkansas at Little Rock is a metropolitan university with an enrollment vacillating between just under ten thousand students to just over twelve thousand students. It is a relatively new institution founded in 1929 as Little Rock Junior College, under the auspices of the Little Rock Board of Education. In 1957 it became Little Rock University, a privately supported four-year institution. Finally in 1969, it became the University of Arkansas at Little Rock, a part of the newly formed University of Arkansas system. Now, like most metropolitan universities, the UALR is almost exclusively a commuter campus. Averaging in ages twenty-six to twenty-seven, students at the UALR tend to be married, divorced, or single parents. Many have served in or are currently serving in the military. Often, their current effort is not their first attempt to earn a college degree. UALR is an institution where faculty are torn between identifying themselves as a Research I University and a Liberal Arts College faculty; they are, in fact, neither. UALR's mission is to engage in applied research, but many faculty trained in the traditional liberal arts have trouble understanding this mission.

In 1982, I became the Writing Program administrator (WPA) in the UALR English department during my second year as an untenured assistant professor. At that time almost all the full-time faculty taught composition, usually comprising half of their four courses per semester load. None of the tenure-track faculty had had any training in rhetoric or composition, though technically neither had I. Of approximately twenty-two full-time faculty only three of us had done any professional reading in writing, though another three had written composition textbooks. As the new WPA, I hired and supervised approximately twenty part-time writing faculty. Our part-time staff was, to say the least, a heterogeneous group. Some had taught part-time for years; some had just returned to Little Rock and were teaching part-time until full-time work came along. Some were high school teachers, and others worked full-time as technical writers and liked to maintain an academic connection. Still others were full-time parents who chose to work part-time while their children were young.

The way we staffed first-year writing was counterproductive to good teaching. Every year we lost approximately one-third of our part-time staff; most part-time faculty worked for us for less than two years before leaving. Ironically, the programs that used Ph.D. candidates as TAs had more stability than we did. As a new WPA, I was young enough and naive enough to think I could change the situation by professionalizing the part-time instructors via workshops on writing theory and practice.

The First Change

Through a fortunate combination of events in the mid-eighties (the hiring of several more writing faculty and the allocation of state money), we were able to institute training workshops for both full- and part-time faculty. The initial training workshops introduced writing process theory—something new to most of the UALR English faculty. The workshops themselves were a combination of actual writing, responding to one another's writing, and discussion of current professional articles. All participants were paid, thus enticing the attendance of the full-time faculty to meetings required for new part-timers. We also instituted a series of "brown bag seminars." With these professional development activities, we revised the composition curriculum to engage current composition theory. Still, the system that we were using to inform ourselves and effect change was not producing the best-possible composition instruction. The program's success depended on a trained, full-time professional composition staff. We needed to devise an institutionally acceptable plan to hire that staff.

On July 1, 1987, when I became chair of the Department of English and JoAnne Liebman (now Matson) became WPA, we both agreed that creating full-time, non-tenure-track positions for composition would be the best way to improve writing instruction. The Dean of Arts and Sciences had hired some full-time instructors with MAs to help teach first-year math; this provided us with a campus precedent, if a faulty model (the math instructors were supposed to teach five courses per semester and had little support). Nonetheless, in her enthusiasm as the new WPA, Matson proposed the idea to the English department, where it was met with hostility and a threat to deny her tenure. We backed off on the proposal.

Two years later, however, in fall 1989, we were faced with a growing number of first-year students. In the middle of registration, the chancellor gave us permission to upgrade four of our part-time instructors to temporary, one-year, full-time employees. They were to teach four sections of writing for both fall 1989 and spring 1990 semesters at a salary of $22,500 plus full benefits. In 1990, the administration agreed to authorize full-time positions to help teach the first-year writing courses. As a result of several developments (including advising of majors and the emphasis on writing majors and minors), our number of majors rose from 60 in 1987 to over 220 in 1993 when the unit split into the Department of English and the Department of Rhetoric and Writing. Though most of the new majors and minors were there for the writing courses, many took upper-level literature courses as well. As a result, the literature faculty began to teach more upper-division classes; also, in my capacity as department chair, I moved a number of literature faculty out of the composition classroom. No one complained because the literature classes had a healthy enrollment—well beyond minimum standards. This move created a staffing need in the first-year composition program.

Moving the literature faculty out of the composition program was more than a staffing issue; it was a matter of excellence in teaching. Many literature faculty, although well-intentioned, saw teaching composition as a duty; they felt that teaching and studying composition was less rigorous, less intellectual, and less important than studying literature or literary theory. In addition, because of their traditional training in literary studies, few had received any training in the teaching of writing, even though many had put themselves through graduate school working as teaching assistants responsible for writing sections. Because their training and intellectual work was focused on literature, most did not fully invest themselves as writing teachers. In my opinion, professionalized part-time faculty were better teachers than full-time faculty who had little or no training in the area and were above mentoring.

Moving to Full-Time Positions

Ironically, the full-time faculty's disinterest in teaching writing became one of our selling points for the full-time instructorships. Realizing that hiring full-time composition instructors would reduce their chances of teaching composition, literature faculty finally accepted the idea of hiring full-time permanent instructors. There were only two points of contention: the first was the issue of *de facto* tenure after the seventh year; the second concerned departmental voting rights. Actually, both of the issues were easily resolved under the University of Arkansas System Policy. The problem is faculty do not always abide by System Policy and neither campus nor system administration tends to enforce it—especially in the touchy area of faculty governance.

UA System Policy allows for hiring full-time faculty with *full* faculty rights at the level of instructor. The one exception is that, by definition, the position of instructor is a nontenurable position. Instructors work on one-year contracts renewable as long as programmatic need exists and yearly evaluation deems it to be appropriate. The English department faculty accepted the notion of permanent nontenurable faculty, with some squirming from local AAUP members. We adopted a hedge policy that gave full-time instructors voting rights in "areas which concerned them." What the faculty failed to realize (as did the dean) was that departments do not have the right to supersede System Policy.

Interestingly enough, as we were beginning to move toward creating full-time instructor positions, the real stumbling block became the provost who had initially been the prime mover. He insisted that the instructors teach five courses per semester; I refused to agree to those terms, citing NCTE and ADE Guidelines on course loads. After two weeks of almost daily meetings, the provost came to a meeting of the English department where the faculty, to a person, told the provost that a five-course load was simply unacceptable and unprofessional. Since I had been meeting with him for days, I was quiet. Then I presented the argument I had been saving: I suggested that he was using the wrong model by comparing first-year writing instructors to first-year math instructors. I then suggested if there was another model on campus it was surely that of journalism whose accreditation agency requires that they teach no more than three courses per semester and have no more than eighteen students per class.

Although the meeting ended with no resolution, the provost asked if there were an appropriate organization to provide reviewers for writing programs. I told him about the Council of Writing Program Administrator's Consultant (WPA)/Evaluator Program, which is as rigorous and thorough as a discipline specific accreditation review. First, the program requires an institution to do an in-depth self-study, and then it brings in two experienced and trained consultant/evaluators for an onsite visit; I was immediately given the "go ahead" to begin the review process.

In the review report, the consultant/evaluators made a key comment in the "Workload" section: "We know of no four-year English Departments where anyone's course load is more than 4/4" (p. 7). The report had the desired effect on the administration. By the end of May, we were authorized to conduct a search for six full-time composition instructors who would teach four sections per semester at $24,000 for a nine month contract with full benefits—a salary roughly equivalent to the local school districts' pay rate for entry level MA teachers. We searched for instructors with at least a master's degree in an appropriate area and a demonstrated commitment to teaching writing as well as an awareness of current theory, research, and approaches to teaching composition. The full-time positions included teaching four sections of freshman composition each semester, performing appropriate departmental and university service (e.g., committee work), and engaging in professional activities (e.g., workshops, conferences, continuing education).

We conducted a regional search and hired six people; all but one were currently part-time instructors at the UALR. With additional authorization, we hired three more people from the pool for a complement of nine full-time instructors: eight women and two men—one African American. There was tremendous competition for those first nine positions, and some local candidates who did not get the full-time positions have never forgiven us and chose not to return as part-time instructors. In reality, we lost some first-rate teachers that way. By hiring this group and giving them secure positions with full benefits (health insurance, retirement), we could ask them to devote all of their many talents and energies to developing the composition curriculum and teaching writing. Now we could expect programmatic consistency and continuity.

Although they were not required to be publishing scholars, the full-time instructors received funding to attend a professional writing conference, regardless of whether they were to appear on the program. Though they were only asked to attend the conferences, most of the instructors started submitting proposals to be on the program. Currently, almost all of them have given at least one national presentation. This last fact confirms what may have been our most important hope in the professionalization process: by welcoming our full-time instructors into the community and by actively encouraging their professional growth, we have seen them develop as professionals far beyond what we could have predicted. I had hoped after winning what appeared to be a major battle in professionalizing the faculty who taught first-year composition that the problems would have disappeared. What we discovered was that we had created a new set of problems, which had to be addressed.

Not a Bed of Roses: The Next Set of Problems

While in the beginning administrative issues were pressing, later we found ourselves confronting a far more complex series of questions: How is an academic department going to function successfully when it has faculty who are different from one another? Should instructors be allowed (and that is the language that was used) to teach anything other than first-year courses? As stated earlier, the English faculty was supportive of hiring the full-time instructors because they really had no professional investment in the writing program. They perceived that teaching composition is service, not intellectual work. Unfortunately, this speaks to one of the central problems present not only in English departments but across the academy: We are a service profession in denial. The positions of most faculty at most colleges and universities, as defined by the employing institution, are positions that combine teaching and service. The faculty, on the other hand, define their positions by their intellectual work.

The problem of who should teach the first-year course was complicated because it emerged on two different fronts. Several of the full-time instructors had worked as full-time technical writers, technical editors, corporate trainers, and writing consultants before taking the instructorships. While their workplace experience made them clearly more qualified, if not more appropriate, to teach our junior-level technical writing class than literature faculty, the English faculty could not accept the idea of anyone without a Ph.D. teaching anything but first-year classes. When UALR changed its core curriculum to require sophomore-level World Literature of all students, we simply did not have enough faculty to cover these extra sections. The administration looked to the instructors to fill the gap. The literature faculty argued against the administration's plan, emphatically stating that only Ph.D.'s in English who were hired with a national search were qualified to teach the course. Eventually the tenure-track literature faculty relented and decided that someone with an MA might be able to teach the World Literature course; however, the literature faculty demanded that new positions be created to teach World Literature with the proviso that instructors already employed would have to become candidates in the search process. This, of course, was to be done in the name of standards, fairness, affirmative action, and department precedent. The English department limited the teaching assignments given to people hired to teach writing. Even I had experienced this limitation. Although my dissertation was in Victorian fiction, I was told when I was hired that I could teach only writing. The only way I could ever teach any literature course would be to apply for a different position and go through a second national search. The message was clear: the department can allow "lesser qualified" people to teach writing, but the standards of who can teach literature must be protected.

Unfortunately, the attitudes held by UALR English faculty are not atypical. They are the function of the classic clash between those who teach applied fields and those who teach in the humanities (see Berlin, 1987; Brereton, 1995; Miller, 1991). Because of this "classic clash," the UALR literature faculty's attitudes toward the instructors are not surprising. The instructors had two strikes against them; they had one less degree, and they taught a course that had no disciplinary prestige.

The Last Straw

As these conflicts developed, my term as department chair expired. I had served six years and wished to step down, but there was really no one to take over. The department, for years, had refused to hire anyone with administrative potential since those candidates interested in administration were thought to be "less serious" about their scholarly work. I resigned myself to reelection, although I was not committed to serving a full three years.

A week before the scheduled election, two tenured faculty members appeared in my office. They wanted to make sure that full-time instructors would not be allowed to vote in the upcoming chair election. Since I had been supportive of the instructors and their status, a group of the literature faculty, of which these two were members, assumed that the instructors would vote as a single block and that I would do their bidding. While the daily business of the department was running smoothly, there was an undercurrent of fear among some of the literature faculty that the instructors might dominate departmental decisions. Nonetheless, I told the two faculty members that I expected to follow university policy on the matter.

I checked with the University System Attorney about non-tenure-track faculty voting rights; he told me, by Board Policy, the department could not limit which faculty were allowed to vote and which could not. He also told me that the dean had the final say in appointing a suitable department chair while voting members of the department only offered a recommendation for a suitable candidate. When I announced the lawyer's decision and my decision to abide by it to the department, the literature faculty refused to cooperate. Memos starting flying in the department with copies to the dean and provost. The dean asked me to hold a series of open meetings with both tenure-track faculty and instructors to "bring the faculty together." Instead of bringing the faculty together, the meetings further divided us. Some of the faculty brought tape recorders to record the discussion. Still, some literature faculty made unproductive and insulting comments about the writing instructors. They equated the instructors with the secretarial staff and then qualified their remarks to assert that the secretarial staff could probably teach better. They implied that the instructors were hired illegally. It went down hill from there.

Finally, in a memo titled, "Where We Go from Here," (March 18, 1993) the provost presented us with the following four possible scenarios:

◆ Scenario One, Status Quo: Department deals with the current issues within the framework of 1986 governance document, as amended in 1990. Dean and provost cease involvement.

◆ Scenario Two: Composition Subunit within department. A defined subunit, including full voting rights for full-time instructors, is responsible for composition program, including selection of composition director. Otherwise functions within 1986 governance framework, as amended in 1990.

◆ Scenario Three: Reassignment of Composition Program and Writing Center (Reporting to University College or College of Education or Provost Office). Another version of this would combine developmental and freshman English, math, and reading with their labs into one division.

◆ Scenario Four: Two Departments—One Literature, One Writing. No description given. (Anderson, p. 2).

At a follow-up department meeting with the dean and the provost, everyone was cordial, but, again, condescending comments emerged, this time about the instructors *and all* of the writing faculty. This meeting, more than anything else, brought home to me the aristocratic mind-set that allows for the exploitation of adjunct writing faculty. Comments made in the public meetings indicated that the literature faculty simply viewed the writing faculty (especially the non-tenure-track faculty) as an inferior professional group not worthy of the voting rights granted by the system and departmental policy. During all the discussions concerning voting rights, the tenured writing faculty (with the exception of two technical writing professors who were literature faculty and chose to stay in English and teach literature after the split) all supported the instructors' full rights to participate and vote. The writing faculty accepted the instructors as colleagues; the literature faculty did not. Ironically, many literature faculty espouse left-wing ideologies and encourage their students to value "difference" in their classes. Yet, when it comes to those issues that are closest to them, labor issues and the governance of the academy, some are aristocrats of the first degree. Once a group sets itself up as being inherently superior to another group—whether that second group is defined by academic degree, gender, or race—the first group cannot value or respect the different skills of the second group.

The Outcome

A few weeks later, the dean showed me the draft of a memo calling for the creation of the Department of Rhetoric and Writing. Although the decision had been made by the provost, implementation of the separation was to be in the dean's hands. Looking back at the four scenarios presented in the provost's memo, I suspect he was leaning toward separation all along. The two crucial issues were programmatic integrity and faculty rights for all regardless of rank.

The problems that occurred as a result of implementation of the new department need to be chronicled elsewhere. However, the new unit had a significant impact on the work lives and professional opportunities for the non-tenure-track instructors. During the first few weeks of the new unit, I assigned two instructors with significant consulting experience to sections of technical writing. It was a highly pragmatic move, not a bold political move, as some surmised. No tenured faculty members were teaching second summer session. We *needed* to offer technical writing; I had two qualified teachers. As they taught technical writing, I freed up sections of composition for other people to teach.

I wish this story could have a fairy tale ending. My professional life and the lives of others at UALR would be much easier. Just five years after its creation, the UALR Department of Rhetoric and Writing was named the university's "Department of Excellence for 1998." We've come a long way in five short, but tumultuous, years. Winning the award has given the unit a sense that the new beginning is still ahead. We recognize that many of the problems we faced in the first five years were vestiges of a department culture that could see difference in faculty roles only in hierarchical terms.

In the Department of Rhetoric and Writing, where full-time non-tenure-track instructors make up more than half the faculty, we still have problems with defining roles—not unlike those we faced in English. The instructors were hired to be teachers first, who were then expected to engage in professional development. However, it seems as though over time they have raised the ante themselves. Since most of them now make professional presentations and some of them publish, they have come to believe that these professional activities are expected—not exceptional. There are complex reasons for our continuing problems, but I don't think they are insurmountable. For example, non-tenure-track instructors try to mimic tenure-track behavior at evaluation time. As a result, teaching, their primary job, is devalued in favor of professional activities (which were originally defined as added value for instructors). I suspect the roots of this are deep within the culture of the academy—especially humanities disciplines, which value scholarship over teaching. My own solution is simple, perhaps naive, still I think effective. For non-tenure-track faculty, I'd reward documented excellence in teaching with merit pay. Nothing seems to engender culture change in the academy more than the reward. To solve the problems, our unit must engage in a culture change.

If we are to succeed and perhaps serve as a model for other institutions, we must acknowledge and accept that our faculty are different from one another. Because we are different, we will play different roles and must be rewarded by different criteria. This is nothing new. However, we get into trouble by trying to implement the old triad of teaching, research, and service. In this schema, service gets relegated to committee work and as a result gets discounted; teaching is what everyone does, so that research is all that matters. Ernest Boyer's Carnegie Foundation Report, *Scholarship Reconsidered* (1990), points out some of the problems with such a method for tenure-track faculty. As deficient a model as it is for tenure-track faculty, it is completely inappropriate for the non-tenure-track faculty with heavy teaching loads.

We must then look at ways to evaluate faculty on the basis of their real jobs—not their imagined jobs. Clear and precise job descriptions will need to be written for both non-tenure-track and tenure-track faculty. These descriptions will differ and must be evaluated differently (including, in some cases, different peer-evaluation committees). Above all, it should mean that job descriptions should coincide with actual work assignments. Faculty who have administrative assignments, for example, will be evaluated and rewarded (including promotion and tenure) for those assignments. Doing so is in the spirit of the WPA's "Evaluating the Intellectual Work of Writing Program Administrators: A Draft" (1996) and the MLA's "Making Faculty Work Visible: Reinterpreting Professional Service, Teaching, and Research in the Fields of Language and Literature" (1996). This also means that tenure-track faculty, because of their credentials, will have teaching assignments primarily in the graduate program and at the undergraduate upper-division while instructors will primarily be teaching first-year writing and some of the junior-level classes. What it really means, however, is that we are all willing to accept these different roles. And here's the rub. In a unit born, at least partly, out of a struggle for faculty rights for all regardless of rank, it is difficult for some to understand that "different" doesn't mean "less than." In order to do so, what we'll need most of all is a mutual respect among all the members of the department, and that, in a culture based on traditional academic values, is perhaps the hardest thing to achieve.

Is the creation of a Department of Rhetoric and Writing outside of an English department the answer for all or most American colleges and universities? The answer depends on the cultures and values within an institution's English department. If an English department is willing to accept that writing faculty are different from literature faculty—meaning that they may have different degrees, different institutional roles, that their research methods and results may look very different, that they may regularly publish collaboratively, that they may engage in program administration as professional activity, and that for some consulting will be a professional necessity—then writing faculty may flourish in an English department. There are, in fact, a handful of departments across the country that appear to have attained such a positive mix. Yet, by establishing work criteria in the field of writing that differ from those present in traditional literary studies, we are not dealing with a subset of English Studies, as the traditional view dictates, but rather the emergence of a new applied discipline. In colleges and universities that are forging partnerships with both public and private organizations outside the academy, writing programs will need to flourish. To do so, as I argue here, most writing programs and their faculty may need to be separate from English departments.

Works Cited

Anderson, J. E. (1993, March 18). *Where we go from here.* Memorandum to Department of English, University of Arkansas, Little Rock, AR.

Appleby, B. C., & Brereton, J. C. (1990, May 17–18). *Review of freshman composition program University of Arkansas at Little Rock.* Report for Council of Writing Program Administrators.

Berlin, J. A. (1987). *Rhetoric and reality: Writing instruction in American colleges, 1900–1985.* Carbondale: Southern Illinois University Press.

Boyer, E. (1990). *Scholarship reconsidered: Priorities of the professoriate.* Princeton, NJ: Carnegie Foundation for the Advancement of Teaching.

Brereton, J. C. (Ed.) (1995). *The origins of composition studies in the American college, 1875–1925: A documentary history.* Pittsburgh: University of Pittsburgh Press.

Miller, S. (1991). *Textual carnivals: The politics of composition.* Carbondale: Southern Illinois University Press.

Modern Language Association Commission on Professional Service (1996). Making faculty work visible: Reinterpreting professional service, teaching, and research in the fields of language and literature. *Profession 96*. New York: Modern Language Association.

WPA Executive Committee. (1996, Fall/Winter). Evaluating the intellectual work of writing program administrators: A draft. *WPA, 20(1–2)*, 92–103.

CHAPTER THREE

The Best of Times, The Worst of Times: One Version of the "Humane" Lectureship

EVA BRUMBERGER

New Mexico State University, Las Cruces

Introduction

The conversation about the marginalization of the teaching of writing in English departments is certainly not a new one. Over a decade ago, in 1987, this already ongoing conversation led to the Wyoming Conference Resolution's opposition of unfair working conditions for postsecondary teachers of writing. Since then, many English departments have sought ways to reduce what Lester Faigley has referred to as "the colonized status of writing instruction" (1992, p. 53). One approach has been to improve material working conditions for writing instructors, many of whom are part-time and/or temporary. However, while the improvement of material conditions responds to several critical problems, it does not fully address the many factors that comprise the "social context for writing teachers" (Robertson, Crowley & Lentricchia, 1987, p. 274). That social context is determined both by material issues—such as salary, course loads, and benefits— and by issues of intellectual community, such as respect, support, and collegiality. Therefore, improving material conditions cannot entirely solve existing problems with the intellectual context for most writing programs, namely their often marginalized position in English departments and the university.

In this essay, I discuss the University of Wyoming's version of a full-time long-term (potentially permanent) lecturer position— sometimes known as a "humane" lectureship. I examine the ways in which these positions improved the material conditions and intellectual conditions of writing teachers at the University of Wyoming; I also analyze the lingering problems that these positions did not address and some that they created. My goal here is to highlight the need for improvement of material issues but also to address the ways in which there are larger issues of department culture and disciplinary history that must be considered when creating non-tenure-track, full-time writing instructorships. In my analysis, I draw upon personal experience, interviews with tenure-track faculty, a survey of lecturers in the department, and local documents. The interviews with faculty focused on the history of the lecturer position, external and internal changes necessary to give the teaching of writing more respect, and awareness and perceptions of lecturers' professional contributions. The survey of lecturers inquired about classroom and non-classroom assignments, professional development activities, research leaves, perceptions of departmental tensions, and specific ways in which to relieve those tensions. Only three of the six lecturers responded. The interview and survey responses enabled me to assess the costs and benefits of the full-time, long-term lectureship and to suggest concrete strategies for improvement that may assist others who have instituted full-time instructorships and wish to improve them or who are seeking to establish such positions.

Justification and Creation of the Extended Term Position

As someone who taught as an "adjunct" for three years before obtaining a full-time lectureship, I know what it is like to be hired from semester to semester, to receive no benefits, and to earn approximately one-half what full-timers at the same institutions did for teaching the same courses. I am well acquainted with the heavy course load, minimal compensation, and lack of job security common to the adjunct positions often held by writing instructors. I am also painfully aware of the sense of isolation—the lack of "colleagues" and therefore of community—that often accompanies these positions and makes professional development difficult, if not impossible. My awareness of such issues solidifies my belief that improving working conditions benefits not only adjunct instructors but also their departments and their students.

At the University of Wyoming, temporary instructors have a better work environment than many adjunct writing faculty at other institutions. They are hired for one academic year at a time, for a maximum of four years, and receive the same benefits as other university employees (although only for the academic year). They are typically hired as full-time instructors rather than course by course, and they are paid approximately $19,000 for teaching eight courses per academic year, including up to one non-classroom assignment per semester, such as tutoring in the writing center. Yet, their limited contracts still put them in a tenuous and marginalized position within the department.

To address these problems, the University of Wyoming created the "probationary to extended term academic professional lecturer" position (P/ET APL) in 1992. The positions, which predate the Wyoming Conference Resolution in their development, were designed to help the department offer continuing employment for excellent writing teachers who lacked Ph.D.s and thus were ineligible for full-time positions. The P/ET APL positions allow the English department to maintain "a cadre of good instructors who were [and are] well-prepared in the teaching of writing" (Constantinides, 1997). The positions were also created to resolve the question of de facto tenure if temporary instructors were rehired for six or more years.

The P/ET APL Position and Its Place in the Department

To meet the criteria specified in the position description, P/ET APLs have a six-year probationary period followed by a six-year renewable contract. Prior to the renewable contract, the P/ET APL position has a yearly reappointment process, which closely parallels that for tenure-track faculty. P/ET APLs are required to be strong teachers and to grow professionally; the position is therefore defined as 78 percent teaching and 22 percent professional development. The load for P/ET APLs is twenty-seven semester credits per academic year, six of which are set aside for professional development. This translates to a 4/3 teaching load, including up to one non-classroom assignment per semester. Courses most frequently taught by P/ET APLs (and temporary lecturers) are Scientific and Technical Writing, Freshman Composition, Introduction to Literature, Writing in a Technical Field, First-Year Composition for International Students, and Oral Skills (also for ESL students). The most common non-classroom assignments are tutoring in the writing center and mentoring graduate teaching assistants.

Most of the P/ET APLs, like their temporary lecturer counterparts, hold master's degrees rather than doctorates, yet they make approximately $5,500 more per year and have a lighter teaching load that creates room for their increased professional development activities. The English department, which currently comprises 6.5 P/ET APLs, 7 temporary lecturers, 21.5 professorial faculty, and 15 graduate students, teaches an average of 156 sections of literature and writing courses per year. Writing courses constitute a substantial percentage of these enrollments; for example, there are often as many as 12 sections (23 students each) of Scientific and Technical Writing offered in a semester (and taught almost exclusively by temporary lecturers and P/ET APLs). Multiplied by two semesters, that is over 550 student enrollments in one writing course alone. There are even higher enrollments in first-year composition, which is predominantly staffed by P/ET APLs.

The department mission statement, although focused on literature, does mention the teaching of writing; however, there is no writing program mission statement and there is no official writing program, which may account for some of the tensions I will allude to that revolve around the intellectual issues associated with writing instruction and the employment of P/ET APLs.

Improvements Accompanying the P/ET APL Position

The professional development component of the P/ET APL position enables—and requires—them to keep current in the field and to interact with colleagues from other institutions, with the expectation that these activities will benefit their teaching and future professional development. The lighter teaching load (as compared to the temporary lecturer load) facilitates this development, and P/ET APLs may apply for conference travel funds that range from four to six hundred dollars per academic year. They also review textbooks, publish articles, and complete other projects for professional development. As Ann Ronald, former Dean of Arts and Sciences at the University of Nevada, Reno (UN-R), says of permanent lecturers in the UN-R English department: "Part of their success comes from the interest they take in rhetoric and composition as a field for intellectual inquiry" (1990, p. 34). A high level of professionalism is critical to the success of these positions at any institution.

As P/ET APLs grow as both teachers and as scholars, they allow for a continuity of intellectual work. They are viewed as permanent members of the department and university communities, and they are eligible to serve on departmental and college-level committees for standard two-year terms, unlike temporary lecturers. Finally, the stability and continuity of the P/ET APL positions benefit students. It is likely that students receive improved instruction resulting both from the professional development and from the security of their instructors; they can establish and maintain relationships with their instructors, taking additional courses from them over the years and relying on them as unofficial advisors. Undergraduate and graduate students may also receive fewer contradictory messages about the value of writing and the teaching of writing when they see their writing instructors are permanent and valued members of the academic community. In short, as Ben McClelland indicated in his 1995 Council of Writing Program Administrators' Consultant Evaluator report on the University of Wyoming writing program, "[P/ET APLs'] terms of appointment, including salaries and benefits, professional development opportunities, and travel funds, are much better than the norm. Indeed, their working conditions are the envy of the majority of the profession's writing teachers" (pp. 12–13).

Issues That Remain Problematic

However, while the creation of these "humane" lectureships has improved working conditions, many problems persist. First, such positions have not addressed the abiding distinction between the teaching of literature and the teaching of writing; in fact, such positions have reinforced the split between the teaching of writing and the teaching of literature. Although most lecturers are trained in literature, they teach virtually all writing courses in the department (with the exception of "creative writing" courses). They are not permitted to teach the 4000-level and graduate-level courses, but an exception is made for the 4000-level Scientific and Technical Writing course, which is taught exclusively by lecturers with "special expertise." There is a clearly visible (and audible) sentiment that a doctorate with a specialty in literature is required to teach literature courses, while a master's degree in any area of English will suffice to teach writing courses—an attitude that serves to further separate P/ET APLs from tenure-track faculty. And, since the English major does not currently include any writing courses, P/ET APLs rarely have any interaction with the department's 140 majors. Unless they serve as mentors to teaching assistants, P/ET APLS also have little contact with the department's graduate students, even though those TAs also teach writing. As a result, even though there is greater inclusion into the departmental culture than that available to temporary lecturers, P/ET APLs are still in a marginalized position in the department and university community.

P/ET APLs separate status is clearly communicated in their material positioning in relation to tenure-track faculty: their different teaching loads, prorata pay, professional development choices, leaves, and voting privileges. Their positions are, of course, defined differently than tenure-track faculty, which leads to many of the distinctions. Professorial positions require 60–75 percent teaching, 20–35 percent research, and 5 percent service, while P/ET APL positions are 78 percent teaching and 22 percent professional development. However, given that teaching is heavily weighted for both positions, and given the university's stated commitment to both teaching and research, one must question whether the salary and teaching load differentials between the two classes of faculty are reasonable. Tenure-track faculty teach a 2/2 load, tenured faculty a 3/2 load, in comparison to P/ET APLs 4/3 load. Many of the literature courses have small enrollments, while the courses taught by lecturers often are writing courses filled to capacity (twenty-three students). For example, Scientific and Technical Writing is typically at capacity and requires each student to submit forty pages of final copy—upward of nine hundred pages of reading for the instructor per section (not including drafts). At the same time, the starting salary for an assistant professor is typically at least $10,000 higher than that for an assistant lecturer (the "equivalent" rank). Granted, the professorial faculty hold doctorates, while most of the P/ET APLs hold master's degrees. However, if the salary is determined by the position, not by the degree, even those lecturers with a Ph.D. are not paid commensurate salaries. The current salary structure clearly indicates that teaching literature is more valuable than teaching writing. The perception is that, as long as lecturers earn less, they will be less respected; put differently, with greater equality in pay, there is likely to be more equality in professional standing. Although it is not realistic to ask that lecturers receive the same salaries as equivalently ranked professorial faculty, it seems reasonable to expect—and to argue for—a more equitable salary structure.

While tenure-track faculty are eligible for sabbaticals, paid leave, and unpaid leave, P/ET APLs are only eligible for unpaid leave. The inherent message in this policy is that P/ET APLs do not engage in scholarly or professional activities that would benefit from sabbatical or paid leave. However, P/ET APLs indicate that they would use paid sabbatical/research leave privileges effectively, primarily by furthering their education and expertise in their field (Brumberger, 1998), which would certainly be beneficial to the department.

A marked difference in voting privileges also separates P/ET APLs from tenure-track faculty. P/ET APLs are only permitted to serve on committees and vote on issues deemed "directly relevant" to them. They may not vote on issues that affect tenure-track faculty (though the tenure-track faculty may vote on P/ET APL issues). For example, although their feedback was certainly solicited and considered, P/ET APLs were not permitted to cast ballots in the selection of a rhetoric/composition candidate this past spring, even though that individual will direct the writing program and will work closely with the lecturers. P/ET APLs' voting privileges are limited in a way that clearly indicates they are a separate—and less respected—class of faculty.

Even in the area of professional development, P/ET APLs may find themselves confined to developing professionally in areas defined by the department, not necessarily by their scholarly interests. Pursuing activities outside one's perceived area of expertise is frowned upon, and that "expertise" seems at times determined more by departmental need rather than by one's own professional interests. For example, one P/ET APL focuses her professional development on technical communication simply because that is what she is most often assigned to teach (Brumberger). Thus, P/ET APLs may find their professional development projects strongly directed by departmental need and may feel discouraged from exploring new directions in their careers, developing new knowledge, and adopting new pedagogical practices.

P/ET APLs, although marginalized in the department, overall, are clearly in a privileged position when compared to the temporary lecturers, who have a heavier teaching load, a lower salary, and no vote whatsoever. Thus, not one, but two "subcultures" now exist within the department, both comprise writing teachers who have a distinct—and less respectable and respected— position within the department's culture. McClelland notes that lecturers in the profession typically "feel condescended to by regular faculty and unappreciated for the workloads they carry" (1995, p. 12). This statement holds true at the University of Wyoming.

These tensions are exacerbated by the fact that most of the individuals who hold probationary-to-extended-term positions were previously temporary. The funding for P/ET APL positions, although initially separate, now comes from the same pool as the funding for tenure-track lines, meaning that hiring more P/ET APLs can conflict with hiring tenure-track faculty. Because the department needs to fill tenure-track lines to maintain both the major and the graduate program, it is unlikely that additional P/ET APLs will be hired until those needs have been met. Compounding this problem is a sentiment among faculty members that any future hires should come from outside the department, making it unlikely that those who are currently temporary will ever be able to change their status within the department, even though that option existed for their colleagues. Understandably, this has led a certain amount of bitterness among the temporary lecturers and deepened the divisions within the department.

Thus, although creating "humane" lectureships (P/ET APLs) has improved material conditions and fostered professional development opportunities, it has not been a completely effective step. And, it certainly has not assured the teaching of writing a position of respect equivalent to the teaching of literature within the department. The disparities that remain point strongly to a differential sense of worth accorded the two enterprises.

Some Suggestions for Further Improvement

To give writing—and writing instructors—an equal place in English departments, we must alter the intellectual culture of those departments and the practices of universities whose mission statements claim to value teaching, including teaching of required courses, while privileging research. This is, of course, far more complex than simply altering material conditions. In order to transform departmental culture, we must first create a "contact zone" in which teachers of writing and teachers of literature can work together productively. In his Council of Writing Program Administrators' Consultant-Evaluator's report, Ben McClelland suggests that "the area of rhetoric and composition has been relegated to a marginal position in the [University of Wyoming English] department's academic mission" (1995, p. 7). This observation is supported by a comment from one of the P/ET APLs, who said, "In terms of APLs and professorial faculty, we are talking about different 'orbits,' different worlds" (Brumberger, 1998). How can we bring those "different" worlds and different "orbits" more in alignment with one another?

McClelland presents some very concrete approaches for reversing this trend and fostering departmental collegiality. Before considering McClelland's recommendations, however, it is important to note both the benefits and the limitations of an outside review process. The obvious benefit is that an outside reviewer can provide an objective assessment of the problems and impartially offer possible solutions to those problems. The limitations are twofold: first, the reviewer cannot possibly approach the task with the extensive knowledge of the department that an insider can; second, implementation of any suggestions that are both feasible and desirable is only a realistic goal if the department as a whole is willing to take ownership of them and work together on their implementation. In other words, the actual changes have to come from within the department itself.

To facilitate such changes, McClelland suggests, first, that literature and writing faculty team-teach courses; second, that distinguished lecturers in rhetoric and composition be invited to speak at the University of Wyoming; third, that literature faculty be more involved in teaching writing courses; and, finally, that the English major be revised to incorporate rhetoric and composition courses. Each of these steps would "provide a common ground for professional conversations between faculty of different areas and between faculty, lecturers, and teaching assistants" (McClelland). These are productive recommendations, but what would it take to implement them?

Team-teaching, McClelland's first recommendation, would encourage development of collegial relationships between faculty members and P/ET APLs and may minimize an "us" and "them" way of thinking. In addition, team-teaching would give each member of the team knowledge of what the other does in the classroom, which could lead to a greater awareness of the goals that the teaching of literature and writing have in common. Unfortunately, team-teaching means that fewer courses can be taught by the department overall, resulting in a less efficient distribution of resources. In a time of limited funds, budgetary cutbacks, and shorthanded departments, such a step is not likely to be approved at the University of Wyoming, although its benefits may outweigh its initial costs.

A distinguished lecturer series, McClelland's second recommendation, would "enable faculty to understand that writing is, in and of itself, intrinsically interesting, that it is an intellectually challenging field of study, one worthy of standing beside literary study" (1995, p. 9). Thus far, the department has included rhetoric as a possible topic for an already existing lecture series and promoted keynote speakers in rhetoric and composition at the

Wyoming Conference on English. However, these lectures will have an impact on departmental culture only if faculty members and lecturers attend. To reduce the different status accorded writing instruction and writing instructors, departmental awareness and understanding of composition as a scholarly field needs to increase. However, this must be a farther-reaching process than simply inviting distinguished lecturers to speak. In some cases, faculty members seem to be unaware of departmental tensions; in others, differences in opinion seem to stem more from longevity in the department and/or profession than from views about the nature of literature and writing per se (Ronald, 1990, p. 35).

McClelland's third recommendation—to have literature faculty teach more writing courses—would help integrate writing and literature faculty around a common enterprise. The chief problem with this approach is that the department is already short of people to teach upper-division and graduate literature courses; adding writing courses to faculty teaching loads would exacerbate this problem. In addition, this approach would promote the idea that anyone with a graduate degree in literature can teach writing, while teaching literature requires special training in that field. A better option might be, as one faculty member suggested, to hire individuals with a strong background in both rhetoric/composition and literature (Reverand, 1997), or to hire P/ET APLs qualified to teach lower division literature courses and tenure-track faculty whose specialty is rhetoric/composition. Since the P/ET APL position would then no longer be primarily for teachers of writing, the division between writing and literature might also be diminished. Unfortunately, resources for new hires are limited at best, so this option is again problematic for financial reasons. However, the department does recognize the need for tenure-track faculty in rhetoric/composition: it recently received permission to hire at a senior level and voted overwhelmingly to do so.

Perhaps the most effective and feasible of McClelland's suggestions is revision of the English major to include writing courses. Such a shift has the potential of sending a clear message to both students and faculty that writing does have a valued place in the English curriculum, that P/ET APLs should be permitted to teach and advise majors and thus bring more students into the department. Since McClelland's report, the department has voted to add minors in creative and professional writing. This will involve designating existing courses as contributing to a minor as well as designing and offering new courses, including some focused on theory. The creative writing minor is already being designed; establishing the professional writing minor will involve extensive input from the new rhetoric/composition faculty member and will probably lead to the hiring of additional rhetoric/composition faculty members.

Interestingly, both the support for and the resistance to changes in the major seem to stem from one and the same perception: the idea that the teaching of non-"creative" writing has purely practical, skills-oriented goals. Faculty members who support adding an option to the major do so primarily because they see a professional writing minor as meeting a growing practical need: preparing students for jobs through what could be considered almost a vocational education (for example, preparing students to be technical writers). The faculty who oppose such a step mirror this same argument. They seem to hold that the work of composition is, as Slevin describes, "marginal to the real . . . work of English departments" (1991, p. 6), which is, of course, the humanistic study of a canon of "timeless" privileged texts.

What is so disturbing about both sides of this argument is the underlying idea that all important academic (as opposed to mundane) discourse within English departments is confined to the literature classroom and that the study of writing is totally separate from the study of literature and the discussion of philosophical ideas. There is a tendency among literature faculty members, as Slevin points out, to view the ". . .work of those in . . . composition . . . as impoverished in both its subject and the intellectual power upon which it draws" (1991, p. 6). In fact, one faculty member suggested that one way in which to give the teaching of writing more respect is to change the content of writing courses to include literary works and therefore to make them more intellectually challenging (Reverand, 1997). It is exactly this attitude that fosters marginalization. Thus, whether the department develops a writing minor or not, the teaching of writing, and by extension teachers of writing, will remain marginalized as long as these misconceptions permeate the department's culture.

Hiring a tenured rhetorician is a significant step toward changing this culture. Not only can she be an advocate for the teaching of writing and, by extension, for P/ET APLs, she can also be a catalyst for the development and implementation of other programs, such as the professional writing minor. And, as a tenured member of the faculty, she will be in a position of power to bring about broader departmental changes.

However, those "in power" do not bear the sole responsibility for changing departmental culture. P/ET APLs can work together to advocate changes in departmental culture. As one individual remarked at the conference at which the Wyoming Conference Resolution was first drafted: "We don't want to face our own roles in the problem, and how we—as people, as teachers, as 'professionals'—are implicated in the very problems we're trying to solve" (Robertson, Crowley & Lentricchia, 1987, p. 277). The APL committee, comprising two P/ET APLs and one faculty member (which handles lecturer personnel issues) could be much more active in addressing instructor concerns. Individually and as a group, P/ET APLs can be more outspoken, instead of adopting the attitude that they are powerless. P/ET APLs can involve nonwriting faculty in classroom observations of their work (part of the annual reappointment process) (Frye, 1997). Another helpful addition would be informal presentations—"brown bag" lunch "talks" perhaps—given by the lecturers themselves on their current work (Harris, 1997). This would be a less formal and more personal approach than a distinguished lecturer series. Finally, publicizing P/ET APLs conference presentations, publications, and other professional achievements in the department newsletter and Arts and Sciences publication might increase respect for lecturer contributions (Hull, 1997).

Departments also need to "search fairly" for instructor candidates (Ronald, 1990, p. 36), hiring outside candidates to fill newly created lecturer positions instead of hiring from within (Frye, 1997). Although this certainly would not be a popular approach with temporary lecturers in the department, it would have several long-term benefits. For example, as one might expect, there are obvious alliances between certain faculty members and those lecturers who were formerly their graduate students. Even in cases where there is no obvious history, I cannot help but wonder if the prior teacher-student relationship lingers in some sense, coloring faculty members' views of P/ET APLs who were once students in the department. As the only P/ET APL to have been hired through a national search, my perception is that the faculty treat me differently—perhaps more professionally—than they do other P/ET APLs in the department. Concomitantly, the other lecturers are often reluctant to accept me as "one of them." In addition, hiring from within restricts the number of new ideas and teaching styles that are brought into the department. Finally, I am inclined to believe that being hired from outside the department makes one less hesitant to speak out in department meetings and to advocate changes in departmental culture, since one is not constrained by preexisting perceptions and relationships. Nor does one carry the "baggage" of having been in a position of much less power and respect within the department in the recent past. In short, hiring from within can lead to a variety of complications and conflicts. As one P/ET APL put it: "This institution is simply too in-bred, and the politics smacks of it" (Brumberger, 1998). Hiring from outside the department through a national search, as is typical for professorial positions, is a much healthier approach for both the department and the APLs themselves.

Finally, McClelland indicates that writing instructors he spoke with at the University of Wyoming underscored the importance of helping writing students learn to think conceptually, "to develop a culture of inquiry," and to "take responsibility as learners" (1995, p. 18). Aren't these goals common to literature classes as well? Doesn't teaching an appreciation of words and language belong in both literature and writing courses? Doesn't an emphasis on being able to express that appreciation belong? To think through problems, whether practical or aesthetic in nature? To explain one's reasoning or argue for one's solution? In short, I would argue that writing teachers and literature teachers often have similar goals for their students—goals that include teaching citizenship skills, preparing students to be active and critical members of a democracy. Writing instruction and literature instruction have many intersections. As a crucial step in assuring writing an equal place in English departments, we must alter departmental culture to include recognition of our common pedagogical goals, not just of our differences.

Separate but Not Equal

Clearly, there are many ways in which "humane" lectureships, such as the probationary to extended term positions at the University of Wyoming, can improve working conditions. And, as clearly, there remain many ways in which those positions themselves can be improved on. As Ronald concludes, "no department should attempt to institute this kind of lectureship without an overt commitment to equality. Too many problems will arise if those under such contracts feel that their work is undervalued, their opinions ignored" (Ronald, 1990, p. 36). However, even if this criterion is met, and the "ideal" lectureship is created, can it bring a farther-reaching equality to English departments? Although the creation of "humane" lectureships is a strong positive step toward elevating an underclass of writing teachers, it cannot by itself address the marginalization that surrounds the teaching of writing. To address these issues, we must also make more global changes to the culture of English departments, working to forge connections and common goals with "nonwriting" faculty on intellectual issues. We need to find ways that our disciplines can support and strengthen each other. Creating a separate track of instructors to teach primarily writing courses in many ways makes this struggle more difficult rather than less so. As our education system has already amply demonstrated, there is no such thing as separate but equal.

Works Cited

Brumberger, E. (1998, May 4). *Survey of English Department P/ET APLs*. Laramie, WY: University of Wyoming.

Constantinides, J., Chairperson of English Department, University of Wyoming. (1997, June 24). Personal interview. Laramie, WY.

Faigley, L. (1992). *Fragments of rationality: Postmodernity and the subject of composition.* Pittsburgh: University of Pittsburgh Press.

Frye, S., Associate Professor of English, University of Wyoming. (1997, September 10). Personal interview. Laramie, WY.

Harris, J., Professor of English, University of Wyoming. (1997, September 8). Personal interview. Laramie, WY.

Hull, K., Professor of English, University of Wyoming. (1997, September 8). Personal interview. Laramie, WY.

McClelland, B. W. (1995, December 7). Report on the University of Wyoming Writing Program in the English Department. Report for Council of Writing Program Administrators.

Reverand, C., Professor of English, University of Wyoming. (1997, September 11). Personal interview. Laramie, WY.

Robertson, L., Crowley, S., & Lentricchia, F. (1987, March). Opinion: The Wyoming Conference Resolution opposing unfair salaries and working conditions for post-secondary teachers of writing. *College English, 49(3)*, 274–280.

Ronald, A. (1990). Separate but (sort of) equal: Permanent non-tenure track faculty members in the composition program. *ADE Bulletin, 95*, 33–37.

Slevin, J. F. (1991). Depoliticizing and politicizing composition studies. In R. Bullock, C. Schuster, and J. Trimbur (Eds.), *The politics of writing instruction: Postsecondary* (pp. 1–21). Portsmouth, NH: Boynton/Cook.

Chapter Four

The Material and the Cultural as Interconnected Texts: Revising Material Conditions for Part-Time Faculty at Syracuse University

Carol Lipson

Syracuse University, Syracuse, New York

Molly Voorheis

Syracuse University, Syracuse, New York

We wish to discuss the efforts to create equitable professional conditions for part-time writing faculty at Syracuse University. After approximately fifteen years of sustained effort on this front, we have made some significant progress, but we are decidedly not where we want to be. The improvements in professional and material conditions for part-time faculty occurred in two stages. The changes in the second stage coincided with the establishment of an independent writing program and were from the early days envisioned as ways to enact and reinforce a new teaching culture. This teaching culture has from the start been exciting, to be sure. It has also demanded a good deal of all of its participants—whether part-time faculty, full-time faculty, staff, or graduate assistants. It has become increasingly difficult to sustain this high level of commitment to change; it has also proved difficult to make substantive changes in the teaching culture that was created in the second stage, given the sensitivities and cultural meanings associated with any effort at change. Syracuse University's writing program houses one of the strongest teaching communities nationwide, and, like all dynamic communities, the program is a complex place to work.

Background: Where We Started

The need to improve the egregious conditions under which part-time teachers of writing functioned was recognized in Syracuse University's English department well before the Wyoming Resolution of 1986 and well before the Syracuse University Writing Program was established, also in 1986. There can be little honor in claiming such priority, since the need to improve conditions had a lot to do with the dire state of conditions at the time. Required freshman English courses were taught by a cadre of teaching assistants and part-time teachers under a rigid, outdated curriculum. The dismal national conditions for part-time faculty were prominent here as well; excellent part-time teachers were treated as forced labor.

In the push for change at Syracuse, the faculty's unhappiness with the state of the curriculum and pedagogy was as much a factor as was the desire to treat part-timers decently. The freshman curriculum had been an exciting one in its early years, in the 1960s; it had ossified by the late seventies and early eighties, however, in large part because curricular and pedagogical concerns were the responsibility of only one full-time faculty member. The part-time faculty particularly bridled at required conformity to rigid curricular guidelines and lack of freedom for experimentation in their courses. The full-time faculty in the department bridled at what they saw as an atheoretical or antitheoretical, formulaic approach to teaching writing.

In the late 1970s and early 1980s, the English department's leadership made numerous efforts to get the university to commit to an outside evaluation of the Freshman English Program and to improvements in the material conditions for part-time employment. Repeatedly, the dean of the College of Arts and Sciences refused both requests. What finally changed the situation was the part-time faculty's investigations into unionizing as a possible way to improve their conditions. This unionization effort brought unwelcome publicity to the university; it also brought the dean's agreement to bring in outside evaluators from the Writing Program administrators. As expected, these evaluators condemned the conditions under which teachers of writing—

part-time faculty mainly—had to function. Before the new Writing Program was conceived and established, it was made clear that the university had to create a more professional environment—both material and pedagogical—for part-time writing faculty. Some important material concessions were already in place by 1986, when the Writing Program was founded: the availability of a limited number of three-year contracts; a long-term commitment to increase the per-section salaries of all English department part-time faculty; and the provision of medical insurance benefits, prorated retirement benefits, and tuition remittance benefits.

At Syracuse, the particular approach to further improving material circumstances for part-time faculty was influenced by a need to update curriculum and pedagogy. The College-wide Planning Committee that established the groundwork for the new Writing Program recommended hiring a faculty of specialists in composition and rhetoric, to be heavily invested in running the undergraduate program. This planning group also recommended the establishment of a Ph.D. program in composition and rhetoric, affiliated with the undergraduate program, as a way to continually ground the undergraduate teaching of writing in developing research and scholarship in the field. The university's plan capped the size of the full-time faculty at ten. Applicants for the first faculty/administrative position recognized clearly that the entire enterprise would fail unless part-time faculty were mentored and given the freedom to take on leadership responsibilities in the four-course undergraduate program. For the most part, the part-time cadre had not had such opportunities before; to become leaders in this new situation would involve their taking substantial risks. Material changes would have to encourage and reward such risk taking.

To illustrate the necessarily complex process and its effects, we will focus attention on three aspects of the new teaching culture that were established to accomplish necessary change: (1) mechanisms that allowed part-time faculty to assume leadership roles with compensation, (2) a merit-tier system to enable a career path for part-time faculty, and (3) peer evaluation of part-time faculty's teaching. As we discuss both the benefits and challenges that have accompanied the efforts to implement these improvements for part-time faculty at Syracuse University, we will argue that the material and the cultural have been in dialogue throughout this process, in complicated ways.

Overview of Material Changes

When the Writing Program began in September of 1986, it immediately became an independent administrative and curricular unit. Two factors combined to enable immediate improvements in the material circumstances for part-time faculty: independence from the English department, and the fact that the new dean of the College of Arts and Sciences was a specialist in ethics, sympathetic to moral arguments for improving the conditions of the part-time faculty. Part-time faculty in writing were for the first time funded for travel expenses. Telephones materialized in their refurbished offices and carrels. Fairly liberal photocopying privileges were extended. Part-time faculty representatives were included in search committees for new tenure-track faculty. Computer technology was made available for their use. And the average salary per section rose considerably. In 1982–83, the average part-time salary for writing teachers at Syracuse was approximately $1400 per section. In 1986, when the Writing Program began, the average salary rose to $2000 per section, and it is now $3173 per section. In fall 1991, part-time faculty contracted for at least five sections per year gained tuition remission benefits for dependents. When new space became available, part-time faculty were given offices interspersed with those of full-time colleagues.

Though important gains were made, part-time faculty have also been extremely vulnerable in times of economic hardship. SU has faced serious budget cuts in the last seven years. There are no longer telephones in every part-time faculty office. Annual increases for part-time faculty most often turn out to be smaller than for other groups on campus. The part-time faculty have been the only employee group on campus ever to lose a benefit— eligibility of dependents for the tuition-exchange program. Since part-time faculty have little visibility and little clout, this event passed unnoticed by the rest of the campus.

Even benefits that have never been officially rescinded re-main elusive. The approval of insurance benefits does not appear to have been documented in any detail. Medical and pension benefits are no problem; other benefits that we thought were available to the part-timers have never been applied, and the university offices at times don't seem to know that these are even available to the part-time group. The benefit problems reveal the anomalous status of part-time faculty on this campus. They seem to be officially classified in the employee categorization system as part-time staff, not as part-time faculty. The University now acknowledges that part-time faculty are eligible for disability payment at the part-time staff rates, which are minuscule. No amount of pressure from the Writing Program has effected the needed improvements.

Material and Professional Mechanisms to Support Cultural Change

"Release" Sections

For its long-term survival, the Writing Program had to find a way to compensate part-time faculty as professionals for taking on leadership responsibilities in the program. Such duties involved leading curriculum-development efforts, mentoring and support-ing experienced teachers, and training new ones. The approach was opportunistic, as the director, Louise Phelps, looked for pos-sibilities within the existing budgetary structure.

As in most writing programs, the instructional budget for the teaching of writing at Syracuse involved two main compo-nents: stipends to hire people to teach one or more sections of one or more of the program's writing courses, and stipends to hire writing tutors. Although there was no flexibility in funding for course sections, and no decrease in the numbers of sections needed, the tutoring budget, always tight, could offer some flex-ibility.

This flexibility got us through the short term. For the longer term, the dean needed to be convinced of the need to establish a limited number of what we called "release" or "discretionary" sections to allow experienced part-time faculty to devote time to coordinate discussions of teachers' groups and to assume some supervisory authority for the members of those groups. A rough formula was established—one coordinator (as these part-time faculty leaders were called) for approximately ten program teachers. In addition, discretionary sections were established for other purposes such as coordination of the program's involvement with basic writers, or work with a variety of departments across the campus. From the outset, the availability of discretionary sections was crucial if part-time faculty were to effectively shoulder leadership responsibilities in the program. Although they have never been entirely removed, the University's recent budget cuts have seriously reduced the number of such sections.

The Opportunity for Representation Outside the Writing Program

Until 1986, part-time faculty were invisible beyond the bounds of the Writing Program. The few intracampus initiatives they took part in brought almost universally high praise for their talents. Until recently, however, these initiatives were few and far between.

In the last five years, however, part-time faculty have seen some professional doors opened for them outside the Writing Program. First, they are now considered eligible to propose curricular innovations for funding through a campus-wide Faculty Instructional Grant Program. Second, after much lobbying by full-time faculty and administrators in the Writing Program, the campus-wide University Senate agreed to allow representation of part-time faculty: two delegates can be elected by part-time faculty across the campus. The achievement required two years of discussion, in which the main objections involved the common perception that adjuncts are transitory and have little connection to the university. The Writing Program defused this objection by proposing that the privilege of representation be restricted to those with more than a half-time teaching commitment at SU, on renewable annual or multiyear contracts. Of the two delegates elected from across the campus, one has always been from the Writing Program. Finally, part-time faculty will have a representative on the recently established search committee for a new vice chancellor for Academic Affairs. We have been less successful in efforts in our own college: Arts and Sciences. Although part-time faculty receive official announcements of all meetings of the college faculty, they are not allowed to vote. The college has also refused requests that part-time faculty be eligible for faculty teaching awards, or that special college-wide teaching awards be established just for them.

The Elusiveness of Full-Time Status

From its inception in 1986, the Writing Program argued for the need to create full-time, renewable teaching positions. At first, the university administration supported this initiative, but it died quickly, meeting strong resistance from the powerful AAUP group on campus, who feared an administrative misuse of the nontenured lines and a degradation of tenure. In addition, the university's lawyers have raised what they consider a major problem: the university's faculty handbook, which governs part-time faculty as well as full-time faculty, specifically states that after six years of full-time employment, faculty gain tenure unless officially denied tenure. Campus lawyers are concerned that even if a contract letter for a full-time non-tenure-track faculty position directly says that there is no possibility of tenure, a lawsuit might result on the issue. We have not given up, but the roadblocks are formidable.

In the meantime, the director received approval from the administration to divert some funds from the instructional budget that had been used for release sections to accommodate nonteaching work by part-time faculty; these funds can now be used as extra stipends on top of a three-section teaching load. Theoretically, then, a part-time teacher can achieve full-time pay this way. However, the reality proves far less desirable, as part-time faculty once again find themselves in a Kafkaesque administrative nightmare with these stipends. At Syracuse University, stipends that supplement regular salaries are paid via extra service vouchers. Because such vouchers are by definition considered supplements to full-time pay, they're processed infrequently and payroll withholdings are far greater than from regular checks. Part-time faculty are left with irregular compensation that they cannot count on—for work above and beyond the normal.

Opportunities for Reward and Advancement: Recognition of Merit in a Tier System

If the Writing Program had not had the possibility to create a career path for part-time faculty, with significant pay increments for increasing responsibilities at different stages of part-time service, we would have been stymied in our ability to keep the best people. Before 1986, salaries of writing instructors increased with time in rank. The only benefit that highly meritorious teachers received was not having to undergo rigorous review each year; three-year contracts were available for a select few. Louise Phelps, the first director of the Writing Program, favored the introduction of merit recognition as a condition of professional life in the program, including monetary differentiation. A system of merit recognition was instituted incrementally. Notably, merit recognition initially came out of the Writing Program's budget and continues to be funded from a part-time faculty salary pool. This system is not without its problems.

In the first year, $300 merit awards were made available; part-time faculty or graduate assistants could be nominated in writing by peers or by full-time faculty. The total funds set aside (approximately $5400 that year) were neither insignificant nor formidable; but these funds served the crucial function of establishing heroes in the new culture. Teachers noted that those chosen for merit bonuses were almost uniformly cited for significant contributions beyond teaching their own classes well. The merit announcements made clear that meritorious teaching would be predicated upon "talking about one's [teaching] in useful ways with other instructors." By definition then, excellence or merit as a teacher involved having a beneficial effect on other teachers, not just on students. Good teachers had to contribute to the good of the community and not just to students in their own classrooms. The merit awards helped establish the basic values of the new teaching culture.

Once the concept of merit pay differentiation was accepted, the Writing Program moved to establish other differentiations that could allow for a career path. In 1989–1990, a committee of part-time faculty representatives met with the director to develop a merit pay plan. This plan is designed around four tiers (four pay categories that compensate teachers according to years of service in the program and professional leadership roles that teachers take up). The length of contracts differs for the tiers as well, with one-year contracts in tier one, and three-year contracts possible in tiers three and four. The plan outlines a normal sequence of advancement through the tiers, while allowing for more rapid advancement based on excellent performance (see Attachment A). One of the important functions of this plan is to identify the types of activities that are considered meritorious, including meritorious teaching as well as demonstrated skill and leadership ability in roles such as mentoring, designing curriculum, participating in evaluation, or writing needed program texts. Only meritorious performance in such activities can move a veteran instructor into tier four, a category designed to serve as exceptional distinction for a small group of outstanding part-time faculty leaders in the program.

Implementation of the merit plan was accomplished smoothly, though the initial discussion raised a good deal of suspicion. A number of individuals were concerned that the tier system would affect the sense of community among the instructors, introducing an inherent sense of competition among teachers. Tension remains between the impetus for equal treatment as a condition of fairness and the differential treatment for differing contributions.

Problems of the Merit Tier System

The merit system was designed to encourage and reward those part-time faculty who were willing and able to take on some of the tough tasks involved in running an innovative writing program. Thus there are sharp distinctions in pay between the entry-level salary (now $2386 per section), the level-one salary (now $2608 per section), and the level-four salary (now $3620 per section). The tier system was planned to create a career path, with incentives and rewards for those who stayed in the program for the long term and who successfully took on a series of challenging assignments. Before the Writing Program began, turnover among the part-time ranks was high. In the last three years, however, an average of only three part-time faculty have left each year, out of a total of forty-three. By far, the majority of the part-time faculty remain for long periods.

1. Dead End: In the seven years since the introduction of the tier system, some part-time instructors have made their way to tier three. These are excellent teachers, but often individuals who prefer to work alone. They do not aspire to the leadership roles that might move them to tier four. Some seem bothered by the fact that excellent classroom teaching brings limits in the recognition they can attain. Other individuals long ago moved into tier four, soon finding themselves with nowhere else to go. Though their pay is much better than it was in 1986, or when they entered the program, it's still part-time pay.

At the time we set up the five-step system, the last tier was envisioned as a gateway, not as an endpoint. That is, we foresaw that tier four might lead to even higher-paying, three-quarter-time positions (which we did have for a time), and that these might lead to renewable full-time, non-tenure-track positions. And these in turn might lead to placement in a full-time administrative staff position within the program, or in full-time administrative positions elsewhere at the university. Three of our former part-time teachers, all working for Ph.D.'s, have garnered such full-time positions—one in the College of Education, supervising student teachers; two working under the vice president for Undergraduate Instruction. But the expected full-time teaching positions in the program never came to be, and the extensive career path we planned was drastically truncated.

2. Slow Progress: One effect of the tier system is that it takes a long time for new teachers to attain the higher levels of pay that the program was able to offer its part-time faculty in the top categories. The program administrators had no trouble convincing the dean that the part-time teachers who distinguished themselves, especially those who were taking significant and challenging leadership positions, should be paid well and encouraged to remain with the Writing Program. How-

ever, we had no leverage with the dean in arguing for high salaries for new part-time faculty. This dean had become painfully aware that the weak link in the program's teaching lay in the large group of teaching assistants (novices to the teaching of writing), and in new part-time faculty, some of whom are relatively new to teaching, some of whom are new to pedagogical practices operating in the Writing Program. We could not have gained dramatic increases in the stipend level for highly meritorious part-time faculty had we been unwilling to create a staged pay system, with newcomers starting at the bottom.

The result is that very talented new part-time teachers, even with considerable experience at other institutions, can earn only $14,000 during the academic year at SU. This can involve a pay cut over what they earned at previous schools. While the system allows for excellent teachers to move through the tiers more quickly than normal, it can still take years until they reach tier three, where the academic-year salary for six sections might reach $20,000. For new part-time faculty with a good deal of experience under their belts, and even with teaching awards on their records, the ethos of the merit tier system and the resulting low pay create some serious morale problems.

3. Effect on the Raise Pool: At SU, it's the Writing Program that gets to decide how much of the annual raise pool it wishes to devote to each of the tiers. Theoretically, the program could devote all of the part-time raise pool to tier one, with no raise for any other tier. Since it's generally the people in the top tiers who are taking on the toughest and riskiest assignments—such as working with groups of new inexperienced teaching assistants—there has historically been a tendency to reward those tiers. That seems fair, but it doesn't address the low level of pay for newcomers. Significantly, since the cost of promotions to higher tier levels also comes out of the total annual salary adjustment pool, not much is left at times for across-the-board section increases.

In recent years, more and more teachers have risen to the top merit tiers, only to find little or no growth in salary from year to year. Those teachers who have already benefited from a merit system now often advocate an alternative approach that would protect the raise pool from being consumed by merit upgrades. On the other hand, teachers with some seniority who are still in lower merit tiers want to keep the tier differentials so they can benefit from the steps. The problem is inherent in a process bounded by a fixed salary pool that must accommodate both annual raises and merit tier upgrades.

Part-Time Faculty Evaluate Their Peers

The final element in the structure of the Writing Program that enabled the creation of professional conditions for part-time faculty involved their inclusion in the design and implementation of the process for reviewing and assessing their teaching. This involvement allows the part-time cadre to have a major say in the most important judgments that affect their professional lives. The impetus for this involvement came from the part-time faculty themselves, out of frustration with the time limitations on Writing Program administrators—who at that time were full-time faculty—that prevented them from providing written feedback on the annual portfolios. In a system in which so much emphasis is given to excellent teaching, and so much hinges on evaluation of quality, the part-time faculty increasingly sought careful and useful feedback on job performance. In the spring of 1989, one group of teachers developed a proposal to solve the dilemma by systematically involving part-time faculty in the evaluation process, with appropriate remuneration. After a year of study and planning and consultation, under the leadership of then Associate Director Patti Stock, a proposed system for peer control of evaluation was approved. This plan, put in place in the spring of 1990, remains a dominant feature of the Writing Program's teaching environment. The plan called for the establishment of a committee called the Teacher Evaluation Committee, composed of up to six part-time faculty, some elected by peers. Until this year, one full-time faculty member sat on the TEC, as did one member of the Writing Program administration.

The Downside of Peer Evaluation

From the beginning, university administrators have complained vociferously about the expense of the peer involvement in evaluation, since part-time faculty are compensated for their participation. For years, the six part-time faculty members all received a section release to participate in the work of the committee, and a part-time faculty member was provided with an additional release section and named as Evaluation Coordinator to supplement the work of the committee. The committee initially cost at least $18,000 to $20,000 per year. We were told over and over by the administration that no other academic unit on campus pays so much just for evaluation. As of 1997–98, the system for remunerating committee members involved only two release sections for the evaluation coordinator (a part-time faculty member), and $1,150 stipends for the part-time faculty members who serve as portfolio readers, reducing the cost for this work closer to $13,000. In the future, we anticipate further reductions.

Over the years, the Teacher Evaluation Committee has had mixed reviews within the Writing Program. While part-time faculty welcome peer participation in the evaluation process, they do not always trust the particular groupings that make particular decisions. There is also a feeling that substantive evaluation has inordinately come to dominate the atmosphere of the Writing Program. A significant component of the program's resources is directed towards evaluation, and a significant portion of every part-time faculty member's time and attention has had to be directed toward the fact of evaluation. That centrality became a source of great complaint.

The New, Improved Peer Evaluation Plan

The Teacher Evaluation Committee has, over the years, generated a variety of proposals to ease the burdensome process of evaluation, and one plan was approved this year for implementation (see Attachment B). This proposal offers a rough equivalent of "tenure"—that is, once part-time faculty have passed a certain stage, they do not have to submit portfolios and undergo evaluations unless they wish to be promoted to a higher merit tier, or to take on new leadership challenges—or unless questions have been raised about a teacher's work. The plan changes the composition of the Teacher Evaluation Committee, so that it includes only part-time faculty, with no administrative or full-time faculty representation. The plan was approved by the program's administration without any consultation with full-time faculty, who have raised concerns about the effects of their lack of representation in the evaluation process. Given this concern, full-time-faculty participation in some form—perhaps nonvoting—is currently under discussion.

The new plan creates a new category of professional writing instructor—the veteran instructor. After at least five years in the Writing Program, a PWI can submit an exit portfolio to the Evaluation Committee, as an application for veteran instructor status. Once approved, such an individual will no longer need to submit portfolios for evaluation, even at the end of contract periods. Veteran instructors will simply present syllabi, student evaluations, and Curriculum Vitae updates annually, a practice similar to what is asked of full-time faculty annually at most institutions. Significantly, it will be the Evaluation Committee composed of part-time faculty who will be determining who has this "tenure" in their ranks.

The Material and the Cultural in Dialogue: Problems in Implementing a New Teaching Culture

From the beginning of the Writing Program in 1986, the program's founding director envisioned the creation of a new teaching culture—one saturated with a spirit of inquiry, a spirit of innovation, and a concern for excellence. The goal was to create a teaching community committed to reflective exploration of teaching, to collaborative participation in teaching projects, and to thoughtful dissemination of ideas and insights. The part-time faculty would be leaders in this community.

Repeatedly, the director called forth the image of the scientific research group as a model for the teaching community she envisioned. Members of a scientific research group work together and separately in close quarters; they talk about their work informally in the lab, in offices, and in regular meetings. They discuss one anothers' research projects, and the related issues and problems, offering advice and support and new ideas. The scientific research group served as the model for a teaching community whose day-to-day talk and activities would focus on the teaching of writing.

Scientific research groups often work in common spaces. To create a space for the Writing Program community's talk about teaching, the director established a structure—coordinating groups of approximately eight to ten teachers, led by part-time distinguished teachers—in which such a teaching community could be constructed in small group settings. The institution of these groups offers a revealing example of the ways that the material changes remained in dialogue with other messages of the culture. What was being changed in the Writing Program beginning in 1986 was not just unfair material conditions for part-timers. In fact, what was changed was a culture, involving values and practices and behaviors. For such a change to work, the material circumstances must fit with the new culture. The changes have to encourage and promote and reward new behaviors and practices, and not contradict them. But material changes also have to be meaningful in the terms of the old culture, or they are not seen as improvements.

The force of the new teaching culture was to emphasize the professional status of the part-time faculty, and to underline their value to the program and to the profession. But the part-time faculty had never before been treated as the professionals they were. When they were required by new contracts to attend mandatory coordinating groups that were announced as offering official and safe locations for weekly "teacher talk," the part-time faculty were both suspicious and puzzled. Though these groups were led by leaders from their own ranks, these leaders were appointed by the administration; thus the groups were often entered with suspicion. While the program identified these sites as generative places for the creation of a new culture, the part-time faculty viewed them through lenses ground in the old teaching culture—or in similar hierarchical environments. For them, the coordinating groups signified close supervision and administrative monitoring, thus undercutting the sense of independence that the part-timers expected of professional treatment. It didn't help that their full-time colleagues were not required to take part in the weekly group meetings (although, in fact, some chose to do so).

The dissonance of conflicting meanings with which different members of the Syracuse University Writing Program invest program practices continues to operate in these groups. Participation is now optional for experienced part-time faculty members, who are instead now asked to choose a focus for their own professional development and to participate to some degree in professional development activities sponsored by the Writing Program. While part-time faculty have pursued a variety of individual projects, many have also begun to miss the regular community of teachers and the opportunities to talk about their work on a regular basis. Some are now attempting to imagine a new incarnation of teacher groups to meet a wider variety of needs. For these teachers, the value of being part of a teaching community engaged in regular, serious teacher talk is no longer a top-down requirement.

Problems with the Teaching Culture

Over time, it has become clear that the problems in the teaching culture are intimately related to the strengths of that culture. They are so deeply embedded in a complex of structures and values that were adopted in the early days that they have proved difficult to address.

1. It's a teaching culture: The first area of difficulty lies in the fact that the Writing Program has been primarily a teaching culture, yet the full-time faculty and now the Ph.D. students have strong commitments to scholarship, often unrelated to teaching. On the whole, the day-to-day experience here reinforces the centrality of teaching in this community. Until this year, the established forums almost universally focused on teaching, which shapes the research agenda of some of the full-time faculty, but not all. In recent years, the ethos of the teaching community has come close to resenting faculty for

protecting their time for their research, and for not coming to many of the excellent presentations and discussions arranged for and by their part-time colleagues. Full-time faculty are often deemed selfish for working on scholarship that is crucial to their function and to their security. The collaborative teaching culture has become so well institutionalized that research, undertaken in time and space protected from the community's demands, is suspected and even disrespected. All groups expect that growth of the newly established Ph.D. Program in Composition and Cultural Rhetoric will have an impact in changing this cultural ethos in ways that worry a number of the part-time faculty.

2. The culture is resistant to change: One of the defining qualities of the Writing Program's teaching culture, noted quickly by new members of the community, is the conservatism that has come to characterize what was envisioned as an innovative and progressive teaching culture. In many ways, ours is basically a libertarian community. The curriculum offers the broadest of frameworks, within which individuals (all but new TAs now) have an enormous amount of freedom to design and implement their courses. That individual freedom, within very general, minimally constraining guidelines, has become a primary value here, closely tied to the professional status of the part-time faculty. The result is that our curriculum is open to individual innovation and experimentation, which can prove exciting for both students and teachers. The downside is that the curriculum can seem scattered and chaotic, with substantial differences from section to section of the same course. We've never chosen to impose a new requirement for all teachers and sections of any course within our undergraduate studio curriculum. Even small changes carry great symbolic significance as possible threats to the valued freedom and to the delicate balances of a complex community's negotiated status quo.

In fact, as the Writing Program's culture has developed and matured, it seems to have deepened its reliance on a set of crucial symbols as a way of defining itself and its values. Many of the primary symbols represent and reinforce the independence of PWIs, the professional status of PWIs, and the parallel nature of their conditions to those of full-time faculty. Any differential in treatment tends to be seen as a denigration of the part-time status. For instance, just as full-time faculty evaluate one another, peer evaluation of part-time faculty has become an important symbol of the PWI's professionalization and of their rigor in upholding the high quality of teaching. Many do not see the need to include full-time faculty on their evaluation committee—just as part-time faculty have not served on committees to evaluate the teaching of their full-time colleagues. This sensitivity brings some major losses for the program as a whole, and for the full-time faculty's involvement in it. Notably, though the program now employs a hierarchy of administrators who could take on the evaluation of part-time faculty teaching, and thus release funds that might be used for part-time faculty in other ways, no proposal for simplifying the process of such evaluation has advocated shifting the responsibility from the part-time faculty themselves. The peer handling of evaluation, with no full-time faculty participation, has developed crucial significance to the PWIs' sense of professionalism. It is not necessarily the best approach for the program as a whole, even for the teaching culture of the program.

Interestingly, full-time faculty in the Writing Program recently opened discussion of plans to include part-time faculty as members of investigation committees to report on the teaching of full-time faculty for three-year reviews, tenure reviews, and promotion reviews. Implicit in such a discussion is the level of expertise about teaching that the part-time faculty can bring to such a committee. The current proposal does not provide for part-time faculty voting on contract decisions, but does recognize the expertise in documenting and assessing teaching. That's an important step.

Over the years, part-time faculty have worked closely with full-time faculty and administrators to create structures and processes and practices and curricula—all of which involved intense discussion and negotiation. To change any of those elements can seem threatening to the part-time faculty. When the program first began, they collaborated with the small existing faculty cadre. Now that the faculty has grown to full size, two assistant directors have been added, and Ph.D. students have joined the community, the part-time faculty fear a diminution of their centrality.

3. Part-time is not full-time, or even close: The Winter 1998 issue of *Forum*, a newsletter for part-time faculty in composition, contains reports from several NCTE representatives to the September 1997 National Conference on the Growing Use of Part-time/Adjunct Faculty (*Forum*, 1998). The meeting included participants from academic organizations representing eight different fields, including the teaching of English. The group issued a statement defining appropriate policies, and calling for action to enact such policies (*ADE Bulletin*, 1998). Of the sixteen "good practices" listed, SU's Writing Program is still deficient in one—a major one. That is, the conference called for equitable salary remuneration indexed commensurately to full-time faculty salaries, rather than per-course rates. We're just not there. For new hires, the full-time-equivalent salary is around $19,000—far below any full-time salary for college teaching. For teachers with many years of excellent performance behind them, the highest full-time-equivalent salary they can attain is currently about $29,000; some of these teachers have been doing excellent work here for fifteen to twenty years at three-quarters-time. In comparison, according to the 1993 report of the AAUP on "The Status of Non-Tenure-Track Faculty," the average salary nationally for full-time faculty in 1987 was $37,000 (AAUP, 1993). Though we've made some progress, the salary levels remain unsatisfactory. And for part-time faculty, annual increases have been embarrassingly minuscule, largely as a result of the particular way the merit tier system is handled here.

In January 1998, the university published a report of a study just completed, which looked at part-time faculty employment here (Syracuse University, 1998). The report basically pats Syracuse University on the back, as using part-time faculty for academic reasons, and not to save money. Such a conclusion clearly does not apply to the large contingent of part-time positions in the Writing Program. Many of those teachers want and need regular full-time salaries. Some of the full-time faculty are committed to working toward that goal, but current conditions on the campus do not portend well for any large-scale change of this sort in the near future.

Conclusion

As an institution, Syracuse University favors entrepreneurial units; and the Writing Program has historically chosen to move opportunistically and incrementally, taking advantage of opportunities that could help us improve conditions of part-time faculty, while recognizing that these opportunities left us with significant problems. At this institution, that seemed the only way to achieve progress. While we fully acknowledge the remaining and resulting problems, we do not feel these outweigh the benefits.

For instance, even though participation in intensive teaching evaluation has come to dominate the professional life of part-time faculty here, remaining a costly element in a limited budget, the process has also reaped tremendous benefits for the program. Certainly peer participants in the evaluation process have gained from the exposure to the thoughtful, rigorous, imaginative, and elaborate planning and reflection documented in the teaching portfolios they examine, and from the careful discussion and deliberation in the committee. Thus far, the program has not been particularly successful in finding ways to disseminate such gains beyond the confines of the committee. PWIs rotate on and off, but out of approximately forty-five PWIs, approximately half have never served on this committee. And only four of the ten full-time faculty have participated. Service as part of this evaluation process has contributed greatly to the growth of individual participants as teachers, but we still need to find ways to broaden that learning. However, even those who can distance themselves from the icon of peer control of evaluation can see substantial gains from the existence of peer participation in evaluation.

Similarly, the existence of the merit tier system provided the means for significantly raising the salaries of highly experienced part-time faculty. The problems we now face were foreseeable from the start, and we chose to take the risk. The tier system in many ways mimics the availability of ranks for full-time faculty. In the case of full-time faculty, each dean withholds a certain percentage of the salary raise pool in order to reward annual merit achievements such as promotions or the granting of tenure. For part-time faculty, however, there is no equivalent college-wide participation. The Writing Program is on its own in having to come up with the funds to reward the equivalent of part-time faculty promotions. Such rewards have to come from the annual part-time salary raise pool. Thus far, the program has been reluctant to limit the number of merit tier moves possible in a year. Only once has the dean of Arts and Sciences stepped in to rescue the program, by providing an additional one-time amount to allow for both approved merit-tier upgrades as well as for minimal cost-of-living increases for the rest of the part-time faculty.

However, it doesn't seem to us inevitable that, at other institutions, the establishment of merit tiers would necessarily be held to the same conditions we face. Our system has to function within a fixed sum of money, as a zero-cost enterprise for the college. We foresee no change in that policy. We will have to make some changes, but these do not invalidate the concept and its benefits.

One significant advantage of the merit system lies in the clear understandings it provides to part-time faculty of what they have to do in order to rise through the ranks, and of when they can reasonably expect such promotions. It demystifies the professional expectations for success. But the tier system also creates significant problems, particularly in the ways it clashes with several other crucial components of the culture. It embodies an ethos of Syracuse's uniqueness, which undermines the ethos of professional conditions for those who come with established credentials from elsewhere. The differentials of the merit system also clash with a coexisting ethos of equal treatment. The combination inevitably brings forth contradictions. Professional part-time faculty from other schools lose their "professional" status in coming here, going to the bottom rungs of the merit ladder. Professionalism for full-time faculty allows for flexibility in hiring conditions—flexibility in negotiating salary and rank, for instance. The lack of flexibility in these and other matters within our current practices speaks against professional treatment of the part-time community. Some changes are in order.

Implicit in our situation is the question of the ultimate value of the changes made here. That is, part-time faculty at Syracuse have gained most conditions that their colleagues elsewhere are clamoring for; the improvements are greatly appreciated, but they have also resulted in some significant difficulties for the Writing Program as well as for the part-time faculty themselves. We would argue that many of the problems are factors of the particulars of the context and history here, and are not inevitable elsewhere. Other problems, we would agree, inhere in the situation of a large cadre of part-time faculty within a research-university environment that includes a smaller contingent of full-time faculty and Ph.D. students.

On the whole, we do recommend to other schools the mechanisms that enabled our achievements: the use of release sections, the establishment of merit tiers, and peer involvement in evaluation of part-time faculty teaching. However, we would not advocate the wholesale importation of such programs into other settings precisely as they exist here. The particular implementations here grew out of a particular context at a particular place and time. As efforts were made to improve the material and professional conditions for part-time faculty in the Writing Program, choices had to be made. Within varying sets of constraints, negotiations were conducted and compromises agreed upon, sometimes after abandoning hope for the entire pie in order to have as many pieces as possible. After twelve years, we have learned the consequences of our choices. While we have identified a range of problems with the policies that were implemented, we also note the ongoing efforts to minimize and to resolve these problems. The recently announced changes to the evaluation procedure, while slow in coming and not free of difficulties themselves, still serve as a case in point. At Syracuse, we have complicated the traditional situation of full-time faculty (and of Ph.D. students) in improving conditions for part-time faculty. It's a tradeoff the two of us find necessary. Our teaching community will and should remain a complex one, but it does not have to be as slow to change as it has been. Growth and change can continue.

We end by noting that there are no mountains in the Syracuse area. The landscape is characterized by formations called drumlins—hillocks formed by glacial drift. This landscape seems to bear a relation to the Writing Program's situation in its mission to improve the conditions of the part-time faculty. We have climbed some drumlins here, each one revealing new ones we have yet to tackle. Tackling one drumlin at a time seems manageable, though there is still a long, long way to go.

Attachment A

Merit Pay Plan for Professional Writing Instructors

Note: The new policy on evaluation presented below, in Attachment B, renders some of the following discussion obsolete. In addition, several sections have been omitted at the end. The full text can be found on the Writing Program's Web site (http://wrt.syr.edu/), in the Teachers' Sourcebook section titled "Merit Pay Plan for Professional Writing Instructors."

The following plan is a 1997–98 revision of the original plan first implemented in 1990–91. The Merit Pay Plan is subject to administrative review and revision at the close of each academic year.

For the purposes of determining merit pay tiers, all section assignments (whether as studio teacher or as writing consultant, regular or specialized) are considered to be of equivalent skill level. The same is normally true of specialized administrative or curricular assignments.

<u>First Year:</u>
All first year PWIs, including former TAs, will be considered probationary hires and will be evaluated at the end of the initial year. Rate for 1997–98: $2,386 per section.

<u>Tier One:</u>
Tier One includes second- and third-year instructors, who will be observed and evaluated yearly and rehired on the basis of program need and performance. An exception is an instructor whose first-year portfolio earned a 2 or better; this instructor is not required to submit a portfolio until after her/his third year of teaching before entering Tier Two. Tier One instructors are eligible for merit recognition, which may facilitate more rapid upward movement, at the discretion of the Director. Rate for 1997–98: $2,608 per section.

Tier Two:
Those instructors who have taught at least a 2/2 load for at least two consecutive years enter this tier automatically upon rehiring following the third year of service. Instructors who do not meet these requirements for load and continuity of service are eligible to be considered for Tier Two on the basis of performance. Tier Two instructors are eligible for two-year contracts; they are observed and evaluated formally on a bi-annual schedule or at the end of the contract period. They are eligible for merit recognition, which may facilitate more rapid upward movement, at the discretion of the Director. Rate for 1997–98: $2,972 per section.

Tier Three:
Instructors can enter Tier Three on the basis of a combination of five years of service and determination of sustained merit and/or special skills. Those not promoted into Tier Three can continue in Tier Two. Tier Three instructors are eligible for three-year contracts; they are observed and evaluated formally on a three-year schedule or at the end of the contract period. Tier Three instructors are eligible for merit recognition, which could facilitate more rapid upward movement. Rate for 1997–98: $3,334 per section.

Tier Four:
Normally instructors enter Tier Four directly from Tier Three, on the basis of sustained merit, special skills, and leadership in the Program. Tier Four instructors are eligible for salaried appointments, if available. Promotion to Tier Four requires five years of service, including a meritorious teaching record over at least the last two years, along with consistently demonstrated skill and leadership ability in special roles (e.g., mentoring, program writing, curriculum design, evaluation) addressing important areas of program need and having positive, broad impact on program life and program development. This is an exceptional category limited to a very small number. Instructors in Tier Four are observed and evaluated every third year. Rate for 1997–98: $3,620 per section.

Note: Downward movement from Tier Four to Tier Three and from Tier Three to Tier Two is possible as decided by the Director, based on the results of a formal evaluation.

Attachment B

New Policy for PWI Evaluation

1. Who Will Submit a Portfolio: Professional Writing Instructors who have taught fewer than five years will continue to present their work in a portfolio for peer review at the end of each contract year.

Professional Writing Instructors who have taught five years or more may achieve veteran instructor status by submitting an exit portfolio for review by the Teacher Evaluation Committee at the end of their current contract period. Veteran instructors will then be required to update their portfolios with annual syllabi, student evaluations, handouts, and a C.V. Veteran instructors are encouraged to continue their professional development with the assurance that their update will NOT be evaluated.

2. Who Will Serve on the Teacher Evaluation Committee: The Teacher Evaluation Committee will be comprised solely of Professional Writing Instructors, including the Assessment Facilitator who will oversee the whole process. Four members will be elected; the Director will appoint at least one more member.

Works Cited

American Association of University Professors. (1993). *The status of non-tenure-track faculty.* [On-line]. Available at <http://www.aaup.org/rbnonten.htm>.

Forum, Newsletter of the Non-Tenure-Track Faculty Special Interest Group. (1998, February). *College Composition and Communication, 49(1),* A1–A24.

Statement from the Conference on the Growing Use of Part-Time and Adjunct Faculty. (1998, Spring). *ADE Bulletin, 119,* 19–26.

The use of part-time and adjunct faculty in instruction at Syracuse University. (1998, January). Syracuse, NY: Office of the Vice Chancellor for Academic Affairs, Syracuse University.

CHAPTER FIVE

Trafficking in Freeway Flyers: (Re)Viewing Literacy, Working Conditions, and Quality Instruction

HELEN O'GRADY

University of Rhode Island, Kingston

One morning, on my way to teach, I found myself flying down the highway, only to realize I was headed the wrong way. Juggling a hectic schedule involving teaching appointments in three different institutions, I had unconsciously confused the routes I had to travel that morning. On the surface, this incident might be amusing, but another signaled its grim reality. Momentarily dozing off while driving one Friday afternoon, I headed the wrong way again, only this time, I traveled across the lane into the oncoming traffic. Fortunately, there were no cars in the opposite lane, and the abrupt jerk of the steering wheel woke me. The demands of part-time teaching, family, and graduate school had begun to take their toll. And it was only February.

Of the many familiar injustices part-timers endure, inequitable salaries and contractual instability emerge as the most pernicious, forcing us to teach concurrently in more than one institution. Although most part-timers no longer fit the stereotypical "faculty wife" image, most are women whose low salaries still mandate their dependence on other sources of income, be they husband, partners, parents, children, or additional jobs. An inequitable salary for some translates into less than a living wage for many others. Consequently, who can afford to teach part-time and who can afford to teach in only one institution become questions of class—and in the case of writing instruction—statistics reveal that to be a gendered class.[1]

Embedded in these realities lies an important question: What are the connections between and among class, working conditions, and instructional quality? For example, my financial status forces me to teach concurrently in more than one institution, further compounding the adverse working conditions I experience within any single institution and inevitably affecting the quality of my teaching at all of them. Considering the question in these terms, other questions become apparent: Who can afford to teach part-time in only one institution? Who can afford to deliver quality instruction? Apparently, class dictates who can avoid interinstitutional teaching and who can work around conditions that adversely affect the quality of writing instruction. Effective writing instruction depends on teachers having sufficient time and energy to prepare classes, to respond usefully to students' writing, and to conduct writing conferences with students outside class during office hours. When writing teachers have neither time nor space (many do not have access to telephones, mailboxes, or offices), their ability to teach effectively is diminished.

Institutional mission statements suppress these socioeconomic inequities even as they promise educational quality to students. While it may not be surprising that mission statements overlook these inequities, it is surprising that radical discourse theorists, particularly critical literacy theorists, also do so.[2] Although a number of writing theorists have called attention to the ways in which teachers negotiate class issues in critical pedagogy (see Gale, 1996; Herzberg, 1994; Knoblauch, 1991; Shor, 1987) and the ways in which college level literacy practices serve to maintain students as an underclass (see Clifford, 1991; Holzman, 1991; Trimbur, 1991), the discourse on critical pedagogy and literacy tends to construct writing teachers as a privileged group. These theorists have focused on class issues related to students' experiences and learning conditions but have failed to study, describe, and theorize the correlation between socioeconomics, literacy instruction, and instructional working conditions for part-time writing teachers; in short, they have failed to examine the conditions under which the majority of postsecondary writing teachers "teach." Although critical literacy theory provides an analytic framework for theorizing this correlation (see Freire, 1993; Giroux, 1987; Shor, 1987), critical pedagogy theorists have ignored class issues related to part-time writing teachers' contexts and teaching/working conditions.[3] Thus, like institutional mission statements, radical literacy discourse relies on the notion that teaching is primarily performed by privileged tenure-track or tenured full-time faculty. Both discourses perpetuate the full-time faculty myth by eliding the material conditions under which many part-time and nontenure track writing teachers work.[4]

For the sake of instructional quality and socioeconomic justice for part-timers, I offer a critical reading of the working conditions of postsecondary part-time writing/literacy teachers in light of the idealized representations of writing teachers' class status in institutional and radical literacy discourses. In doing so, I employ Paolo Freire's idea of problem-posing education through which

> people develop their power to perceive critically *the way they exist* in the world *with which* and *in which* they find themselves. . . . [Thus,] the form of action they adopt is to a large extent a function of how they perceive themselves in the world. (1993, p. 64)

In Freirean theory, self-perception and reflection require demythologizing (p. 64). Additionally, Freire emphasizes the importance of contextualizing teachers' as well as students' situations when he urges both teachers and students to "reflect simultaneously on themselves and the world without dichotomizing this reflection from action"(p. 64). In Freire's view, therefore, developing the critical consciousness necessary for critical reading extends beyond mere consciousness raising: it involves reflection, dialogue, and action.

Thus, using Freire's framework to reflect on my own underclass status as a part-time writing teacher, I address the contradictions in the institutional discourse in mission statements and in radical discourse about literacy. I'll begin by discussing contradictions inherent in institutional mission statements, supporting my arguments with the results of surveys I conducted of part-time writing teachers' participation in interinstitutional teaching. Next, I'll discuss the contradictions in radical literacy discourse. Finally, reading through the lens of critical literacy discourse, I'll offer a way to (re)view the part-time problem and suggest ways to address it. In doing so, I wish to extend critical literacy practices to include how we read, write, and speak about the part-time problem and, ultimately, how we address it. How we assess and talk about part-time labor issues can lead to a more productive vision of higher education and literacy instruction and, I hope, more productive ways to create better working conditions for the part-time faculty largely responsible for college writing instruction.

Institutional Mission Statements and Contradictions

Although institutional mission statements dictate various goals and priorities, a constant is their claim to providing quality instruction. However, as James Slevin points out, institutions undercut their mission by employing a "neglected, badly paid, with no hope of security, adjunct composition faculty" (1989, p. 2). Although undergraduate catalogs focus on the value of writing instruction in educating America's citizens and preparing future leaders, such value is not evident in writing teachers' devalued status—a status that affects part-time faculty morale and the quality of their teaching (pp. 2–3). Slevin's remarks echo the position of the National Council of Teachers of English in their Conference on College Composition and Communication's "Statement of Principles and Standards for the Postsecondary Teaching of Writing." The "Statement" specifies that "the quality of writing instruction is today seriously compromised" by the practice of overrelying on part-time and/or temporary appointments. CCCC explicitly connects working conditions with instructional quality. Recognizing the "extraordinary contributions that so many of these [writing] teachers have made to their students and schools," CCCC draws public attention to the working conditions of teachers who "work without job security, often without benefits, and for wages far below what their full-time colleagues are paid per course," as well as to the working conditions of many writing teachers who "are forced to accept an itinerant existence, racing from class to car to drive to another institution to teach." Such conditions "undermine the capacities of teachers to teach and of students to learn" (1). This connection between working conditions and instructional quality was also affirmed at the 1997 Summit on Part-Time/Adjunct Faculty in Higher Education when many participants expressed their concern that the overuse of part-timers is diminishing instructional quality as well as exploiting many adjuncts (Leatherman, 1997, p. 14).

Although concern for quality instruction exists in mission statements and statements issued by professional associations, institutional practices reveal the gap between projection and reality. For example, some institutions boast a low student-to-teacher ratio and claim to offer small class sizes and individualized attention. While such a ratio may prevail within individual classes in one institution, the proportions can explode when the figures are multiplied by the total number of students a writing instructor might have to teach interinstitutionally. This ratio holds up when we interpret it from students' contexts but not from teachers' contexts. Institutions cannot boast favorable student/teacher ratios and quality writing instruction if they account for total interinstitutional numbers of students taught per instructor in a given semester. For example, one mission statement where I have taught claims, "A low student-to-faculty ratio enhances the University's mission." Although the percentage of part-timers is lower at this institution than at others, the statement suppresses the identity of its faculty members and hides the fact that the majority of its writing courses are taught by temporary underpaid and overworked graduate teaching assistants and part-timers, a number of whom hold interinstitutional appointments. Interinstitutional teaching results in student loads in excess of CCCC's recommended limit of sixty students per writing teacher a semester. CCCC bases its sixty-student guideline on the following rationale:

> The improvement of an individual student's writing requires persistent and frequent contact between teacher and students both inside and outside the classroom. It requires assigning far more papers than are usually assigned in other college class-

rooms; it requires reading them and commenting on them not simply to justify a grade, but to offer guidance and suggestions for improvement; and it requires spending a great deal of time with individual students, helping them not just to improve particular papers but to understand fundamental principles of effective writing that will enable them to continue learning throughout their lives. (1989, p. 4)

Limiting the number of writing students per teacher establishes a condition crucial to providing teachers the time and energy to teach effectively. Teaching more than sixty students a semester cuts down on the amount of time for conferencing with individual students and the numbers of drafts teachers can read, or even the amount of writing that can be assigned. Even though the sixty-student limit may be adhered to within one institution, interinstitutional teaching confounds the ratios. For instance, I have taught as many as five courses in three institutions in one semester and have regularly taught courses without any contract at all, receiving compensation well after I have turned in grades. Very often, my course load exceeded that of a full-time faculty member. Like other part-timers, I tend to load up on courses in the fall because fewer courses are offered in the spring.

To measure my experience against the sixty-student guideline, I calculated the numbers of writing students I had taught interinstitutionally each semester over a period of six and a half years, or thirteen consecutive semesters. The figures show a teaching load in excess of sixty students for six of these semesters (see Table 5A). Teaching more than sixty students a semester did cut down on the amount of time I could conference with individual students and the numbers of drafts per assignment to which I could respond. Also, I think it is important to distinguish between applying the sixty-student guideline within one institution as opposed to more than one institution. Teaching sixty students full time in one place is not the same as teaching them part time in more than one place. For example, multiple preparations with multiple appointments multiplies time spent negotiating different institutional philosophies and different student demographics, not to mention the time driving from one place to another. It's just not the same.

My own experience with interinstitutional teaching led me to conduct a survey of my colleagues teaching writing part time during the fall of 1996 (see Figure 5.1). My goal was three-fold: to determine the numbers of students my colleagues taught interinstitutionally, to show ratios of full- to part-time faculty who taught writing (see Table 5B), and to determine the extent to which part-timers taught *inter*institutionally in excess of sixty students (see Table 5C). To avoid being institutionally specific, I have used the letter designations "A," "B," and "C" to refer to the institutions I surveyed. All three are co-educational institutions located in the Northeast; they offer liberal arts and sciences programs, professional programs, as well as selected graduate programs. Institution A has an approximate enrollment of 13,700; institution B has 9,100, and C has 3,800. At institution C, which had the largest response rate of 60 percent, the percentage ratio for full- and part-time faculty in the English department was 57/43 respectively. Based on the total number of part-timers responding to the survey, 56 percent taught interinstitutionally, and 100 percent of these taught loads exceeding sixty writing students

TABLE 5A. Number of Students Taught Per Semester

Semester	Total Students	Writing Students
Fall '90	84	84
Spring '91	70	70
Fall '91	90	90
Spring '92	40	27
Fall '92	87	55
Spring '93	59	38
Fall '93	65	44
Spring '94	58	37
Fall '94	88	67
Spring '95	96	72
Fall '95	48	48
Spring '96	48	26
Fall '96	96	96

Number of institutions in which you taught   _____

Number of courses you taught   _____

Number of writing courses you taught   _____

Number of other courses you taught   _____

Total number of writing students you taught   _____

Number of developmental students you taught   _____

Number of nondevelopmental students you taught   _____

FIGURE **5.1.** *Survey to part-time writing faculty, fall 1996.*

TABLE **5B.** Full-Time and Part-Time Faculty Teaching Writing, Fall, 1996

Institution	Number FT	Number PT	Number GTAs*	% FT/PT
A	27	14	21	66/34
B	26	28	N/A	48/52
C	20	15	N/A	57/43

* Graduate teaching assistants represented to show institutional reliance on other temporary and partial teaching appointments.

TABLE **5C.** Interinstitutional Part-Timers Teaching Writing, Fall 1996

Institution	Total PT*	Response Rate		Interinstitutional PT **		Teaching 60+ Students**	
	N	N	%	N	%	N	%
A	14	6	43	3	50	2	67
B	28	5	18	4	80	2	50
C	15	9	60	5	56	5	100

* These numbers represent total part-timers teaching writing as well as total part-timers surveyed.
** These percentages are based on the total number of part-timers responding to the survey.

during the fall 1996 semester. Institution A yielded a response rate of 43 percent, showing a full-time/part-time percentage ratio of 66/34 with 50 percent part-timers teaching interinstitutionally. Of these interinstitutional teachers, 67 percent teach sixty or more writing students. At institution B, which had only an 18 percent response rate, the full-time/part-time percentage ratio was 48/52 with 80 percent of all part-timers teaching interinstitutionally and of this, 50 percent teaching sixty or more students.

Although the scope of my research encompassed only three institutions, more representative and formal surveys will likely confirm a similar overreliance on interinstitutional writing instruction. This kind of formal research could yield the empirical data needed to determine the extent that institutional practices impinge on the working conditions necessary to ensure teachers' ability to fulfill pronounced commitments to deliver quality instruction.

Claiming favorable student/teacher ratios, university mission statements tend to advertise the total number of full-time faculty within an institution without indicating how many of those full-time faculty work off the tenure-track. One of the rhetorical purposes of citing full-time faculty statistics is to attract students by reassuring them that their courses are staffed by "full-time faculty" or even just "faculty." For example, the mission statement at another institution where I have taught, advertises, "Undergraduate courses at the University are all taught by faculty, not by teaching assistants." The statement, however, fails to mention that the faculty includes a large number of part-timers and, of this total, a large number comprises interinstitutional part-timers. Furthermore, this institution classifies its part-timers as staff, not faculty. However, these classification discourses erase the experience of interinstitutional teachers such as me. For example, at the abovementioned institution, I have taught courses while holding another part-time appointment plus a partial teaching assistantship respectively at two other colleges. So in my case, I am not only considered "nonfaculty" but also I am an interinstitutional teacher and a teaching assistant. As I shift gears driving to my teaching jobs at various institutions, I also shift subjectivities, moving in and out and between part-time and teaching-assistant status, a tradeoff between status as well as degrees of exploitation.

Distinctions in status are more evident in some institutions than in others. For instance, at one institution, my contract stipulates "that you inform the students at the beginning of the semester, at mid-term, and in the week before final exams that, because of your temporary status, you cannot assign grades of 'Incomplete' except in cases of real emergency, in which it must be approved by the department chairperson." However, at another institution, I not only teach without a contract but I also have been permitted and expected to assign incompletes. At the first institution, my contractual obligations are clearly delineated but at the expense of having to denigrate myself professionally in front of my students. At the second, my obligations are noncontractually enforced, and I have been expected to work with students following course completion, which I have done—gratis. Ironically, the distinctions in status become a tradeoff between professional denigration and further exploitation.

In addition, I have come to realize the incongruity in preparing students for professional status and success given my own underclass status. For instance, the mission statement at another institution where I have taught, promises, "The education provided . . . has as its objectives preparation for advancement in professional areas." Sadly, though, this institution hindered such advancement for its own writing faculty since the focus was on students' socioeconomic status while ignoring teachers' underclass status. In this instance, the contradiction was even more ironic since I taught business communications, which meant I was facilitating professional advancement for my students while piecing together a full-time appointment at two other institutions.

I lasted only two semesters teaching in three places. Despite the prospect of incurring more financial instability by giving up one of my three jobs, I decided the costs to my sanity, my safety, and the quality of my teaching WERE too high. Even before my potentially fatal highway incident, I had been concerned about having to race from one school to another—sometimes distractedly—trying to arrive on time. Finally, another driving incident forced me to cut back. At the beginning of one semester, I didn't make it on time for my first class; I had deceived myself into thinking I could handle three places. I thought I could swing the interinstitutional commute, but I had not budgeted enough time to travel from one institution to another. I arrived ten minutes late for class, and the students had already left. Fortunately, another part-timer who had been assigned a course she did not want to teach was permitted to swap with me.

The conditions that I have described expose the gap between the rhetoric and reality in mission statements. Part-time faculty do not occupy the privileged status implied by institutional mission statements; moreover, the conditions under which we teach—especially inequitable, unlivable salaries, contractual instability, high class loads—work against delivering quality instruction. To deliver the quality instruction advertised in such statements, we need just and equitable salaries, reasonable teaching loads, benefits, office space, mailboxes, telephones, clerical support, access to copy machines, as well as time and reasonable support for research, scholarship, and professional development.

Thus, demystifying the rhetoric of faculty life in institutional mission statements involves (re)reading and (re)viewing the texts of mission statements while acknowledging the contexts of part-time faculty's working conditions. Freire names constraining contexts "limit situations," and in Freireian problem-posing education, the teacher and students work to gain critical consciousness by "demythologizing the false interpretations . . . [by] reading within the social context to which it refers" (Freire & Macedo, 1987, p. 157). Radical literacy discourse has reflected upon the ways in which literacy practices enable or constrain students. Critical literacy discourse in particular has been especially valuable in examining how critical teaching empowers students to recognize and reflect on their own limited situations. In focusing on the ways oppressive literacy practices affect students, however, these theorists have ignored the status of the majority of writing/literacy teachers. This discourse, like that of institutional mission statements, assumes that all teachers occupy a privileged status and thus perpetuates the full-time myth while constructing an idealized image of teachers' working lives.

Radical Discourse and Its Contradictions

Critical literacy discourse has enriched our knowledge of the ideological, theoretical, and pedagogical challenges and conflicts that occur in teaching students from diverse socioeconomic backgrounds. In particular, Bruce Herzberg, Xin Lu Gale, and Cy Knoblauch provide thought-provoking inquiries and reflections about critical teaching. For example, Bruce Herzberg recounts the challenges in trying to get his students in his freshman writing class, which included service learning, to see beyond the "individual and symptomatic" in "the ways literacy is gained or not gained in the United States" (1994, pp. 309–10). Herzberg relates how difficult his "students find it to transcend their own deeply-ingrained belief in individualism and meritocracy in their analysis of the reasons for the illiteracy they see" (p. 312). Similarly, Cy Knoblauch examines the problems inherent in critical teaching in the face of middle-class students' firm belief in individualistic and meritocratic ideology, wondering, "Are these heirs to American wealth and power in fact the oppressor (re)incarnate, already too corrupted for Freirean dialogue since they have so much to gain from not listening?" (1991, p. 15). In these critiques, radical discourse has theorized the correlation between literacy practices and socioeconomic relations of power pertaining to students' contexts but has generally ignored teachers' contexts.

As exceptions, Cy Knoblauch and Xin Lu Gale reflect on their own teacherly contexts. For example, Knoblauch asks the following question:

> What is the meaning of "radical teacher" for faculty in such privileged institutions—paid by the capitalist state, protected from many of the obligations as well as consequences of social action by the speculativeness of academic commitment.(1991, p. 16)

Knoblauch admirably asks an important and courageous question, interrogating the privileges that accrue to faculty teaching in such institutions, the most obvious of which are their salaries.

Heeding Freire's insistence that teachers as well as students should "reflect simultaneously on themselves and the world" (1993, p. 64), Knoblauch contextualizes his experience from his own point of view and class status, and rightly so, but in doing so, questions the ways privilege is unevenly distributed between full- and part-time faculties within institutions. His reflection begs the question, "What is the meaning of radical teacher for [part-time] faculty [especially interinstitutional part-time faculty] in such privileged institutions—paid by the capitalist state [but paid inequitably]?" (16). Knoblauch's question does not account for the working lives of the majority of writing teachers.

Similarly, Xin Lu Gale also focuses on her own teacherly context when she questions the position of teachers in relation to their institutions. Citing faculty obligations as "cultural agent[s] hired by the institution to perform pedagogic acts" (1996, p. 129), Gale asserts that faculty simultaneously

> owe their loyalty to the institution, the dominant culture and discourse are obligated to teach students normal discourse even though edifying teachers are suspicious of its hegemonic power and critical of many of its basic assumptions. (p. 129)

This description speaks from Gale's context and for faculty who are privileged and positioned to engage in her kind of critical reflection and speculation. However, her description ignores the material effects of the dominant culture and hegemonic power that constrain the lives of the majority of writing teachers.

Gale further extends her reflection to elaborate writing teachers' roles in exposing students to a multiplicity of discourses, but rejects the notion that discourse is ideologically positioned. Furthermore, she sees the positive end results in students' and teachers' exposure to many discourses as follows:

> Most important, perhaps both the teacher and students will obtain greater satisfaction from the realization that they have communicated with new people, experienced new feelings, gone through new adventures, and succeeded in keeping the conversation going. (1996, p. 130)

Then, in recounting the presumed pedagogical and human satisfaction that accompanies the process of introducing students to a variety of discourses, Gale asks, "What more can a writing teacher ask for than this?" (p. 130)—a question that, in effect, erases the material conditions of the majority of writing teachers by presuming that psychic satisfaction is virtually all teachers need.

Gale's speculation invokes the "psychic reward" myth that Eileen Schell successfully argues against—the myth that women are intrinsically motivated to seek part-time work and are supposedly content to accept psychic capital as pay (1998, p. 36), or as Gale adapts it—the assumption that writing teachers occupy a privileged class and do not need the materialities of equitable pay. Additionally, in locating the source of this psychic satisfaction in the reward of "keeping the conversation going," Gale tends to uphold dialogue as an end in itself, which stops short of Freire's insistence that reflection and dialogue are bound up with transformative action.

Knoblauch's and Gale's self-reflective analyses address the status of radical teacher only from a privileged subject position and, thus, tend to idealize teachers by perpetuating the full-time faculty myth. If the question "What is the meaning of radical teacher?" were answered from the point of view of an interinstitutional teacher, then the contradiction in using an exploited labor force to teach writing would be more apparent. Additionally, in tying teachers' obligations to the dominant culture because they are paid by a dominant cultural institution, Gale begs the following questions: "What then are part-time teachers' obligations when they are not paid equitably? Are their obligations less?"

In other instances, radical discourse has idealized teachers by focusing on "what" and "how" to teach while again ignoring the status and working conditions of the "who" that teach. For example, two decades ago, Richard Ohmann criticized English textbooks, claiming their authors encouraged balanced positions and avoided conflict and resistance; instead, he contended that such texts promoted the middle way in argumentation, that they presented argumentation as a form of discourse by which "social choices are made by rational debate, in which all have equal voice"—a supposedly balanced process but one in which "power is played down" as well as the "relations between ideas and material circumstances" (1976, p. 181). According to Ohmann, social and economic influences are absent, in these textbooks, and students are without identities or political contexts (p. 182). Following this line of reasoning, John Clifford has argued that "little has changed" since Ohmann's criticism that "the rhetorics from the seventies privileged the middle way while denigrating strong positions, conflict, and a committed sociopolitical agenda" (1991, p. 43). In particular, Clifford criticizes *The St. Martin's Guide* for creating "the illusion that we can transcend ideology with three well-developed paragraphs of evidence, that we can somehow change the minds of others in a rhetorical vacuum freed from the pollutants of prior social alignments" (1991, 44). Overall, objections to these composition textbooks center on the way they suppress critical consciousness by producing students who are passive, adaptable, manageable, and dominated. In these instances, teaching and learning become what Freire terms practices of domination.

The foregoing critiques of postsecondary literacy instruction demonstrate how radical discourse has theorized class issues related to students' experiences, especially how students are relegated to an underclass and disempowered, as well as how their experiences are decontextualized and idealized. Although the examples show how critical teaching has sought to further critical literacy practices by contextualizing and demythologizing students' experiences, overall, the focus has been on the ways radical discourse has interrogated the *what* and *how* to teach but in a manner suppressing the identities of the *who* that teach and the conditions under which they teach in relation to critical literacy concepts.

Ironically, in ignoring the working conditions of part-time writing teachers, radical discourse has in effect decontextualized teachers and their experiences. Henry Giroux emphasizes the need to discuss teachers' contexts as requirements for successful critical teaching when he argues that teachers cannot practice critical literacy unless appropriate ideological and material conditions exist to support that teaching (Freire & Macedo, 1987). He further indicates that the struggle is "not only around the issue of *what* and *how* to teach, but also around the *material conditions* that enable and constrain pedagogical labor" (Intro., 26). These conditions include those affecting teachers as well as students. Although Giroux does address this issue in connection with secondary schooling, he does not explicitly relate it to postsecondary literacy teachers' working conditions.

Even when theorists successfully focus on ideological and material conditions, they have done so only from the perspective of students' "limit situations." For example, focusing on literacy as an ideologically positioned set of practices, a number of theorists have admirably called attention to how some practices relegate students to an underclass while maintaining other students in a privileged class. Moving away from a reified and narrow notion of literacy as a set of skills, these theorists have analyzed how literacy and class have become conflated in regulating socioeconomic access while tracking and keeping students in their place (see Brodkey, 1987; Holzman, 1991; Lunsford et al., 1990; Stuckey, 1991; Trimbur, 1991). Such theories focus on teachers' complicity in reproducing an underclass. Naturally, I have examined my own pedagogical and theoretical posture. But in doing so, I have realized that focusing on teachers' complicity can overlook the similarities between students and part-time writing instructors who are themselves denied professional working conditions and are an "underclass" within academe. Those of us who teach interinstitutionally to earn a livable wage spend inordinate amounts of time driving from institution to institution, and our teaching effectiveness is often diminished by our course loads and commuting schedules. Teaching large numbers of students diminishes not only prep time but also the time available for reading, evaluating assignments, and conferencing, as well as research and scholarly activities. Even if part-timers had more time, professional access and advancement are still regulated because the majority of jobs in writing instruction are non-tenure track. Thus, adverse working conditions and the inaccessibility of tenured positions perpetuate part-timers' marginalized status.

Critiques of the ways in which student access to quality education is regulated offer a parallel in understanding how part-timers are economically tracked and trapped and challenging the notion that literacy automatically empowers and promotes socioeconomic mobility. Michael Holzman contends, "Full employment is not necessarily an overriding societal goal" and "ideological forces or simply those of commerce can be sufficiently persuasive to insulate groups from active participation in the economy," resulting in "an economically superfluous underclass" (1991, p. 302). Holzman sees the justification for an underclass as "ideological rather than economic," explaining "some children [are prepared] for lives in factories and fast-food stores, others for lives designing or directing those factories and services" (p. 302). In these terms, illiteracy is a marker, rather than the cause, of the underclass in American society, the majority of whom are "women who are black and poor" (p. 303). Speaking standardized English, or assimilating literacy practices of the dominant class, supposedly arbitrates economic success, but very often, access to this literacy is regulated and controlled by the ability or inability to pass gender-, class-, and racially biased standardized tests, thus perpetuating cultural inequities. As J. Elspeth Stuckey explains, "the test reduces to poverty or maintains in [poverty] entire segments of the economy" (*Violence*, p. 118). Those segments maintained are tracked into vocational training destined to become hamburger wrappers or data entry clerks, not because of cognitive deficits but because of the ideological demands of a capital economy. Stuckey aptly sums it up, "The teaching of literacy, in turn, is a regulation of access" (p. 19). And I would add, a regulation of access for part-time teachers as well as students. For I have come to believe the question "Who can afford to teach?" is an inversion of "Who can afford to learn?"

Although inequitable literacy practices have relegated both students and part-time writing instructors to an underclass, literacy continues to be mythologized and valorized as a reified set of skills having a causal relationship with socioeconomic success. Students are socialized to believe in the potential of an upwardly mobile status accessible as the result of acquiring literacy. When they fail to measure up to literacy standards, they are relegated to an underclass within the academy, falsely led to believe their literacy status prevents economic success. As in the Freirean banking model, "Education thus becomes an act of depositing, in which students are the depositories and the teacher is the depositor" (1993, p. 53). The myth here assumes literacy as cultural capital—a reified product—mass produced, mass consumed, equally accessible to all and responsible for economic success. Literacy teachers possess and produce it while students acquire and consume it.

As the myth would have it, writing teachers, then, should be at the top of the meritocratic ladder by virtue of their possessing such a large volume of cultural capital. However, part-timers' actual underclass status cuts through this myth. Part-time writing instructors experience the same kind of failed meritocracy as students; that is, only a certain percentage of good-paying jobs exist at the top of the hierarchic ladder for both students and teachers. Those whose access is cut off have to settle for the bottom rung or no rung at all.

While illiteracy is assumed to be the cause of students' underclass status, economic or individual factors are assumed to be the cause of teachers' underclass status. Unlike students, part-timers are led to believe their status is the result of economic necessity or individual failure. Although decreased federal and state funding has been a real challenge for institutions, a recent study has shown the insufficiency of the "economic necessity" argument. In a study of 183 college and university faculty's collective bargaining contracts, Gary Rhoades, professor of higher education at the University of Arizona's Center for the Study of Higher Education, found that constraints on part-timers were due to budgetary flexibility, not economic necessity. In particular, Rhodes noted a proportionally related increase/decrease in the part-time/full-time faculty ratio over the last twenty-five years as well as a large increase in administrative and nonfaculty professional positions, the latter of which are usually nonunionized and aligned with management (1996, pp. 655–56). Increasingly, faculty in American universities and colleges are becoming managed and highly stratified professionals (p. 656).

Reading through and against critical literacy discourse serves as a lesson for all of us in higher education—a reminder that we need to apply critical literacy reading practices to our own employment conditions for the sake of quality instruction for students and employment equity for part-time writing teachers. Critical literacy practices demystify the ideal image of teacherly employment constructed in institutional and radical discourses and serve as a basis for reconfiguring the part-time problem. As we continue to reflect critically on this problem, I hope we can go beyond mere consciousness-raising to dialogue and action.

Rearticulating the Part-Time Problem

How then should we talk about overreliance on part-time writing instructors? And how should we address this overreliance? On one hand, decreased federal and state funding presents a real challenge to higher education; on the other hand, cutting instructional costs and exploiting part-time faculty undermine institutional commitment to quality instruction. College faculty need to resist justifying the present and future overreliance on part-time writing instructors in terms of economic necessity and inevitability. We cannot rely on the myth of economic necessity; instead, we need to link the working conditions of part-time faculty to issues of instructional quality. Department and division chairs need to connect working conditions and instructional quality when submitting budget requests for improving part-time faculty's working conditions. Budgetary flexibility needs to be balanced with issues of quality. At the Summit on Part-Time/ Adjunct Faculty in Higher Education, attention was called to the need to reorganize budgeting to meet educational priorities (Leatherman, 1997). The value placed on effective writing within and outside the academy should make teaching conditions in writing instruction one of our highest educational priorities. Overall, institutions need to question the growing administrative, managerial, and capital construction costs incurred at the expense of instructional costs.

As I argue early on in this essay, radical discourse scholars and practitioners need to extend their field of inquiry to address part-time faculty's working conditions in light of their critiques of oppressive literacy practices. In general, I hope all discourses within academe dealing with marginalization, domination, and liberation would see the need to address the part-time labor problem. Eileen Schell has already argued for viewing the part-time problem as a gendered class issue and has appealed to feminists to use coalition building as a strategy to improve working conditions for women within the academy. This appeal can be extended to all critical literacy theorists and practitioners, as well as theorists involved with African American, postcolonial, and gay/lesbian studies. Cary Nelson has suggested that we need "a national debate among all in higher education about the ethics and instructional consequences of current and emerging employment practices" (1997, p. 180). Writing and literature departments can begin this dialogue by organizing and scheduling university and collegewide forums that address the link between employment equity and quality education.

Economists, sociologists, and education professionals can be instrumental in extending their expertise to collect more complete data and conduct more studies on the use of part-time labor. Gary Rhodes argues that we need further research disaggregating the work and experiences of part-time faculty (1996, p. 654). More studies on interinstitutional teaching need to be undertaken as well. His recommendation is especially important since aggregated studies do not account for discipline-specific working conditions nor do they determine the fields in which part-timers are concentrated, namely the fields in which faculty teach lower division students (pp. 654–55). Clearly, these studies would be important to radical critiques and speculation about academic class stratification and the growing imbalance between academic managers and faculty. In addition, such studies would provide the empirical data needed to argue more successfully about the effects of working conditions on instructional quality.

As I conclude this chapter, I am on the road again, beginning another semester of interinstitutional teaching as I complete a doctoral dissertation in rhetoric and composition. I wonder how I can squeeze in some proactive steps to address the part-time problem. I have already attended four noncontractual, noncompensated meetings at two institutions. The full-time faculty were paid since they are on salary, but the part-time faculty were not. At one meeting on curricular planning and design, fourteen writing faculty were present: three full-time and eleven part-time, seven of whom teach interinstitutionally. Before the meetings, the three full-time faculty, two of whom are tenure-track and one already tenured, sent a memo to the university administration requesting that part-time faculty be given a stipend for meeting attendance. However, the administration refused on the grounds that there wasn't enough money. At the first faculty meeting for the writing program, the full-time faculty distributed copies of their memo, during which time I publicly commented that the administration would never require the cafeteria workers to work two days without pay. I mentioned these workers because they had had contractual disputes with the administration in past years. After the meeting, a number of part-timers discussed boycotting the next meeting. However, we eventually decided to attend the meeting because we were afraid of not being rehired the next semester. We also knew that if we did not attend, we would not have curricular input and would be uninformed about issues affecting our classroom practices. In short, we were concerned about how it would affect the quality of our teaching.

Although I'd rather expend my limited time and energy on my teaching, I'm still wondering about the next step. Once again, I turn toward the liberatory practices of critical pedagogy. Freire links problem-posing education to "futurity" and to human beings

> who move forward and look ahead, for whom immobility represents a fatal threat, for whom looking at the past must only be a means of understanding more clearly what and who they are so that they can more wisely build the future. (p. 65)

Freire's words give us hope for improving part-time faculty's working conditions; we need his visionary thrust to help us accomplish the seemingly impractical. If we do not take steps to address the growing use of part-time faculty, we become complicit in failing to deliver educational quality, and we become complicit in the injustice of generating and perpetuating an underclass of part-time writing instructors.

Notes

1. See Eileen Schell's argument that part-time writing instructors constitute a gendered class of workers ("Gypsy Academics and Mother-Teachers": *Gender, Contingent Labor, and Writing Instruction*. Portsmouth, NH: Heinemann-Boynton/Cook, 1998).

2. I use the term "radical discourse" to include theorists whose critiques are class-based, which would include critical literacy and pedagogy theory associated with Freire, Giroux, and Shor. I also use the term to include scholars who may not necessarily identify themselves as critical literacy theorists but who employ a class-based critique of literacy practices.

3. Although critical literacy discourse has treated teachers' working conditions on the primary and secondary levels, it has generally ignored such conditions on the postsecondary level.

4. In "The Feminization of Literacy," J. Elspeth Stuckey theorizes the correlation between and among literacy, race, gender, and class. Although her critique acknowledges the exploitative working conditions of part-time women teachers, it categorizes full-time and part-time women as an "exploited" female class. While Stuckey's analysis acknowledges literacy work as a gendered class issue, she elides important differences between women teaching writing part time and those teaching writing full time. Also acknowledging connections between literacy and class in "Teaching for Literacy," Miriam Chaplin persuasively critiques the correlation between teaching/learning and relations of power in literacy practices. Although her analysis calls attention to how overrelying on part-timers to teach writing "minimizes the importance of literacy education" (p. 103), it touches only briefly on the part-time problem.

Works Cited

Brodkey, L. (1987). Postmodern pedagogy for progressive educators. *Journal of Education, 169*, 138–43.

Bullock, R., Schuster, C., & Trimbur, J. (Eds.). (1991). *The politics of writing instruction: Postsecondary*. Portsmouth, NH: Boynton/ Cook.

Chaplin, M. T. (1991). Teaching for literacy in socio-cultural and po-litical contexts. In M. C. Hurlbert & M. Blitz (Eds.), *Composition and resistance* (pp. 95–104). Portsmouth, NH: Boynton/Cook.

Clifford, J. (1991). The subject in discourse. In P. Harkin and J. Schilb (Eds.), *Contending with words: Composition and rhetoric in a postmodern age* (pp. 38–51). New York: Modern Language Association.

Freire, P. (1993). *Pedagogy of the oppressed*. (M. Bergman Ramos, Trans.). New York: Continuum. (Original work published 1970)

Freire, P., & Macedo, D. (Eds.). (1987). *Literacy: Reading the word and the world*. South Hadley, MA: Bergin & Garvey Publishers.

Gale, X. L. (1996). Teachers, discourses and authority in the postmodern composition classroom. Albany: State University of New York Press.

Giroux, H. (1987). Introduction. In P. Freire & D. Macedo (Eds.), *Literacy: Reading the word and the world* (pp. 1–27). South Hadley, MA: Bergin & Garvey Publishers.

Herzberg, B. (1994, October). Community service and critical teaching. *College Composition and Communication, 45(3)*, 307–319.

Holzman, M. (1991). Observations on literacy: Gender, race and class. In R. Bullock, C. Schuster, & J. Trimbur (Eds.), *The politics of writing instruction: Postsecondary* (pp. 297–305). Portsmouth, NH: Boynton/Cook.

Hurlbert, M. C., & Blitz, M. (Eds.). (1991). *Composition and resistance*. Portsmouth, NH: Boynton/Cook.

Knoblauch, C. H. (1991). Critical teaching and dominant culture. In M. C. Hurlbert & M. Blitz (Eds.), *Composition and resistance* (pp. 12–21). Portsmouth, NH: Boynton/Cook.

Leatherman, C. (1997, October 10). Growing use of part-time professors prompts debate and calls for action. *The Chronicle of Higher Education*, A14.

Lunsford, A. A., Moglen, H., & Slevin, J. (Eds.). (1990). The right to literacy. New York: Modern Language Association.

Nelson, C. (1997). *Manifesto of a tenured radical*. New York: New York University Press.

Ohmann, R. (1976). *English in America: A radical view of the profession*. New York: Oxford University Press.

Rhoades, G. (1996, November–December). Reorganizing the faculty workforce for flexibility: Part-time professional labor. *The Journal of Higher Education, 67*, 626–59.

Schell, E. E. (1998). *Gypsy academics and mother-teachers: Gender, contingent labor, and writing instruction*. Portsmouth, NH: Boynton/Cook.

Shor, I. (Ed.). (1987). *Freire for the classroom: A sourcebook for liberatory teaching*. Portsmouth, NH: Boynton/Cook.

Slevin, J. F. (1991). Depoliticizing and politicizing composition studies. In R. Bullock, C. Schuster, & J. Trimbur (Eds.), *The politics of writing instruction: Postsecondary* (pp. 1–21). Portsmouth, NH: Boynton/Cook.

Statement of principles and standards for the postsecondary teaching of writing. (1989, October). *College Composition and Communication, 40(3)*, 329–36.

Stuckey, J. E. (1991a). The feminization of literacy. In M. C. Hurlbert & M. Blitz (Eds.), *Composition and resistance* (pp. 105–113). Portsmouth, NH: Boynton/Cook.

Stuckey, J. E. (1991b). *The violence of literacy*. Portsmouth, NH: Boynton/Cook.

Trimbur, J. 1991. Literacy and the discourse of crisis. In R. Bullock, C. Schuster, & J. Trimbur (Eds.), *The politics of writing instruction: Postsecondary* (pp. 277–295). Portsmouth, NH: Boynton/Cook.

II

Collectivity and Change in Non-Tenure-Track Employment: Collective Bargaining, Coalition Building, and Community Organizing

The Real Scandal in Higher Education

WALTER JACOBSOHN
Independent Scholar

Experience, though noon auctoritee
Were in this world, is right ynough for me
To speke . . . .
                    CHAUCER, *"Wife of Bath's Prologue"*

Introduction

Tenured radicals, cushy jobs, ivory towers are images the public associates with professors and the academy. As inaccurate as these popular caricatures of tenured faculty are, they bear absolutely no resemblance to more than half of the teachers in the academy: higher education's contingent faculty. The exploitation of part-time and adjunct faculty and graduate student teaching assistants is the most ignored issue facing higher education today perhaps because it is the most serious. The litany of disgraceful working conditions that contingent faculty experience needs to be repeated again and again: pitifully low wages (close to minimum wage in many cases); no health care in most cases; no job security; no voice in faculty governance; no time to pursue research that would enhance their own and others' professional practice; and no respect. Dramatically increasing numbers of adjunct, part-time, and temporary non-tenure-track faculty and graduate student teaching assistants in the United States—who among them teach more than half the courses offered in academia—are essential to the operation of most colleges and universities. In some, adjunct faculty teach 100 percent of the courses offered.

Speaking as an adjunct faculty member, I must note that our experience as dedicated teachers is essential to the education of the diverse students with whom we work; in part, our experience is valuable because we have learned much about our students and from one another as we have moved from college to college during our weekly intercampus commutes. Sharing our common experiences enhances our essential work: We swap not only horror stories but also coping strategies for handling the work we have been hired to do. Unfortunately, the sense we make of our experiences too often goes undocumented and unpublished because we lack the luxury of time and the venues to make connections among the theories of professional practice developed by established faculty. Our personal experiences, our common experiences, and the lessons we have learned often go unheard and unrecognized. Nor do we find time to introduce, conduct, and sustain a desperately needed dialogue with tenure-track faculty about the changes that are taking place in higher education under our eyes, but without our acknowledgment.

Changes in higher education's student body, in its expectations of faculty, and in the uses it is making of information technologies make it clear that we must study and understand the work experience of higher education's contingent faculty. Mining the experiences of these faculty—the canaries in the infrastructure of an educational system we are creating to serve us in the twenty-first century—has much to teach us, has the potential perhaps to inform us about some surprises that may be waiting for us just around the corner. Without a dialogue based on the experiences of faculty who teach service courses, extension courses, clinical courses, provisional courses, understanding of the current state of higher education and how it must change will be seriously uninformed. The course of action the academy is currently pursuing may be counterproductive to its goals and its well-being, to say nothing of its ethics.

In this essay, I reflect on the work of part-time adjunct faculty in light of the working conditions at Long Island University–Brooklyn, where I taught for seven years. I also describe attempts made in that setting to redress the problems of part-time adjunct faculty in higher education. Writing this essay has been difficult for me because I write out of anger and frustration. I have read many intelligent and articulate essays about the pros and cons of employing contingent faculty in higher education, and I find it difficult to identify with the dispassionate and distanced language these articles employ. I cannot repress entirely the irritation I feel when I hear glib analyses of the operations of power and privilege in texts and presentations. I believe that this language has failed us, has failed to reveal the problems that we have created and that we face in all their complexity, seriousness, and destructiveness.

The Personal Is Political

Long Island University (LIU) is the eighth largest private university in the country with over 24,500 students. It has numerous branch campuses and three main campuses: C.W. Post (Brookville), Brooklyn, and Southampton. The Brooklyn campus, where I taught as an adjunct associate professor in the English department, has more than 9,500 students, most of whom are nontraditional, first-generation college students, immigrants, and/or members of ethnic minorities.

The May 1997, LIU–Brooklyn commencement featured an impressive array of guests. Honorary degrees were awarded to Bella Abzug, Ralph T. Branca, Henry Louis Gates, Jr., Wynton Marsalis, Hazel W. Johnson Brown, Hylan Garnet Lewis, and Robert P. Moses, the guest speaker. Named after the long list of student awards in the commencement program were the Officers of the University, the Board of Trustees, and the Brooklyn Campus Full-Time Faculty, all 215 of them. No mention was made of the more than 573 part-time, adjunct faculty at LIU–Brooklyn, some of whom had been teachers in the LIU community for over twenty years, even though part-time, adjunct faculty teach over 60 percent of the courses offered on the Brooklyn campus. In some programs, such as the Bushwick program, where I taught from 1993 to 1997, part-time adjunct faculty taught 100 percent of the courses offered until the spring of 1998 when full-time positions were created as the direct result of pressure from the state accrediting board.

The situation is even more ironic when we consider the fact that enrollment increases caused by ill-advised changes in the CUNY system—changes that essentially end open admissions in that system—have led to exponential increases in the LIU–Brooklyn student population and its part-time adjunct faculty. Complicating this situation is the fact that adjunct faculty course loads are being cut: Fewer adjuncts teach a "full load" of nine credits a semester, making it likely that these adjuncts will have less incentive to invest in the LIU community. Who will take their place? How many students who received awards at the 1997 commencement benefited from the encouragement and inspiration of these faculty members? How do we insure the continued quality of future students' education?

The 1997 commencement ceremony was disturbing for me because it honored an impressive array of civil rights activists and public figures who have contributed to making our society more equitable even as it reduced to invisibility a substantial number of the faculty who had served as the graduating students' teachers. The ceremony also disturbed me because for some time before 1997, some of us in the part-time adjunct ranks in LIU–Brooklyn had been working to make ourselves, our working conditions, and our contributions to the university more visible.

The Problem of Invisibility

The invisibility of LIU–Brooklyn's contingent faculty was evident when we adjunct, part-time instructors began to organize in 1992. After reading the union contract carefully, a small group of colleagues, Michael Pelias, an adjunct associate professor of philosophy, and I realized that we had full rights as members of a closed union shop, and that these rights were being denied to us. We decided to find out how many part-time faculty there were at LIU–Brooklyn so that we could seek fair representation on the union executive committee; however, no one could tell us the number. Until we had access to union records we had to go around counting, department by department. When we did get access to union numbers, we identified even more than the 423 we had counted. Presented with the figures, the full-time faculty and the administration still took three years to acknowledge our numbers. The same story can be told about almost every unionized or nonunion campus in the United States. Fortunately for us, on campuses such as LIU–Brooklyn where adjunct faculty pay dues to a union, records exist and are accessible.

The union at LIU–Brooklyn is led by five officers (president, vice president, secretary, grievance chair, and treasurer) and a twelve-member executive committee who are elected to two-year terms and given released time from teaching to fulfill their functions. This union, formed in 1970, before part-timers' numbers and working conditions were a problem, was initially radical and proactive. Until 1980 most benefits the union gained were shared by all faculty. However, beginning in 1980, as the result of a grievance procedure brought by a part-time faculty member, the union began to trade away the salaries and rights of part-time, adjunct faculty in exchange for full-time faculty benefits. Adjuncts were not represented on the union executive committee until the mid-1980s, and even then they were seldom influential. Although no policy to this effect appeared in writing, there was a tacit understanding that no adjunct would run for election and official recognition.

Writing instructors comprised the greater number of those who participated in phone trees, information gathering, and petition signing in the "Adjunct Association," begun in 1992. "Leadership" of our association fell to Michael and me. We were the only ones convinced that we could make a difference, the only ones who felt we had nothing to lose. Because Michael and I shared goals, we were able to bypass debates about strategy and method that often impede action in larger organizations. Although we were effective within union meetings, we had only enough energy to maintain and pursue adjunct initiatives within the union. As a result, we and our association enjoyed the benefits and suffered the problems of an organization without a hierarchical structure. While we were able to be efficient, particularly at the outset of our work, our organization lacked mechanisms and roles for recruiting members to fulfill the loosely defined roles of a larger core group. Constant recruitment is necessary if real change is to be made by an organization such as ours whose membership consists of a transient population, something the Yale graduate students have managed to do with some success.

Success is a thrill in a small group; disappointment, however, can be very hard to bear. Criticism by colleagues is also hard to bear. Although the majority of adjunct faculty in LIU–Brooklyn in 1992 wanted Michael and me to represent their interests, in the views of some, we were co-opted by what was then a predominantly white-male union power structure and by the interests of the full-time faculty. These colleagues had an exaggerated sense of the power that Michael and I possessed. Other colleagues striving for better working conditions for adjuncts were inclined by background and education to move on to better positions very quickly, and they were right to do so. They left the university or refused to invest any more energy in our endeavor.

Even though the beginnings of our efforts were modest, when we canvassed as many adjuncts as we could and encouraged them to run for election to the union executive committee in spring 1993, six women and men, ranging in age from twenty-two to seventy-seven, agreed. The association's phone tree organizers called hundreds of faculty, full- and part-time alike, to campaign for our candidates. All six were elected. We shocked the hell out of full-time faculty delegates, who could barely speak to us when we arrived for our first union meeting.

Our work to organize looked much like the work of those on other campuses who have tried unionization. Across the country, adjunct faculty, temporary non-tenure-track faculty, and graduate and teaching assistants are calling for union representation. A surprising number have successfully aired their issues in a public forum (e.g., the Yale University graduate students—GESO). But the truth is that most faculty unions are run and supported by senior faculty; neither junior faculty nor part-time faculty are willing or able to devote the time to become part of the union structure. In many unions, part-timers split off (by choice) from the tenure-track faculty union or are forced into a separate bargaining unit; those separate units, however, are not a panacea. Such divided arrangements can work only as temporary measures for part-time adjunct faculty because contingent faculty are expendable. Furthermore, the nature of their temporary, part-time work means that, as a group, contingent faculty cannot achieve continuity of union participation and leadership. Having full-time and part-time adjunct faculty in the same union has its dangers. It was clear to us in LIU–Brooklyn that although we part-time faculty had an equal vote with full-time faculty, we did not have equal power. If our gains were too many, full-time faculty would abandon the union or reduce the proceedings to undermine our initiatives. Still, in LIU–Brooklyn, and I would argue in most other places as well, there is a better chance of achieving beneficial change for all faculty in one union. There is a better chance of gaining adjunct faculty's objectives by convincing full-time faculty that our best interests are theirs as well.

Our joint work with full-time, tenure-track faculty did produce some modest gains at LIU–Brooklyn after the 1993 union election. For example, the schedule for adjunct faculty pay was adjusted from three checks a semester to coincide with the monthly pay schedule of full-time faculty. We achieved this beneficial change by circulating a petition to all faculty. Most were glad to sign. Not without significant effort, we also gained other benefits from the union negotiations and strike of 1994: access to parking, emergency loans, a self-paid group health care plan, and a 1½ percent larger salary increase over three years than that given to full-time faculty. In the larger issues, though, we made hardly a dent: a pay scale that better reflected the contributions adjunct faculty make to their students and the institution, systematic promotion of dedicated part-time adjunct teachers to full-time positions, and health care for long-term adjuncts that is at least partially supported by the university.

A positive understanding of unions and union representation was already in place when we began our work at LIU–Brooklyn on behalf of adjunct faculty; the acceptance of the role of adjunct faculty in the union was also in place by the time I was elected secretary of LIU–Brooklyn's union in 1996, but these conditions were not enough for substantial changes to be made.

Gerald Graff and Gregory Jay make an argument essential for an understanding of the particular role faculty unions and associations must undertake:

> Theorizing the practice of entire institutions of higher educa-
> tion means thinking from the viewpoint of conservatives, liber-
> als, and others with whom we work, not just from the viewpoint
> of radicals. This calls for a model of education in which we
> engage with those who hold the "wrong politics and will not
> take our assumptions for granted, that is, a model in which
> ideological opponents not only coexist but cooperate. . . .This
> means respecting those with the "wrong" politics, and even
> accepting the risk that they may change us. (1995, p. 209)

It is important for those of us who wish to become agents of
change to remember all individuals, including those who hold
what some call the "right" and the "wrong" politics, need to be
educated about the dimensions of part-time, adjunct faculty work
and working conditions in higher education. No informed edu-
cator can be comfortable with the situation; it is neither normal
nor healthy nor in their best self-interest.

At LIU–Brooklyn, once we became members of the union
executive committee, we were dealing with the way the power
structure operates in our university, some of that operation was
boring, seemingly irrelevant from our perspective. However, we
knew we could not hope to change anything until we accepted
this apprenticeship; only when we demonstrated to our colleagues
that their interests were ours could we persuade our union colleagues that our agenda was theirs. We attended every union
meeting, joined in discussion, and voted on issues not directly
connected to adjunct faculty. Michael and I discussed which committee would do what, chaired committees ourselves, and completed research on health care, contractual language at other
universities, and distance learning initiatives. These issues—sometimes removed from our own—were important to others.

Constructing and Enacting Power

In 1982, Cara Chell described simply and cogently the life of a
part-time faculty member. She makes the following insightful
observation:

> So far, I realize, my examples include only women. That's part
> of the system, you know. Most of us have employed husbands

and therefore can better afford exploitation. At least we have health insurance. Perhaps most of us are more used to being exploited, can stand up under it better, rationalize it longer, maybe enjoy it? (1982, p. 38)

Even as this statement calls for an end to "taking it," it reminds us that the current practice of employing contingent faculty in higher education often preys on those who are "used to it."

As a student of noncanonical literature and postcolonial theory, I might have anticipated what participation in the adjunct union movement in LIU–Brooklyn taught me: Part of our success in creating a movement and gaining the recognition of our full-time colleagues lay in the fact that Michael Pelias, adjunct in philosophy, and I, the two members of our initial core, had high personal and professional opinions of ourselves. We were used to the idea of our own privilege. Both of us are white males from upper-middle-class, well-educated families. Furthermore, we became involved in the union very soon after we became adjuncts. Perhaps we hadn't learned "our place."

More and more, however, the ranks of part-time faculty include individuals accustomed to thinking that the world belongs to them, individuals accustomed to thinking that exploitation happens to others. These individuals have experience with the business policies and practices that guide administrative decisions. Gappa and Leslie illustrate my point in *The Invisible Faculty:*

> a successful unionization campaign was led by two retired business executives who had considerable experience in corporations that were unionized, one in legal affairs and one in human resources. Both individuals knew how to organize and lead a union and how to negotiate a contract, and they felt it was important to do so on behalf of their fellow part-time faculty members. (1993, pp. 80–81)

This is not to say that the increasing numbers of individuals used to seeing themselves as powerful in part-time faculty ranks necessarily create more activism, often it is to the contrary. I have been approached by more than a few white males who want to commiserate with me about how highly qualified white males have been degraded in the job market because of affirmative action. They take refuge by imagining a conspiracy against the most deserving—themselves—and often refuse to see that they share a situation with others who, although not them, are no less qualified. Their attitude reaffirms the kind of petty identity politics and not so invisible racism that rears its head when the economic situation gets tough. These individuals hold themselves aloof, hold onto the sense of their own privilege. And, of course, many full-time faculty in powerful positions find it in their self-interest to bolster this point of view.

However, at LIU we learned that the inclusion of this relatively new group among the exploited opened up new possibilities. The self-esteem of people who have a hard time accepting victim status makes them ready to stand up and fight. More and more Ph.D.'s and highly qualified people from various professions are entering the ranks of part-timers. The truth is, the adjunct faculty delegates to the LIU–Brooklyn union were listened to because we had "qualifications" that our full-time faculty colleagues valued. Our group numbered a labor lawyer, a judge, and several Ph.D.'s. If anyone needs to be reminded of just how little has really changed in an era of women's studies, African American studies, and the now disappearing affirmative action programs, this piece of LIU–Brooklyn history should serve as a case in point. My predecessor, one of three women on the executive committee, was an older woman married to a successful business man. Her intelligence, commitment, and hard work seemed to count for little among full-time faculty members. Perhaps not surprisingly, a woman union officer from a working-class background was the most outspoken advocate of adjunct faculty concerns.

Currently, with the influx of new faculty and a renewed interest in the union, there are seven women and many more junior faculty on the executive committee of the LIU–Brooklyn union. The new president of the union (summer 1998) is a woman, the first ever at LIU–Brooklyn, and she has stated for the record her willingness to call a strike on issues that pertain directly to adjunct faculty (e.g., health care insurance)—something her predecessor refused to do. This new president was the choice of the majority of full-time faculty. On some level, it would seem that our efforts to change the union and attitudes of full-time faculty have had an effect; however, real changes in the way LIU–Brooklyn and other universities do business still must be made.

Whether higher education and unions will come to grips with the problem of the growing use and abuse of contingent faculty remains to be seen. Four integrally related situations that have kept effective protest against these problems from taking shape will have to change. The four deterrents I have in mind include (1) the inability of contingent faculty to form a cohesive and broadly based political identity among themselves because of what I call "adjunct passing"; (2) the inability of contingent faculty to form a cohesive and broadly based political identity among themselves because of the temporary nature of adjunct positions; (3) media and market forces; (4) the refusal of full-time tenure-track faculty to accept their complicity in the phenomenon or to deal with the crisis that it is producing in higher education.

Contingent Faculty: Politics and Identity

There are obvious reasons for the growth and persistence of the large body of adjunct faculty in America. Colleges and universities are being charged to run institutions like a "failing business— a business that concentrates on short term goals and short term profits" (McVay, 1994). Another reason is the relative lack of politicization of adjunct faculty. Lack of time, investment in other "full-time" activities, a general sense of helplessness, and fear of losing their positions have often been cited as explanations for this inability to act regardless of the part-timers' level of anger and frustration. As Gappa and Leslie explain,

> Dissatisfaction with second-class status was almost universal among the part-timers we interviewed. Over and over again, whether they were aspiring to an academic career or teaching one night a week as specialists, part-timers constantly alluded to their status in a bifurcated academic career system. They expressed anger and frustration about their treatment, work loads, salaries and benefits, and lack of appreciation of their efforts. They often felt deep anxiety about the temporary and indefinite nature of their employment. Many expressed clear annoyance over their lack of consultation and involvement in decisions affecting them, an annoyance that was only exacerbated by their feeling that protesting or demanding a more substantive role would jeopardize their continued employment. (1993, p. 43)

Two other reasons are less frequently discussed: the understandable reluctance of part-time faculty to affirm their identity as adjunct faculty and the no less surprising refusal of full-time faculty to recognize their complicity in creating the status and working conditions of contingent faculty. Without these acknowledgments by part-time, adjunct and full-time, tenure-track faculty, there can be no coherent political movement to redress the growing use and abuse of contingent faculty in higher education.

It is not so much the individual differences such as age, economic status, and the various reasons for taking on part-time employment that underlie part-time faculty's reluctance to affirm their work. It is their reluctance to assume the political identity associated with their role in higher education. Most part-time faculty do not want to acknowledge that the institution in which they work exploits them shamelessly, that it does not value them as members of its community. Most full-time faculty do not wish to acknowledge this situation. And when part-time faculty do affirm their institutional identity, they sometimes find it difficult to maintain a sufficient sense of self-worth to enable them to change their working conditions and to act in solidarity with peers who may not want to step forward. Furthermore, many full-time faculty would just as soon not think about the extent to which the dollars that support their salaries and research leaves are generated out of the work and working conditions of their part-time colleagues.

In the "Introduction" to *College for Sale,* Wesley Shumar explains that

> it is hard to recognize the operation of power on one's doorstep; easier and more comfortable to think about how the global economy is affecting itinerant fruit pickers or unemployed steel workers someplace else. And then many younger university intellectuals and their marginalization are made invisible by their own strategies of survival. They resist and deny being identified as temporary, part-time, or flexible, because it deligitimates them. This denial helps to maintain the illusion that fragmentation goes on always elsewhere; in the field, at smaller universities, in the Third World; not at the center, not here, not at my university, in my department. Neither the older generation, still benefiting from the remnants of an older and more gracious (to university pro-

fessors anyway) past; nor the younger one, shut out and struggling, wants to consider the implication of the political process
that we are inevitably part of. Who could blame us? (1997, p. 4)

Many part-timers take refuge in their vocations as teachers—a
role that confers a great deal of power and intellectual and emotional satisfaction. Vocational satisfaction is especially reassuring to those individuals who take part-time roles based on their
love for teaching and other generous motives that have no basis
in economics. Yet only "being there for your students" is a temporary refuge in a system that severely challenges teachers' ability to give the best they have to offer, a system that erodes their
freedom to do what is best (and I am not even talking about the
larger principles of academic freedom here), a system that
disempowers teachers in a way that inevitably disempowers students. Regardless of their teaching ability and dedication, without the various forms of institutional support available to full-time
tenure-track faculty, part-time faculty's students are shortchanged.
What kind of lesson does this cavalier disrespect for their instructors teach students? What kind of attitude can part-time
instructors have about an institution that disregards them totally? Is it not, then, inevitable, perhaps only right, that instructors let their students know that their teaching and their students'
learning is not being supported.

Teaching is not an isolated act. It takes place in a community. When part-time faculty do not acknowledge their status,
they are enacting an ideology that degrades them and their students. I call this practice "adjunct passing." Ultimately, of course,
the instructor is "there" less and less. Passing as a respected professional is not only degrading to its practitioners but also to
others in the community who ignore it, tolerate it, or oversee it.
It serves to make the working conditions of adjunct faculty almost impossible to change. Furthermore, it also encourages students to just pass. It validates students who are seriously
disinterested, unwilling to speak up, in school only for the degree, and suspicious even of that.

Students, increasingly courted as paying customers but unclear
about their roles in a future society and unsure that the creden-

tials they are getting are going to help them, are more and more alienated from the process of education. (Shumar, 1997, pp. 174–75).

By invoking "passing," a metaphor from the experience of African Americans, I do not equate the struggles and sufferings of part-time faculty with this group; rather, I mean to reveal some of the structures involved in disempowerment and some of its insidious effects on those who participate in it, even in the academy, whether they be part-time faculty, full-time tenure-track faculty, or academic administrators.

Americans seem to be ill equipped to deal with class analysis or to assume political identities when they have mobility and can escape the situation. Only in extreme cases, when there are overwhelming numbers of exploited individuals with no mobility, have labor movements been successful. The new temporary workforce of struggling "consultants" has not identified itself yet as a coherent group; nor can it without help. The intrinsic problem with assuming an adjunct identity is that you can leave it or the institution in which you hold it. This situation reminds me of the dilemma of Johnson's protagonist in *The Autobiography of an Ex-Coloured Man* (1927). The very fact that the protagonist can pass as white dramatizes his experience, opens possibilities to him, but it also creates his identity crisis.

Without understanding the problem of adjunct identity, we cannot find the resolve necessary for action. Contingent and full-time faculty have to make the first move that all twelve-step programs spell out. They have to acknowledge: "I am an exploited worker—an accomplice in the commodification of knowledge." "I am a privileged academic benefiting financially from the work of exploited colleagues."

Maybe it is time for all of us to realize that the creation of another class of faculty in higher education will not solve the problems it is intended to solve. The shift toward the market economy in universities does not make for a better or even more profitable enterprise except in the shortest of terms. We are suffering as much from what Shumar calls our perception of market forces and their inevitable consequences (pp. 140–41). Furthermore, the current marketing of education and reliance on a temporary academic workforce in this process poses another problem. What happens to the "product" we are selling so well? According to Shumar, "Workers resist, consumers get bored, and the product is criticized for lacking substance. Education in America today is coming under increasing attack for not being what it is imagined to be" (p. 141). It seems that there is much more to facing the future of higher education than simply commodifying what it produces and making sure it is packaged attractively.

Market Forces

It is by now common practice to theorize the implications of the late capitalist system of production, of post-Fordism in terms of the Japanese model of industrial production, and of the influence of corporate economy on academic institutions. Increasing investment in academic administration and dwindling allocations for faculty and faculty support services is well documented (Aronowitz, 1994; Nelson, 1997; Shumar, 1997). Most academics take such analyses and the effects they document for granted, but we do so at our own peril. For instance, in *The Invisible Faculty*, which examines part-time faculty from an administrative perspective, Gappa and Leslie quote an anonymous part-time faculty union leader to support their claim that the use of part-time faculty is not a temporary phenomenon.

> Part-time faculty are a modern fact of life and a useful flexible resource. They are emerging as a rational alternative to the elite institutions in a different kind of university that can extend itself in less expensive ways to a greater segment of society. Without part-time faculty, we would still be an elite organization. If you want mass education and modern access, the use of part-time faculty is the model for how to do it. (1993, p. 110)

The question is *what* will be extended to the general public in a useful way in the future. Will it be the work of knowledgeable, secure faculty or will it be the efforts of harried, overworked, temporary faculty who are unable to raise issues about their working conditions because such political action might cost them their jobs? Though some see the advent of distance learning as the greatest threat to the teaching profession, I would argue that the greatest threat is our attitude toward teachers. Whether it be in a virtual university or a traditional classroom, teachers' ability to teach remains the most important element in our educational system. If we continue to devalue our teachers, all education will suffer.

The models now being adopted to make education more accessible to more people, technologically and economically based models, are for the most part neither good business measures nor good academic practice; furthermore, they are causing a variety of short- and long-term problems. As privileged tenured professors become less numerous and contingent workers become the norm, academics find ourselves in the same situation that other contemporary industrial workers find themselves:

> At the most minimal level, Japanese style production requires a type of cooperation between labour and management that undercuts traditional trade union bargaining about the character of the work performed. Insofar as it also demands a dual labour market, a structural division between core and temporary workers, it introduces a fundamental obstacle to effective solidarity action. (Foster and Woolfson, 1989, p. 60)

Furthermore, referring to corporate investment in the north of England, John Foster and Charles Woolfson remind us that "any move which weakens the bargaining power of labour will not just undermine wages and conditions but also militate against the longer-term social and political conditions for real economic growth" (p. 61). Once the sense of a faculty as a community is destroyed by the introduction of a two-tiered system, our ability to produce a "superior product" is seriously jeopardized.

What academics must do is very similar to what workers in the industrial sector must do if we and they are to resist the more egregious effects of "corporate think." As the authors of "Corporate Reconstruction and Business Unionism: The Lessons of Caterpillar and Ford" conclude, we must ensure

> that all improvements in productivity are bargained and not imposed; and that there is no introduction of a dual labour

market (and subcontract labour). More positively, [we must garner] the wider political strength which can compel the state directly to counter the planning of corporate capital. (1989, p. 66)

We need state regulations that mandate the percent of part-time faculty an institution may hire in proportion to the number of full-time tenure-track faculty it employs. The only reason that there will now be full-time faculty at the Bushwick branch campus of LIU–Brooklyn is that state regulations intervened. This intervention changed what years of talking could not. If universities cannot take charge of their own houses, the state will need to step in.

We were able to mount a strike at LIU in 1994 because an inexperienced chief negotiator for the university, working under the direction of a contemptuous board of trustees, made the mistake of offering faculty a 1 percent raise. Before he could "negotiate" a higher number, we called a strike. As soon as he offered a 6 percent increase, the strike was over. The next time the contract was up for negotiation (1997), the same negotiator was wiser. He offered a 15 percent increase, 5 percent per year, over three years. The negotiating committee had nothing to work with. Our base of support was gone. Too many full-time tenure-track faculty would have danced naked in the street had that sum been quid pro quo for the salary increase.

Other issues bit the dust, including adjunct health care and a carefully worked out system of raises that would give junior and adjunct faculty proportionately higher raises than those awarded to senior faculty who were earning close to six figures. Even issues of interest to all faculty disappeared in the rush to accept this offer (e.g., including dental care for tenured, tenure-track, and senior part-time faculty in the health insurance package). In addition to the raise it offered, the university administration sent letters of misinformation about their money offer to faculty. This tactic helped to end the 1994 strike, and it worked again in 1997. In these letters, the administration reported that the union negotiating committee had refused a 5 percent raise in starting salaries—for no visible reasons. The reasons were perfectly visible. The negotiating committee proposed that part of the raise offered be used to achieve a more equitable pay scale for all faculty by initiating a step scale for raises instead of providing a 5 percent increase across the board. The negotiating committee also proposed that some of the funds be used to support adjunct health care.

The administration represented the union negotiating committees' proposals this way:

> On April 30, 1997, the LIUFF gave to the administration committee a written proposal which proposes that those starting salaries be increased by only 3%. We pointed out to the LIUFF that we had offered C. W. Post 5%. Nonetheless, the LIUFF insisted on the 3%. (Sutton, 1997)

Even educated people seem to find numbers magical. Indeed, many faculty failed to even look at the adjective "starting" and were incensed that we had refused a raise of 5 percent. We all knew that the majority of the full-time faculty would refuse to strike and that most of those who had said that fairness and not money was their real goal would either stay away from the proceedings or acquiesce quietly. This is not to say that lack of action by faculty was the sole reason for the failure of these initiatives. The union did not offer its membership compelling reasons and explanations that moved them to action.

Unions need to take the high ground if they are to appeal persuasively to their membership. Teachers' unions need to give new meaning to terms such as compensation and working conditions. There is no ethically higher ground for a faculty union than combating the exploitation and abuse of its members. Perhaps if the issues of adjunct faculty were given the priority they deserve, these unions' efforts would be more successful.

Full-Time Tenure-Track Faculty and the Crisis in Higher Education

In "Going Public," Linda Ray Pratt recounts a fairly typical anecdote:

> I recall a faculty member in a state university declining to join the campus union with the explanation that to join would be to say

to the governor, "I am your employee." Though he was about to become a zero-percent-pay-raise employee of the state, his image of himself as free of the muck of money and politics was more valuable to him than the actualities of the job. (1995, p. 37)

Full-time faculty do not like to see themselves as workers, including most of those who are part of a union. Countless times faculty have informed me that they are more concerned with the "issues" than money, but more often than not, their actions or nonactions belie their words. Most experienced union participants know money is the bottom line, whether it is expressed in terms of job security or the issues surrounding tenure.

Descriptions of full-time faculty's reactions to the graduate union strike at Yale are revealing. In reference to Yale faculty's reaction to the strike, Michael Bérubé writes: "The weight of prestige in the collective faculty imaginary should not be underestimated here" (165–66). As insecurity about their imagined prestige increases, so too does faculty's need to preserve it, whatever the price. Toni Morrison draws our attention to the phenomenon in her analysis of Willa Cather's *Sapphira and the Slave Girl*. Morrison describes the "mistress" not as mean and vindictive but as desperate, as one

> whose social pedestal, whose social spine rests on the pedestal of racial degradation; whose privileged gender has nothing that elevates it except color, and whose moral posture collapses without a whimper before the greater necessity of self-esteem, even though the source of that esteem is a delusion. (1992, pp. 25–26)

When Morrison holds up a mirror to the operation of power and its effect on ethical principles, the image she reveals looks all too familiar.

Whether we are readers of Morrison or Cather or Gilman (*Herland*, originally published in 1915), we see images of power relations at particular moments in time, images that figure in the movements of women and members of minority groups to be treated fairly and equitably. These images give a sense of how deeply full-time tenure-track faculty are invested in the status of part time, adjunct faculty. Whether Yale's faculty are distinguishing themselves from other schools, or full-time faculty are distinguishing themselves from contingent faculty, inequity and unfairness is the result. Higher education will suffer the fallout as surely as our society suffers the injustices it has tolerated and advanced.

At LIU, I argued for a proposal that called for the creation of non-tenure-track "lecturer" positions that would serve as a form of promotion for long-term, qualified adjuncts, in effect converting part-time lines to full-time lines. The plan was for these lines to eventually become tenure-track positions, and in the meantime for them to have three- to five-year time limits.

I had a problem with both the arguments of those who opposed the creation of these positions and the hypocrisy of colleagues who espouse radical scholarly positions and turn their backs on the implications of those positions for their everyday lives. The argument that irritated me most was that the new "lecturer" position would create second-class academic citizens. Higher education is already filled with faculty who are treated as second and third classes. Those who advanced this argument seem to regard the adjunct faculty already in their midst as either invisible or as members of some other species. Tenure-track faculty who already rely on adjuncts to teach the majority of undergraduate courses in higher education have not yet realized that academic freedom and tenure are what they will relinquish next.

Another argument I found frustrating was one that a radical union officer offered to picketing faculty to persuade them not to vote for adjunct faculty concerns during the 1994 LIU–Brooklyn strike. The argument was that all part-time faculty had second jobs and more money than full-time faculty. There were no figures or surveys to support this argument, except ones the Adjunct Association had produced that contradicted the argument. Since the proposal the adjuncts had made would only have granted the full-time contract to individuals who did not have full-time jobs, the logic of this argument was hard to follow.

At LIU–Brooklyn, more real change has come through the efforts of relatively conservative faculty or those from working-class backgrounds than from the self-identified "radicals" at LIU–Brooklyn. When push comes to shove, I have found many radicals concerned with their self-interests and not with the common agenda, even when the common agenda involved "causes" they espouse (e.g., health care for domestic partners).

Full-time faculty often fail to see that they are responsible for adjunct faculty, and that ultimately, it is in their self-interest to take part in this process of changing not just the inequities associated with part-time faculty work, but with the very direction in higher education is moving. In *Manifesto of a Tenured Radical*, even as Cary Nelson offers a level-headed view of the changes that need to be made in higher education, he also offers part-time faculty this cautionary advice:

> Too many tenured faculty respond to the job crisis by wondering whether they can get through their careers without having to deal with it. Of course everyone concerned should press their tenured colleagues to act, but I would not count on them to do so. In any case, it is probably naive to imagine that a mass movement for change will come from above rather than below. (1997, p. 166)

Nelson's advice is good and not so good. Nothing would have happened so far if part-timers had not begun to empower themselves, yet the single most important reason that faculty have not organized to resist overuse and abuse of part-time adjunct faculty is the distinction that is made between the goals and aims of tenure-track and contingent faculty. The situation reminds me of a moment from Rebecca Harding Davis's *Life in the Iron Mills*.

In a visit by the owner and some companions to a mill, two of the characters, Doctor May and Mitchell, engage in a discussion. May, who does nothing about it himself, is disturbed that although Mitchell understands how the degradation he has seen prevents workers' access to the finer things of life, he nevertheless maintains his distance from the problem: "Go back, Mitchell! You say the pocket and the heart of the world speak without meaning to these people. What has its head to say? Taste, culture, refinement? Go!" (1972, p. 38).

Mitchell responds by saying nothing.

> He turned his head indolently, and looked into the mills. There hung about the place a thick, unclean odor. The slightest mo-

tion of his hand marked that he perceived it, and his insuffer-
able disgust. (p. 38)

When Mitchell finally speaks, he says, "It would be of no use. I
am not one of them" (38). Going on, he observes:

> Reform is born of need, not pity. No vital movement of the people's
> has worked down, for good or evil; fermented, instead, carried
> up the heaving cloggy mass. Think back through history, and
> you will know it. What will this lowest deep—thieves, Magdalens,
> negroes—do with the light filtered through ponderous Church
> creeds, Baconian theories, Goethe schemes? Some day, out of
> their bitter need will be thrown up their own light bringer—their
> Jean Paul, their Cromwell, their Messiah. (p. 39)

Like Davis's, my own purpose in this "aside" is both deadly serious and satiric. Creeds, theories, schemes are as much a part of
the part-time faculty mind-set as they are of their full-time counterparts. Though they often do not want to acknowledge it, full-
time faculty are already down here with us with their noses
sticking out of the mud. We need to acknowledge our mutual
interdependence—the presence of the others on the same boat—
or we will all sink. Where is that recognition that could begin to
mobilize coherence of action? For all intents and purposes, we
are the light bringers—"we," part-time, non-tenure-track, full-
time, tenure-track, and graduate student teaching assistants who
must move together to ensure the integrity of higher education in
the United States today.

What Was Achieved at LIU–Brooklyn?

In the years after the 1994 contract, part-time adjunct faculty in
the LIU–Brooklyn union spent most of our time trying to make
sure that the contract spelled out the gains we made during negotiations. The first copy of the new contract that we received con-
tained inaccuracies about part-time matters; none of them to our
benefit. A year before the 1997 contract negotiations, a new initiative was launched by one of the senior, most respected members of the faculty. He called for equal pay for equal work in

some form of prorated salary. Although his initiative renewed interest in adjunct faculty concerns, most people who approached me wanted me to denounce it as "unreasonable." This faculty member was listened to at first because he was critically responsible for helping to save the university from fiscal crisis and shutting its doors in the early eighties—a time very different from the present one when enrollments are booming and classrooms are overcrowded. Quickly, however, people wanted to dismiss his arguments. It goes without saying that no counterproposal to improve the lot of part-time faculty was offered. Without this solitary faculty member, few people would have given adjunct issues a thought. It would be naive to suppose that we could have gained such a hearing on our own; once again the necessity for faculty to work together to ensure just and equitable working conditions was clear.

In many ways part-timers' presence was responsible for initiatives in the LIU–Brooklyn union that would have been unimaginable without our demands. Full-timers used our demands to create pressure for their own agenda, which was created as an alternate to our demands. LIU–Brooklyn's administration needed to give somewhere. They created new full-time positions and wrote the creation of these positions into the contract (i.e., forty new positions for the 1997–2000 contract with the "intent" of creating ninety or more). This kind of contractual initiative and obligation was unheard of before our plan to "convert" part-time positions into full-time ones.

It is possible that the administration "intended" to do this anyway, as they now contend. Nevertheless, introducing the possibility during contract negotiations heralded a new direction for the union and how it might involve itself in university affairs. As a result, the union's interests are no longer confined to salaries and tenure. They now include a new more proactive vision for the university. We began to change the health care provisions, reversed lower wage increases for adjuncts.

Even when full-time faculty union leaders supported our causes, faculty as a whole did not. For example, they did not support the use of 1 percent of their 5 percent raise to provide health care for adjuncts. It is their hearts and minds that must change—be changed—if gains are to be made. Too many full-time faculty are suffering a siege mentality that refuses a sortie, and this is something that can be changed.

There is a new spirit at LIU–Brooklyn, and that spirit is open to taking on some of these challenges. Not only is the union more proactive but also LIU–Brooklyn students are entering the discussion. They have published a special front-page story, dealing with the abuse of part-time faculty, in the school newspaper, *Seawanaka*. The administration needs now to rethink the argument, a long-time staple of union negotiations, that it must make arrangements on the LIU–Brooklyn campus that match the arrangements it makes on LIU's two other campuses, even though the faculty and students on those campuses differ in character and needs from those on the Brooklyn campus.

Conclusion

By 1997, economic necessity, if nothing else, led me to move on. After a summer of contract negotiations at LIU–Brooklyn in 1997, I took up a non-tenure-track instructorship in a private college in New Jersey that, of course, does not have a union. Ironies abound. This position, though, is in many ways a delight. I am a teacher, and for a brief moment I felt like a respected professional. My ideas are accepted as contributions; that makes me a stronger teacher. I feel a new burst of energy. I take on projects that I would not have had time for before. Yes, this job is tenuous, likely to last only two or three years. It is hard work, but it is good work—work that restores me even as I do it. In the meantime Michael Pelias continues the good fight at LIU and keeps me apprised. Perhaps after all his years of selfless work, one day the LIU–Brooklyn union will see fit to recognize some portion of his dedication.

I continue some things, too. I continue to be angry at how the academy is unremittingly represented in the media. An article by W. H. Honan recently appeared in the *New York Times* (Jan. 4, 1998) and presents the debate about higher education in polarized terms—downsizing an anachronism versus maintaining the status quo. Not one mention of part-time faculty even appears in the article. I continue to worry about the proliferation of vitiated position statements such as the "Statement on the Growing Use of Part-Time and Adjunct Faculty," recently published in *Academe* (Jan./Feb. 1998).

For the AAUP or the CCCCs or the MLA to proffer guidelines for the proper use of adjunct faculty is meaningless. Now it is time for departments, colleges, and universities to speak a different language—the language of action. Unfortunately, we have come to the point where any action is better than no action. If we do not act now, the corporate academy and "market forces" will use the stranglehold we have given them to finish us off with a flourish—all of us—graduate students at Yale, instructors in community colleges, tenure-track faculty in comprehensive universities. It is time for the "Brahmins" and the "untouchables" (*Academe*, 1998, 57) to articulate common cause. Our very ability and power to speak is in question. Now is the time to acknowledge our common cause and to recognize these facts: Most students in higher education are now being taught by temporary laborers. Higher education as we have known it in the United States is gone. It is, however, reclaimable. To do so, we must move—quickly, together.

Works Cited

Aronowitz, S., & DiFazio, W. (1994). The jobless future: Sci-tech and the dogma of work. Minneapolis: University of Minnesota Press.

Bérubé, M. (1997). The blessed of the earth. In C. Nelson (Ed.), *Will teach for food: Academic labor in crisis*(pp. 153–178). Minneapolis: University of Minnesota Press.

Bérubé, M., & Nelson, C. (Eds.). (1995). *Higher education under fire: Politics, economics, and the crisis of the humanities.* New York: Routledge.

Cather, W. (1940). *Sapphira and the slave girl.* New York: Knopf.

Chell, C. (1982, January). Memoirs and confessions of a part-time lecturer. *College English, 44(1),* 35–40.

Davis, R. H. (1972). *Life in the iron mills; Or, the korl woman.* New York: The Feminist Press.

Foster, J., & Woolfson, C. (1989, March/April). Corporate reconstruction and business unionism: The lessons of Caterpillar and Ford. *New Left Review, 174,* 51–66.

Gappa, J. M., & Leslie, D. W. (1993). *The invisible faculty: Improving the status of part-timers in higher education.* San Francisco: Jossey-Bass.

Gilman, C. P. (1979). *Herland.* New York: Pantheon Books.

Graff, G., & Jay, G. (1995). A critique of critical pedagogy. In M. Bérubé and C. Nelson (Eds.), *Higher education under fire: Politics, economics, and the crisis of the humanities* (pp. 201–213). New York: Routledge.

Honan, W. H. (1998, January 4). Ivory tower under siege: Everyone else downsized; why not professors? asks a growing chorus of business-minded leaders. *New York Times,* national edition, pp. 4A–33.

Johnson, J. W. (1927). *The autobiography of an ex-coloured man.* New York: Knopf.

Lauter, P. (1991). *Canons and contexts.* New York: Oxford University Press.

McVay, C. (Ed.). (1994, November 7). *pro-fess-ing: an organ for those who teach undergraduates, 5(6).*

Morrison, T. (1992). *Playing in the dark: Whiteness and the literary imagination.* Cambridge, MA: Harvard University Press.

Nelson, C. (Ed.). (1997a). *Manifesto of a tenured radical.* New York: New York University Press.

Nelson, C. (Ed.). (1997b). *Will teach for food: Academic labor in crisis.* Minneapolis: University of Minnesota Press.

Pratt, L. R. (1995). Going public: Political discourse and the faculty voice. In M. Bérubé and C. Nelson (Eds.), *Higher education under fire: Politics, economics, and the crisis of the humanities* (pp. 35–51). New York: Routledge.

Shumar, W. (1997). *College for sale: A critique of the commodification of higher education.* Washington, DC: The Falmer Press.

Statement from the Conference on the Growing Use of Part-Time and Adjunct Faculty. (1998, January/February). *Academe, 84(1),* 54–60.

Sutton, G. (1997, August 22). *Update on negotiations.* Memorandum to LIU–Brooklyn Campus Faculty, Brooklyn, NY.

Faculty at the Crossroads: Making the Part-Time Problem a Full-Time Focus

KAREN THOMPSON

Rutgers University, New Brunswick, New Jersey

P art-time America Won't Work." That's the bold and ambiguous slogan on the poster in my office. It is intentionally ambiguous. The Teamsters mean to convey two things: 1) that part-time employment will not effectively run the country's industries; and 2) that these part-time employees may withhold their labor in order to make that point. United Parcel Services (UPS) drivers recently dramatized these messages to the nation with their successful strike. Examining their situation may help us focus on certain aspects of our own problems in higher education—and may even hold a few lessons for us as well.

Many of us have noted parallels between the UPS strike and growing trends in academic labor. Steve Finner of the American Association of University Professors' (AAUP) Washington office circulated this statement from Peter King of the *Los Angeles Times*:

> In this highly visible strike . . . what seems to resonate the most are union complaints about the proliferation and treatment of part-time workers. It doesn't take a subscription to the *Wall Street Journal* to grasp what has been happening across the American workplace. The UPS teamsters are fortunate that delivery work can't be farmed out to the Third World, that computers can't drive trucks. (August 10, 1997)

Responding to King's statement, Finner commented: "58% of the UPS teamsters unit are part-time, while 40–50% of all undergraduate courses are taught by part-time faculty. And computers can and are teaching courses." I'll add that 43 percent of all faculty nationwide are part-time, and that figure is a conservative estimate (NCES, 1993) since data for this constituency is seldom kept systematically. One thing, however, is certain: that figure *is* going up.

There *are* a large number of part-time employees in our industry, and trends are clear: part-time faculty are replacing full-time faculty—through attrition, if not directly—at a rate that will do-in the teacher/scholar profession by 2030 if left uncorrected. Tenured faculty are not just losing ground to part-timers. Full-time non-tenure-track faculty are on the rise, bringing the percent of non-tenure eligible faculty to at least 60 percent (NCES). Tenured faculty represent no more than a quarter of the profession now. In a wonderful speech at the University of Cincinnati, Amy Elder (1996) characterized tenured faculty as an endangered species, concluding that the difference between the dodo bird and the professor remains to be seen. Let's heed her warning.

We can agree there *is* a problem, but not everyone agrees that it is really all that threatening. At an interdisciplinary Conference on the Growing Use of Part-Time/Adjunct Faculty a couple of weeks ago in Washington, a variety of papers reproduced the spectrum of opinion.

A university president defended the use of part-timers by relying on the need to keep costs and class size down while pointing to the wonderful contributions made by part-time faculty (Adamany, 1997). This "administrative school of appreciation" is a view frequently held by administrators, a view laden with myths and false generalizations (e.g., most part-time faculty are employed full-time and professionally someplace else). This is the wishful-thinking view, attractive to shortsighted managers who hope that part-time faculty will not count, even as they solve the institutions' financial crises. The concrete manifestation of this resistance to acknowledging part-timers' plight presented itself to me once at a statewide conference on the "problem of adjuncts" in New Jersey. Dominated by administrators, this seemed to be a meeting about how to continue to encourage adjunct teaching without spending any money. The facilitator introduced one session by telling us that we would discuss anything except financial concerns—giving coffee-mugs-to-adjuncts was one suggestion that emerged during the discussion. The University of Phoenix and other institutions that virtually staff their whole faculties with part-timers contribute widely to acceptance of the view that adjunct faculties are well functioning and content—at least on the surface.

Some say the problem we're addressing resides in the job market; it is a problem of supply and demand. These folks say "over-production" of Ph.D.'s has created a buyers' market for universities. This view generally de-emphasizes or ignores the erosion of full-time lines and the fact that every fall my part-time colleagues and I are in high demand to cover courses—at the last minute. Appealing to full-time faculty and administrators, this view allows faculty the sense that they are making policy, the illusion that they might redirect negative trends. The common shortsighted response, proclaiming a need to cut back on graduate programs, will not only limit access to higher education, it will also reduce the need for graduate faculty and the problem will continue to snowball. There's no escaping the real economic problem involved here: labor exploitation.

Another frequently held attitude revolves around subcontracting, or outsourcing; this view sees a bifurcated (or trifurcated) faculty where full-time faculty remain the "core," while full-time non-tenure-track and part-time faculty circulate on the margins. Like the "administrative school of appreciation," adherents of this view believe that treating the marginalized with a bit more respect (inclusion at meetings, office space, recognition) might solve the problem. Judith Gappa and David Leslie, in their book *The Invisible Faculty,* stress this type of approach. This viewpoint, however, may easily degenerate into another form of wishful thinking. Economic problems demand economic solutions.

A more likely, but even more threatening, scenario has been put forth by Charles Handy of the London School of Business, who predicts a "shamrock" model for the future. The first leaf of his "shamrock" has administrators as the "professional core." He sees tenured faculty as a second leaf of "subcontractors" who can serve as "experts" that are "almost in the wings." He sees tenure as being restricted to a certain block of years with faculty living portfolio lives, employed when needed. (Sounds marginal to me.) The shamrock's third leaf is the "independents" or "hired help" as Handy says. These are the "temporary, part-time, semi-skilled workers helping out at peak times." (Gypsy scholars.) Handy does not mention graduate students, but maybe they would be the stem since they are the one workforce feeding all the others. So there must be room on the margins for lots of folks (Handy cited in Edgerton, 1993). The growth of the University of Phoenix ("Drive Thru U," as James Traub called it in the *New Yorker*) whose employee structure closely parallels Handy's model, should warn us of dangerous trends ahead.

A more recent view develops the concept of the "faculty member as bureaucrat," a way of conflating administrators with professors. The idea is to get faculty to see themselves as benevolent managers able to make positive change in their new roles. This faculty bureaucrat view, put forth by Richard Miller in his new book, *As If Learning Mattered*, says there IS something wrong with the big picture, but the best way to fix it is by infiltrating the bureaucracy (rather than resisting) and manipulating from within. This is a good way to help faculty see their ties to the administration as closer than those to other instructors. Examined from another angle it might be seen as a divide-and-conquer strategy. More intriguing than other distracting approaches, and perhaps more variable, this view either presupposes a vigorous system of faculty governance—something many of us have seen turn nearly moribund—or some other more vital form of faculty organization. Or, it may be likened to TQM (Total Quality Management) approaches where the illusion of cooperative enterprises distracts us from the problems at hand.

All of these views seem optimistic because they ignore the exploitation of a growing sector of academic employees; they deny the trend that full-time faculty are truly on the wane, and/or they refuse to acknowledge cost-driven mismanagement of the labor force by our institutions. By allowing this trend to continue, we insure the further decline of quality in higher education while we abandon our responsibility as academic leaders.

So Who Exactly Is Responsible?

The growing ranks of part-time faculty threaten to extinguish altogether the shrinking numbers of tenure-track faculty in the profession. Aren't part-time faculty themselves contributing to the general decline in postsecondary education with their lack of commitment to the institution, their lesser credentials, their limited scholarship, and weakened morale? Even worse, their willingness to teach under more-than-full-time workloads for what barely approaches the minimum wage without any kind of fringe benefits makes it more difficult to argue for increased compensation for regular full-time faculty, more difficult to resist efforts to make health care premiums employee-paid. Add to these explanations the fact that part-time faculty seldom identify themselves, let alone speak in their own defense, and the result is a constituency begging for exploitation while dragging the whole profession down. We have all heard of individuals who are willing to work for no pay at all, to satisfy their "calling," or "to get a foot in the door." Where do they get the idea this is an apprenticeship or the Peace Corps?

But maybe we should not blame the victims; part-timers *are* the most powerless in this equation. They are so isolated and marginalized, seldom meeting with colleagues and rarely included in decision-making procedures at any level. More significantly, they are part of a national trend toward contingent labor, where downsizing has become the way of the world and Manpower, Inc. is the largest private employer in the country.

What about the secure tenured faculty, complacently allowing all this to go on, even contributing as they turn their heads—or worse, as they administer writing programs? These are the faculty who need someone to teach the low-level courses that bore them. These are the faculty whose own salaries may depend on economizing someone else's. They are the ones whose aloof attitudes blind them to the plight of their own graduate students and to the erosion of their own full-time lines. There are even retirees, professors *emeriti,* who continue to teach postretirement for no pay, further confusing the profession with volunteer work.

But wait a minute. Tenured faculty themselves are facing massive cutbacks, loss of their traditional governance role, and aggressive attacks on academic freedom and tenure. The word is out that regular faculty are sometimes held responsible for raising the funds for their individual salaries through outside grants. They, too, are the victims of the corporate strategy.

So who is really making these decisions? Who is managing these scenarios? Our administrators find part-time faculty to be irresistibly cost-effective. How else could these savings be achieved with such total flexibility? Administrators can solve their financial woes while making virtually no long-term investment. One institution actually advertises for ESL instructors to work for a term or two initially without pay as a kind of probation. These are shortsighted managers par excellence: whittle down the permanent staff, increase outside contractors, and make sure you take care of yourselves. Administrative costs are often the fastest rising part of any university budget. In the Handy model, or at institutions such as the University of Phoenix, administration represents the most permanent portion of the budget. This is particularly true where high-tech trends have kept capital costs at a minimum, using distance education to avoid library purchasing, building maintenance, on top of economizing through low-cost adjunct teaching.

There's probably another side to this story as well, but it's a case for someone else to make—about bad legislators, ineffectual governors, inadequate state budgets, and diminished federal aid. Education is supposed to be a priority for our government, yet cutbacks continue, especially as economizing remains more attractive than reenergizing. Government representatives have not yet taken marginalized constituencies seriously. Perhaps they will when adjuncts and part-time faculty become more effectively organized—or when full-time faculty and their associations see the self-interest in focusing on these issues. The point is—and it's an old point—if we are not part of the solution, we are part of the problem. Let's talk, then, about solutions.

I believe the centerpiece of any solution to the part-time faculty problem must be *pro rata* compensation. Removing the economic incentive is the only way to prevent further erosion of the profession and protect the quality of higher education. It is also the honest way to acknowledge the contribution of part-time faculty. It is the only way to prevent part-timers from serving as a cheap labor force, to prevent regular faculty from being devalued, and to prevent shortsighted administrators from taking advantage.

In addition, other parts of the solution would have to include professional treatment, a grievance procedure for resolving discrepancies, and a system of public accountability or accreditation to support these standards. It is crucial that the public—parents, students, taxpayers—be clearly informed of the impact these policies have on education. Institutions that provide positive examples of implementing fair employment and educationally sound programs must be publicly acknowledged, just as violators of these policies are publicly criticized. This recommendation emerged last fall at the interdisciplinary Conference on the Growing Use of Part-time/Adjunct Faculty, and it was reiterated in the Modern Language Association's Report from the Committee on Professional Employment (1997).

The economic incentive can be shifted. As Pierre Walker points out, "If students and parents who pay tuition know which institutions guarantee stable learning environments by employing more full-time tenured or tenure-track faculty members, they may well choose to give their dollars to those institutions" (1998, B6). Accreditation agencies must clarify their standards and implement them carefully. As a matter of fact, many of these principles have already been included in a variety of policy statements. There are the AAUP's, the AFT's, the NEA's, the CCCC's, the MLA's, and so forth. Getting them on to an action agenda must be the next step.

We have many good ideas in these statements—academics always do. The question is how do we get from here to there? Perhaps the UPS Teamsters can offer us a few lessons.

First, everyone knows who the UPS drivers are—they wear uniforms and drive matching trucks. Many of us know our individual drivers, and they often know us by name. Is there anything remotely like this situation among faculty? Some of us belong to departments so large that we do not even know each other; full-time faculty certainly often do not associate with part-timers; students never know who's who. This situation needs to be addressed with some consciousness raising.

Consciousness takes slightly different forms depending on whether you're full-time or part-time. For part-timers, it involves visibility—identifying yourself and your position to your students; showing up at the meeting you were barely invited to attend; speaking up at that meeting; writing letters to administrators, editors, and so on. For full-time faculty, consciousness involves sticking your neck out—discussing the issues openly with colleagues, raising these concerns at the meetings you already attend, committing yourself to positions in writing. For everyone, consciousness means we take this problem seriously—we move it from the back to the front of our minds.

When UPS Teamsters went on strike, full-time employees led the way with full-time and part-time employees working together, with part-time issues right up there alongside full-time concerns. The combination of high participation by part-timers in the strike and the full-timers' willingness to fight for part-time workers' concerns was key to the strikers' victory. This kind of unity, internal collegiality, means that full-time and part-time faculty need to talk to each other. Yes, it can happen. Full-time faculty will not catch the plague and part-timers will not be struck dead. Once we talk to each other we might discover that we have common concerns, such as pricing part-time faculty out of the market to save the profession and protecting the future of higher education. When we talk, it becomes easier to initiate joint projects and activities. Organizing for collective bargaining may be an option, but even addressing the issues at forums or approaching administrations together is extremely productive.

At Rutgers, internal collegiality was instrumental in the successful creation of a new bargaining unit for part-time lecturers in 1988. Full-time faculty supported our organizing drive; some even participated by supplying lists of contacts and some just by spreading the word. In whatever way full-time faculty participated, their encouragement was key. As our organizing passed from an overwhelming four-to-one election into a three-year protracted struggle for a first contract, support from the full-time faculty continued. Still, other outside forces needed to be mustered.

External collegiality involves making alliances. Faculty at research institutions have important bases of unity with TAs/GAs and post-docs, as well as part-time faculty. At Rutgers we have a unique situation: Full-time faculty and TAs/GAs share the same bargaining unit. Common ground also exists between faculty and support staff, unionized or not, where having the same employer and participating in the same institutional mission brings us together. Alliances with students and their organizations make it possible to counter the myth of tuition-salary trade-offs, while reemphasizing the central purpose of our work: educating students. Again, at Rutgers, we forged many of these alliances through contract struggles, but also around other university concerns: tuition hikes, administrative priorities, and student democracy. We attended and spoke at student rallies. Students came to our media events, and we developed important connections. Once alliances are established the challenge is to sustain these relationships, making them part of faculty's regular organizational work.

Beyond the institution, there are crucial coalitions to be forged, with other public interest organizations in the state, with parents in communities, alumni, and legislators. These are more difficult constituencies to reach. At Rutgers, for instance, writing to every corporate contributor was easier than sending letters to the alumni. But parents and taxpayers might well be the crucial constituencies to reach. They want to know how their money is being spent. Public opinion about professors is at an all-time low and as Stanley Aronowitz warns in his article "The Last Good Job in America":

> We know that the charges against us—that university teaching is a scam, that much research is not "useful," that scholarship is hopelessly privileged—emanate from a Right that wants us to put our noses to the grindstone just like everybody else. So far we have not asserted that the erosion of the working conditions for the bulk of the professoriat is an assault on one of the nation's more precious resources, its intellectuals. (p. 108)

If we are to refute such charges and stem the assault, we must do it in alliance with students, parents, and communities who understand what is at stake. Coalitions of this sort make for external collegiality. UPS drivers built theirs based on the solid, long-term relations they had developed with their customers as well as the Teamsters' ties with other unions. For us coalition-building means working with students as well as other campus bargaining units. Graduate student employees may be the crucial players here: as both students and employees. Perhaps that is also why they are the most actively organizing sector in academia today. They are in the unique position to bridge the gaps between faculty, students, staff, parents, and so on.

Finally, the UPS strike was an example of sustainability–the willingness to persist. The UPS Teamsters were prepared to stay out, to walk their picket lines for as long as it took. Likewise, we must have the determination to continue raising these issues for as long as it takes to redress them. We have to send a message that clearly indicates we are neither giving up on nor giving away our institutions. I can think of no other single factor that has influenced the success of part-time faculty at Rutgers more than insistently pursuing our goals. The opposition hopes we will tire, or retire, in the face of endless obstacles and delays. We will not. Our willingness to persist, however, must also include a willingness to renew—to revise our structures and strategies to adapt to a changing world, to bring younger faculty into the leadership of our organizations, and to reexamine and revise our comfortable and traditional approaches.

Almost ten years ago, Carolyn Heilbrun, who combines academic work as a professor with popular work as a writer of detective fiction, offered some good advice to many of us in her memoir *Writing a Woman's Life*. That advice applies more than ever today:

> Many of us who are privileged—not only academics in tenured positions, of course, but more broadly those with some assured place and pattern in their lives, with some financial security—are in danger of choosing to stay right where we are, to understand each day's routine, and to listen to our arteries hardening. I do not believe that death should be allowed to find us seated comfortably in our tenured positions. . . . Instead, we should make use of our security, our seniority, to take risks, to make noise, to be courageous, to become unpopular. (1988, pp. 130–31)

Consciousness, collegiality, and constant renewal, or more simply visibility, unity, and persistence. It sounds like a group of citizens organizing to defend the future and not relying on their institutions to do it for them—and that's just who we have to be and what we have to do.

Works Cited

Adamany, D. (1997, September 26–28). *A university president reflects on the role of adjunct faculty in the contemporary research university.* Presentation at the Conference on the Use of Part-Time and Adjunct Faculty, Washington, DC.

Aronowitz, S. (1997, Summer). The last good job in America. *Social Text, 51*, 93–108.

Edgerton, R. (1993, September). Upside-down thinking: A conversation with Charles Handy. *Bulletin of the American Association for Higher Education.*

Elder, A. (1996, October). *Academics: Why are we an endangered species?* Talk at the University of Cincinnati Teach-In, Cincinnati, OH.

Finner, S. (1998, Spring). American Association of University Professors general listserv. aaup-general@aaup.org

Gappa, J. M., & Leslie, D. W. (1993). *The invisible faculty: Higher education at a crossroads.* San Francisco: Jossey-Bass.

Heilbrun, C. (1988). *Writing a woman's life.* New York: Norton.

King, P. (1997, August 10). The battle of Hayward: A dispatch. *Los Angeles Times*, p. A247–248.

Miller, R. E. (1998). *As if learning mattered: Reforming higher education.* Ithaca, NY: Cornell University Press.

Modern Language Association Committee on Professional Employment. (1997, December). *Final report.* New York: Modern Language Association.

National Center for Education Statistics (NCES)/U.S. Department of Education. (1996). *Fall staff in postsecondary institutions, 1993.* Washington, DC.

Traub, J. (1997, October 20 & 27). Drive-thru U. *The New Yorker*, pp. 114–22.

Walker, P. A. (1998, May 29). The economic imperatives for using more full-time and fewer adjunct professors. *The Chronicle of Higher Education*, p. B6.

How Did We Get in This Fix?
A Personal Account of the Shift to a Part-Time Faculty in a Leading Two-Year College District

JOHN C. LOVAS
De Anza College, Palo Alto, California

Voted into existence forty years ago, the Foothill–De Anza Community College District has always tried to lead. In 1962, *Time* magazine described Foothill College as "a mountaintop among U. S. junior colleges—the fastest growing segment of U. S. higher education." Founding President Calvin C. Flint said, "Some junior college has to be the prototype of what a junior college can do. Why not Foothill?" (p. 56)

Four years earlier, in September 1958, announcing the thirty-four full-time faculty that would meet its first classes, the Mountain View *Register-Leader* noted "more than a third of the faculty has doctors' degrees while the state junior college average is 10 percent." The article also reported that "the largest number of instructors (6) are teaching in the field of English."

After describing some of the new full-time faculty, the *Register-Leader* article reported further:

> Twelve part-time instructors will augment the Foothill faculty. They will teach in the evening along with 13 instructors from the day faculty. The part-time evening instructors will teach primarily in the fields of electronics and engineering and are being drawn from Sylvania, Lockheed Missiles Systems Division, Hewlett-Packard Company, Ampex Corporation, and Stanford Research Institute.

In 1998, as I write this essay, I am serving as interim dean of Language Arts at De Anza College (founded in the same district in 1967) with a full-time faculty of 48 and a part-time faculty of 105, assigned to teach writing, reading, speech, literature, and two fields that did not exist when Foothill opened in 1958: technical communications and English as a second language.

The work of researchers in higher education creates a context for these data. Jack Schuster reports that for all of higher education the proportion of faculty members who are part-timers grew from 22 percent in 1970 to 44 percent in 1997 (1997, p. 2). Judith Gappa and David Leslie note that in some community colleges 60 percent of all faculty are part-time. In one district they studied, the humanities and communications division had 31 full-timers and 130 part-timers (1993, p. 112).

While increasing numbers of part-time faculty across postsecondary education are well documented, the use of part-timers in community colleges is not so well documented and even less well understood. Although *Teaching English in Two-Year Colleges* (1974) presents excellent profiles of three note-worthy community colleges (Forest Park, in St. Louis; Hinds, in Mississippi; and Staten Island, in New York City), and gave substantial attention to issues of gender and race, no reference was made to part-time faculty in the "Staff" descriptions in any of these profiles. Presumably, the numbers were not great and the status of part-time faculty was not an important departmental concern in the community colleges described.

Since Foothill opened in 1958, the junior college has become the community college, and a variety of two-year institutions have remained the fastest growing segment of higher education. The federal government has established the Hope scholarship program to put a two-year college education in reach of every American who seeks it. And technology institutions, such as those from which Foothill drew its first part-time faculty, have fueled the information revolution, pioneering the transistor, the silicon chip, the personal computer, and the Internet.

Focusing attention on particular geographic and local settings, studies such as Judith Gappa and David Leslie's *The Invisible Faculty* (1993) and D. Sharon Miller's 1992 dissertation,

The Impact of the Preponderance of Part-time Faculty on the Mission of the Two-Year College, contribute to a needed body of knowledge about the two-year college and how it is staffed. Gappa and Leslie base the conclusions they draw about part-time faculty in the two-year colleges on data collected only from community colleges in New Jersey, Ohio, and Florida. Miller bases her discussions on her survey of a group of Arizona community colleges.

In this essay, I hope to contribute to our need for a fuller understanding of this complex issue in higher education—the overuse of part-time faculty in the two-year college—by offering a detailed account of the experience of a large and nationally recognized California community college district. How did Foothill–De Anza Community College go from relying almost entirely on full-time faculty to teach English to a circumstance where currently more than 50 percent of all sections of English at my college are taught by part-time faculty? To describe the shift, I examine patterns and trends in this district, one that has been part of the educational engine that created Silicon Valley (Stanford University, University of Santa Clara, and San Jose State University all played critical roles). I draw on a number of local data sources and reconstructed memory. My own participation in these developments will be the focal point of my discussion of the important forces impinging on Foothill and De Anza that have led to a transformation of these institutions and their teaching faculty. My information and perspective come from serving in a variety of roles in the early years of my professional life in the Foothill–De Anza Community College District: assistant chair of my division, president of the American Federation of Teachers local union, chief negotiator for faculty salaries and benefits precollective bargaining, and chair of the constituting meeting of the exclusive bargaining agent elected by the Foothill–De Anza faculty. It goes without saying that this account has both the strengths and limitations of personal narrative. Others would no doubt tell the same story differently.

My narrative supports a number of claims about how the current excesses and abuses in part-time hiring and assignments developed. In my telling, I will demonstrate the following points:

♦ The basis of the excessive use of part-time faculty lies in a complex set of arrangements in which taxpayers and legislators, college boards and administrators, and full-time faculty have strong vested interests.

♦ A strong faculty union that includes all teaching professionals provides the best mechanism to bargain for equitable pay and benefits.

♦ Improvements in working conditions for part-time faculty are most likely to come when part-time faculty themselves organize and advocate in a variety of professional organizations.

♦ Effective state legislation establishes a framework for addressing these issues, but requires funding mechanisms to support improvements.

♦ The situation remains largely a zero-sum game (shifting inadequate resources among various categories of employees and programs) until the public at large, especially the voting taxpayer, can be convinced that the quality of higher education depends on maintaining a full-time professoriate.

Foothill–De Anza Community College District: Changes in Teaching Faculty

Demographics have become a cliché for explaining every social and economic phenomenon of the last several decades. Even still, shifting demographics in northern Santa Clara County seem a key to understanding what happened at Foothill–De Anza and, I think, at most two-year colleges in America. They also explain, in part, how I came to join the Foothill faculty, and later, the De Anza faculty.

In the early 1960s, community leaders of Palo Alto, Los Altos, Mountain View, and Sunnyvale projected great economic development in Santa Clara County. They also saw the children of the baby boom moving through their school systems. Twelve years old in 1958, the first baby boomers would reach college age in 1964. Foothill hired over fifty faculty in 1964, matched that number again in 1965, and approximated it in 1966. De Anza opened in 1967, with the Foothill faculty dividing itself to provide the core faculty for De Anza. Today, enrollments have outstripped all projections. The campuses were conceived to serve about 5,000 students each. Now De Anza alone serves 24,000 students, or about 13,000 full-time equivalent students.

Gappa and Leslie note one development that occurred as the sheer numbers of the baby boomers outran the planners:

> Community colleges, overwhelmed by growing enrollments and diminishing budgets, and remaining faithful to a tradition of open access, were forced into increasing use of part-time faculty beyond any reasonable limit or plan they might have had. (p. 128)

At the same time that the baby boomers arrived at college age, two significant political developments shaped the demand for higher education. The Vietnam War produced a new wave of veterans with veterans' benefits. The civil rights movement triggered soul-searching throughout higher education about what was then called "institutional racism" and, more recently, "structural barriers to the success of minority students." Numerous outreach and support programs, including forms of affirmative action that have now become commonplace were initiated in community colleges in an effort to increase both access and success for categories of students that barely existed in 1968.

In addition, various forms of continuing education for adults, including adults with baccalaureate degrees and higher, became an increasing part of the community services mission of colleges such as at Foothill and De Anza. Some of these programs were supported by a special community services tax that community college districts could levy against property owners. Others were supported by the general operating funds, which were comprised in roughly equal measure of income from local property taxes and state funds approved by the legislature. Therefore, initially, community colleges had access to resources that could accommodate some, but not all, of their rapid enrollment growth.

Almost concurrently, the sharp increase in high school graduates produced by the baby boom had been augmented by veterans (usually in their twenties, but older than high school graduates), growing numbers of post-baccalaureate adult learners, and newly recruited minority students, especially African Americans and Latinos. In Mountain View, we also saw the beginning of a trend that would later become significant in our district, Southeast Asians (especially Vietnamese) locating near Moffett Field, a Naval air station. The aftermath of the Vietnam War would trigger a wave of refugees and immigrants that also impacted Foothill and De Anza. By 1998, De Anza enrolled over 2,400 Vietnamese American students.

Shifting to Part-Time Faculty

As early as 1968, I began to observe practices that spurred the shift to a heavy reliance on part-time faculty. Full-time hiring began to level off at the same time community colleges were motivated to expand their offerings to serve a variety of new constituencies. Very often, new programs were located off campus, in community centers, downtown storefronts, or local elementary and high schools. They were offered at times and places less attractive to full-time faculty, who preferred a compact schedule on campus. Thus, a pattern was established: expansions of programs were staffed by part-time faculty. Gappa and Leslie report similar experiences at other community colleges (e.g., Cuyahoga Community College) (1993, pp. 208–9). This approach to staffing meant less risk to the colleges. If a new program did not generate the expected enrollment, it could be canceled. The part-time faculty member would be paid for meeting one or two classes and let go with no further obligation on the part of the college. Another practice that developed at this time took advantage of part-time hiring to enable cancellation of courses with low enrollment. If a full-timer were teaching a course with low-enrollment, the course could be cancelled, the full-timer reassigned to a section originally assigned to a part-timer, and the part-timer could be dismissed. In an Arizona district, Miller reports that part-time faculty generated 57 percent of the instructional effort but were allocated just 27 percent of the instructional salary dollars. She adds:

> Based on salary alone, a student credit hour generated by full-time faculty cost $126.83 while one generated by part-time fac-

ulty was done so at a cost of $49.33 per SCH. In other words, the cost was 2.57 [times] more for full-time faculty than for part-time faculty. (1992, p. 103)

Very quickly, college administrators saw part-time faculty as the key to institutional flexibility. At first, this might just have been in staffing marginal off-campus classes in the community. But state-funding practices also encouraged this kind of "flexibility." In California, community college funding is based on "Weekly Student Contact Hours" or WSCH (pronounced "wish"). From year to year, the legislature would make changes in the funding formulas or in the maximum level of funding permitted. As long as community college districts had local-taxing authority, colleges could react to change in the levels of state funding by seeking an increase in local taxes.

When those increases were modest, local taxpayers were willing to vote for higher taxes. However, the wave of baby boomers hitting higher education coincided with, perhaps even encouraged, developing taxpayer rebellion movements. The counterculture activities and social activism of many students and some faculty created resistance in both voters and some political leaders, not the least of whom was California's governor, Ronald Reagan. My personal suspicion is that these developments were interrelated, though I do not know how to demonstrate that. Whatever that connection may be, the pattern is fairly clear: the baby boomers started entering colleges in the mid-sixties and by the early seventies, sources of funding for higher education were overwhelmed. In California, the community colleges lowest members of a three-tier system of higher education (University of California, California State University, and California Community Colleges), were the least effective at lobbying the legislature.

When the state economy slowed down and reduced state revenues, community college funding remained static, often failing to meet inflation increases. However, increased reliance on the property tax by both K–12 school districts and rapidly growing community colleges created pressures that led to a statewide taxpayers' revolt in the form of Proposition 13, passed in 1978. This measure essentially eliminated the power of local boards to levy tax increases since a 2/3 vote was now required.

These competing pressures came together in the mid- to late 1970s: rapid increases in enrollments, rising inflation that undermined faculty and other employees' buying power, flagging taxpayer support for education. Where did flexibility lie? In hiring part-time faculty at rates that approximated 40 percent of the salary paid full-timers, and without benefits? Enrollment increases could be accommodated, salary increases that kept pace with inflation could be provided for full-time faculty, with no increase in the tax rate. This solution accommodated the three interest groups with the most influence on institutional decision making: the voter-taxpayer, the college board and administrators, and the full-time faculty. Part-time faculty had virtually no voice in decision making at any level.

Institutionalizing a Part-Time Faculty in California's Community Colleges

Since the mid-1970s, California community colleges have been structurally dependent on the hiring of part-time faculty. The system could not function, its mission could not be carried out, if part-time faculty work was limited to the original conception of it: some specialists from local industry would offer specialized courses in the evening.

Decisions to rely heavily on part-time faculty did not come from strategic planning; rather, a set of economic and social pressures impinged on the colleges, and decision makers managed those pressures by taking the line of least resistance. That may explain why current discussions about over-reliance on part-time and adjunct faculty seem so full of rationalization. No one thought through the long-term implications of this approach twenty-five years ago. We just did it.

How did faculty, especially part-time faculty, respond to these developments? Let me offer a series of anecdotes that suggest, on a personal level, how these policies played out and how they have led to some formal ways of limiting the worst of the practices.

In 1967, in my third year of teaching at Foothill, I was named assistant chair of the Language Arts Division and primarily assigned to hire, schedule, and evaluate part-time faculty to teach in evening and newly developing off-campus classes. The San Francisco Bay area attracts many professionals, including many academics. It was commonplace for me to arrive at my office hours to find a prospective part-timer waiting for me, résumé in hand. No appointment, no call in advance. At least twice, candidates seeking work accosted me as I left my classroom.

One way for an aspiring candidate to get a foot in the door was to propose a unique class that might appeal to some segment of students. Candidates would pitch their special course (I can remember one in *Latin in Translation*, another in *Native American Poetry*) and make their case. Often, we would schedule the course. If it drew twenty or more students, the candidate had a job. If not, we canceled the class. In the late sixties, *Children's Literature* became extremely popular. We kept adding sections, until one spring we offered five sections at various times and places. We had overreached. Two were canceled. No matter. The cancellations did not affect full-time faculty load, and the college had no expenses to speak of—certainly none that were identified.

Paradoxically, the growing reliance on part-time faculty coincided with the development of increased power for two-year college faculty in California. The pattern of development of faculty organizations in Foothill–De Anza is a case in point. It includes most of the ways faculty groups have attempted to control conditions of their work.

In the early days of Foothill College, salaries, benefits, and working conditions were handled through a relatively informal process. The superintendent-president, business manager, and two other top-level administrators would meet with several faculty appointed by the president of the faculty association (primarily a social entity, but also a device for establishing leaders who could speak for the faculty as a whole). This group was called the Finance Committee. The committee would hold weekly meetings in late winter and early spring with no formal agenda. The superintendent and business manager would describe current financing conditions—prospects in the legislature, growth in property valuation, effects of current tax rates—while faculty members would talk about the importance of maintaining excellence, the pressures of inflation, and the need to stay in the forefront of salaries and benefits. Very often, these meetings had the flavor of bull sessions—lots of free-flowing talk, especially from the college leadership. Many faculty felt constrained from speaking frankly in these sessions.

Just in time for the annual faculty-recruiting season, an administrator on the committee would say something such as "I think we're talking about 4.5 percent this year." And that would be the salary increase recommended to the board of trustees. As best I could tell, administrators used these discussions to get a feel for faculty concerns and to probe for what would get relatively broad support. Nothing even resembling a negotiation ever occurred. The superintendent-president was fond of the "family" metaphor, and it was often invoked during these meetings. As the head of the Foothill family, he would let everyone know the current situation, and then decide what was best for all concerned.

By April 1970 a somewhat more formalized process had evolved. In a memorandum from the Faculty Finance Committee to the District Finance Committee, the opening paragraph concludes: "We have enumerated these proposals in terms of priorities; but we feel that all of the items are of utmost importance in budget considerations and hope that they will be swiftly adopted and implemented." (As you can see, such rhetoric is not the language of bargaining.)

The following list includes the seven proposals in order of priority:

1. Cost of living (using the Federal CPI, from March to March)

2. Sabbatical leave (shorter term to qualify, higher pay while on leave)

3. Summer school (equal pay for equal work, we argued)

4. Career pay (increasing an incentive award for those at the top of the schedule)

5. Professional salary schedule (a proposal to improve pay beyond COLA)

6. Work experience pay (crediting work experience for placement on the salary schedule)

7. "Because we recognize the policy of 'equal pay for equal work,' we believe that <u>evening school salaries</u> should be improved to a percent of contract basis as soon as financially feasible."

I quote the last proposal in its entirety since it addresses pay for part-time faculty. From this remove, two points strike me. We used the word "policy," as though this principle was already agreed to. It certainly was not practiced anywhere I knew about. The other point is that several years later, after collective bargaining and formal contracts were established, we did achieve the "percent of contract basis" for part-time pay. So while this proposal had the lowest priority in 1970, by 1980 it had been bargained for successfully. To provide context, the salary schedule for 1969–70 provided a range from $8,240 for a teacher with less than a master's degree and no teaching experience to $16,160 for a teacher with a doctorate and twelve years of experience. An additional six years of experience could earn a professor in good standing an additional $600 per year in incentive pay.

The early impulse to establish formal faculty organizations to represent faculty interests (e.g., pay and working conditions) did not come primarily from dissatisfaction over the existing situation. Foothill faculty had comparatively favorable teaching loads and consistently placed statewide in the top five for salaries. However, the paternalistic style of decision making rankled many faculty, most of them in the humanities, and most of those in English. These faculty wanted a more formal structure, one that would allow conversations to take place on a more equal footing.

As a first move, in 1965 faculty formed the Foothill Academic Senate, an entity recently authorized in the Education Code, as two-year colleges began adopting governance structures more like those of higher education and less like those of K–12 schools. The senate became the formal body for faculty participation in academic governance at the college. In general, the senate would appoint faculty representatives to college committees that provided for such participation. Significantly, part-timers were not included in the senate.

Even then, the Education Code included a provision intended to limit over-reliance on part-time faculty. The code specified that noncontract faculty (part-timers) could not be assigned to more than 60 percent of a full teaching load in a given year. By implementing this code, the legislative intent was to prevent hiring faculty full-time at part-time pay rates. Should a district assign an instructor to more than 60 percent of a full workload, the instructor could claim a full-time contract based on the percentage taught. Thus, if a college assigned an instructor 72 percent of a load, the instructor had a legal claim to a regular contract at 72 percent of a full workload . When a group of faculty filed a class action suit under this provision, community college districts fought the issue in court and lost. Known as the Peralta Decision, the court ruling affirmed that exceeding the 60 percent rule earned a faculty member a contract based on full-time pay (*Peralta Federation of Teachers*, 1977).

Several dozen faculty in California received these Peralta contracts. But the institutional response was not to reduce reliance on part-time faculty. Rather, elaborate information systems and administrative procedures were instituted to insure that part-time faculty did not exceed 60 percent of a full load. Here is an example of substantial costs incurred to monitor the work of large numbers of part-time faculty that simply are absorbed in the overall cost of administration. At Foothill–De Anza, a district-wide data base of all part-time faculty was created. Division deans and other schedulers had to regularly monitor assignments. Because the 60-percent rule applied to districts, and not to individual colleges, multicampus districts had to track assignments in all departments and on all campuses. Many colleges adopted conservative assignment policies, limiting all part-timers to 50 percent of a full load, to allow for a fudge factor when "errors" in assignments were made. In fact, in English at Foothill and De Anza, a full load of composition courses comprised eight five-quarter-unit courses. Four such courses added up to 50 percent. One more course put the instructor over 60 percent, so the effective limit became four courses per year. This fact alone required hiring more part-time faculty. For example, if one hundred sections of composition per year are taught by part-time faculty, twenty-five different instructors must be hired. If each could teach five sections per year, only twenty instructors needed to be hired. The administrative costs of interviewing, hiring, training, and evaluating those extra five instructors are simply absorbed into general operational costs. I am not aware that any college attempts to identify these costs separately.

Because part-time instructors could teach in more than one district, the only way most could earn a living wage was to teach in two or three separate districts—these instructors are now widely known as "freeway fliers." In the late sixties, I recall a conversation with a young man I had hired to teach two sections of composition at Foothill College. He expressed great frustration with teaching—and appeared exhausted. As we talked, I learned he was teaching, concurrently, seven sections of English composition at four different colleges. Not surprisingly, he left teaching the next year.

In 1966, the superintendent-president proposed a work schedule in which faculty could be assigned to teach on Saturdays and raised some academic freedom issues about text selection. These proposed policies led a small group of faculty (most of them in English) to form Local 1676 of the California Federation of Teachers (AFT, AFL-CIO), with heated opposition from both administrators and many faculty. Only about twenty faculty joined Local 1676. This action triggered a number of organizational responses.

By 1968, Foothill and De Anza faculty issues were represented by various groups: the Foothill College Faculty Corporation, a chapter of the California Teachers Association (CTA); Local 1676 of the California Federation of Teachers; the Foothill Academic Senate; and the De Anza Academic Senate. Not many faculty understood just how each group represented them. The most aggressive group was the small union local. They competed with CTA for memberships. CTA offered a range of financial services, especially a convenient credit union and insurance plans. While CTA had no special provisions for part-time faculty, the November 1971 edition of the AFT local's newsletter made this offer:

ATTENTION PART-TIME FACULTY
Since there now may be more part-time certificated employees than full-time in this district, it is time they be given an opportunity to be represented by a professional organization. For this reason, the Union Council has recommended to the membership that a part-time dues rate of $35.00 per year ($3.50 tenthly) be

established for part-time teaching faculty. [The dues for full-time faculty were $65.]

All part-time teachers—day, evening, Saturday, extended campus—would be eligible for Union Special Services programs and all other benefits of membership. To provide proper liaison and communication, a representative of part-time members would be appointed to the Union Council.

This effort to organize part-time faculty did not sit well either with district leaders or with the majority of faculty leaders. The following year, while president of the AFT local, I worked with a chemistry instructor, who had been awarded a Peralta contract for 75 percent of load, to survey all part-time faculty about issues of concern to them (e.g., whether they preferred part-time work to full-time work; whether they would accept full-time employment if it were offered). We received over 150 responses; over 60 percent of our respondents indicated they preferred full-time teaching. My efforts to present this material to the district board of trustees was sabotaged by the new district chancellor (a title upgrade from superintendent). While I met all the deadlines required, he held the item for "consultation" so that it would not appear formally on the agenda. His action forced me to present the results of our survey more informally in the Oral Comments portion of the board meeting.

Most instructive about this incident was that the following fall, the chancellor conducted the district's first official survey of part-time faculty. By framing their questions differently and getting a much larger response, the administration were able to claim that only about 30 percent of part-timers sought full-time employment. Even today, these figures vary widely from discipline to discipline. It is nearly impossible to find a full-time teacher for many computer languages. The same has long been true for real-estate courses. On the other hand, about 80 percent of humanities part-time faculty indicate interest in full-time assignments.

While this initiative, by a small group of AFT faculty, to survey part-time faculty was widely criticized and initially resisted, later a variation of it became institutionalized. The initiative taught those of us involved an important lesson: Success comes not just from raising an issue in dramatic terms, but from persistent follow-up, from ensuring that the issue remains in front of decision makers. At this time, we also began to learn lessons that other groups of organized workers in education had learned earlier.

For example, in 1965, the California legislature adopted the Winton Act, which created an entity called the Certificated Employees Council. The K–12 schools regularly used this device, but it was rarely used by community colleges. The council gave "meet and confer" rights to faculty organizations on a proportional representation basis. Collective bargaining was not yet legal for school districts in California, so the "meet and confer" process was the only legally defined means for a faculty to address issues of salary and working conditions. Although the board of trustees could still adopt policies unilaterally and no bilateral, binding contracts need result, the board had to meet with faculty representatives.

Partly as an organizing device, and partly as a hedge against a new chancellor, the AFT local invoked the Winton Act. While Senates could not compete for seats on the Certificated Employees Council (CEC), the other four organizations competed for the nine seats. When it became apparent that all salary and benefit proposals would be developed by the CEC and discussed with the chancellor in that framework, the deans of the evening colleges on both campuses encouraged a group of experienced part-time faculty to form their own organization: Faculty Association for Continuing Education (FACE). In 1973, the hundreds of part-time faculty who joined FACE qualified the group for three of the nine seats on the CEC, which now reflected five faculty organizations, none holding more than three seats. The presence of FACE representatives on the CEC led to more emphasis on improvements in part-time faculty working conditions.

Collective Bargaining at the Local Level

In 1975, SB 160, the Education Employment Relations Act, established the legal framework for faculty in K–12 schools and community colleges to choose an exclusive bargaining agent and to negotiate binding contracts with boards of trustees. In this, the final year of the CEC, the group was chaired by a part-time faculty member, a real estate instructor who proved a very skill-ful negotiator. Even more important, the FACE group provided critical support in the collective bargaining election that took place in the 1976–77 academic year when the faculty of the two colleges decided to elect an organization of their own construc-tion rather than to affiliate with state and national teachers' or-ganizations. In spring 1977, the Foothill–De Anza Faculty Association (FA) was formally constituted and sought to negoti-ate a contract.

Formulating membership provisions in the new bargaining agent was controversial and sensitive. Some college districts of-fered part-time faculty membership on a fractional basis. Some districts asked part-time faculty to form bargaining units sepa-rate from full-time faculty, in effect pitting one group against the other. After considerable debate and wrangling, the Foothill–De Anza FA constitution included part-time faculty on a full-voting basis regardless of their teaching load. The FA could go to the bargaining table knowing it represented every faculty member hired in the district. The dues structure was constructed on a sliding scale, based on salary. Thus senior faculty paid dues of well over twice what junior part-time faculty paid. This structure has proven durable and resilient. The FA continues to keep sala-ries and working conditions among the most desirable in Cali-fornia, and part-time faculty serve in critical leadership positions in the union.

Where the first contract negotiated at Foothill–De Anza in 1978 ran about five pages, the most recent contract, titled "Agree-ment between Foothill–De Anza Community College District and the Foothill–De Anza Faculty Association, July 1, 1995–June 30, 1998," has 198 pages. The regular participation of part-time fac-ulty in decision making and the imperative to serve that large portion of its membership has led the FA to negotiate these pro-visions in the contract:

1. Pay from a salary schedule that takes into account both formal training and previous teaching experience. Additionally, a stan-dard provision of the contract establishes that any cost-of-living increase negotiated will be routinely applied to the part-time faculty salary schedule, ensuring that part-time salaries, though lower than full-time, do not fall further behind due to inflation.

2. While part-time faculty are not eligible for tenure, the contract does provide "reemployment preference" to all who have completed five quarters of satisfactory teaching. These reemployment rights are based on seniority, so that part-time faculty who have served the longest will first be offered assignments (after all full-time assignments have been made).

3. Part-time faculty may be bumped from an assignment by a full-timer before a term begins, but deans may not bump a part-timer after the term begins without incurring a costly penalty (50 percent of pay in the first week, 75 percent after that).

4. Part-time faculty required to attend staff meetings, serve on professional committees, or participate in co-curricular or extracurricular activities of the college must be compensated on an hourly basis keyed to the part-time salary schedule.

5. A federally required choice among three retirement programs: FICA (social security), STRS (California's teacher retirement system), or PARS (a district-sponsored alternative retirement plan).

6. After six quarters of employment, part-time faculty are provided one day per quarter of personal necessity leave. Sick leave accumulates at one and a half days per quarter.

7. While full-time faculty have preference for summer session teaching assignments (not part of regular teaching load), part-time faculty have some rights of preference.

8. Part-time faculty with reemployment preference are eligible for funding from the Professional Conference Fund to meet expenses of attending professional meetings.

9. Part-time faculty with reemployment preference who teach at least 50 percent of a load get medical insurance on a partially subsidized basis and at rates based on the entire employee group.

These provisions mean that Foothill and De Anza part-time faculty receive higher pay than at any of our neighboring colleges. Most part-time faculty say the working conditions are better here than most other two-year colleges in the area. Yet the situation remains a far cry from "equal pay for equal work." The 1995–96 part-time schedule represented 70 percent at the low end and 55 percent at the high end of the full-time schedule. And since "part-time temporary faculty" [the term used in the contract] can teach no more than 60 percent of a full load, earning power is further constrained.

In the fall of 1998, part-time faculty from a number of California districts initiated a new statewide organization for part-time faculty. Veterans of working district by district to improve conditions, these faculty now believe they must also establish a clear and independent voice statewide. This development fits my claim that improvements are most likely to come when part-time faculty organize and press their concerns themselves.

Collective Bargaining at the State Level

Bargaining for an agreement in each district can bring real improvements, but legislative action creates the context in which bargaining can take place. In 1972, the Community College Council of the California Federation of Teachers persuaded an assemblyman to introduce a bill requiring equal pay and job security for part-timers to the California legislature. However, success did not come until 1988, when AB1725, the community college reform act, was adopted. The landmark provision of that legislation established that full-time faculty should teach 75 percent of the total hours of instruction offered by a community college, the so-called 75–25 law. The initial legislation provided incentive funding for districts to move toward that ratio. For three years, real improvements were made. Then, a California recession dried up funding, but the colleges kept hiring part-time faculty.

Part-time faculty continue to make progress in securing improved working conditions, albeit slowly. Recently, legislative action authorized payment for one office hour per week per course taught for part-time faculty. On the face of it, this seems a significant improvement. But the legislation simply authorized local boards of trustees to establish such an arrangement through the bargaining process. The state will provide 50 percent of the cost of compensating the faculty member, but no money for constructing office space to hold the office hour. The Foothills–De Anza FA has reached tentative agreement for part-time faculty office hours in its current round of contract negotiations. Legislators can tell their constituents they have responded; the colleges and their faculties, however, still must expend considerable effort and allocate their limited resources to implementing the practice.

While incremental gains are important, they do not significantly influence the situation. Underfunding of the colleges remains at the root of the problem. The current president of the
Community College Council of the California Federation of
Teachers, Tom Tyner, emphasized this point in an E-mail to Tom
Nussbaum, Chancellor of the California Community Colleges.
In order to reach that 75 percent mandate, Tyner advocated support for a bill that would add two thousand full-time positions
to the California community colleges for each of the next five
years: "California's community colleges have a legal mandate to
reach 75%/25% full-time/part-time teaching hours, yet the system is at an all-time low of 58%/42% currently."

Tyner argued further:

> The 2000 jobs in AB1714 will cost around $60 million, given
> the cost of salary + benefits minus the cost of the part-time fac-
> ulty positions that the new jobs would replace. It is not going to
> be inexpensive to begin reversing a part-time hiring pattern that
> has continually escalated for over twenty-five years, but if we
> don't bite the bullet now, the situation will soon deteriorate be-
> yond control. . . . there is certainly money . . . to finance AB1714.
> (E-mail, February 6, 1998)

Changing the equation will require a sea change in the usual
faculty-administration-trustees approach to this issue. The leaders of each group too often duck their own role in the current
situation, preferring to lay blame on another group. All community college leaders—as well as those in other segments of higher
education—must see that their own long-term self-interest will
be served by persuading the voting public that funding quality
higher education should be at the forefront of every policymaker's
agenda.

The complexity of this issue requires that several avenues be
pursued simultaneously and persistently. To that end, I suggest
five areas for action:

1. Governors, legislators and trustees must be made aware of
the significant threats to quality in this massive shift to part-
time teachers. Campaigns must be mounted among students,
parents, and business leaders to support significant new fund-

ing to improve the quality of undergraduate teaching. As part of those efforts to improve teaching, full-time jobs and sound accountability measures must be the cornerstones of the new funding.

2. Create new coalitions among the range of professional organizations, including faculty senates, faculty unions, and discipline-specific associations to inform the public and the civic leadership of the deleterious consequences of creating a part-time teaching workforce in higher education. The Conference on the Growing Use of Part-Time/Adjunct Faculty, held in Washington, D. C., in September 1997, provides one good starting point for these efforts. Since funding decisions are primarily at the state level, national organizations need to encourage coalitions between state affiliates and the other groups lobbying on behalf of funding improvements for higher education.

3. Equally important, and probably more difficult, promoting cooperation among all institutional types (universities, state colleges, small liberal arts colleges, community colleges, proprietary postsecondary schools) will be critical. The current environment encourages simply shifting new growth to institutions most likely to use low-paid, part-time staffing. Developing extension and distance learning programs that rely excessively on part-time faculty will undercut the arguments for establishing new full-time positions. Whatever state body holds responsibility for coordinating the various segments of higher education should be pressed to take leadership on these issues of promoting a high quality, fully professional faculty in every segment.

4. In the process of developing these efforts at public education, professional groups must clarify the goals of their efforts. Here are some possibilities:

> (1) every class taught by a full-timer or former full-timer (those who retire, job share, or voluntarily seek a reduced assignment), except for visiting scholars, writers in residence, special expertise;

(2) every class taught by a full-timer or permanent part-timer;

(3) California's goal of 75 percent of all classroom hours taught by full-timers;

(4) supplementing full-time tenured faculty with a new class of nontenured full-time, full-pay faculty.

To be effective, all professional groups engaged in improving teaching conditions for part-time faculty will need to establish common ground and common purposes.

5. Finally, at the local level, faculty within a college or department can make real improvements. Once we recognize the reality that large portions of instruction are presented by part-time faculty, each of us can take steps to insure that students get the same quality of instruction and the same access to their instructors, regardless of that instructor's employment status. Sharing office space with a part-timer, offering informal mentoring, insisting that all departmental communications reach every faculty member, regardless of status, and arranging department support services convenient to part-time faculty are actions within reach of every full-time faculty member.

In all of these efforts, teaching professionals must focus on the central issue: insuring that all qualified students in any American university or college get the opportunities and challenges they deserve.

Works Cited

Agreement Between Foothill–De Anza Community College District and the Foothill–De Anza Faculty Association, July 1, 1995–June 30, 1998.

American Federation of Teachers. (1971, November). *Newsletter of the Foothill College Federation of Teachers, Local 1676*, AFL-CIO.

College chief lauds first J. C. faculty. (1958, September 18). *Mountain View Register-Leader*.

Fast climb at Foothill. (1962, March). *Time, 30*, p. 56.

Gappa, J. M., & Leslie, D. W. (1993). *The invisible faculty: Improving the status of part-timers in higher education*. San Francisco: Jossey-Bass.

Miller, D. S. (1992). *The impact of the preponderance of part-time faculty on the mission of the community college*. Unpublished dissertation at the University of Arizona.

National Council of Teachers of English. (1974). *Teaching English in two-year colleges: Three successful programs*. Urbana, IL: Author.

Peralta Federation of Teachers, Local 1603 v. Peralta Community College District. (1977). 138 California Rprtr 144. California Court of Appeals.

Proposals for 1970–71 academic year. (1970, April 17). Unpublished memorandum, Foothill Junior College District. Palo Alto, CA.

Schuster, J. H. (1997). *Reconfiguring the professoriate: The part-timer phenomenon and implications for the academic profession*. Unpublished paper presented at the Conference on the Growing Use of Part-Time and Adjunct Faculty in Higher Education, Washington, DC.

Tyner, T. (1998, February 6). *Re: Weekly e-mail update*. [On-line posting].

A Place to Stand: The Role of Unions in the Development of Writing Programs

NICHOLAS TINGLE
University of California, Santa Barbara

JUDY KIRSCHT
University of California, Santa Barbara

For over ten years, several times each quarter, a group of librarians and lecturers—nontenured and nontenurable faculty at the University of California at Santa Barbara—have gathered late on Friday afternoons. Collectively, these are the formally elected officers of the University Council of the American Federation of Teachers (UC-AFT) local executive board. Similar locals meet on each of the eight campuses of the University of California system. We meet to figure out what can and should be done about the following such questions:

◆ Who has and who has not written articles for the Local's quarterly publication, the *Forward*

◆ Where can we find another student recruiter to help get more lecturers and librarians to join the Union

◆ What is the time line for starting a grievance against the UCSB administration for unilaterally declaring that lecturers shall get no more merit raises

Over the years the people on the executive board have changed. Some participate for a year or two, some for three or four, a couple for more than ten years. The issues change constantly. Some have been insignificant; some have gone to the heart of working conditions for lecturers and librarians. Always the intent of the board has been to oversee and protect the labor rights of lecturers and librarians as stated in the UC-AFT contract (the Memorandum of Understanding or MOU) as it is defined through ongoing negotiations with the statewide administration of the University of California.

At meetings of our local board, we are regarded, by our younger colleagues, as old hands. Tingle was present at the inception of the union; most of his "leisure" time, from 1983 to 1986, was spent in union meetings, walking the campus, distributing flyers, knocking on doors, and posting notices. He continues to recollect with amazement the fear unionizing seemed to provoke among members of the Senate Faculty, some of whom indicated they no longer felt free to speak to him (as if he were a spy), and among his colleagues. Kirscht joined the union in 1988, served as president of the local from 1991 to 1993, and as southern vice president for the statewide organization from 1993 to 1996. For Kirscht, working with the union has represented a baptism by fire into the institutional workings of the university. While she swung, at times, between anxiety and terror, the experience increased her confidence that unions can make a difference. If freedom is, as Hegel said, the recognition of necessity, then Tingle and Kirscht, in union work, have recognized a necessity and exercised a freedom.

Our purpose, however, is not to recount our personal experiences but to explain why lecturers of the University of California system unionized, to discuss how unionization affected the development of one UC writing program, and, most important, to show how unionization has affected the ideals and self-concepts of lecturers working in a large research university system. Lecturers are hired to teach within institutions where research is valued above all else and where status, among those who do research, is measured by how few classes one teaches. The teaching-centered professional interests of composition lecturers simply do not coincide with the interests of the research institution. The result is an invisible wall, as real and as corrosive as any class barrier, between those who teach (particularly those who teach "skills" rather than "content"), and those who conduct research. Those who teach skills are, by definition, temporary, needed only to remediate students' deficient high school education and not considered bona fide members of the university community.

Unionization has taught us this hard lesson. Few of us started our academic careers believing that universities operated with values similar to those of Dow Chemical. Most of us yearned for the protected environments higher education seemed to afford. Working with the union, however, has shown us that for nontenurable faculty, the university has values no different from any other corporation. Lecturers enjoy less job security than researchers, than staff, than groundskeepers—all of these workers are considered more central to the mission of the university than those who teach writing, elementary math, or beginning foreign languages.

The iron law governing the employment of lecturers, and all "temps" for that matter, has been and always will be economics. We are not privy, of course, to the university's official thinking on the issue, but a look at the prevailing economic conditions of the late seventies suggests why the university began to use the lecturer hiring category. By 1979, the halcyon days of indefinite expansion that had characterized the fifties and sixties were over. The university, constrained by drops in state revenues after the passing of Proposition 13, which limited property tax revenues, began to tighten its belt. But the belt was hard to tighten. The system was "tenure-heavy." This heaviness, in turn, hampered "programmatic flexibility." Students, meanwhile, voting with their feet, flocked to universities and to departments within universities most likely to enhance career prospects. Departments of business-economics bloomed; classics wilted.

The hiring of faculty under the rarely used job classification of "visiting lecturer" appears to have been a short-term solution to these problems. Theoretically the classification might allow quick hires for departments like business-economics in need of persons to teach accounting, and quick fires, once the exigency passed. In practice, while departments across campus made use of the classification, pools of lecturers began to form, especially in English departments, where writing was taught and in the languages where instructors were needed for introductory courses. In 1979, the UCSB English department had three or four visiting lecturers; by 1984 it had fifty, most of whom were on 100 percent nonemergency one-year renewable appointments, all teaching eight classes a year exclusively in the freshman writing sequence.

While the university administration viewed the use of lecturers as a response to a short-term economic need, these faculty, in fact, were meeting long-term educational needs that the traditional research faculty had little interest in or competence to fill. Theorists in economics were not accounting teachers, theorists of French literature were not language teachers, and theorists in English literature were not composition teachers. While lecturers were increasingly hired as professional educators, the university administration remained wedded to a view of lecturers as satisfying a short-term economic need. This view was perhaps reinforced by the fanciful notion that, if suddenly and for no apparent reason the quality of entering students dramatically improved, there would be no need for teachers at all.

Lecturers were hired on what were officially described as one-year "self-terminating" contracts. "Self-terminating" meant the university legally did not have to give cause, explanation, or reason should it decide not to renew a contract. Indeed, one strict interpretation of "self-terminating" suggested that the university neither had to give cause nor did it have to tell the lecturer that his or her contract had not been renewed. If a lecturer did not receive a new one-year contract, he or she would make the logical inference that the contract had "self-terminated." An instructor receiving a contract had to keep in mind the self-terminating nature of the contract and its term limitations; after one had received eight such contracts, one would never receive another. In 1983, the university reduced the number of such contracts one could receive from eight to four. This became known as the "four years and you are out" rule.

The imposition of this ceiling was the trigger to the unionization of lecturers in the UC system. In 1983, the American Federation of Teachers took this "rule," at its own expense and at its own initiative, before the California Public Employee Relations Board, (PERB), the state appointed board of lawyers and judges that hears all labor disputes. The board ruled the policy illegal (*University Council*, 1983). In the predownsizing world of 1982, the board, whose experience was mostly in labor law, could find no rational reason for firing a competent instructor to be replaced by another person with no experience, only because the experienced person had served four years. This decision taught the lecturers of the UC an important lesson: the university's employment practices were not considered rational beyond the walls of the ivory tower and the courts were willing to face off with the university. In the years that followed, we saw this lesson repeated over and over.

In 1983, on the basis of this widely publicized victory, the AFT ran for and won ratification from the vast majority of lecturers as the official representative of all lecturers in the UC system. After two years of arduous negotiations—during which the university denied the need for trained teachers and claimed lecturers were not faculty—a contract was hammered out (*FORWARD*, 1). The hammering was done on the university side primarily by a former labor organizer, to whom the university paid $70,000 a year, and on the AFT side, by four lecturers pro bono. Because the university would allow no release time for the lecturer negotiators, all, under the stress of work and biweekly negotiating sessions, were warned by their personal physicians to drop out of the negotiating team before they irreparably damaged their health. For others who follow this road to unionization, we would add a second lesson: never try to bargain with the university without both legal and union professionals at the table. The imbalance of power and experience at the table resulted in a final contract that was probably among the weakest ever produced in the history of American labor.

Despite its weaknesses, however, that first contract initiated changes in lecturers' and librarians' lives. Though lecturers traded away, for example, the right to strike, the contract did spell out in clear and enforceable detail that lecturers, after six years of one-year self-terminating contracts, were eligible to be reviewed for three-year contracts. If a lecturer was judged excellent in the three categories of teaching, professional development, and program service, he or she would receive a three-year contract, renewable indefinitely as long as the lecturer continued to perform at a level of excellence and, most important, as long as the position for which he or she was hired continued to exist. If the lecturer did not pass the performance review, he or she was severed from the university and could not be rehired at that campus.

This key article of the MOU, it was hoped, would satisfy the university's fear that unionization meant the retention of inferior personnel while insuring those who did pass the review a reasonably stable professional life.

Without the union, without the contract, without the possibility of job security for lecturers, the Santa Barbara Writing Program as it now exists would not have been possible. Though the lecturer faculty had been growing for years, the teaching of writing was still considered an occasional occupation for graduate students in English. No program and no sense of the teaching of writing as a distinct and professional enterprise had developed or could have developed under preunion circumstances. The interests of graduate students and the department in which they worked rested with literature. Nor would the "floating bottom" of lecturers on one-year self-terminating contracts have afforded the kind of personnel necessary to establish a permanent program. The self-interests of persons on such contracts would and should lie with their personal and professional futures and not with a writing program from which they would be fired in four years. The contract and the possibility it presented of extended employment made possible a convergence of self-interest and program development.

This is not to say that unionization alone made program growth possible. Though it was an essential brick in the edifice, a number of other factors were at work also. In 1984, before the contract but not before the prospect of unionization had reared its head, the English department created the position of co-chair in charge of lecturers and the writing sequence, which at that time was a two-quarter first-year sequence (three quarters for those who did not pass the UC assessment exam). The position, moreover, was given to the only person in the department with professional expertise in writing, and an office was constructed in the English complex to house this person. Lecturers received their mail in the English department mailroom, but their mail slots were separated from those of the tenured and tenurable faculty by a large orange strip.

The creation of the position of co-chair, the new office, and the orange strip suggest Max Weber's iron law of bureaucracy was already at work. The situation was being "rationalized."

Oranges and apples, the law holds, cannot be kept in the same container; lecturers in composition and the tenured faculty in literature were apples and oranges. Unionization in 1986 drove home that fact. The possibility that lecturers might be in place for an unpredictable number of years meant that they might begin, willy-nilly, to exert a degree of influence on department affairs, even though they were allowed to serve on no department committees. Moreover, the instructor review process instituted by the contract would drain the resources of English department staff and possibly the time of English department faculty. In a scene Weber might have predicted, lecturers arrived at work one morning in 1988 to find that their offices and mailboxes, along with their chair, had been moved to another floor.

Though it would take five years, an external review, an internal review, and the report of a Senate Faculty committee to turn the de facto separation of the writing program from the English department into an institutional reality, it became clear far sooner that this "rejection" by the English department was another essential brick in the building of an autonomous program. During that period, the English department chair continued to sign the contracts of lecturers, but the everyday reality was one of separation and independence. The co-chair, with the assistance of lecturers, ran the daily affairs of the program. Committees were put in place, one for each of the different writing courses taught, and lecturers served on the central administrative committee.

Less dramatically, but significant still, lecturers lobbied for and eventually acquired a telephone in each office, albeit with two and sometimes three people on the same extension. They obtained developmental grants for the study of pedagogy. One group of five lecturers, dubbed the " videocell," used their grant to videotape their classes; over the course of a year, biweekly discussions of pedagogy followed. Eventually, the group produced an instructional video, wrote and published two articles. Lecturers, as a whole, began to subscribe to the journals pertinent to the discipline of composition, and (usually at their own expense, since they were denied access to travel money) they attended and presented research at professional conventions. Buoyed by the contract and the possibility of security that it afforded, lecturers in the late eighties began to view themselves as participants in a professional discipline and to build the foundations of an autonomous program, which was officially recognized in 1991.

While under the institutional control of the English dpartment, the writing program faculty saw themselves as serving the needs of the English department, as teaching what the English department faculty did not want to teach, and as serving as training faculty for English department teaching assistants. Granted relative autonomy, the program began to assert its own definition. New lecturers, for example, were hired for their education and teaching experience, and the program began to see itself as serving the general student population. "Service" ceased to be a dirty word; indeed, the writing program became one of the few places on campus where teaching was the primary value.

This evolution occurred, however, without the blessings of the institution and was not bloodless. Indeed, the signing of the first UC-AFT contract in 1986 marked the beginning of a four-year court battle between the union and the university. In 1987, when those lecturers who had already served six years came up for the first performance reviews under the contract, the university's strategy became clear. On three campuses (Los Angeles, Santa Barbara, and Santa Cruz) they denied that the positions held by all but a handful of the eligible lecturers were needed, insisting that new appointees could fill them just as well. The Santa Barbara administration justified its action as the need for "fresh blood." Though it was not clear whether this referred to the need for a transfusion (understandable on a "tenure-heavy" campus) or a good meal, this interpretation of "need" essentially eviscerated the contract. On the Santa Barbara campus, ten of fourteen lecturers were denied review. Clearly the university had set up a quota.

The UC-AFT immediately filed "Unfair Labor Practice" charges against the UC administration on two campuses, Los Angeles and Santa Cruz, adding Santa Barbara to the list a year later (*University Council*, 1987/1988). The ensuing four-year legal battle over the words "long-term need" could not have been carried on without the extraordinary endurance and commitment of the executive director (who was himself a lecturer who had been denied review) and the council president, a lecturer in the speech department at UCLA. Collaboration with the librarians also proved invaluable, for they provided stability during those rocky years. Though they had battles of their own, no such battle threatened their professional existence as the attacks on lecturers did. They, as we were fond of saying in those days, "had real jobs." Equally important was the necessity of belonging to a large nationwide union. The AFT and CFT (the California branch of the AFT) paid two-thirds of the legal costs of that and other battles. Though the University Council has recently come to question the fit between the AFT and the interests of UC lecturers, the lecturers could not have carried on their initial battle with the university without the funds afforded by the national union.

As the court battle dragged on, the novice union members became seasoned veterans. At both council and local levels, lecturers learned to read labor contracts and file grievances. The lessons learned during this period may save other nascent unions a good many casualties. Most important, locals learned not to give up in the face of the weak contract. The locals that filed grievances against their administrations, whether or not they thought they could win, kept their programs fairly well intact simply because the administrators knew they would be challenged. Where there was no one to pay attention or no one willing to fight, programs were decimated. Giant though it is, the university of California behaves differently when it knows it is being watched.

Furthermore, union boards learned that the system has two Achilles' heels. First, granted almost total autonomy by law, the UC does not like outside public agencies (like PERB) meddling in its affairs. Its claimed need for "academic freedom" was truly its most powerful weapon against contract restraints; however, the union members present felt that by using that weapon indiscriminately to thwart every request for commitment to its teaching faculty, the administration conveyed the attitude of being unaccountable to anyone, including the court.

Second, the university does not like adverse publicity. Campus units that made sure their local presses and radio stations received news of mass firings, or mass refusal to review lecturers for three-year appointments, made sure their administrative officers had to face the press and explain their actions. Universities are loath to appear as less than model employers or as less than fully committed to the education of the public's children. The university, the union found, would far rather deal with the lecturers than explain to the public why they were firing experienced teachers simply because they had served competently for six years.

The years 1989–91 marked a watershed in both the systemwide union battle and the local struggle of the UCSB Writing Program. In 1989, the court decided in favor of the UC-AFT in the Santa Cruz and Los Angeles cases, and the UCSB program review committee of the Academic Senate recommended granting autonomy to the writing program. The administrative law judges of PERB stated the university had not made a case that there was any "programmatic need" (academic freedom to establish and eliminate programs) to deny lecturers review for three-year contracts. According to the court, the fact that the university could not see changes in need into the indefinite future was not sufficient cause to deny three-year need, and that the university's ability to change programs was sufficiently protected by the existing contract (*University Council*, 1987). After an offer to settle with the union on weaker terms aborted, the university appealed the decision, promising another long delay. Nevertheless, the message was clear: the courts were not sympathetic to the university's case.

On the local front, the recommendation of autonomy and the subsequent granting of that status by the UCSB College of Letters and Science had a profound effect on the writing program. Free of its institutional tie to the English department, it could now address its university-wide function. Under the leadership of its own lecturer with security of employment (a tenured position), the faculty set about writing its own program goals. By faculty committee consensus, it replaced the literature-based courses with a writing-across-the-disciplines approach to composition instruction, while spreading the two quarters' required sequence across the four years and developing upper-level writing courses in academic and professional specialties. It initiated new relationships with other campus departments by linking its introductory-level courses to general education courses across campus and in the engineering school. It gained the right to accept or reject graduate student teaching assistants from the

English department based on their performance in composition and to require training in composition as a condition of employment. In addition, the program began to recruit teaching assistants from departments other than English. In 1993, it earned the right to review its own personnel cases. After ten years of struggle, composition lecturers had finally won the right to have their performance judged by their peers, rather than by faculty with no knowledge of composition.

In 1991, with the Santa Barbara case still pending at PERB, the UCSB administration made its last effort to deny the need for long-term lecturers, refusing to review two writing program faculty. The UCSB local, through the council, filed a new "Unfair Labor Practice" charge (*University Council,* 1991). Throughout the court years, the leaders of the UCSB local had argued that, where educational program goals depended primarily on lecturers, continuity was necessary to create programs of academic excellence. This argument seemed eventually to gain credence with administrators. The granting of autonomy to the UCSB program was, of course, a great boon to this argument. Whether the program had indeed helped prove the case or whether the systemwide administration had simply lost confidence in its ability to win at PERB, they offered to settle both the old and new charges out of court. When their original offer to simply save the two lecturers' positions was refused, they accepted the union's demand for a real policy change. They stated simply that (at the UCSB campus only) if the courses formed a permanent part of university requirement and were taught primarily by lecturers that would constitute "need" for a long-term position and entitle the lecturer to review. Thus ended the "needs" battle at UCSB. At this one campus, at least, the need for long-term lecturers to fulfill on-going needs of the university became an accepted fact of life. Both UCSB lecturers and administrators have enjoyed five years of relative labor peace. One attempt to deny merit increases to lecturers was turned back by PERB (*University Council,* 1994), but most grievances have been settled at the local level. Though such settlements were not ideal, they have wrought small improvements in the working lives of lecturers and in their institutional identities. For example, lecturers have also won nonvoting seats on faculty legislature committees and service on these committees has afforded invaluable opportunities. Lecturers have become more visible to their senate faculty colleagues and more knowledgeable about the intricate and sometimes arcane workings of the university administration.

This radical change, of course, would have been impossible had the UCSB administration not accepted the settlement and acted in good faith in the ensuing years. This has not been the story on all campuses. When the appeal decision was handed down on the original cases, the university won back some ability to deny review for economic reasons, and writing programs at some of the other campuses did not weather the court battles as well as Santa Barbara. The structure of the campuses, the location of the writing programs and the administrations' attitude and strategies also varied. At some campuses there were not enough lecturers to provide a critical mass. In short, the reasons for the uneven results were not monolithic, though California's economic crisis of 1990–96 surely played a major role on all campuses. On the Santa Barbara campus, the writing program now numbers twenty-three full-time lecturers, rather than fifty, and the library has lost some twenty positions.

Much of the turmoil can be laid at the door of the university regents' chosen method of dealing with California's recent economic crisis. Basically, the regents bailed out the system with retirement funds, offering repeated "golden handshakes" to senior faculty in order to hire cheaper, younger faculty. This thrice-repeated technique decapitated departments all over the system, leading to a desperate scramble for positions and recruitment monies. In this scramble, the "soft money" used to hire lecturers and librarians diminished. Cost-of-living salary increases for lecturers and librarians, which had traditionally been the same as for tenurable faculty, were "decoupled" to free funds for recruiting. The librarians, whose contract came up for negotiation first, fought valiantly against this amendment and won some measure of equity back; nonetheless, the salary gap has certainly widened.

The University of California behaves more and more openly like the corporate giant it is. Harvesting enough funds for super-science faculty and labs means hiring more and more part-time temporary faculty to fill the holes left in the classrooms. Furthermore, new titles are appearing on faculty rosters; at UCLA, 40 percent of the undergraduate classes are taught by persons with "visiting" and "adjunct" titles, suggesting that new classes of temporary faculty are being created. The union is currently exploring the nature of this new "hidden" faculty and its contracts. But the very capacity of the university to invent new hiring categories for "temps" may make the relative stability of union membership and three-year contracts look more attractive to academic faculty than it has in the past.

Against this backdrop, the UCSB Writing Program continues a steady, if somewhat schizophrenic, growth. On the one hand, the writing program now offers a minor in professional writing, and an external review panel of composition experts found the program "cutting edge." On the other hand, the program has lost its quarters to a much smaller unit because those in charge of space during major remodeling forgot that the program existed. The program has negotiated with the English department for further training for graduate students teaching writing—an event that simply could not have happened five years ago—but is so technologically poor that the use of technology in the teaching of writing is stymied.

Despite all of this, however, the UCSB Writing Program has a degree of stability, autonomy, and acceptance rare for programs staffed with non-tenure-track faculty, certainly rare in the UC system. This success is not accidental. Key to the program's survival and growth are these events: (1) collective action (the union won three-year contracts that provided a permanent faculty); (2) separation from the English department, where its interests could never be primary; (3) development of a cross-disciplinary curriculum, including linked classes that took program faculty out of their isolated ghettoes and built relationships across campus; (4) membership on university-wide committees, giving program faculty increased visibility and therefore gradual acceptance as an integral part of the university community.

None of this means the existence of a separate writing program can be taken for granted; none of this means UCSB's tenured faculty considers us peers. What it does mean is that helpless acceptance of an underclass role is suicidal; we must maintain the attitude that created the union and sustained it through its infancy. UCLA Writing Program lecturer, Susan Griffin, (also past council president and recently appointed state coordinator of the UC-AFT), expressed this attitude perfectly when asked how she got into union work: "I'm from Chicago. I'm Irish. I don't like to be pushed around" (1997, 3).

We realize that the picture we have presented here is not rosy. Perhaps most difficult to accept is that the university is indeed a corporation, and that our lot is not that different from that of other American workers. From executives to line workers, employees are becoming "temps." Historically, a central factor militating against the more inhumane excesses of capitalism has been and continues to be unions and the threat of unionization.

For unions the bottom line always will be a fair wage for a decent day's work. But since their inception, unions have also always been about the attempt of workers to make their labor meaningful. Work at McDonald's is not meaningful. Fry cooks report that they do not have to know how to cook a burger to prepare a Big Mac. They simply respond to a series of bells and whistles that signal when to flip the burgers or turn the buns. They make no decisions. In a scene B. F. Skinner might have admired, a person simply responds to stimuli. If teachers wish to preserve the autonomy of their work and the potentials for commitment and creativity implied in that autonomy, if they wish their work to remain meaningful, unions afford a means by which they may collectively begin to assert control over the circumstances of their labor. Making their work meaningful is inseparable from providing a meaningful education for students.

Works Cited

FORWARD, 1.2. (1996, December). Newsletter of UC-AFT Local 2141. University of California, Santa Barbara, CA.

Griffin, S. (1997, November). *UC-AFT Perspective, 3.*

University Council of the American Federation of Teachers v. Regents of the University of California. State of California, Public Employees Relations Board, Decision #SF-CE-57-H, (1983, April 27).

University Council of the American Federation of Teachers v. Regents of the University of California. State of California, Public Employees Relations Board, Decision #SF-CE-272-H, LA-CE-235-H, (1987, November 17).

University Council of the American Federation of Teachers v. Regents of the University of California. State of California, Public Employees Relations Board, Decision #SF-CE-287-H, (1988, December 19).

University Council of the American Federation of Teachers v. Regents of the University of California. State of California, Public Employees Relations Board, Decision #SF-CE-287-H & #SF-CE-320-H, (1991, July 23).

University Council of the American Federation of Teachers v. Regents of the University of California. State of California, Public Employees Relations Board, Decision #SF-CE-349-H, (1994, June 7).

University Council of the American Federation of Teachers v. Regents of the University of California. State of California, Public Employees Relations Board, Decision #SF-CE-340-H, (1994, December 16).

CHAPTER TEN

Same Struggle, Same Fight: A Case Study of University Students and Faculty United in Labor Activism

ELANA PELED
Harvard University, Cambridge, Massachusetts

DIANA HINES
California State University, Long Beach

MICHAEL JOHN MARTIN
San Francisco State University, San Francisco

ANNE STAFFORD
San Francisco State University, San Francisco

BRIAN STRANG
San Francisco State University, San Francisco

MARY WINEGARDEN
San Francisco State University, San Francisco

MELANIE WISE
San Francisco State University, San Francisco

On Thursday, December 12, 1996, we, a group of non-tenure-track writing faculty, gathered in a classroom at San Francisco State University (SFSU) awaiting the start of a scheduled meeting of our union, the California Faculty Association (CFA). We wondered how many of our colleagues from the Department of English and other departments on campus would attend this meeting. What kind of crisis would it take to prompt our colleagues to leave their stacks of papers, anxious students, and other meetings to attend this one? In a bureaucracy that encourages classism and often pits the haves against the have-nots, the tenured and tenure-track against lecturers and graduate teaching associates, who would come to join this fight, who would take the time and make the effort? Though we had not been without allies and friends up to now, these last-minute doubts gnawed at us. But as lecturers, students, union representatives, tenured and tenure-track faculty alike filled the seats and spilled into the hall, we knew that today we would not stand alone. In fact, the day's events would demonstrate the importance of enlisting student support and fostering solidarity among all ranks in the fight for fair university employment practices, especially in the face of the ongoing weakening of the status of academic professionals.

The purpose of this meeting was to inspire faculty to join together in a fight against the university administration, which at the time of the meeting had threatened to leave a group of fourteen lecturers in English composition and ESL jobless. With this decision, the administration made it clear that lecturers were regarded as faceless servants of a flexible fiscal budget, dispensable as the first course of action in an apparent budgetary shortfall. People—ranging from members of the group of fourteen, who were to have lost their jobs, to union officials and representatives of student activist groups—spoke to the assembled group about the inequities of the university system. They spoke of the price students and faculty pay for this way of operating, and, ironically, the unforeseen loss of revenue that the university was likely to sustain by canceling classes desperately needed by high-paying international students as prerequisites to upper-division coursework. Following the speeches, everyone gathered outside the humanities building, where another, larger group—students, staff, and faculty alike—were awaiting their arrival. A space was cleared in the center of the group, and a street theater performance characterized the carefree manner in which university officials hire and fire the faculty who do approximately half of the teaching on our campus. Each lecturer immediately affected by the proposed layoff stepped forward, with a suitcase in hand, as a mock-administrator called her name from a list. The role-playing administrator then proceeded to give the lecturer a "kick in the pants" and send her "packing." The performance was followed by more speeches, most notably from the CFA state secretary and the student body president. Following the speeches, those present donned placards and picket signs, and to the beat of a drum, began their procession across a campus visibly adorned with high-cost construction, all the while chanting slogans and enlisting fellow students, faculty, and staff to join in their march.

At their destination, the administration building, the dean of Faculty Affairs awaited their arrival. The protesters gathered, made more speeches, and then presented a stack of petitions— some 2,300 signatures gathered in a period of less than three weeks by the disgruntled students and faculty—to the dean. The event ended with cheers and shouts for the university administration to employ fair employment practices.

Planting the Seeds of Discontent

The situation that gave rise to the protest began in mid-November, when fourteen lecturers in English composition and ESL received notification that they would not be scheduled to teach the following spring semester. Most of the fourteen had several years of teaching experience at the university; nine had received full academic-year contracts the previous September. Each instructor had every reason to expect to be rehired for the spring. That fall, because of an "administrative error," the university had accepted two thousand more students than it could accommodate. A tremendous strain was placed on the required, core courses most often elected by first-year students and taught nearly exclusively by part-time lecturers. Certainly, it is common for teachers of core courses such as composition to have several students trying to over-enroll during the first weeks of a semester, but the fall of 1996 saw teachers fighting their way through seas of students who lined the halls outside of classrooms already filled to capacity. English department staff were bombarded with angry students demanding that the university meet their course needs. Most had expected that the university would try to accommodate the needs of those fall students locked out of freshman writing courses by increasing the number of sections offered in the spring. No one was prepared for the news that sections of spring composition courses were being reduced; instructors were to be laid off; students were to have fewer chances to complete their freshman course requirements.

University officials argued that "budgetary constraints" necessitated the spring semester "scheduling crisis." The chair of the English department carefully explained his understanding of the situation: For many years it had been the practice of the English department to "borrow" from their spring budget during the fall in order to provide courses to meet demand; in the spring, when the budget was not sufficient to support enough courses, the department turned to the administration for an "augmentation" to their budget. For at least a decade, the department had received the additional funding. But in 1996, for unstated reasons, the administration turned down the department's request. By not providing an augmentation, the administration forced the department to scale back. Indeed, graduate and upper-division courses were scheduled to be cut back as well, and tenured faculty were being asked to give up release time in order to teach some of the basic writing and freshman composition courses typically taught by part-time faculty. Department officials speculated that with this move the university administrators sought to "punish" the department for its long-time practice of employing such "expensive" lecturers when the courses could be taught by cheaper graduate teaching associates, a practice popular at universities around the country.

Actual notices of the layoff[1] went out to the faculty affected on Wednesday, November 6. The coordinator of the composition program set up two meetings, for the following Tuesday and Wednesday (November 12 and 13), to discuss what came to be known as the "scheduling crisis." A previously announced English department meeting was scheduled to take place at a later time on the same Wednesday, November 13, and the lecturers at the earlier meeting decided to "take over" the later meeting, to make the agenda the fourteen faculty members in the department who were losing their jobs, their incomes, and their livelihoods.

Union representatives attended the English department meeting to offer their support. They explained that a process for filing grievances was in place and helped to create momentum for organizing more immediate action. A subsequent meeting was set up to give the affected lecturers and the union representatives an opportunity to discuss the possible actions. At that meeting, a number of committees were created—one to contact the press, one to organize the protest, one to circulate petitions, one to write a street theater scene, and one, consisting of union members only, to proceed with an inquiry into the manner in which instructional funds had been distributed in the fall. It was this committee who discovered that money promised by the state for faculty cost-of-living increases had never made its way to academic departments. The money slated for English alone could return several courses to the spring schedule.

Meanwhile, a separate group was taking action of its own. During the English department meeting, a reporter from the student newspaper sat quietly at the back of the room. The next morning, the front-page headline read "SPRING CLASSES CUT." With that headline, students received their first notice that they would face increasing difficulties enrolling in English classes. The fight had begun.

Why Students Were So Eager to Join the Fight

The reporter who attended the English department meeting continued to follow the story. She conducted interviews with affected faculty members and union representatives, attended every open meeting on the "crisis," and saw to it that the story was updated weekly in the student newspaper. In fact, student activism was not limited to the efforts of one eager reporter. Student government officials also became involved. The student body president drafted a letter to the president of the university stating his concern that the university was disregarding the needs of its students, many of whom would be lining up again in the spring for English classes. Our former writing students became valuable allies. They circulated petitions and gathered student signatures. Since they were not currently enrolled in our classes, we could no longer affect their grades and therefore could not be accused by the administration of coercing them into taking action on our behalf. And a group of student activists already organized to battle recent antiaffirmative action legislation (Prop. 209) joined in the effort by taking the petitions from class to class and by posting flyers and painting signs for the march across campus. This last group saw that the threat to their teachers' jobs was also a threat to them and to their future success as educated members of society. These students, for whom the state was making it difficult for those already in college to complete their education, willingly joined in our efforts. Likewise, graduate students in the composition and ESL programs circulated petitions as well. As future teachers, they understood that they too might one day become lecturers subject to unfair employment practices.

It should come as no surprise that so many students were willing to help. In California, a precipitous decline in state support for public education has occurred at all levels—a pattern that began twenty years ago with the passage of Proposition 13. At the same time, our student population has been transformed because of open enrollment and recent waves of immigrants who speak languages other than English. In order to master the critical thinking and writing skills needed for successful participation in their academic and working lives, these same students now need even more support from their writing teachers. They know that learning to write English effectively is an important step on the road to overcoming the racial and class prejudice they often face. They know that our classes help them to gain access to the privileges of a culture in which economic disparities and mean-spirited legislation keep those who most need an education from obtaining that goal. Sadly, examples of legislation impeding the educational access and progress of diverse students have proliferated: Proposition 209, which abolished all affirmative action policies in college admissions in California, has already resulted in a 52 percent drop in minority enrollment at UC Berkeley for fall 1998; CUNY in New York has just barred all students needing remedial work from enrolling; and our own California State University system has just required students needing remediation to complete that work in just one year.

Stories of students taking five and six years to complete their undergraduate degrees are commonplace at SFSU, and many of those admitted in the fall of 1996 soon learned that they would be forced onto the five- or six-year track because adequate sections of required courses were unavailable. For many students, pursuing a college degree requires tremendous sacrifice, often placing a hefty financial burden on them and their families. Lengthening the time required to complete their degrees only increases this burden and may discourage some students from continuing. With students clamoring for more sections of required courses, the university's firing of fourteen lecturers seemed the height of folly—or arrogance. Members of the campus community became equally angered, committed to the cause, and more than ready to fight. Collectively we realized that these layoffs foretold a darker future for teachers and students at SFSU. Our vociferous response proved to be one that the administration could not ignore.

Composition courses provide an essential rung on the ladder to students' success, and students are acutely aware of the many ways the rungs of that ladder are being weakened. To them, the loss of our jobs was one more attempt by those in power to place obstacles in their way. To support us was to fight for themselves, for their education, for the justice they rarely receive but so deserve.

The Politics of Teaching Composition in the Classroom and Beyond

That students are aware of the sociopolitical importance of their English courses should not come as a surprise, especially at a highly politicized campus such as SFSU, where many members of the community see their education in larger contexts. Composition instructors, too, often incorporate the politics of language acquisition and use into their courses. In fact, the English composition program at SFSU is, in many ways, unique, for SFSU is one of few schools to offer both a master's degree and certificate program in English composition. These two programs serve as a training ground for future teachers of composition. At SFSU, applicants for lectureships are required to complete an extensive application process that includes a three-hour screening exam and an interview conducted by a committee of both tenured and lecturer faculty. This rigorous process ensures that the highest quality of instruction is maintained.

And indeed, in certain ways lecturers at SFSU are afforded more professional consideration than many of our colleagues nationwide. Those of us who teach half time receive a full benefits package. Those of us in English who teach a full academic year are entitled to be rehired in the following year before new lecturers can be hired. We have offices with windows, telephones with voice mail, computers with e-mail. But while we may have more than our colleagues on other campuses, we are undeniably a part of a vulnerable labor force, treated with little respect or consideration for the work we do or the preparation we bring to that work.

We often locate the genesis of our poor working conditions in the open admissions movement of the 1970s. As record numbers of nontraditional students flooded our traditional English classrooms, the story goes, the university was hard put to supply both adequate numbers of classes and fair terms of employment. While open admissions certainly paved the way for the excessive use of part-timers, we can trace our problems even further back than that. In fact, Robert Connors traces these problems back to the 1880s after the first Harvard entrance exam revealed that few of its entering freshmen could pass a standard test of correctness. Responding to these results, and to the general perception among Harvard's elite that linguistic standards in this country had sunk well below those in Britain, President Eliot resolved to exclude from college any freshman who had not completed a writing course involving extensive hours in writing "labs." The focus of rhetorical training, then, shifted from oral discourse, which had been the backbone of the classical education for hundreds of years, to written discourse. And as teachers were charged with reading and responding to hundreds of themes that poured in weekly and spending many hours in student-teacher conferences, their workload mushroomed. This increased workload diminished the status of composition, so that scholars who were more concerned with establishing themselves in distinguished careers pursued oral rhetoric rather than written composition.

The separation between oral rhetoric and written composition has everything to do with the status of composition in English departments today. When composition split from rhetoric, it also split from rhetoric's more prestigious roots in philology and literary history. Instead of focusing on classical languages and philosophy as rhetoric did, composition focused on the writing of the burgeoning middle class, whom administrators perceived as more practical in spirit than the sons of the upper class who had traditionally filled college classrooms. Composition teachers provided basic skills for these new students' success in a growing economy. Clarity and correctness became the focus of instruction. So when we hear talk today that we are doing remedial work, "the least professional teaching the least able," we can be sure we are still reeling from the split between written and oral discourse, between what English departments came to see as the scientific statement versus the poetic statement, and the logical statement versus the mythical statement. James Berlin says that others characterized the split as the impoverished rhetorical statement versus the privileged poetic statement, two separate and unequal groups (1990, p. 108).

This characterization certainly coincides with the two-tiered system that we now have in many English departments, which house what Connors calls, "a privileged literature faculty enjoying benefits that the composition underclass lacks" (1990, p. 108). This definition fails to accurately describe the work that professional composition teachers actually do. The fact is that teachers who are conversant with the intellectual tradition of composition, knowledgeable about the research, and experienced in using current methods in the classroom know something that untrained writing teachers do not. We know that every time we write assignments that call for critical argument or aesthetic judgment, every time we instruct students in heuristics or the relationships among audience, writer, text, we draw on principles from classical rhetoric. When we instruct first-time freshmen on how to parse an argument, compare multiple perspectives, or apply a theoretical model, we draw on research in cognitive and social psychology. When we bring our students together in groups for research, peer editing, and critical inquiry, we draw on sociological and linguistic theory. In spite of the fact that these lessons transcend the skills and drills that people have associated with writing classrooms for much of this century, they have not transformed our status.

Many campuses still staff their writing classes primarily with literature M.A.'s who have little or no composition training—as if a degree in English somehow intrinsically qualifies one to teach writing. Still other campuses staff their writing classes with graduate students who are given fifteen minutes of advice and nudged into service. In contrast, composition professionals have been rigorously trained to teach writing. We have—as Martin Nystrand suggests in a thorough study of the intellectual development of our field—a professional discipline concerned with the reader-writer-text relationship and the teaching of both "formal and rhetorical considerations" (1993, p. 268).

But because many of us temporary faculty do not have Ph.D.'s or Ed.D.'s, we can be asked to teach fifteen units a semester (the tenured staff's limit is twelve) and still be deemed ineligible for the standard fringe-benefit package of health insurance and retirement benefits. Working conditions such as these not only exacerbate divisions between faculty but also constrain students' access to higher education as well. Decreasing numbers of permanent, full-time faculty mean students continually find it more and more difficult to achieve their educational goals. Rather than providing students with the opportunities and the tools they need to succeed in life, the university is becoming an active participant in the dissolution of the middle class. The increasing use by the university of part-time instructors contributes to this dissolution in other ways as well, as these faculty members are finding it harder and harder to earn a living wage. Currently, more than half of all university faculty are non-tenure-track "part-time" instructors who often earn less than civil servants who collect garbage or clean streets in their communities.

Making this situation apparent to students is only logical, for many students arrive at the university believing that their education will serve as their ticket to the American Dream; they are certain that the instructors they find in their classrooms have already arrived. When those illusions are shattered, students are unlikely to sit back passively and accept a similar fate. When they recognize the kinship that exists between their own precarious social positions and the precarious positions of faculty, particularly composition faculty who teach a course in which they receive individual instruction, they will be willing to join our fight, as the situation at SFSU has demonstrated.

Lest you think such a fight is a futile exercise, our struggle demonstrates otherwise. On the day of the march, thirty-three days following the announcement of the cutbacks, three-quarters of the affected faculty had been given spring schedules; by the semester's start, all affected faculty had been offered classes and returned to their previous status. We doubt the situation would have been reversed, or at least not reversed within the time frame that it was, had we not raised our collective voices as loudly as we did. In the words of one union activist, "Don't believe for a minute that there is no money. There's money! If an earthquake hit tomorrow and all the windows were blown out on the administration building, they'd find the money to replace them." As the outcome attests, the funds did exist to prevent this "scheduling crisis." Money does exist, in the university, in the state, to create full-time jobs for part-time employees working full-time schedules. This money needs to be made available to academic units so that they can operate more effectively, in a manner that serves not only the students these departments are constituted to teach but also the faculty they hire to accomplish their goals.

In an ironic move, one made perhaps in an effort to bring closure to this situation, the campus president boldly announced at the start of 1997–98 that the academic year would be the year of the lecturer! While we appreciated the acknowledgment, we are sorry to report that our status has not changed—we are as vulnerable to layoffs as ever. And so we should not be pacified by empty words meant to smooth ruffled feathers. Our situation is far more serious. We must continue to speak out, to raise our voices, to represent our interest in the intersection between employment equity and educational quality. Students engaged themselves in our cause at SFSU because they recognized that our cause was their cause. The failure of the university to rehire fourteen English composition and ESL lecturers meant that students would not be able to find places they needed in required courses.

Our experience at San Francisco State University taught us an important lesson, a lesson with implications for building on student-faculty coalitions where employment equity is linked to issues of educational quality. What we have to do now is to engage tenure-track faculty, university administrators, and state legislators in fighting for our cause if we are to achieve the recognition and status we deserve, and to maintain educational standards and opportunities as well. Beyond these measures, we need to engage the media in our struggle to remind the public of the important role of higher education. We need to remind the public of the important role that teachers play in our colleges and universities and to inform them of the steady erosion of their working conditions. The treatment of part-timers within the system speaks to a much larger problem—the threatened erosion of students' access to a quality education.

Note

1. Note that the situation could not officially be called a layoff. The lecturer contracts given each fall indicate that "employment as a lecturer is contingent on enrollment and instructional need sufficient to justify the prospective employment as determined by the Dean of the College." Apparently, the university felt that enrollment and instructional need were not present, in spite of the enrollment crisis taking place on campus. Union officials were ready to file a grievance with the university based on this discrepancy.

Works Cited

Berlin, J. A. (1987). *Rhetoric and reality: Writing instruction in American colleges, 1900–1985*. Carbondale: Southern Illinois University Press.

Connors, R. (1990, Fall). Overwork/underpay: Labor and status of composition teachers since 1880. *Rhetoric Review, 9(1)*, 108–126.

Nystrand, M., Greene, S., & Wiemelt, J. (1993, July). Where did composition studies come from? An intellectual history. *Written Communication, 10(3)*, 267–333.

CHAPTER ELEVEN

Climbing a Mountain: An Adjunct Steering Committee Brings Change to Bowling Green State University's English Department

DEBRA A. BENKO

I n an article published in *Profession 1997,* Katherine Kolb asks, "How much longer, then, before adjuncts follow the Yale students' example?" Kolb responds to her own question, "Quite awhile" (100).[1] At Bowling Green State University (BGSU), a regional university in rural/small town Northwest Ohio, serving approximately 19, 000 students, the English department's Full-Time Temporary/Part-Time Steering Committee, a committee of adjuncts, has indeed been working to improve conditions for its members. In fact, former steering committee member, Mark Graves, in an e-mail to the author dated January 10, 1998, suggests that the committee may serve as a useful example to adjuncts elsewhere who are pursuing change in their own departments:

> I think the Steering Committee at BGSU has effected real change along the lines that most schools can follow. I doubt that most untenured teachers could adopt the radical stances seen at Yale. (M. Graves, e-mail to the author, January 14, 1998)

First established ten years ago for several years and then revived three years ago, the BGSU steering committee serves as an ad hoc union. Advocating for nontenured faculty, the committee has become a force for change in the English department until that future day when union organization occurs and formal collective bargaining is achieved university-wide. The steering committee is not a formally elected committee. Any adjunct faculty member in the department can be a member or attend meetings. Currently, 25 percent of adjunct faculty are active in the committee and increasing participation is a goal for next year. Various adjunct faculty on the steering committee have also served as representatives to all of elected departmental committees, including the newly created writing program committee, ensuring greater voice to steering committee concerns and more recognition in the department. In turn, the steering committee keeps its minutes open to tenured and probationary faculty in an effort to create awareness of the circumstances of adjunct faculty and promote alliances for change.

Based on a review of the steering committee's history and interviews with past and present members and the English department co-chairs, I will show what the committee has achieved, what remains to be done for adjuncts here, and how the committee may serve as a useful example for adjuncts at other universities trying to improve their working conditions.

In 1997–98, I was in my second year as a part-time instructor in BGSU's English department. Before that, I was awarded a university dissertation fellowship and a doctoral teaching position in the department. In these roles, I was only partially unaware of the exploitation of adjuncts and graduate students in what has been a disastrous job market; moreover, I was sufficiently aware of adjunct issues to know of the work of the steering committee. Without a full-time position after my fellowship year, my only career option as an ABD hoping to finish the dissertation seemed to be part-time teaching.

I knew that I wanted to be actively involved in helping to improve conditions for adjuncts in the department, especially since they were working to achieve health care benefits for part-time instructors. After receiving a contract late in August, I joined the ranks of part-time instructors. I also received an invitation from an adjunct colleague to attend the first steering committee meeting of the 1996–97 academic year. Subsequently, I volunteered to work with a health care subcommittee to prepare a university-wide survey of part-time instructors' opinions of the need for and type of health care plan they wanted to receive. At that point, the steering committee's activities demonstrated committed, but not openly activist, fervor.

Scholars, such as Cary Nelson, who have written about the exploitation of adjuncts and graduate students have called on marginalized workers in the academy to unionize. In *Manifesto of a Tenured Radical*, for example, Nelson writes, "At the very least it is time for job seekers to work together to explore what collective power they might have" (1997a, p. 166), and "teaching assistants and adjunct or part-time faculty should unionize" (p. 180). In the anthology *Will Teach for Food*, Nelson states, "All the contributors believe those employees who cannot negotiate better salaries and working conditions as individuals should consider collective bargaining as an alternative" (1997b, p. 6). Coming from a blue-collar background, I agree with Nelson's statements; I believe the ultimate goal of an adjunct group such as the BGSU steering committee should be university-wide collective bargaining. Many of my tenured and non-tenured colleagues agree.

The question that had to be asked at BGSU's English department in 1996–97 was this one: What steps can be taken immediately to improve working conditions for adjuncts before coalitions can be formed and a union can be organized and recognized? The American Association of University Professors' (AAUP) longstanding effort to organize a faculty union at BGSU was voted down in 1994. As for the example of the Yale graduate students' efforts to form coalitions with unionized clerical and service workers that Nelson recommends to others (1997b, pp. 19–20), the possibility did not exist for us. Only the campus police are currently unionized at BGSU. As Kolb notes, most adjuncts living from paycheck to paycheck and traveling from campus to campus may not have the financial resources to strike for even as long as the Yale graduate students did. Because we are operating in a nonunion shop, do we merely accept exploitation until radical change can be precipitated, or do we take the intermediate steps we can toward change? The steering committee's strategy was to climb a mountain it wanted to move.

Kolb notes that "there are formidable barriers, both practical and psychological, to organized resistance by temporary faculty members" (p. 101). Nevertheless, these barriers were at least partially broken down by the formation of BGSU's English department Temporary Faculty Committee, which became known as the steering committee during the 1987–88 academic year. The steering committee appears to have been formed and led by several members of the temporary faculty with input from most of the temporary faculty. An August 22, 1988, memo sent to all adjuncts notes the significant accomplishments of the committee's first year. Committee members established representation on three department committees, including the Central Advisory Committee (CAC), the department's policymaking group; the Promotion, Salary and Tenure Committee (PST); and the General Studies Writing Program Policy Advisory Committee (GSW), which was "newly reinstated" (Klein, 1988, p.1). A three-year plan to increase pay was implemented, and office assignment and supply procedures were improved (p. 1). In addition, four task force proposals were approved. These outlined improvements to implement in the future, including "continued salary increases, fringe benefits, and improved working conditions for temporary and part-time faculty"; granting nontenured faculty eligibility for the university Master Teacher Award and departmental research/travel money; and urging university administrators to establish lecturer positions and to pay part-time instructors "proportional salaries and benefits" (p. 1).

About the goals for the 1988–89 academic year, the second year of the steering committee's existence, Klein states in a memo:

> Our first goal this year *must* be to win the right to vote within the English department. Without this, we will never have the respect and equality we are fighting for. . . .Our long-term goals include lobbying the administration for further pay hikes and medical benefits. (1988, p. 2)

Members of the steering committee also drafted and distributed a "Temporary Faculty Handbook" for non-tenure-track faculty in the English department, which included information on teaching loads, class attendance policies, office hours, supplies, and duplicating procedures. Under the auspices of the University Faculty Senate, the steering committee also conducted and tallied a university-wide survey to gather statistics about part-time and

temporary faculty. In March 1990, in conjunction with department administrators, the steering committee conducted another
survey of adjunct faculty in the English department. One survey
question boldly asks, "If any or all of our requests for job stability, salary increase, and benefits (issues being discussed by Faculty Senate and the Department), are not met within a reasonable
period of time, what actions do you suggest be taken by the Department or by Temporary English Faculty Members?" (steering
committee survey, March 1990). The adjuncts responding called
for various measures ranging from a teach-in, refusing to sign
contracts, urging the department to refuse to staff first-year writing courses, working toward unionization, and a strike.

Steering committee members had supported a resolution proposed by Alice Calderonello, a full professor who is now co-
chair of the English department and then-chair Les Barber. The
Barber-Calderonello resolution, which was under consideration
in Faculty Senate spring semester 1989, would have created full-
time nontenured continuing lecturer positions and continuing
part-time faculty. Although the resolution was not approved, one
year later in spring 1990, the Faculty Senate did consider and
approve a new resolution creating the lecturer rank (BGSU Faculty Senate Executive Committee Minutes, February 20, 1990).
In order to protect tenure, the number of lecturers in a given
department may be equal to no more than 25 percent of the number of tenured faculty. In recent years, the number of lecturer
positions approaching this quota has been approved for the English department and greater job security has been achieved for
those experienced temporary faculty members who have won
these positions.

Once the lecturer rank and other benefits had been achieved,
the steering committee was inactive for several years. Since it
was reactivated in fall 1995, it has grown more influential and
achieved greater recognition from department administrators in
response to crises concerning adjunct hiring and scheduling issues; it has also continued to work toward ongoing institutional
change.

In 1988–89, there were twenty-three part-time instructors,
two permanent part-time instructors, ten one-year instructors,
and three renewable instructors in BGSU's English department.

In 1997–98, there were thirty-four part-time instructors (fall semester) and twenty-six part-time instructors (spring semester), one permanent part-time instructor (a unique category that has been phased out), four one-year nonrenewable instructors, six renewable (for up to five years) instructors, and five lecturers in a department of twenty-eight tenured and probationary faculty members. Due to attrition of retiring tenured faculty and demands of the general studies writing program requirements, more adjuncts are needed now than in the past because tenured faculty never teach composition. The number of nontenurable faculty positions has steadily increased during the past decade. Despite advances, such as winning proportional voting in the English department, many of the issues of concern to adjunct faculty remain: access to health care benefits, increased security, and a need to work toward building university-wide coalitions and a collective bargaining unit.

One crucial challenge that steering committee members made to university policy was initiated in the summer of 1996. Committee members fought the implementation of the No Hire Rule, which would have prevented adjuncts who had served for five years as full-time instructors from being rehired to teach part-time in subsequent years. Administrative concern about de facto tenure lingered although steering committee members argued that temporary instructors were in nontenurable positions and therefore should be eligible for part-time teaching. According to Julie Haught, a lecturer in the English department and a member of the steering committee since fall 1995, it was this issue that "encouraged us to become more active" (personal interview, January 13, 1998). English department administrators had been informed of the implementation of this no hire policy in February 1996. However, the two instructors in the English department who would be most effected by this policy had not been notified. Both applied for part-time teaching and were informed during the summer that they were eligible to teach in the fall. Thus, they were shocked to receive a letter saying they could teach a maximum of one section in the fall and could not expect to receive any sections in future semesters because of the no hire policy.

Learning of this situation, steering committee members met with department administrators and drafted a policy explaining why the No Hire Rule should be set aside and stating why those who had completed five-year instructorships should be allowed to continue their employment with the university as part-time instructors. In a subsequent meeting, the steering committee, department administrators, and the dean of the College of Arts and Sciences agreed to eliminate the No Hire Rule. Andrea Van Vorhis, a member of both the original and current steering committees, was one of the instructors affected by the No Hire Rule. In an e-mail to the author dated January 14, 1998, she gives the steering committee credit for helping her obtain a part-time instructorship in the English department:

> I know that had I been alone in this, there would have been no way for me to get . . . [department administrators at the time] to do anything about the policy. . . . Without the Steering Committee I probably would not be teaching here right now. To me, the Steering Committee is sort of a miniature version of a union without which part-time instructors would be left to fend for themselves and remain virtually powerless and subject to exploitation, unfair practices, and abuse. (A. Van Vorhis, e-mail to the author, January 14, 1998)

The steering committee was able to respond to this situation and effectively propose and achieve change. Playing the role of union negotiators, the steering committee managed to get administrators to see the impact of the No Hire Rule from the perspective of adjuncts.

In its October 15, 1996, proposal to set aside the No Hire Rule, the steering committee pointed out that it was "not necessary to protect against the possibility of accidental or de facto tenure, since the (university) charter makes it clear that tenure is not an option for temporary faculty, whether full-time or part-time." The steering committee asserted that preventing post-five-year instructors from teaching part-time at the university would, in the current job market, be a "'use them then loose [sic] them' policy" (Steering Committee, October 15, 1996). Because of the steering committee's success in setting aside the policy, experienced instructors who wish to continue teaching part-time after serving full-time contracts may continue to do so at BGSU.

Perhaps the greatest achievement of the steering committee thus far has been less tangible than a specific policy change. Annmarie Pinarski, who served two years on the steering committee, notes the significance of the very recognition of the steering committee in an e-mail to the author dated January 15, 1998:

> the Committee established itself . . . as a presence within the English Department. As a result . . . others could no longer ignore the needs, requests, demands of part-time faculty. . . . at some point the "higher ups" began to acknowledge that the Steering Committee was not going to disappear, but rather functioned as a serious force within the department. (A. Pinarski, e-mail to the author, January 15, 1998)

The steering committee has given adjuncts a collective place to take their concerns and has been acting on those concerns to the extent that other department constituencies, including administrators, must now reckon with them. Julie Haught believes the steering committee's greatest impact has been to provide "a unified voice for marginalized faculty because without a committee, there's no problem with ignoring part-timers. . . . administrators hear silence as no problem rather than marginalization" (personal interview, January 13, 1998). The English department's new co-chairs (since fall 1997), Ellen Berry and Alice Calderonello, support this point of view. While both note that "full-time faculty in positions of power have to be behind change," Ellen Berry says that the "Steering Committee has challenged people in power to act" (personal interview, January 13, 1998). The steering committee has been united both in supporting the interests of part-timers and in working toward change that empowers adjuncts.

In July 1997, steering committee members signed a formal grievance charging violations of departmental policy and fair hiring and scheduling practices, which had been brought to its attention by adjuncts.[2] Acting through the university's Faculty Personnel Conciliation Committee procedures, the steering committee conciliated the grievance, and departmental committees have been formed or expanded to address writing program and personnel concerns. The steering committee has demonstrated its ability to remain a united coalition throughout a conflicted situation despite the fact that it is not a formal union with collective bargaining power.

The steering committee has actively worked toward establishing health care benefits for adjuncts. In 1996–97, we surveyed all adjunct faculty university-wide to establish the desire and need for access to health care benefits for part-time instructors. We plan to use the results of this survey to argue before a faculty senate subcommittee that a resolution for proportional health care benefits be drafted and passed. One area in which the steering committee is just beginning to make progress is increasing departmental, university, and community awareness of the exploitation of adjuncts and the need to implement change. Steering committee members have been preparing a newsletter regarding adjunct issues.

The steering committee model can have a positive impact not only for adjuncts but also for undergraduates, tenured faculty, and administrators. For example, the lecturer position created at BGSU, with the help of steering committee support, contributes to the continuity of instruction for undergraduates, which facilitates retention of first-year students, a current priority of BGSU's administration and faculty. Simply put, the strongest argument an adjunct committee using the steering committee model can make is that what is good for the adjunct is also good for the institution's educational mission. Indeed, this was the argument the steering committee used in defeating the No-Hire Rule: not hiring post-five-year instructors part-time would cause the university to lose some of its most experienced undergraduate instructors.

Future goals for the steering committee include a commitment to working toward coalitions with adjuncts in other departments on campus in order to unionize; however, realization of this goal of unionization is probably at least several years in the future. Ellen Berry, English department co-chair, agrees that "organizing adjuncts in other departments and more publicity" are goals the steering committee must continue to work toward (personal interview, January 13, 1998). At the same time, Alice Calderonello, English department co-chair, points out that there must be "intercollegiate coalitions" including faculty and administrators to effect change in "the institutional structures that cause material conditions that affect part-timers" (personal interview, January 13, 1998). There is much that remains for steering committee members to accomplish in order to achieve equitable working conditions for adjunct faculty at BGSU.

In the past, the steering committee has met on a monthly basis. The grievance action of summer and fall 1997 took a demanding toll on those who participated in those efforts, as frequent meetings were required and the conciliation process was often daunting. However, despite this exertion, the steering committee has been remarkably united in contentious situations and dealt with internal conflict through open discussion and consensus building. Adjuncts who are not members of the steering committee have felt free to bring specific problems and issues to us and have seen us as a collective that can work for changes in the department. While academics in general may not be prone to confrontation and activism, steering committee members have found ourselves in a situation where our very lack of job security and our precarious situation within the department have created a strong sense of purpose and bonds that have enabled us to put aside any minor differences and work toward change and improved job situations for all adjuncts. Although department administrators are not always supportive of the steering committee's initiatives and the grievance last year unavoidably placed us in an adversarial position with the department, communication between tenured faculty and the steering committee has improved under the current department co-chairs of Berry and Calderonello. Politics and self-interest always enter in to any desires to bring about major change especially in an environment of systemic exploitation and hierarchy. However, Berry and Calderonello are working with the steering committee to foster improved working conditions and greater academic freedom for adjuncts. The changes brought about due to the grievance such as the GSW committee may not yet have resulted in all the improvements the steering committee would like, but the mechanism has been put into place for change, education, protest, and dialogue to occur.

Alongside finding changes for the better, I also made some disheartening discoveries as I conducted the research for this article. Reading the list of steering committee accomplishments in the 1987–88 academic year, its first year of existence, I realized how many of the "future goals" named then have yet to be accomplished ten years later and how some of the gains once achieved, such as conference travel money for adjuncts, have since been taken away. This past semester, travel money for adjuncts was again budgeted thanks to steering committee member efforts. In some ways, it seems as though adjuncts are fighting to return to what was the status quo ten years ago rather than moving forward. Andrea Van Vorhis voices concern in her e-mail to the author: "In the future, I hope, the group can continue to move beyond being more or less a defense mechanism and help improve working conditions for part-timers in general—health care, etc." (January 14, 1998).

The historical record created by the file folders containing past and present steering committee minutes, memos, and other documents underscores the importance of sustaining and renewing a committee membership that will work toward long-term goals in improving working conditions even as short-term goals are met. Part-time and non-tenure-track faculty are notoriously difficult to organize, as many have pointed out, because we have multiple and often competing obligations. We have demanding teaching responsibilities (sometimes at multiple institutions) and competing demands made on our time as some of us take on nonacademic work to stay afloat financially. Some of us are completing our graduate education as we work part-time and are trying to publish and improve our professional profiles. In addition, family obligations also take precedence, as many of us are parents raising children on limited budgets. These demands often make it difficult for part-time faculty to organize, especially since many of us face only short-term contracts and are unsure of our future at the institutions where we work. These competing obligations and pressures coupled with the transience of our work often prevent coalition building. Nevertheless, despite teaching three or four sections a semester and teaching at one or more campuses, we have formed a standing committee that agitates for improved working conditions.

I believe that the steering committee concept may serve as a model for adjuncts at other institutions who wish to work toward change within their departments. I would recommend that adjuncts interested in forming their own steering committee consider listing both their short-term and long-term goals. As I noted earlier, the steering committee has been able to achieve many short-term goals, but we are still working on achieving long-term goals. Being able to note the successes and drawbacks we have had gives us more strength to keep working on what we have not been able to achieve yet. Also, keeping a history is important, so that interested parties can know what has been achieved in the past and what has been lost. It has been easier for the steering committee to achieve goals for which there is a pre-existing precedent recorded. Establishing an open dialogue with department administrators as far as possible is essential. The steering committee has invited various administrators to meetings in the past to discuss programs and to clarify policies in an open atmosphere. The contingent nature of adjunct positions also makes publicizing meetings and recruiting new members regularly important. Those establishing a steering committee should make minutes available to all adjunct and tenured faculty, not just to committee members; adjuncts who may not be able to participate in the group will then still be aware of its work and know that it is a resource, and tenured faculty members will be made more aware of the issues and how they might aid the group's efforts.

For me personally, joining the steering committee facilitated a return to activist roots of my college days that had been effectively buried on all but a theoretical level throughout the course of graduate school and becoming an adjunct instructor. I have a nonrenewable full-time instructorship for 1998–99. Despite the fact that this position seems a luxury after two years of part-time teaching, I am well aware that the finite status of a one-year instructorship is still a precarious position, and I plan to be active in the steering committee again next year. In fall 1996, I thought I was joining the committee to help tally surveys on health care concerns. In the process, I learned again the importance of acting and speaking, the importance of not being silent, not being silenced. As Adrienne Rich reminds us, "The politics worth having . . . demand that we delve still deeper" (1979, p. 193). The adjunct situation is a national problem that is not going away any time soon given that the number of adjuncts increased by nearly 70 percent from 1984 to 1994 (Lesko, 1995, pp. 22–23). Much still remains to be done, but the steering committee has brought about important changes. As Julie Haught concludes, the "Steering Committee allows part-timers a voice in the department, and it's a voice that has to be heard" (personal interview, January 13, 1998). Thanks to the steering committee, adjuncts in BGSU's English department now feel a sense of genuine empowerment.

Notes

1. Case studies and analyses of the Yale graduate students' collective action are documented in Cary Nelson's edited collection *Will Teach for Food* (1997).

2. It should be noted that quotes from past and present steering committee members in this article do not reflect whether they participated in the grievance action, and I have spoken only in general terms about that action to protect confidentiality of those concerned.

Works Cited

Berry, Ellen, professor, English Department, Bowling Green State University. (1998, January 13). Personal interview, Bowling Green, Ohio.

Bowling Green State University Faculty Senate Executive Committee minutes. (1990, February 20). Bowling Green, Ohio.

Calderonello, Alice, professor and co-chair, English Department, Bowling Green State University. (1998, January 13). Personal interview, Bowling Green, Ohio.

Haught, Julie, lecturer, English Department, Bowling Green State University. (1998, January 13). Personal interview, Bowling Green, Ohio.

Klein, R. (1988, August 22). *Memorandum to the steering committee*, pp. 1–2. Bowling Green, OH: Bowling Green State University.

Kolb, K. (1997). Adjuncts in academe: No place called home. *Profession 97*, 93–103. New York: Modern Language Association.

Lesko, P. D. (1995, November/December). Think the root of the 'adjunct problem' is funding? Think again. *The Adjunct Advocate*, 22–27.

Nelson, C. (Ed.). (1997a). *Manifesto of a tenured radical.* New York: New York University Press.

Nelson, C. (Ed.). (1997b). Between crisis and opportunity: The future of the academic workplace. In C. Nelson (Ed.), *Will teach for food: Academic labor in crisis* (pp. 3–31). Minneapolis: University of Minnesota Press.

Rich, A. (1979). Women and honor: Some notes on lying. In A. Rich, *On lies, secrets, and silence: Selected prose 1966–1978,* (pp. 185–194). New York: Norton.

Steering Committee Survey. (1990, March). English Department, Bowling Green State University, Bowling Green, Ohio.

Steering Committee. (1996, October 15). *An approach to the "no hire" rule.* Bowling Green, OH: Bowling Green State University.

III

Rethinking Non-Tenure-Track Faculty Roles and Rewards

Distance Education: Political and Professional Agency for Adjunct and Part-Time Faculty, and GTAs

Danielle DeVoss
Michigan Technological University, Houghton, Michigan

Dawn Hayden
Michigan Technological University, Houghton, Michigan

Cynthia L. Selfe
Michigan Technological University, Houghton, Michigan

Richard J. Selfe Jr.
Michigan Technological University, Houghton, Michigan

A Difficult Position

In November 1997, Dawn Hayden was teaching composition as a part-time, adjunct instructor in the department of English at a large university in the Southeast. The department chair, faced unexpectedly with the need to staff a new distance-education[1] course in advanced composition for the spring semester of 1998, asked Hayden to take on the new class. Hayden's initial response to the assignment illustrates some of the complex problems encountered by adjunct faculty, part-time teachers, and graduate teaching assistants (GTAs) who are asked to take on such courses in schools and institutions that are increasingly using distance education as a strategy for coping with constricted budgets, declining enrollments, and changing student populations:

Because I taught advanced composition in a traditional classroom, I really didn't think it would be difficult to translate my course into a distance-education offering. As a mere adjunct instructor and a new graduate, I was flattered to be asked to try this new teaching technology.

My graduate advisor had taught the first distance education course in composition at our university two years earlier, so I immediately went to her for advice. Her advice was unequivocal: Decline the opportunity! But the challenge of doing something new with my teaching, of pushing myself further, and of accumulating marketable experiences overrode her good advice. I accepted.

It is no coincidence, we believe, that adjunct faculty members, part-time teachers, and GTAs (especially those who teach composition) are the people who most often face these kinds of decisions about distance-education assignments—especially in connection with composition classes. According to a recent study sponsored by the Modern Language Association, adjunct and part-time teachers and GTAs, for example, teach between 52 percent of first-year composition courses at institutions granting four-year degrees and 95 percent of such courses at institutions granting advanced degrees (Laurence, 1997). In the nation's two-year colleges, part-time and adjunct faculty account for more than 50 percent of all faculty (Stock, 1998). Thus, such teachers constitute a larger proportion of the national teaching population for distance-education courses in composition than do tenure-track faculty.[2] In addition, some of these teachers have often acquired more technical expertise than conventionally-educated tenure-track faculty in English studies. In some cases, this is because their graduate education is more recent and, generally speaking, has exposed them to computer-supported instruction in their own careers as students. In other cases, these teachers may be more technologically oriented because they are more likely to teach in computer-supported first-year composition programs that require a knowledge of online literacies. Moreover, given the often precarious working conditions under which part-time and adjunct faculty and GTAs may labor, these instructors are typically more willing to take on risky assignments—such as distance-education teaching—to secure continued funding. Finally, given their strong commitment to undergraduate education and reflective practice, part-time and adjunct teachers and GTAs are often the teachers who most regularly update their repertoire of teaching skills, approaches, and pedagogical understandings to take advantage of the most effective innovations in teaching. As a result of all these factors, part-time and adjunct faculty and GTAs are increasingly faced with the complex set of problems that come along with distance education.

The decisions that grow out of such circumstances, to some extent, also reflect our discipline's uncritical acceptance of technology-rich instruction (Selfe, 1998) and the related pressure to offer our courses at a distance (see, for example, Gladiuex & Swail, 1999; Sherron & Boettcher, 1997). The reflective anecdote that Dawn Hayden began above and continues in more detail later in this chapter helps illustrate how problematic *and* exhilarating these choices can be. It also reveals many dilemmas that part-time and adjunct faculty and GTAs face at the personal, local, institutional, professional, and national levels.

In this chapter, we explore distance education as one important site in which English studies professionals can make productive and important change—particularly by increasing the power that part-time and adjunct workers (who comprise approximately 43 percent of the English studies workforce as indicated by Stock, 1998) can exert on some of the decision making and policymaking that shapes their professional lives. We begin by describing some of the challenges and drawbacks attendant to distance education in English studies departments within American higher education. We present Dawn Hayden's experience as a specific case study because it illustrates some problematic aspects of current distance-education practices. We follow by identifying specific strategies that can improve conditions for adjunct, part-time, and GTA stakeholders in distance-education literacy programs. We conclude by bringing several theoretical perspectives to bear on the potential of distance education.

The stakeholders who have written this chapter represent the parties we believe must form productive relationships if distance-education programs are to prove effective: Danielle DeVoss, a Ph.D. student at Michigan Technological University, currently holds a graduate teaching assistantship (GTA) and a graduate research assistantship (GRA) in the rhetoric and technical communication program. Dawn Hayden, also a Ph.D. student in the same program, was—at the time of the experience we describe—a part-time, adjunct instructor. Cynthia Selfe is a tenured, full professor and the chair of the humanities department at Michigan Technological University, as well as the immediate past chair of the Conference on College Composition and Communication. Richard Selfe is an adjunct professor and holds a professional technology related staff position in the same department. Together, we would like to build a case for attending critically to the development of, training for, and institutionalization of distance-education curricula. We are convinced that English studies professionals are in a particularly powerful position to influence such curricular decisions at local, institutional, and national levels if we act in concert and with keen attention to the power relations among all stakeholders in these endeavors.

We Can't Simply Say "No," Nor Can We Simply Keep Saying "Yes"

It is as true at the beginning of the new century as it was at the close of the last: English studies teachers cannot afford to ignore technology. We do not have the luxury of following Sven Birkert's advice to "refuse it" (1994, p. 229). Such an intellectual move is not only misguided at the end of the twentieth century, it is also dangerously shortsighted. Literacy instruction—at all levels of education—has become, over the last two decades, fundamentally and inextricably linked with technology. Teachers are now faced with students who *must* know how to communicate as informed thinkers and citizens in an increasingly technological world. Technology has become part of our responsibility as literacy educators—whether or not we want it to be so.

In part, we face this situation because the new generations of students who enter English studies classrooms have been raised to understand literacy instruction as a set of practices that take place *primarily* in electronic environments. Eighty-seven percent of high school students, for example, now write on computers by Grade 11 (Coley, Cradler, & Engel, 1997). Further, 89 percent of "teachers and the public" now believe that the Internet adds value to teaching and learning specifically because it "reduces the costs teachers spend on classroom activities" (*MCI Nationwide Poll,* 1998). Similarly, in American homes, 86 percent of parents are convinced that a computer is *the* one "most beneficial and effective product that they can buy to expand their children's opportunities" for education, future success, and economic prosperity (*Getting America's Students Ready,* 1996, p. x). Finally, in the American workplace, approximately 70 percent of jobs requiring a bachelor's degree or an advanced college degree now require the use of computers (Snyder, 1992).

These statistics, as Richard Selfe (1995) has noted, attest to the fact that the lives of college students today are, in many cases, both qualitatively and quantitatively different from those of students in past generations—and that these differences have direct implications for instruction in distance-learning environments. A few additional demographic facts about students help to make this point more clear:

◆ In 1991, fewer than half the states in the U.S. had more than 67 percent of their student population register as full-time. There are also several states where less than half of the students are considered full-time ("The Nation," 1993).

◆ Nationwide, the trend toward part-time status has been increasing—from 32.2 percent in 1970 to 41.3 percent in 1980 to 43.2 percent in 1990 (Snyder, 1992).

◆ Over the last several decades women have become an increasingly larger percentage of the student population: 1960 (37.6 percent); 1970 (41.2 percent); 1980 (51.4 percent); 1990 (54.5 percent). And, as a group, women consistently make up approximately 80 percent of part-time students. (Snyder, 1992).

◆ Older students are also an increasingly larger percentage of the student population ("The Nation," 1993).

◆ Almost half of the adult U.S. population engages in some part-time education or training, and part-time enrollments are growing three times faster than full-time enrollments (Gladieux & Swail, 1999).

As Selfe (1995) pointed out, the students described by these demographic snapshots often work full time; they have families; they are returning to school to retrain, and they are often unable to commute to schools during the hours that conventional instruction is available. As a result, a central strength of traditional education—the face-to-face interactive exchange in a physical classroom—is a significant burden to a growing number of students. To provide alternative approaches to education that better suit these students, a "range of unconventional providers have entered the postsecondary marketplace, offering instruction and credentials in new settings, on flexible schedules—and increasingly by way of distance-learning media" (Gladieux & Swail, 1999, p. 11). Such efforts have proved increasingly successful, as well. It has become clear, then, that unless English studies programs consider the option of distance education—unless we consider the alternative of delivering educational content in new ways that meet the needs of a new population of students—we risk losing touch with growing numbers of Americans who both want and need higher education.

However, if we cannot afford simply to ignore the converging forces of literacy instruction, technology, and distance education, nor can we afford simply to embrace such complex changes without concern. We cannot, for example, forget that the cultural formations of technology and literacy have become linked in ways that now exacerbate some educational and social inequities in the United States rather than addressing them productively (Selfe, 1998)—and that distance education threatens similar effects. As a recent report by the College Board (Gladieux & Swail, 1999) noted:

> Virtual universities will only help those who have the necessary equipment and experience to be comfortable with . . . technologies. While computers may seem ubiquitous in today's society, their distribution is highly stratified by socioeconomic class. . . . Online access is similarly stratified by income. And white households are twice as likely as black and Hispanic households to have access to computers and online services. . . . In fact, there is evidence that students with the greatest need get the least access. (p. 17)

Indeed, in the American school system as a whole and in the culture that this system reflects, computers continue to be distributed differentially along the related axes of race and socioeconomic status, and this distribution contributes to ongoing patterns of racism and to the continuation of poverty (Selfe, 1998).

It is a fact, for instance, that schools primarily serving students of color and poor students continue to have less access to computers, and access to less sophisticated computer equipment than do schools primarily serving more affluent students or white students. And, it is also a fact that schools primarily serving students of color and poor students continue to have *less* access to the Internet, *less* access to multimedia equipment, *less* access to CD-ROM equipment, *less* access to local area networks, and *less* access to videodisc technology than do schools primarily serving more affluent and white students (Coley, Cradler, & Engel, 1997).

In other words, the poorer students are less educated, and the less educated they are in this country—both of which conditions continue to be closely correlated with race—the less likely they are to have adequate access to sophisticated electronic literacy environments. Hence, the national effort to support literacy instruction within technological environments has *not* resulted in a better life, or more democratic opportunities, or an enriched educational experience for *all* Americans, as most of us might wish for. Rather, it has served to improve education only for *some* Americans. In a formulation that many teachers of English studies will feel most keenly, the effort to expand literacy instruction into technological environments has served to ensure the continuation not only of literacy but also of illiteracy and its reproductive relationship to poverty and racism.

Further, we cannot afford to ignore the relationship between the development of distance education and the uses and abuses of part-time and adjunct employment. Sir John Daniel (1997), vice-chancellor of the Open University in the United Kingdom, a vocal proponent of distance education, and an advocate of "mega-universities" claims that distance-learning institutions capable of handling 100,000 to 500,000 students per year, like the Open University, are a productive way of handling the crises facing education in the twenty-first century. In 1996, however, the Open University employed 7,376 part-time teachers and only 815 full-time teachers. Eighty-nine percent of the Open University's teaching staff had no common physical site at which to meet, talk, or learn from each other. Although Daniel celebrates the trend to reduce costs by hiring academic professionals on a part-time basis, it is also true that many of these institutions accomplish some of these reductions by requiring part-time teachers to work under difficult conditions that all but ensure ineffective education. Teachers at Turkey's Anadolu University, for example, are assigned an incredible 454 students per instructor per year (Daniel, 1997, p.14).

Other problems have also been identified with distance education. One recent report by the Institute for Higher Education Policy ("What's the Difference," 1999) reviewed research studies on distance education, indicating, that the drop-out rates for such classes exceed the drop-out rates for conventional classes by anywhere from 15 to 31 percent. In addition, the entrepreneurial momentum that characterizes many distance-education efforts often creates difficulties for professional teachers. As a recent article in the *Chronicle of Higher Education* indicated, the aggressive marketing of distance-education companies who now sell their wares to university communities is prompting many teachers to wonder whether such instruction has become "vendor-driven" rather than "educator-driven" (Blumenstyk, 1999, p. A29).

Finally, we cannot afford to embrace distance education and technology-based learning if, in the process, we lose sight of the humanistic values that form the foundation of our discipline's continued strength. In a 1995 article, "Surfing the Tsunami: Electronic Environments in the Writing Center," Richard Selfe described the technological tsunami that threatened to overcome some English studies professionals with a vague, but increasingly worrisome sense of dehumanization. Selfe outlined a case for integrating communication technologies into departmental and institutional structures in ways that counter such dehumanizing effects. Specifically, he argues for

◆ paying critical attention to the power relations characterizing technology-based education,

◆ maintaining a strong focus on individual students' experiences and the value of those experiences, and

◆ examining the importance of personal communicative relationships between all stakeholders in projects that involve technologically supported environments for literacy instruction.

With such challenges in front of us, it is clear that English studies, as a profession, faces a complicated set of changes associated with computer-based distance-education efforts. Changing student populations, workplace requirements, and cultural expectations seem to indicate that distance-education efforts will continue to expand. However, there are very good reasons to be skeptical of distance education and technologically based education—chief among them, the problems and inequities associated with technology-based literacy environments and the growing problems of staffing such learning environments in ways that assure humane and professional working conditions for teachers, especially part-time and adjunct faculty and GTAs.

Looking at distance education from these cultural and institutional vantage points, English studies professionals *should* feel conflicted. Whereas appealing reasons draw us to distance education, appalling hiring trends and working conditions discourage us from embracing it whole heartedly. Unfortunately, distance-education efforts are no less complex when undertaken on a more limited basis, within one department or institution.

The Complicated Case of Real Life: Dawn Hayden's Story of Distance Education

To be more fully understood, the issues associated with distance education are best examined in the context of the lived experiences of educators—particularly those part-time teachers, adjunct faculty, and GTAs so often assigned to develop and teach these courses. And so we continue Dawn Hayden's story:

It was still early in the fall term. My department chair told me that the distance education department would contact me and a series of training sessions would be arranged. Before I realized it, Thanksgiving break came and went, and soon final exams were upon us; the semester was over and I had heard nothing from the distance education department. With Christmas break on the horizon, I began to worry a bit about how I would handle teaching in this new environment. I called the distance education department and explained my situation. The secretary told me to call the instructional technology department and to speak with the director. So I did. The director of instructional technology had never heard of me and had no idea that I was scheduled to teach a class in a few weeks. She informed me that I had missed all of the training sessions. She suggested that I stop by her office and pick up a handbook created specifically for distance-education teachers. And so began my introduction to teaching on television.

At this point, my knowledge of teaching on television consisted of one major piece of advice from the coordinator of instructional technology: "Anything you do in your traditional classroom, can be done in the distance-education class." I was offered a second piece of advice when I sought feedback about the face-to-face course from students in the advanced composition course I taught in the fall. We talked about what they liked, what worked and what didn't work. I also asked students about distance education courses: Did they like them? What worked and what didn't and why? I explained that I was planning to teach the same course through distance education the next semester. One student shook his head and said, "Miss Hayden, it isn't going to work." Armed with this additional piece of advice, I took a deep breath, sat down, and planned my course, incorporating traditional teaching tools I used in my face-to-face classrooms. I created a syllaweb, an electronic discussion list, and a variety of online writing assignments.

When the night came for the class to begin, I was more nervous than I had ever been before. The classroom looked more like an auditorium than any classroom I had ever taught in. I had to sit up on a stage behind a desk. At least fifteen feet away from the nearest row of student seats, I was surrounded by television monitors. I squinted into hot, bright lights and a huge television screen, trying to look at the students. Students, sitting in rows at long tables, contended with large, antique microphones. When I tried to look directly at my students, it was as if I were teaching to myself. As the distant sites finally began to check in with the technician, I had another unpleasant surprise. Rather than the original ten sites that I had expected and the thirty-three students I had agreed to, I now had twenty-three sites and fifty-three students, well over the twenty-three-student maximum enrollment for composition courses at the university. And, the six students who were registered to attend at my site had magically turned into twelve.

Later I learned that another professor was also teaching advanced composition via distance education, and he was teaching his course entirely online. Some of his students were sitting in my class, some of my students were online in his class. His students had my textbooks, and my students had his textbooks. Two distance-education advanced composition courses were being offered; both had the same section number for the university site, and were scheduled to meet at the same time in the same classroom. It was an administrative disaster. It took me over an hour of class time that night just to figure out what had happened. This type of administrative confusion was a continuing trend throughout my distance-education teaching experiences: It would always take me an inordinately long time to address course "business."

The course business took so long to accomplish, in part, because of the technology the students and I had available for our use. We had one-way video and two-way audio. This meant that students at distant sites could see and hear me. The students at my site and I could hear, but not see, them. Much to my surprise, and contradictory to what I had been told by the instructional technology staff, many students had access neither to e-mail nor to a computer. All of my plans for creating outside discussions via e-mail, electronic discussion lists, netforums, and so on, were thwarted.

I was confined to my chair at the front of the classroom with the camera generally focused on me. The technicians I worked with were either unable or unwilling to have the camera follow me around the classroom, so there I sat—the talking head of advanced composition. I experienced a range of emotions while teaching that class—usually frustration, but occasionally exhilaration. I was stubborn and determined to provide my students with the best possible distance-education learning experience despite the inappropriate technology I was forced to use. My teaching mission became how best to "connect" the onsite students and myself with students we could hear but not see.

Over the last year or so I have had the opportunity to review some of the tapes of that class. After hours of viewing course videos and reviewing forty-five pages of notes, I am able to make these observations:

◆ Four weeks into the course, I was still not sure of the exact number of students and sites participating in my course.

◆ I repeated myself often. The "normal" business of class that might take five minutes at the beginning of a one-site, onsite class takes more than twice that amount of time at a distance.

◆ I asked an average of twelve times during each of the five classes I reviewed: "Is that clear?" or "Does everyone understand what I'm talking about?"

◆ None of the people on camera—not my teaching assistant, my guest lecturers, nor me—looked directly at the camera. This is rather disorienting for viewers who are positioned more as voyeurs watching the course being taught than participants in the learning experience.

◆ Students at my site did not make eye contact with me. Instead, they watched one of several television monitors placed around the classroom. So when I looked out into my "classroom," I saw faces turned away from me. This was disconcerting and left me feeling again as if I were teaching myself.

◆ When students spoke into the microphone, they generally didn't identify themselves. The effect on viewers is that of hearing "disembodied" voices floating out of the air. It was disorienting and disruptive to my thought process. I couldn't see someone raise her hand to ask a question, so students were forced to interrupt me when they had to ask questions.

◆ In three later tapes, I seemed to be more relaxed and was able to laugh and joke with my onsite students. Yet, it still seemed difficult to relate to or with students at the distant sites. I referred to them on two occasions as "the folks out there in TV land." This seems to exaggerate the "us" (those of us at the main site) and "them" (those at other sites) dichotomy I already felt.

◆ For the most part, I was the kind of teacher I like the least: a "talking head." Not being able to move around the classroom and not having the camera pan in on the students forced me to be the focus of the camera lens.

◆ One major difficulty frequently mentioned by students from the distant sites was the length of time it took for them to receive their papers and comments from me. The administrative system mailed student papers to the distance education department on campus, which, in turn, logged them and then sent them via interoffice mail to my department. It could take anywhere from three to seven days for me to *receive* a paper. If I were able to review the paper immediately upon receipt (which wasn't always feasible), log it in, and return it, it would still be another three to seven days before the student received my comments. On average, this meant that it took anywhere from six to fourteen days from the time a student handed in her work to the time it was returned to her. (That is, of course, if nothing got lost, sent to the wrong site, or misplaced.)

◆ Frequently technology interfered with the teaching of the course. On one occasion we lost an entire site because of a thunderstorm. I was scheduled to conference with the site and was unable to do so during that class period. This forced the students to communicate with me either via e-mail or through a long-distance phone call. That same evening at another site, students had to try out several microphones before they could find one that worked. This meant that when I asked them to respond to me, they were unable to do so, and I assumed that they were not present. It was not until an hour into the class that they were able to communicate with me.

◆ Toward the end of the course (the eleventh week) I was able to conduct video conferences with groups at different sites. I did this in much the same manner as I would in a traditional classroom. I photocopied my comments on student essays. The students had their essays with them, and we conducted a discussion of my comments and student questions. I could not see the students' faces, but they could see mine. I asked them direct questions and they offered direct responses to me. I knew who I was talking to at which site because I addressed the students on an individual basis. I also called on group members to respond to the questions I had regarding a particular essay, and members, as a group, had the opportunity to conduct a discussion with me.

Understanding that "distributional changes are changes in the relative power of social forces as a consequence of the change in the mode of communication" (Deibert, 1998, p. 67), allows me to account for the loss of control I experienced when trying to teach a writing course via distance education. Outside of the immediate environment, I could no longer control who spoke or when. In one respect, I was forced to respond to my students on their terms, when they wanted me to. This shift of control left me feeling frustrated and unsure of myself as a teacher. Looking back through notes and transcripts from the course, it seems that the majority of my interchanges with my distance-education students were chaotic. Disembodied voices frequently questioned all aspects of the course—assignments, due dates, grading policies—and I frantically tried to respond to each and every question. I repeated myself over and over again, wasting time in inefficient efforts to overcome distances that were exaggerated by the use of this technology.

It is clear that some distance-education systems provide us with a rich medium of exploration and study (see, for example, Rodrigues, 1999). But the creation of a writing community is a vital component of successful composition teaching. Personally, I am happiest with my teaching when I'm interacting directly with students, when I can respond not only to their voices but also to their quizzical glances and blank stares. I agree with Anson (1999) that "for the most part the new capacities conferred by electronic means have not enhanced the awareness that teaching might be conceived as something other than one teacher before a classroom of students" (p. 262).

The medium of information transmission had changed, and the message was affected. I am convinced that although the distance-education environment encourages the "teaching head" syndrome, with some hard work it can be avoided when it is inappropriate.

If we agree with O'Donnell (1996) that "the ability of the institution to survive depend[s] on its ability to adapt itself to the new technological environment" (p. 46), then it is imperative that we learn how to make use of distance-education learning environments. We must learn how to manipulate them to meet our pedagogical goals. If we do not take an active and questioning look at our goals and motivations for teaching within a distance-education system, we run the risk of missing the chance to develop this medium in a way that can constructively affect education as a whole.

In Terms of Agency

So how can English studies professionals participate in the project we identified earlier in this paper—making distance education a site from which to enact productive change in the power relations between part-time, adjunct, and graduate-student teachers and the individuals (tenure-track faculty, department and university administrators, technology staff members, etc.) who participate in decision making and policymaking in higher education? What specific strategies might help improve conditions for adjunct, part-time, and GTA stakeholders in distance-education literacy programs?

Certainly, we know that cultural, social, economic, and political pressures to explore distance-education opportunities will *not* diminish in the foreseeable future (see, for example, Gladieux & Swail, 1999; Sherron & Boettcher, 1997). More traditional colleges and universities will continue to be faced with declining residential enrollments and will push for reaching student populations by distance education. This means that English departments and composition programs will be asked to develop and deliver courses and programs in a distance-education format. Such a recognition also means that department chairs—who depend on administrative goodwill and money to pay for departmental operations—will ask part-time and adjunct faculty and GTAs to take on such course assignments. Recognizing that part-time and adjunct faculty and GTAs are more likely than conventionally educated tenure-track faculty to have experienced teaching with technology, chairs will ask these faculty—inclined to take on the risk of such assignments given the precarious nature of their funding situation and their willingness to experiment—to accept such courses. Chairs will ask these versatile and effective teachers—

with their track records in a range and number of their course assignments, with their commitment to effective teaching, and with their focus on educational excellence—to become distance-education faculty. In sum, chairs will continue to recognize that part-time and adjunct faculty and GTAs have a clear stake in seeking new and marketable teaching skills in an increasingly competitive educational environment, and that these faculty are some of the most likely department members to do a responsible job in adapting instruction effectively to these new teaching environments.

Given these pragmatic realizations, how can we change the working conditions for adjunct and part-time faculty and GTAs who are asked to take on a distance-education assignment? What advice can we offer faculty who must choose between what could be difficult teaching circumstances and the opportunity to develop a new, marketable teaching expertise? What responsibilities can university administrators, department chairs, tenure-track faculty colleagues, and technical staff members take on in support of such efforts?

To begin, we suggest that departments of English and writing programs consider the strategy of forming teams of stakeholders to work on distance-education issues, and that these teams involve as diverse a membership as possible: part-time and adjunct faculty, GTAs, tenure-track faculty, departmental and university administrators, and technical staff members. This suggestion rests, in part, on theoretically and practically based recognition and respect for understandings that a range of informed social agents can bring to bear on educational issues like those surrounding distance education. As Giddens points out, social institutions do not simply "work 'behind the backs' of social actors who produce and reproduce them" (1979, p. 71); rather, all social agents have a deep and penetrating understanding of the local social situations in which they work—every competent member of every society knows a great deal about the institutions in that society; furthermore, the nature of such knowledge is not simply "incidental to the operation of society, but is necessarily involved in it" (p. 71).

If we recognize the potential of this kind of locally situated knowledge, we also recognize that part-time and adjunct faculty and GTAs have much to contribute to distance-education efforts: knowledge of how specific schools, districts, colleges, and universities might better fulfill their missions through distance-education efforts; knowledge of particular families, communities, and cultures that distance-education efforts might help institutions of higher education reach; understandings of individual students, teachers, administrators, board members, politicians, and parents whose lives are affected by distance-education programs; knowledge of the working conditions distance-education efforts generate.

This kind of "situated knowledge" (Haraway, 1995, p. 175), we speculate, is multiplied by the involvement of different stakeholders in any distance-education effort, and promises to offer a "more adequate, richer, better account" (p. 178) of the complex social formations associated with computer-based learning environments. Although we recognize that all situated perspectives are also partial—Haraway calls this kind of understanding a "coyote" way of knowing (p. 189)—we suggest that the practice of involving as many stakeholders as possible in discussions of distance-education issues can help us avoid the trap of offering overly simple answers to the complex challenges of distance education.

It is true that this way of understanding social agents and their local knowledge has certain intellectual implications—especially for this chapter and our purpose in writing. If we respect the real nature of coyote knowledge, we understand that the perspectives of specific social agents, no matter how valuable and accurate from any one particular vantage point, are locally situated, and, thus, limited and partial. Hence, in the remainder of this section, we caution that our own advice is also contingent and tactical, and based on a limited understanding of local conditions.

In the sections that follow, we offer three different kinds of strategies that may prove useful to colleagues: strategies that can be enacted by individual teachers, strategies that can be enacted within the context of specific distance-education programs, and strategies that can be enacted within the context of national professional organizations. The effectiveness of these strategies and their usefulness and value to individuals will, of course, depend, on the conditions and circumstances under which those involved labor, the particular constraints they encounter within their departments and institutions, the particular distance-education efforts in which they are involved, and the professional organizations with which they are connected, among other factors. We also realize that the approaches we are about to suggest to teachers, technicians, and administrators entail additional work, but we think that the difficulties Dawn Hayden faced and the technological and demographic forces influencing English studies illustrate why this kind of multilevel involvement at local, institutional, and national levels is so necessary.

Strategies for Individual Teachers: "Questioning Builds a Way"

Perhaps the most useful strategy we can suggest to teachers—especially part-time and adjunct faculty and GTAs making decisions about distance-education courses—is that of asking questions. As Martin Heidegger noted, "questioning builds a way" (1997, p. 1) of structuring the most appropriate relationship between humans and the technological environments within which they have come to understand the world and function. Hence, before, during, and after undertaking a distance-education assignment, we suggest that teachers engage themselves and other distance-education stakeholders (e.g., students; administrators; staff members; other part-time and adjunct faculty, and GTAs who have taught distance-education courses) in intensive questioning. Administrators, technical staff members, and other faculty can assist in this effort by setting up social mechanisms for listening—making every attempt to pay attention to the pedagogical, fiscal, and logistical needs and visions of teachers for both humanistic and business-related reasons.

If we all listen well enough, answer and ask enough important questions in connection to distance-education efforts, we can construct improved working conditions for teachers who engage in such efforts. And, simply put, it is only through this collective effort to improve working conditions that we have a chance of creating *sustainable* distance-education programs that attract high-quality faculty.

Many of the questions we suggest below are designed to identify the departmental and institutional support structures already in place for distance-education classes. Because few institutions are ahead of the distance-education curve, however, teachers can expect to contact several administrators, technical staff members, and advisors before they are able to obtain accurate information and responses to these questions. Indeed, the level of difficulty or ease teachers encounter in getting answers to these queries is one indication of a department's and institution's preparedness for dealing with distance-education issues.

♦ Does the responsibility for distance-education courses rest with a home department or with a unit elsewhere in the university (e.g., continuing education, distance education)?

♦ Who is the primary administrative contact person for various kinds of distance-education questions (e.g., student registration, immediate and long-term technical problems, professional preparation, student complaints)?

♦ In what ways are distance-education courses comparable to more conventional courses on the campus (e.g., numbers of students, location, logistics, scheduling, teaching support)?

♦ How much does a distance-education course pay? How does this rate of pay compare with that of a conventional course? Is additional pay provided for developing instructional materials? Who will own the copyright of those materials or control their use after the class has ended?

♦ Will this work be considered part of a departmental teaching load or will it be an overload class?

♦ What type of training and support is available on campus for less-experienced distance-education instructors (e.g., access to a knowledgeable technician as the class is being planned and taught, access to a center for teaching support that will help in assessment and instructional improvement efforts, access to experienced teachers who will allow others to review their syllabi and to observe their classes)?

♦ What type of distance-education technologies are available for the course (e.g., two-way interactive video, one-way video, two-way audio, e-mail, the World Wide Web, asynchronous or synchronous conferencing systems, integrated Web-based grading and instructional systems)?

◆ How many sites will be involved in the instruction effort (e.g., an on-campus classroom, remote sites)?

◆ How many students will be on site, off site, at each site? Does this number match the class-size policy of the department for conventional classes?

◆ Can distance-education teachers get access to student academic profiles before the class begins?

◆ What are the prerequisites for the course (e.g., a knowledge of the school's distance-education system, a basic knowledge of computer-based communication strategies, previous course work, some face-to-face meetings), and who checks to see that the students have met them?

◆ How will assignments, materials, and textbooks be provided to students (e.g., online, postal mail, Federal Express)? How will students' work be submitted to instructors? How quickly can work be turned around?

◆ If quizzes or tests are given, are proctors required and made available at each site?

◆ How will distance students be able to contact instructors if they have specific questions?

This list of questions, of course, is a limited one and one that teachers should add to using a knowledge of their own local conditions. In addition, as we have suggested, the most powerful approaches to answering these questions will involve a multiplicity of perspectives. If departments and institutions can assemble a diverse team of individuals to address distance-education issues (e.g., adjunct, part-time, GTA, and tenure-track teachers who may have taught distance-education courses; administrators involved in such efforts; staff members who support such efforts), teachers who are asked to take on such courses have access to multiple sources of local understandings.

Strategies for Departments and Institutions: Working for the Involvement of Multiple Stakeholders

At the level of programs, departments, and institutions, a productive engagement with distance-education issues must allow for wide variations in social, political, economic, and ideological goals, as well as wide variations in the involvement of teachers, students, administrators, citizens, and communities. In recognition of this fact, we provide the following suggestions:

- Programs, departments, and campuses that undertake distance-education efforts constitute teams of stakeholders to administer and advise on such programs—with the purpose of assembling multiple perspectives on distance-education issues. Among the possible members for such teams, consider students, faculty of various ranks and status, department or unit administrators, technical staff members, and parents. Among the tasks that such groups might productively adopt are the following: creating a set of scheduling priorities that will provide adequate online access for faculty, classes, individual students, and technical staff members (all of whom have differing needs and goals for distance-education facilities and systems); choosing digital systems that allow for important pedagogical values; identifying budgetary priorities that balance expenditures for many competing pedagogical approaches; setting an acceptable level for access; deciding on professional development opportunities that can lead to excellent teaching; and working with libraries, community centers, and other public places to provide for low-cost access to computers for citizens who do not have direct access to technology.

- Campuses that employ a significant proportion of part-time and adjunct faculty and GTAs to teach distance-education courses should involve a similar ratio of such individuals in decision-making and policymaking groups. Hence, if 60 percent of distance-education courses are taught by part-time or adjunct faculty, 60 percent of the representation on committees and groups charged with setting distance-education policy (especially policies about working conditions) and direction should also come from this group.

- In campuswide distance-education committees, documents, and policies, institutions should avoid establishing one, overly narrow, official version of distance education, or a version that privileges only one, narrow version of online literacy. The most robust and sustainable distance-education efforts will include the input of various disciplines, stakeholders, and campus units, and multiple forms of literacy practices and values. Dawn Hayden's experience—in which she had to apply simplistic broadcast-learning technologies to the teaching of content typically presented in robust, interactive, and collaborative literacy environments—provides a cautionary tale in this regard.

◆ Because all distance-education efforts involve the practice of technologically supported literacies, institutions and departments need to involve teachers of English, composition, and language arts at all levels. Such professionals can identify practical ways of applying current scholarship and research on literacy to the work done in distance-education facilities and programs.

Strategies for the Profession: Paying Attention to the Effects of Distance Education

We have maintained throughout this chapter that the complex social formation of distance education can provide a site from which English studies professionals can make productive change. More specifically, for the purposes of this collection, we argue that distance education is a site from which we can begin to address working conditions for adjunct and part-time faculty and GTAs. Such efforts, however, cannot be undertaken by any single set of players—and certainly not by adjunct and part-time faculty and GTAs alone. The power relations associated with such appointments often places contingent faculty at a distinct disadvantage in arguing for new systems, new policies, new training programs, and new distance-education pedagogies.

Hence, we also maintain that it is the responsibility of *all* English studies professionals to take some responsibility for getting national organizations to attend to distance-education issues. In this section, we conclude by providing the following suggestions for professional action:

◆ Create guidelines and standards for the working conditions of English studies professionals employed in distance-education environments, or update existing documents to take the new situations generated by distance-education efforts into account. Such documents—the *Guidelines for the Workload of College English Teachers* (NCTE, 1987), the *ADE Guidelines for Class Size and Workload for College and University Teachers of English* (MLA, 1980), or *Statement of Principles and Standards for the Postsecondary Teaching of Writing* (Conference on College Composition and Communication, 1989)—for instance, could help set reasonable professional standards for class size or course loads in distance-education efforts; appropriate levels or routes of involvement for part-time and adjunct faculty and GTAs in such efforts;

and methods of assessing distance-education resources, pedagogical approaches, and student performance. Such documents might also assist departmental and program administrators as they argue for increased resources to support distance-education programs.

◆ Recognize that if written language and literacy practices are our professional business, so is technology and distance-education efforts. This recognition demands a series of carefully considered and visible professional stands on a range of distance-education issues now under debate in this country: for example, on issues of access to distance-education technology and electronic literacy environments, on issues of funding for distance education programs in English studies, on issues of assessment in distance-education efforts, and on issues associated with the ownership of distance-education materials (e.g., syllabi, videotapes, Web sites, online transcripts of class discussions). We need to engage in much more of this kind of professional activism, and more consistently.

◆ Conduct additional research and scholarship focused on English studies classes taught in distance-education formats and programs. A recent report by the Institute for Higher Education Policy ("What's the Difference," 1999), for example, indicates that current research has a number of shortcomings, among them: emphasizing "student outcomes for individual courses rather than for a total academic program," taking into account "differences among students" and accounting for their individual learning styles, explaining the higher drop-out rates associated with distance learning, and identifying the impact of individual technologies rather than the interaction of multiple technologies (pp. 23–28). We would also benefit from additional examinations of the systems and cultural formations associated with distance-education, and how such formations shape the working conditions of various English studies professionals—among them, part-time and adjunct faculty and GTAs. In addition, we would benefit from historical examinations of the patterns (e.g., staffing, salaries, course loads, class sizes, attrition rates, performance assessments) established thus far in distance-education programs.

◆ Help all English studies teachers—including part-time and adjunct faculty and GTAs—get useful professional development in both preservice and inservice venues and support for distance-education efforts when they choose to undertake such activities.

◆ Make sure that we do not teach English studies professionals simply to participate in distance-education efforts; but rather, to pay attention to the issues that result from (and contribute to) such efforts, by using the tools of technology criticism, social theory, and computer studies to create an informed profession and to help individuals develop their own critical consciousness about distance education and technology use.

Back to the Beginning

In concluding this chapter, we return to the potential of distance-education programs as a site for productive social action. Such programs may well prove to be environments within which we can begin to think carefully about and address the working conditions of part-time and adjunct faculty and GTAs. At this point in time, distance-education programs are relatively young and their structuring within complex university and social formations has just begun. Money and resources are flowing into these programs—although such resources are not always used in the ways we might like to see. We may be able to take advantage of this unsettled, if contested, terrain to affect productive change in these programs by targeting improved working conditions for part-time and adjunct faculty and GTAs as an initial goal.

And this project, in turn, may yield for the profession of English studies a richer sense of the potential of distance education. We do not remember often enough how to value the diversity and the contributions that adjunct and part-time faculty and GTAs add to English studies and composition programs. But, as Latour (1996) reminded us, stories *always* lack richness and accuracy when they are told from a single perspective. In the case of distance-education efforts, the multiple perspectives that part-time and adjunct faculty and GTAs can contribute to our understanding may allow us to assemble a more robust and accurate understanding of distance learning as a social formation. And, if we can pay respectful attention to these perspectives, we may be able to imagine a future for distance education of which we can all be proud.

Notes

1. By distance education, in general, we refer to instruction that is delivered to learners in locations geographically remote or dispersed from

the environments a teacher inhabits. More specifically, in this paper, we refer to computer-supported distance education—instruction delivered online via e-mail, bulletin boards, MOOs and MUDs, the World Wide Web, or other electronic literacy environments.

2. The growth of part-time and adjunct faculty populations in higher education is staggering. In 1960–61, part-time and adjunct faculty accounted for 35 percent of all faculty in higher education; in 1998, the total had grown to 43–44 percent.

Works Cited

ADE guidelines for class size and workload for college and university teachers of English: A statement of policy by the Association of Departments of English. (1980). New York: Association of Departments of English.

Anson, C. M. (1999, January). Distant voices: Teaching writing in a culture of technology. *College English, 61(3),* 261–280.

Birkerts, S. (1994). *The Gutenberg elegies: The fate of reading in an electronic age.* New York: Fawcett Columbine.

Blumenstyk, G. (1999, April 9). The marketing intensifies in distance learning: Some educators value the options, others fear vendors set the agenda. *The Chronicle of Higher Education, 45(31),* A27–28, A30.

CCCC Executive Committee. (1989, October). Statement of principles and standards for the postsecondary teaching of writing. *College Composition and Communication, 40(3),* 329–336.

Coley, R. J., Crandler, J., &. Engel, P. (1997). *Computers and classrooms: The status of technology in U.S. schools.* Princeton, NJ: Educational Testing Service, Policy Information Center.

Daniel, J. S. (1997, July–August). Why universities need technology strategies. *Change, 29(4),* 10–17.

Deibert, R. J. (1997). *Parchment, printing, and hypermedia: Communication and world order transformation.* New York: Columbia University Press.

Getting America's students ready for the 21st century: Meeting the technology literacy challenge. A report to the nation on technology and education. (1996). Washington, DC: U.S. Department of Education.

Giddens, A. (1979). *Central problems in social theory: Action, structure and contradiction in social analysis.* Berkeley: University of California Press.

Gladieux, L. E., & Swail, W. S. (1999). *The virtual university and educational opportunity: Issues of equity and access for the next generation.* A Policy Perspectives Report from the College Board. Washington, DC: College Board.

Haraway, D. (1995). Situated knowledges: The science question in feminism and the privilege of partial perspective. In A. Feenberg and A. Hannay (Eds.), *Technology and the politics of knowledge* (pp. 175–194). Bloomington, IN: Indiana University Press.

Heidegger, M. (1977). *The question concerning technology.* New York: Harper & Row.

Latour, B. (1996). *ARAMIS or, the love of technology.* (C. Porter, trans.). Cambridge, MA: Harvard University Press.

Laurence, D. (1997, September 26). *Data on staffing in undergraduate English programs, Fall 1995.* Presentation at the Conference on the Growing Use of Part-Time and Adjunct Faculty in Higher Education, Washington, DC.

MCI nationwide poll on Internet in education. (1998). Washington, DC: MCI.

The nation: Educational statistics. (1993). *The Chronicle of Higher Education, XL* (Almanac Issue), 7–46.

National Council of Teachers of English. *Guidelines for the workload of college English teachers.* (1987) Urbana, IL: Author.

O'Donnell, J. (1996). The pragmatics of the new: Trithemius, McLuhan, Cassiodorus. In G. Nunberg (Ed.), *The future of the book.* Berkeley: University of California Press.

Phipps, R., & Merisotis, J. (1999). *What's the difference: A review of contemporary research on the effectiveness of distance learning in higher education.* Washington, DC: The Institute for Higher Education Policy.

Rodrigues, D. (1999). Models of distance education for composition: The role of video conferencing. *Kairos, 3(2).* [On-line]. Available at <http://english.ttu.edu/kairos/3.2/index_f.html>.

Selfe, C. L. (1998, May). CCCC chair's letter. *College Composition and Communication, 50(2),* 300–304.

Selfe, R. (1995). Surfing the tsunami: Electronic environments in the writing center. *Computers and Composition, 12(3)*, 311–322.

Sherron, G. T., & Boettcher, J. V. (1997). *Distance learning: The shift to interactivity* (CAUSE Professional Paper Series #17). Boulder, CO: CAUSE.

Snyder, T. D. (Ed.). (1992). *Digest of education statistics, 1992*. Washington, DC: U.S. Department of Health, Education, and Welfare. Education Division, National Center for Education Statistics.

Stock, Patricia Lambert. (1998, February). Untitled article in Forum: Newsletter of the Non-Tenure-Track Faculty Special Interest Group. *College Composition and Communication, 49(1)*, A12–A13.

CHAPTER THIRTEEN

The Scholarship of Teaching: Contributions from Contingent Faculty

PATRICIA LAMBERT STOCK
Michigan State University, East Lansing

AMANDA BROWN
Syracuse University, Syracuse, New York

DAVID FRANKE
SUNY Cortland, Cortland, New York

JOHN STARKWEATHER
Onondaga Community College, Syracuse, New York

A metalogue is a conversation about some problematic subject. This conversation should be such that not only do the participants discuss the problem but the structure of the conversation as a whole is also relevant to the same subject.

—GREGORY BATESON, *Steps toward an Ecology of Mind*

Ten years ago, with the release of *Scholarship Reconsidered: Priorities of the Professoriate*, Ernest Boyer and his associates in the Carnegie Foundation for the Advancement of Teaching challenged those of us in higher education to reconsider and expand the definition of scholarship that currently drives our work. Arguing that higher education in America can remain vital only if it develops a more creative view of the work of the professoriate, Boyer urged us "to move beyond the old 'teaching versus research debate,'" and to reconsider scholarship in terms of four separate, but overlapping kinds of academic work: the scholarship of discovery (work that adds to human knowledge and to the intellectual life of the academy), the scholarship of integration (work that makes connections between and among knowledge developed within disciplinary communities and that places disciplinary knowledge in broader contexts), the scholarship of application (work that emerges when academics' theories and practices interanimate one another), and the scholarship of teaching (work that transmits, transforms, and extends knowledge to others, some of whom may themselves become scholars).[1]

Emerging as it did amid a sea of reports finding serious fault with the quality of university-level teaching in America, it is not surprising that educators in colleges, universities, and professional associations began to address Boyer's challenge in discussions of the scholarship of teaching.[2] The American Association of Higher Education took up the challenge in the context of discussions of educational reform, faculty roles and rewards, and more recently in discussions of new career paths in higher education. In an early publication emerging from these discussions, *The Teaching Portfolio: Capturing the Scholarship of Teaching* (1991), Russell Edgerton, Patricia Hutchings, and Kathleen Quinlan note the authority that Boyer's theoretical construct—the scholarship of teaching—contributes to their interest in improving the quality of teaching in higher education. Grounding their practical concerns in Boyer's concept, they write:

> At bottom, the concept [of a scholarship of teaching] entails a view that teaching, like other scholarly activities . . . relies on a base of expertise, a "scholarly knowing" that needs to and can be identified, made public, and evaluated; a scholarship that faculty themselves must be responsible for monitoring. (p. 1)

To demonstrate the existence of a base of expertise about teaching, Edgerton, Hutchings, and Quinlan draw readers' attention to work that Lee Shulman, professor of education and psychology at Stanford University and Boyer's successor as president of the Carnegie Foundation for the Advancement of Teaching, has conducted with colleagues in Stanford University's

Teacher Assessment Project. In a body of empirical studies of effective teachers' practice and in the theory of pedagogy that Shulman has built upon those studies, Edgerton, Hutchings, and Quinlan find a knowledge base about teaching that they require.[3] They find particularly generative Shulman's concept of *a pedagogy of substance* (pedagogy that transforms disciplinary knowledge into student understandings) because it provides means for identifying and assessing the different shapes that effective teaching takes when different teachers teach the subject matter of different disciplines to different students in different settings.[4]

To demonstrate that it is possible for teachers to represent their work to one another and for peers to evaluate the quality of one another's teaching based on representations of that teaching, Edgerton, Hutchings, and Quinlan draw readers' attention to the work of the Canadian Association of University Teachers and Peter Seldin, professor of management at Pace University. Based on these bodies of work, they identify the teaching portfolio as a means by which teachers may represent their work for peer review.[5] What attracts Edgerton, Hutchings, and Quinlan to the teaching portfolio is its potential to "capture the complexities of teaching"; to "place responsibility for evaluating teaching in the hands of faculty"; to prompt more reflective teaching practice and the improvement of teaching; and to "foster a culture of teaching and a new discourse about it" (1991, pp. 4–6).

Since publication of *Scholarship Reconsidered* and *The Teaching Portfolio: Capturing the Scholarship of Teaching*, a steadily growing number of colleges and universities have begun to require faculty in tenure-eligible roles to include among the materials they submit for reappointment, tenure, and promotion evidence of their scholarship of teaching, more often than not in the form of teaching portfolios, composed sometimes of specified documents (e.g., a statement of a philosophy of teaching, sample syllabi, student evaluations) and sometimes of self-selected ones. While such a requirement sends an important message— the academy values the scholarship of teaching as well as what Boyer calls the scholarship of discovery—it too-often positions preparation and discussion of teaching portfolios exclusively within the practices and discourse of evaluation.

When academics publish for critical review what Boyer calls contributions to the scholarship of discovery, works composed to advance or enrich understanding of unresolved or emerging questions in their fields of study, the focus of their attention is usually on problematic issues in their fields of study. By contrast, however, when faculty submit teaching portfolios to committees entrusted with their reappointment, tenure, and promotion, they tend to illustrate the ways in which their teaching fulfills generally held concepts of already-valued teaching practices. From a rhetorical perspective—in light of the audience, purpose, and occasion for the composition of these portfolios—this is not surprising.

Teaching portfolios designed to explore the problematics of teaching rather than display the achievements of teachers, while few and far between, do exist and are read for the insights into teaching that they provide, rather than for displays of teaching accomplishments, by colleagues who are invested in and grappling with the teaching projects and issues explored in those portfolios. Our point is not that faculty who present their contributions to the scholarship of discovery do not also offer the best examples of that work for review. Rather, our point is that the contexts within which and the purposes for which teaching portfolios are typically read and evaluated differ from those in which articles and books understood to be contributions to the scholarship of discovery are read and criticized. Rarely are teaching portfolios read as contributions to a scholarly community's investigation of a perplexing problem, as contributions that push, extend, even challenge a body of existing and shared discourse and discursive practices.[6] More often, portfolios are read as artifactual evidence of individual teachers' achievements in transmitting an already-existing body of knowledge in practices and courses that readers will find familiar. In other words, they are rarely read as teaching discoveries, which leads us to question whether Boyer's distinguishing the scholarships of discovery, integration, application, and teaching from one another for the purposes of drawing attention to scholarship's many faces and emphases may be read as leaving grounds for the "old 'teaching versus research' debate" still in place.

If teaching portfolios are to figure as more than a body of portraits of effective teaching; if they are to figure as contributions to a scholarship of teaching, as Edgerton, Hutchings, and Quinlan suggest that they have potential to do, they will need to be composed and read as discoveries about teaching and the subjects taught, as evidence of the integration of new and familiar understandings of teaching and the subjects taught as well as scholarly applications of what is known about teaching particular subjects to particular students in particular times and places. In them, teacher-scholars working in communities (whether those teachers be connected in time and space by their responsibility for realizing a coherent curriculum with a particular group of students in a particular program, department, college, or university, or teachers connected across contexts by their responsibility for teaching a common course such as Introductory Composition) will need to find insights into practices, issues, and questions that teaching communities have defined as problematic about teaching the subject(s) they teach to the students they teach under the circumstances in which they teach.

In the decade since publication of *The Teaching Portfolio* and widespread use of the portfolio as evidence of the scholarship of teaching, a demonstration of how teaching portfolios can and do figure as contributions to a discourse of teaching and to the improvement of teaching in a culture with a commonly agreed upon pedagogical project, remains unfulfilled.[7] Why? Perhaps it is because faculty in programs and departments in which a discourse of teaching exists and in which teaching portfolios are read and valued for the quality of their contributions to that discourse, for the scholarship of discoveries about teaching that they make public—while they do exist—are few and far between. Perhaps it is because a disproportionate number of those few and far between communities are ones in fields such as composition studies, fields in which large numbers of part-time and adjunct faculty have been hired to fulfill the community's teaching responsibilities. And perhaps it is because it is not customary for scholars and administrators in higher education to look to contingent faculty for guidance in the development of new bodies of scholarship, even—as in this case—when it makes sense to do so.

In an effort to address this gap, we draw readers' attention to a program whose declared purpose has been to form a culture of teaching, a writing program in which part-time and adjunct faculty have been supported and encouraged to develop a scholarship of teaching that is informed by theory and practice in the broader field of composition studies, a field originally called into being by the introductory composition course (often entitled Freshman English) that its practitioners were challenged to invent and teach.[8] We believe that programs such as this one have much to teach us about the potential of teaching portfolios "to capture the complexities of teaching," "to prompt more reflective teaching practice and the improvement of teaching," "to foster a culture of teaching and the development of a discourse about it" (Edgerton, Hutchings, Quinlan, pp. 4–6), and—we would add—to demonstrate that the scholarship of teaching is not one among several overlapping scholarships but a holistic scholarship of discovery, integration, application, and teaching, all at once, altogether.

Syracuse University Writing Program

Established in 1986 in accordance with a set of heuristic planning documents, the Syracuse University Writing Program was designed to enable its ten tenure-track faculty, approximately seventy professional writing instructors, and fifty graduate student teaching assistants enrolled in the Department of English to do two things collectively: (1) to construct the program's four-course studio writing curriculum and (2) to conduct inquiries into their teaching and their students' learning that would enable them continuously to assess and amend the program's planning documents, its curriculum, and their teaching practices.[9] In other words, from the outset, teachers in Syracuse's Writing Program have been about the business of developing a scholarship of teaching that would emerge from and inform their critical teaching practice simultaneously.

Among the activities in which teachers develop a scholarship of teaching are the following ones: Teachers meet in groups of ten to twelve in contractually required weekly gatherings to discuss matters arising in their current teaching; some meet in self-appointed groups to develop or revise one or another of the four studio writing courses that constitute the program's spiral curriculum; some write for or edit issues of *Reflections in Writing*, a program journal that publishes teachers' and, occasionally, students' research; some plan, organize, conduct workshops, or otherwise participate in one of the program's two annual miniconferences; some organize or participate in *Conversations in Composition,* colloquies of issues or authors of special interest to them; some co-plan and/or co-teach one or another studio writing course. All compose teaching portfolios.[10]

Early on, it was determined that if part-time and adjunct faculty in the Syracuse Writing Program were to be recognized as the professional writing instructors they had been entitled, they themselves would have to determine the standards for their teaching and be responsible for judging whether or not those standards were being fulfilled to their satisfaction. As a result, a process and practices for peer evaluation were developed by professional writing instructors in collaboration with program directors (see Lipson and Voorheis, this volume). Teaching portfolios were chosen to be the vehicle that instructors would use to represent their work for peer review.[11] It was decided that each portfolio would represent three perspectives on an instructor's work: (1) the instructor's, (2) the instructor's students', and (3) the instructor's colleagues'. Each would include self-selected artifacts of instructors' teaching (e.g., syllabi, writing assignments, comments on students' papers, case studies of student writers, students' writing, reports or transcriptions of conversations in which the instructor discussed curriculum development projects). In each case, instructors would compose a reflective essay to introduce peer reviewers to the materials they chose to collect in the portfolio and the "argument" they wished to make based on those materials.

From the outset, teachers in the program have composed teaching portfolios not only to represent their teaching to one another for contract and merit review but also to collect, reflect on, and place in dialogue with one another a constellation of conversations underway in the program (e.g., those taking place in contractually required teacher discussion groups, those taking place in curriculum development groups, those taking place in mini-conferences) and a constellation of teaching genres of their own and their colleagues' composition (e.g., syllabi, writing assignments, commentary on student papers, classroom observations, case studies of student writers, articles written for the in-house journal). Like all texts that are written for the purpose of developing the ideas and practices of a community, in the Syracuse Writing Program teaching portfolios and their contents are public and influential documents not only because they serve as the basis for promotion and merit reviews but also because they constitute one body of this teaching community's published literature, within which, against which, in terms of which the meaningfulness and usefulness of new contributions are read and evaluated.[12]

In our view, teaching portfolios and the genres of teaching they contain—composed as they are, in and for the benefit of a community invested in the ideas and practices they define, describe, and model—constitute a discourse that documents a base of expertise that is made public, evaluated, and monitored by faculty themselves. At its core, this discourse does something that Lee Shulman describes as constitutive of the "new" scholarship for which Ernest Boyer called. It makes the ideas and practices it documents accessible for exchange and use by other members of the community (Shulman, 1998).

The Reflective Essay: A Window onto the Scholarship of Teaching

All discourse is intertextual. The discourse in which a scholarship of teaching develops is no exception. Because instructors in the Syracuse Writing Program recognize the reflective essays they compose to introduce their portfolios to peer readers as occasions to bring conversations, inquiries, and genres of teaching and learning into dialogue with one another, these essays may be understood as intertextual examples of the discourse of the community. As such, they can serve as telling examples of the nature of a scholarship of teaching that is being developed in large measure by adjunct and part-time faculty in the field of composition.[13]

In this essay, we present substantial chunks of reflective essays that two instructors in the Syracuse Writing Program—Amanda Brown and John Starkweather—composed to introduce their teaching portfolios to peer reviewers. We do this for six reasons: first, to support our argument that a substantial scholarship of teaching is being developed in the academy by adjunct and part-time faculty who teach, inquire into their teaching and their students' learning, and publish the results of their inquiries in various venues that include, but are not limited to, teaching portfolios; second, to illustrate how these essays integrate, apply, and extend conversations under way, genres under development, and understandings in place in the Writing Program and in the field of composition studies.

Third, we present these excerpts to illustrate the kinds of contributions that instructors in the writing program value. Peer reviewers who read their teaching portfolios asked Brown and Starkweather to publish their reflective essays broadly in the program for the benefit of us all. Brown was invited to integrate the materials that she collected and discussed in her portfolio into her reflective essay in order that the essay might be read more easily by colleagues without access to her entire portfolio. Starkweather was invited to publish his reflective essay in the in-house journal, *Reflections in Writing,* that was to be devoted to advanced writing, a topic that Starkweather explores in his reflective essay.

Fourth, we present them to demonstrate the different ways in which instructors' teaching portfolios typically document, explore, theorize, and problematize one or another studio writing course and its relationship to other courses in the writing program's four-course curriculum;[14] fifth, to illustrate how teaching portfolios in the writing program figure as discoveries gleaned from "experiments in teaching and learning" rather than as reports of accomplished executions of already-established practices;[15] sixth, to demonstrate that instructors compose these essays for an audience of colleagues they know will evaluate them on the basis of their usefulness—what Gary L. Anderson and Kathryn Herr might call their practical validity[16]—as well as for the discoveries they advance about teaching and learning in composition studies.

As we reread the reflective essays that introduce Amanda Brown's and John Starkweather's and others' teaching portfolios in the Syracuse Writing Program, we find ourselves reading a multivocal literature that Gregory Bateson would likely have called a metalogue, a conversation about a problematic subject in which the structure of the conversation is also relevant to the subject (1972, p. 1). It is a literature composed of context-specific allusions. In this way, it is not unlike other literature of particular disciplinary communities, which is composed of allusions to known scholarship and to address questions of concern in the field in which it functions. It is a literature composed of multiple genres, many of them also context-specific. In this way, it is not unlike literatures that have developed at the intersection of different discourse traditions, such as the literature that emerged as sociolinguistics. It is a literature that achieves such universality as it may achieve through its acute particularity. In this way, it is not unlike anthropological literature. It is a literature that documents events from the perspective of those who are living through those events. In this way, it is not unlike phenomenological research. It is a literature that accounts for what it describes. In this way it is not unlike a theoretical argument. And it is a literature that envisions more successful future practice even as it reflects on past practice. In this way it is not unlike a utopian literature. We use the term *utopian* here in the same sense that Richard Rorty uses it in his important book *Contingency, Irony, and Solidarity* (1989). In Rorty's view, we have "no way to step outside the various vocabularies we have employed and find a metavocabulary which somehow takes account of all *possible* vocabularies, all possible ways of judging and feeling" (p. xvi). As part-time and adjunct faculty in the Syracuse Writing Program construct images of their future work with colleagues and students, they do so in "narratives which connect the present with the past, on the one hand, and with utopian futures on the other" (p. xvi).

Because the function of instructors' reflective essays is not only to introduce and explain materials they have included in their portfolios but also to make those materials available to peers for use in the creation of better courses, in the development of better practices, in their professional growth and development, instructors typically follow one of H. P. Grice's cardinal rules of conversational implicature (1975): Speaking in familiar terms, they say something meaningful about one or another topic under discussion in the program.

Amanda Brown's Reflective Essay (1992)

When Amanda Brown begins the reflective essay she writes to introduce her 1992 Teaching Portfolio with reference to a project she is working to develop with twelve other instructors in the Writing Program that positions teachers and students as co-re-searchers of literacy learning, she signals her readers that she composed her portfolio to contribute to ongoing discussion of communal work in the Odyssey Project. [17] Whether or not her readers are involved in the project's development, Brown knows that they have heard about it and are interested in it:

On the first day of class and often throughout the semester, I told my students about the nature of the Odyssey Project, its purposes and goals, as well as the fact that it was a new idea for Studio I that my fellow Odyssey instructors and I would be necessarily planning and revising as it unfolded. An instructor in my coordinating group always used the phrase "driving at night" to refer to the experience of trying to work through as well as pull off new teaching projects. I borrowed the phrase in speaking to my class about the uncertainties and excitement we would encounter; I claimed the expertise of an experienced driver, but called upon them for flexibility, a bit more patience, and thoughtful feedback along the trip. The journey would require more care and energy on my part and theirs to reach the point toward which we were all headed together, but would be something of a shared adventure. I hoped this set a good tone for my students and me as we began our work in Writing 105 (WRT)using our writing and reading to inquire into the development of effective literacy practices, that is practices of writing and reading.

With her opening words, Brown makes clear to her portfolio readers that she will be relating her discussion of the Odyssey Project to other conversations in the writing program (e.g., conversations among the group of instructors with whom she talks about teaching weekly). Because she plans to focus her discussion on the new course she has developed, Brown also alerts readers to the fact that she is engaged in, and is engaging her students in, a valued program practice: collaborative research. While she may be teaching a new course, an unfamiliar one, she is an expert, an "experienced" driver, whose course is constructed of thoughtful planning and sound practices for teaching composition.

To illustrate one way in which scholarship of teaching is being developed by part-time and adjunct faculty in the Syracuse Writing Program (through careful examination of the work students are able to produce as a result of program teaching and curricula), we reproduce a substantial portion of the version of the reflective essay in which Brown places in dialogue her syllabus, writing assignments, conversations that took place in her coordinating group[18] and in the Odyssey Project Planning Group, one of her students' class magazines, and her student evaluations to support the "argument" her teaching portfolio advances. We also reproduce portions of Brown's reflective essay to highlight one of the defining characteristics of the scholarship of teaching that is being developed in this teaching culture: In it, students' and teachers' work inform one another reciprocally.

After introducing the subject of her portfolio (her work with colleagues to develop an Odyssey section of WRT 105), Brown turns readers' attention to the course itself:

> The first unit worked pretty well. In my portfolio, I have included the class magazine of literacy autobiographies. The following assignment that led to this class magazine asked students to theorize their own literacy development:
>
>> Be sure to consider the negative influences as well as the positive; often the difficulties in the development of one's literacy will tell as much or more of the real story than the successes. So consider both those events and forces that supported its development as well as those that constrained its development. Try to theorize about what drove and what hindered your development. Once you have reached some conclusions, and it's O.K. if they are somewhat tentative ones, organize your paper to communicate those claims clearly to your reader.
>>
>> I expect the papers to go beyond surface narrative to an analysis of the significance of what you are recording about the develop-

ment of your literacy. . . . Do not shy away from representing important complexities; do not make your story much simpler than it was.

To me the most difficult task I asked of students in this assignment
was to theorize their literacy learning. When I asked students to theorize,
I was asking them to name and analyze those phenomena that supported
their literacy development as well as those that undermined it; and, if possible, to account for why their literacy was supported or undermined by
the things they identified. Students were able to do this to varying degrees. Some theorizing is evident in the papers of Linda, Larry, and Jane.
For example, Linda tries to figure out why she was so much more successful as a reader than as a writer:

> . . . Reading and writing eventually became two separate enti-
> ties. . . . I knew that there were types of books out there that I
> could enjoy because I had read them when I was younger, but
> there was no evidence of a writing style or type that suited me
> best. One of the main reasons was because I didn't have to write
> until high school. . . .
>
> I often ask myself, what is it that makes me have this inferi-
> ority complex about writing? There are two possible solutions
> that I can offer myself. First, in my formative years, my mother
> carefully taught me the basics of reading, but there was no nur-
> turing for writing. The subconscious message that I got from both
> my mother and school was that I could put writing off until later—
> that it wasn't as important. And when I had begun to get writing
> assignments for homework, I felt I was too old to go to my mother
> for help. By the third grade I did all of my homework without pa-
> rental supervision, so going to her in the ninth and tenth grades
> seemed too awkward for both of us. So, I kept quiet and struggled
> through writing as best as I could.
>
> The second possible reason may be that I put pressure on
> myself because I feel pressure from society to write well. I stress
> myself out trying to express myself correctly and also appeal to
> the reader and the teacher. . . .

The content of several [students' literacy autobiographies] were amazing (e.g., Tuan, a student who was unable to complete the course, wrote
of his mentoring experience in his native South Vietnam and in his first
school in Massachusetts); the insights in others were equally amazing (e.g.,
with self-awareness and openness, Sheila explains her antiliteracy bias
and theorizes about her relationship to a literacy which she identifies as
something apart from her):

My most vivid, and therefore most important, memories revolve around people and actions, not reading and writing. People are much more rewarding when the petty competition of grades is disposed of. This is where I get my concept that the study of people is more important then [sic] either literacy or the study of literacy. [Earlier in the paper, writing in responses to her peers' developing literacy autobiographies, Sheila indicates the reasons for her disinterest in texts, for her preference for engagement with people. At this time in her thinking about these issues, she understands these preferences as mutually exclusive.]

Maybe it was not only this lack of early motivation and cute bonding experiences but also a general feeling of unease which made me undesirous of reading. You see, my parents did not fail in trying to instill in me a love for reading. They never tried. It was not a lack of positive influences which kept me from reading at an early age, but a lack of influences at all. . . . They were not fairy tale parents, and I have never expected them to be so.

To sit down and devote your attention to an inanimate object you must trust your environment. The real world was odd enough without reading fantasy stories. And when my parents neither punished nor rewarded my actions, accomplishments do [sic] not seem to mean that much.

Sheila goes on to note her desire to keep up with the others, citing examples of fooling those around her into thinking she knew certain literacy skills; the importance of her second-grade teacher's attention; the continuing motivation to compete for attention from teachers; and the pain of excelling when it functioned to separate her from her peers in later grades, grades in which teachers did not pay so much attention to individual students or perhaps their need to be popular with their peers.

Len's literacy autobiography also goes into negative experiences of literacy development. Both Sheila and Len had trouble later, making me believe that their difficulties were deep-seated. Initially I thought each, especially Sheila, who was a very fine contributor in class discussions, would gain real ground over the semester, but both Sheila and Len chose not to invest themselves as fully as was necessary for them to be successful in the more complex, later projects in the course. I think, but may be wrong as they were anonymous, that Len is the student who wrote in his student evaluation of the course that he did not get enough "basic writing." We needed to talk more about what he meant by "basic writing" and what he needed to do to attend to his own writing needs. I regret this concern getting by me. But my larger question here is whether their histories were haunting them, perhaps causing them to have less tolerance for the frustration that other students were willing to meet, address, and push past as they undertook challenging projects? Their experience suggests to me that negative literacy experience is not easily countered, even in a Studio dedicated to the project.

Directing her discussion to peer reviewers, Brown illustrates and analyzes the quality of her students' responses to her first writing assignment. Following her analyses, she raises a question for future study: Do the frustrations of students' prior literacy experiences influence the extent to which they are willing to meet, address, and push past challenges, even in courses designed to help them overcome their frustrations and improve their literacy?

Returning readers' attention to the course that is the focus of her discussion, Brown composes her retrospective with her sights on the future, with what she will do "next time":

The Ethnography Unit, Unit II, took two full-fledged passes to be worthwhile. The first drafts that students produced in response to their studies of the literacy practices and cultures of groups on the Syracuse University campus were full, but too report-like. The discoveries they were making as a result of their inquiries and observations were minimal; maximizing those discoveries was the purpose of the project. In our discussions, teachers of the Odyssey sections of WRT 105 decided to do some revising of the parameters of the ethnography assignment. Originally we had asked students to compose ethnographies focusing on literacy practices of the groups they were studying. As we revised our assignment, some of us did not require our students to focus on the literacy practices. The sacrifice of the literacy focus was made in response to the difficulties students had in finding a suitable group to study that would work for them in a practical way.

Some of my students continued to focus on the literacy practices of the groups they were studying (e.g., Larry, football literacy; Kathy, art vocabulary; Sam, the use of Spanish in the student organization, *La Casa*). Others, however, did not (e.g., Tiffany had a very good ethnography of the Outing Club—full of discoveries about the club community, but with little to do with literacy, unless you count her analysis of the typical opening joke at the meetings.) Currently, I think that next time I will ask students for an ethnography of the literacy practices in a course they are taking at the time.

The challenge the students found in doing the second unit of the course led me to ask them to revise what became their first "final drafts"; I was determined to have them go back and push for discoveries because these discoveries were the intellectual purpose of the project. I could not bear to let go of our investment in the project without students' experiencing its intellectual virtues. In this rewriting project, all students revised their papers purposefully. Still their achievements varied. John, for example, writing about the lacrosse team, recorded more observations and asked further questions about the significance of what he could see in the interactions of members of the lacrosse teams and their coach, but he never understood the ethnographic project as Larry did. Larry defined in detail what constituted football literacy for a group in his dorm to which he belonged: the "gridiron junkies." In his ethnography, Larry named the common experiences or themes in their backgrounds that led the junkies to their interests and practices. He inquired into how what constituted "football literacy" for his group did not constitute it for another community. In this way Larry replicated classroom discussions in which we determined that what constituted literacy for the Amish did not constitute literacy for the "English" community.

I had much to reflect on as I taught, and I do again now as I rethink this ethnography unit. For example, fulfilling this assignment, a technically weak writer, such as Tracy, who examined the contrasting styles of her three art-studio teachers and theorized the significance of what she observed about their teaching, composed a better essay than students who wrote well, described fully and accurately, but did not discover anything much that they didn't know at the beginning of the paper. An example of this kind of ethnography is Kevin's paper on the football team. Kevin as an insider, a manager of the SU team, and son of someone who worked for the Buffalo Bills, could report much interesting information to his less-knowledgeable readers. But all he had to tell got in the way of an inquiry of his own into the meaning of what he could see. He learned some things—he was able to articulate more about competition between players in practices, particularly pre-season practice, for "rights" to "repetitions" of elements of their kind of plays during practice and the cycle of privilege players could enter once they got the repetitions. (The more practice of one's plays, the better a player performed, the more practice time the player was assured.) My point is that the paper might read well, but in terms of the project's goal of having students discover new knowledge in the course of doing the ethnography, it did not succeed as well as a paper such as Tracy's, a paper that does not read as well.

Another intended effect of this project was to train ("train" sounds like a lower form of teaching, but it was a lot like training in the repetitious learning of a small, basic move) students to move from concrete support to claims. We had an interesting discussion about "observations," finally defining them as claims that are developed over time—that are not apparent in an initial "viewing" no matter how clear the view. This definition for the purposes of getting at the rewards of ethnographic observation was one our class developed as a research community develops its common understandings of the object(s) of its study. Perhaps the training my students will carry away with them from this work is the practice of supporting claims and "observing" past the surface of things. For example, in his paper written about the conflict between wrestling and academics, Joe's success with his ethnography of a dorm group who played video games and studied together, carried over to his next paper. From the beginning of the semester, Joe expressed himself awkwardly in his writing. In his final paper, he still does so at many points. Furthermore, in his final paper, Joe is still unable to make connections beyond his own experience, but what he continues to do that he first did in his ethnography, is to proceed through inquiry to interpret experience, in this case not others' but his own. The claims of the paper are well supported and complicated, because he is trying to be faithful to what his inquiry actually uncovers.

Disappointed with the third part of the course, Brown offers her peer reviewers a self-evaluation of her work:

In their final paper, I asked students to project themselves forward, but by design, or maybe I should say because of time constraints, they never had the potential to go all the way with this move. The handout describes the project:

This paper has been referred to as "the theory paper." What does that mean? By theory I mean a range of possible things. For some of you it will mean analyzing experience and coming to some conclusions about it. Some of you began to theorize in your literacy autobiographies when you reflected on your own experiences with reading and writing, analyzed that experience, and came to some conclusions as to the meaning of it (i.e., the support of my parents was key to my success; for me competition was most important; my failures were due to giving in to peer pressure and rebelling against my parents' overly strict attitudes; all my success was due to certain key teachers and all my troubles to my need to be a basketball hero). You might want to take one of the ideas you considered in your own autobiography (or one that was there but you didn't consider) and reconsider it in the larger context of any or all of our readings (Rose, Dillard, Fishman, Rodriguez, and Freire) and the experiences of your classmates (class magazine of literacy autobiographies). Or start with an idea from one of the readings and make connections to other readings or to your own experience, experience that may or may not have been considered in your autobiography. There may also be connections to be made to your ethnographic work, but in any case to examine, observe, and make claims about the meaning or significance of these ideas, you will need to work as carefully as an ethnographer. By thinking about experiences in new ways and making connections, you will be making discoveries as you did as an ethnographer.

What is theory? Analysis, observations, claims, conclusions, accounts, definitions, visions, perceptions, insights, beliefs, values, assumptions, concepts, and/or ideas. By working to articulate such theory, we make more visible our beliefs and assumptions—by making them more visible, we can see what problems they present and revise them for strength and usefulness.

Students entered this project uncertain of how to theorize about some aspect of literacy although most had made pretty good choices of topics for these three- to four-page papers; they seemed feasible and of real interest to them. Students began their work to understand the task of theorizing about their own experiences in one of three ways. Some launched into wholly new territory (e.g., Sheila analyzed her letter writing; Sam evaluated our studio class through the lens of Freireian thought). The largest group focused on one aspect of their literacy experience, and as they worked to analyze it more thoroughly and relate it to other experiences and readings, they developed broader claims (e.g., Adam indicated how he had to change his previously successful literacy practices when they no longer served him; Tiffany wrote about the use of standardized testing for groupings in public school; Kevin about assigned aspects of readings; Joe about the interference both positive and negative of sports with academics; Nick of the influence of having Greek spoken at home and English at school; Jane on the principle of reinforcement; Karen on the effect of siblings on one's literacy development). A couple of students (e.g., Larry and Linda) expanded the original analyses they had developed of their literacy learning in their autobiographies, this time making connections between their experiences and the experiences of others. The best thing about these third papers was the topics students picked—they owned them, and they were topics of broader significance. But students' visions of what could be done with the papers outstretched their reach.

One problem they faced was unfamiliarity with the messy, highly qualified, rarely-across-the-board nature of claim-making. For example, Nick ended up in a quandary because of his expectations that he needed a theory that would work for both him and his brother about the effects of their parents' unfamiliarity with American education and difficulty with English. He also confused an analysis of the reasons for his difficulties, with the idea of making excuses for his difficulties which he would not allow himself to do. A paper that met my initial modest hopes for the assignment was Linda's, which took an appropriate topic, both in nature and size, and theorized about it. Linda's topic choice required her to account for phenomena that had roots in her own experience but moved her beyond it. She was concerned with why it was more difficult to develop as a writer than as a reader. She introduces her paper with a description of its project:

It is intriguing that many of my friends including myself have had more problems with writing than reading. But why? Is it the American educational system, our parents, fear of competition or just plain lack of interest? In my final paper for Writing studio 105 I will discuss the psychological reasons and hopefully offer a solution to this problem.

Linda's text indicates that she is beginning to discover and create new knowledge through her ability to inquire and theorize. This was the kind of thing I imagined students doing with the third project. As a paper it is not bad; with a rigorous rewrite it could be good—interesting and thought-provoking to the reader, satisfying to Linda. I could see the effects of her work in ethnography and in class in this last paper. Her ethnography was about a newspaper on campus, *The Black Voice,* which she had joined as a reporter during the course of the fall semester, but she could not get enough distance from it to make many ethnographic discoveries. Her ethnography improved, but did not take leaps. In her final paper, however, she works ethnographically to extend the claims she made about her own literacy learning in her literacy autobiography to claims about the literacy learning of others. She also talks about the educational system and the role of positive feedback to a developing writer. Her voice is much stronger than it has previously been.

Linda's is not the best paper. Sam's and Larry's are more successful. Her's, however, does represent growth. Sam and Larry were strong students in September; their success is continuous. In this third project, Linda can be seen as growing as a writer, as can Tiffany, Joe, and John. Speaking generally, students' achievements in composing the final "theory" paper range from Karen's and Stacy's papers which are so simple as to be trivial, to Sam's paper which is entirely theoretical and Larry's which is an excellent mix of experience and theory.

Most significantly, there was a large group of B-minuses (5) from students from whom I expected better. If it hadn't been the last paper with no chance for a rewrite, these grades would have been *C+*s. For example, Adam's paper didn't go far enough into what it means for a student to have to change a successful approach to writing papers, an approach that has served the student well, an approach the student does not wish to relinquish; Adam just reports that giving up an outgrown literacy practice was a problem for him and some others. He simply details the negatives of such an experience. Adam, Nick, and others were the ideal candidates for another ten days of the semester in which we could rewrite these texts, complicating, developing, and qualifying their ideas through conferencing and rewriting. They and the others had the ability and—now—the material to develop into papers that would have been as effective as Linda's or

Joe's. Had these students composed the papers they were on the verge of composing, the course would have ended more successfully in my mind.

It's not that the products of students' writing in writing courses are most important, but to move through a process to a reasonably sound paper that handles the intellectual requests of the assignment is an experience that students should have, especially at the end. And it is an experience that teachers need to see their students have. Given what did happen in my course, I ended up writing extensive commentary on students' papers and course work, duplicating their papers, and mailing them to students at home. This was the best I could do.

In the midst of my initial disappointment, I was angry. The semester is so short; why don't we require that students take more writing courses beyond the two studios? And if they do not, why don't more, many more, teachers in other areas of the university pay attention to students as writers? Is assigning the development of writers to the writing program allowing others to forget their responsibility to these developing thinkers? Why don't we just get them coming and going; in writing class and in biology, in art history and in fashion design—write, write, write. They have all this potential and not enough time to have them realize it. As I mailed their papers to my students, I became calmer. Perhaps they will spiral back to think about writing as they proceed. If they join an Odyssey section of WRT 205, they surely will because our teachers' group is talking about these issues even now and planning for ways to address them in the WRT 205s that we will teach in the spring of 1993. Still, I'd like to see these students do more, I think in particular because they were so invested in their last inquiry, their last paper—it belonged to them, and they knew it, but they couldn't quite see at the end of the semester how to push it forward more successfully. I hope that they have an opportunity to go back to this kind of paper again.

Several months after she submitted her teaching portfolio for review—responding to an invitation to integrate materials in it into her reflective essay for the benefit of readers who would not have her portfolio materials at hand for easy reference—Brown added to her earlier reflections on the course, again with her sights on her future teaching and the Odyssey Project curriculum.

As I have worked to piece this document together, I have of course been able to see my teaching of last semester better than I did a month ago. In reviewing my student evaluations my favorite group of comments were those that categorized the class as difficult, but worth it. I wanted them to be challenged; however, I also wanted them to see the intrinsic rewards that can come through dealing with the frustration. I also liked the couple of comments about the combination of flexibility and structure, with an understanding about the rationale for flexibility (e.g., "I would recommend this course because the teacher is open for student comments and ideas and has a relaxed policy. You are challenged by the assignments, but when there is a problem the teacher makes considerations to get the best results and the best efforts and ideas out of the students").

As far as revising the course, I intend to give more time to the third project; I speculate about redoing the first literacy autobiographies for the third unit, with an even greater emphasis on theorizing, and theorizing better in view of reading each others' work and in view of all the readings and thinking the class did in Units I and II. This kind of project might accommodate itself better to the amount of time at the end; and be a way of having students realize how their thinking, knowledge, and theorizing abilities developed over the semester; while still asking students to make the intellectual move toward theory at the end of the course. In addition, I think more highly of the quality of the community of inquiry we established, not only through rereading these documents, but in light of the fact that three students (Sam, Sheila, and Linda) have signed up for independent Odyssey projects this semester. Finally, there are many design elements of the course that have fed into my pilot of Odyssey 205 this semester, most notably an interest in the use of autobiography as a means of teaching rhetoric, and in the use of ethnography/case study projects. The more I consider my teaching in the fall, the more I realize how much I have learned from this particular course and how greatly it is affecting my current teaching.

With images in mind of the next version of the course that was the focus of her portfolio and the first version of the sequel course that she will teach the following semester, Brown's portfolio figures not only as a contribution to a scholarship of teaching that is expert, public, evaluated, and monitored (Edgerton, Hutchings, and Quinlan, 1991) but also as one that is useful and exchangeable (Shulman, 1989). Those of us who were working in the writing program with Amanda Brown had much to learn from her teaching portfolio. It influenced our practice. It did so by re-presenting student texts to the community both as compositions in which students made knowledge and as texts from which teachers might learn about their practice. In addition to learning more about how to read student texts and how to use those readings in the service of better teaching, the teaching community was provided effective examples of teaching genres that individual instructors might wish to adapt or adopt to improve their own teaching (e.g., assignments, the syllabus, and other genres that Brown included in her portfolio).

Brown's re-presentation of the complexities of learning and teaching makes more than one semester's teaching, more than one teacher's teaching available for critical review. As she asks questions about how she structured a course and about how her students handled the invitations to learning that her assignments provided them, Brown implicitly invites her colleagues to ask such questions of their own teaching and of their students' learning. When she documents her "anger" at the arbitrary length of the semester, which does not allow students to develop their abilities more fully, she also tells us that she chose to continue the semester's work with her students' in summer correspondence. Thinking explicitly about how she will teach Odyssey 205, Brown reassures herself and reminds her colleagues that her students will go on to other learning experiences in a community in which she has been their first—but will not be their only—teacher, in which she introduced them to a subject they will continue to study. In the fall, she will teach the students of other instructors, instructors with whom she is sharing insights about curriculum and teaching practices, instructors who are frequent visitors and consultants in each other's classes. Those instructors will find her students in their courses. Students do not learn everything they will learn in one course; teachers do not teach everything that can be taught in one course. The community of teachers and students must accomplish the larger project of literacy teaching and learning together. When Brown's colleagues read her teaching portfolio they learn not only what an effective teacher has learned from her practice but also what they must do next to extend and enrich that practice.

John Starkweather's Reflective Essay (1998)

Readers of the reflective essay that John Starkweather composed to introduce his 1998 Teaching Portfolio believed that we had much to learn from his collaborative experiment in teaching and learning also. They encouraged Starkweather to publish the essay in an upcoming number of the program's in-house journal that was to focus on advanced writing courses. When it appeared in *Reflection in Writing* (Spring 1999), [19] Starkweather's essay had another layer of reflection built into it just as the sections of Amanda Brown's reflective essay that we have reproduced here have an additional layer of reflection appended to them.

Starkweather does not devote his reflective essay, as Brown did, to close readings of students' work and what those readings have to teach him and his colleagues about developing a new course, rather he names pedagogical interest and questions that guided his planning and teaching of WRT 305:

Trying to lead a small group of juniors and seniors through a sustained, sophisticated research and writing project encompassing an entire semester brought into sharp focus several key issues in my teaching that I had long been thinking about in the very different contexts of WRT 105 and 205. Specifically, I was interested in two questions: (1) How do I manage some real unity of action or focus within the classroom when people advance toward their goal at very different rates, thus coming to a particular week's session with, potentially, very different needs and expectations? and (2) How do I balance individual attention with other modes of instruction?

While teaching WRT 305 has not brought flashes of mystical insight or easy answers to these questions, it did prove to be an ideal location in which to explore them. This was true for several reasons. First of all, the class was small, with an enrollment of only seven students, so I had time to observe the impact of different activities on each student's performance. Second, I knew from the outset that I would need to make more use than is my customary practice of presentation and moderation as teaching modes: the course Dawnelle Jager and I had designed included some conceptually difficult readings, including ethnographies, ethnographic theory, and critiques of ethnographic methodology. In order to succeed in their own projects, students needed to understand and make use of this material, even though it might at first baffle and frustrate them. Because this was an advanced writing studio, I also theorized that students would need to manage and take control of their own projects and assist each other to a much greater degree than I would expect in WRT 105 or even in WRT 205. They needed to become the experts. They needed to know much more about their work than I could possibly hope to, to travel in terrain that was potentially quite unfamiliar to me. Fumbling and false starts were to be expected and would be an essential part of the process as they found their way into their site, their focus of study, and their methodology. In this situation, groping was permissible (maybe even laudable) for them, but economy of motion was essential for me. I had to find the best possible interventions to help them figure out where they were going and what they had to do next even though I might not myself know exactly what their destination was. I had to help them remain confident that they could gather useful data, make sense of their observations, and transform a mass of confusing raw material into successful ethnographies.

After he tells readers that teaching WRT 305 added other questions to those with which he began the course, questions to which he sought answers during the course of the semester ("What is 'advanced' writing? How is it different from what we ask of students in 105 and particularly in 205?"), Starkweather presents the argument of his portfolio reflection. Directing readers' attention to a WRT 305 class session and a colleague's written description of that session, which he included as supporting material in his teaching portfolio, Starkweather demonstrates how observations of teaching when conducted among colleagues engaged in a common teaching project can become the basis of generative inquiry and theory building:

> The 305 class that David Franke [the Professional Writing instructor who observed Starkweather's class for purposes of evaluation] attended and has written about for my portfolio observation [which was included with the article Starkweather wrote for the inhouse journal] is as convenient a window as any through which to peer in looking for insights that may help answer my fundamental questions. Repeated readings of his write-up have led me to theorize that four modes of instruction (coaching, facilitating or managing, moderating, and presenting) are available at any moment. In addition, someone, either the student or the instructor, must make a decision about whom the student will consult for help, thus adding the rhetorical question of choosing an appropriate audience. The possibilities include (1) a student talking to herself about her writing; (2) a student talking to her peers about her work; (3) a student consulting experts in the field about her work; (4) a class talking all together about their work; (5) a student talking with his teacher about his work; and (6) a teacher talking to students about their work. I want to consider how I chose (or followed students' leads in choosing) these modes of instruction and rhetorical situations at several points during the evening in question.
>
> **The Student Talks to Herself about Her Work**
> As David mentions, I began this class by asking students to write detailed analyses of what each thought he or she needed to accomplish during this class period. In a lower-level studio, I would expect several people to say, "I don't know." Here, I anticipated useful analyses that could be translated quickly into a workable plan of action. This proved true in almost every case. One or two students did want to consult a detailed list of stages

for the process of writing up, revising and analyzing field notes that I had constructed based on recent readings and class discussion of Margery Wolf's *A Thrice-Told Tale* and Robert Emerson's *Writing Ethnographic Fieldnotes*. I therefore placed this list within easy reach so people could use it as needed. As the session progressed, I asked students to begin making a list of questions their notes were leading them to ask or to write brief interpretive memos to themselves saying what they "really" thought about a detail in their field notes. All of these activities put me in a "coaching" mode, one with which I'm extremely comfortable.

The Student Talks with (One or Many of) Her Peers about Her Work
Occasionally, I found myself wanting to create a situation where two particular students would work together. I'm finding that this kind of informal, spontaneous "facilitating" often works better for me than big pre-planned peer workshop sessions. Here, I can get the right people together at the right time, and I can reinforce the idea that sharing work and getting feedback is something we do all the time, not just when and because the teacher tells us to. By this point in the semester, students in this small and very congenial group had formed easy working alliances. I only intervened to create situations where I saw a good reason to do so, which I articulated to both parties in inviting them to work together. I tried always to be careful to ask, "Does that sound useful to you at this point?" This informal consultation of peers can also be pushed to another level in a comfortable atmosphere. In the following weeks of the class, I found myself asking people quietly, "Would you like to run that by the whole class?" More often than not, they decided that this sounded like a good idea. Because I was discreet about it, they could also gracefully say, "Naw . . . maybe later!" Where they agreed, it was sometimes to seek a solution to a dilemma they faced, but just as often it was to share a breakthrough with others: "Here's my problem, and here's what I'm doing about it." When I can facilitate this kind of interchange, it allows students to demonstrate expertise and see each other as valuable resources for shared problem solving.

Talking to Students about Their Work
This comes in two varieties: when they come to see me and when I go to see them. The question here is to what extent do I pick the timing and the context of our interactions? To what extent do I allow them to take the lead? Wherever possible, I prefer that they initiate the discussion. However, that leads to two problems: (1) those who seldom initiate, and (2) those who seldom cease initiating. In the case of this class, "Mike" (who impressed David with his immortal insight into the Rotary Club, "Pancakes are power!"), is an extremely outgoing person—probably off the end of the Meyers-Briggs scale for "extrovert!" He would willingly engage me endlessly during a class, not from any lack of social skills or regard for his classmates, but rather from plain enthusiasm. I also had one or two stu-

dents who could be prone to "going it alone." This dynamic, I decided, would only be altered if I found ways to alter it. Written materials like the list of stages I've already mentioned encourage a kind of interaction with me even when I'm otherwise engaged: the student can consult them at will. They also easily lead to specific questions the student may feel comfortable posing, thus mediating a more direct interaction. I am also becoming a master of the searching glance, "Are you well-focused and productive, or could you use my help?" Finally, I began experimenting with short, spontaneous bursts of presentation to the entire class as a way of punctuating, focusing, contextualizing, and unifying key moments during a class. For instance, David notes that at 8:49 on March 19, I called the class together to confront them with two "big questions," which I felt had grown out of the evening's work so far, and which I believed would help everyone in the room, either immediately or in the not-very-distant future. I am coming to realize that several small segments of clearly teacher-centered activity serve to clarify the point of seemingly disparate activity going on during a class. It's a way of saying, "Here's what we've been doing and here's why we've been doing it." This can make the difference between a session where there's diversity of activity with clarity of purpose and a session that seems chaotic and baffling to students.

The Student Talks to Experts in the Field about His Work
In his observation, David says that students in this course were asked to write "in" the genre of ethnography "and on it." Reflective statements discussing aspects of their final products were indeed a part of the course design. We were asking our students to become knowledgeable, self-conscious practitioners of this genre. To do that, they needed to read and understand models of ethnographic writing. They also needed to understand some of the theory and discussions of methodology accumulating around the genre. I had expected that students would find some of this material tough going. They did. By the time David visited my class, however, they had navigated through the worst of it. Earlier in the semester, he would have seen me engaged in a good deal of "moderating" and "presenting." During the session under discussion, I had a decision to make. Should I ask students to engage directly and as a group with the readings assigned for the evening? Since the chapter from Wolf was her study "The Woman Who Didn't Become a Shaman" and my main purpose in using it at that point was to help students see the relationship between her thesis, the evidence she gleaned from her field notes, and her analytic discussion tying the two together, this introduction seemed premature, given that every student in the room had identified himself or herself as still moving toward a thesis. I knew all members of the class were likely to be well-prepared to take part in a discussion of the article and that we could have adequately analyzed the features I have just named. However, I was not sure that this analysis would have moved anyone significantly closer to declaring a thesis. I was further worried that it could be a time-consum-

ing activity. Thus, I decided it could easily wait until the next week. During that following session, I did in fact start by asking everyone, "Okay, so exactly what is Wolf's thesis? What other key claims does she make and connect to that thesis?" I wanted students to see the readings as tools, to be used when relevant. I also wanted (because this was an advanced-level course) to reemphasize the idea of repeated readings of difficult texts, of finding your way slowly into materials from other disciplines than your own.

In conclusion, as Starkweather acknowledges the value of making tacit knowledge explicit, he theorizes not only his own but also the community's teaching:

I have tried to elaborate a few of the many tactical decisions I made during the class session described in David's observation. In doing so, I have tried to clarify my (otherwise likely unconscious, intuitive) rationale for a given intervention at a given moment. Understanding the reasons I might have chosen a particular instructional mode at a particular time with a particular student is useful; investigating the ways in which various strategies interact and reinforce each other seems even more fruitful. What I have attempted here is to lay out for myself a basis for further consideration within the framework of "reflective practice" in a studio environment. At this point, I have reached some conclusions that seem sound enough for further testing and elaboration.

First of all, while I labeled this class as a "transitional point" in the semester, I am coming to believe that any studio writing course constantly puts students in a "transitional point." In order to make progress, they must always be moving from one stage or activity toward the next. Almost any moment in a course thus presents both impediments and the possibility of a discovery that will allow the student to move past their present barrier.

Also, I want to revisit my (actually somewhat cavalier) statement to David that "an ideal writing class would operate entirely by conference." This is an exaggeration highlighting an important idea. In conferences with students, I constantly ask them, "What's good about what you've done so far? What do you think still needs work? What do you need to do next?" Students are continually challenged to analyze and evaluate their own work, not merely to "do" it and ask me to judge it for them. As David put it in another context, I am "not the main drama." Finding ways to make a classroom function at a high level without taking center stage has always been a central concern of studio teachers. This semester, I found myself making two distinct moves which I think helped me to shift emphasis toward student activity in WRT 305: (1) using writing as the core of the course; and (2) asking students to decide what tasks to perform and how best to complete them. Both of these bear further discussion.

1. In the class that David observed, students spent most of the evening reading and writing. A great many of the activities were constructed to help students make discoveries about their own texts. Variations on practices such as annotating, coding, and writing analytic/interpretive notes and memos allowed students to stand outside their own work, to name for themselves what they were trying to do. They were using writing to function on a metacognitive level. Urging students to frame for themselves (or each other) and write down as many questions as possible based on their field notes was another important way to center this class session on writing. Discovering key questions that need answering is a very fundamental task; more and more it seems to me the underlying basis of both critical thinking and organizational planning.

2. In helping students figure out what to do next, I see my role as twofold: (a) asking them to articulate for themselves—and for each other and me—what they have done and what might be preventing them from moving forward; (b) offering a clear scheme of stages or steps toward the finished product, thereby allowing them to locate themselves and identify potentially useful procedures for solving their problems. Simply put, I'm talking about offering much more sophisticated and complete maps of the writing process than we would normally offer even in WRT 205. This kind of "schematic," as I like to call such maps, is there for them to call on as needed, and (in the case of my 305) was based on a number of sources, including their own ideas for useful activities and suggestions rooted in both Wolf's *A Thrice-Told Tale* and Emerson's *Writing Ethnographic Fieldnotes*. (The "list of stages" that I have referred to earlier is an example of one such schematic.) The key is having students make informed choices about what to do and what resources can best help them.

Reminding readers of the overarching question that framed his inquiries into teaching and learning in his WRT 305, Starkweather shares with colleagues the answers he has developed:

This last point leads me back to the "new" question this course has forced me to pose for myself, namely, what is "advanced" writing (or, what is an "advanced" writing course). My consideration of interventions in this one session of WRT 305 allows me to offer two tentative answers to that question. Both involve saying what I think students should be able to do more effectively as a result of taking such a course. Advanced writers should be able to conceptualize and execute a writing process appropriate to the task at hand in a way that is more sophisticated and more self-conscious than they could have done earlier in their development as writers. They should also be able to draw as needed on a wider variety of tools and models to help them envision and complete a given writing task. In this sense, I think of WRT 305 (and 405) as courses where students apply in a rigorous and useful way the techniques they learned in WRT 105 and the analytic skills in analyzing and judging models they practiced in WRT 205. Part of David Franke's last 205 portfolio, for example, asks the student to select a journal in his or her field of study and write the first page of an article that could appear in that journal. I'm saying to my 305 students, "Okay, now write the rest of it!" If I get them to make use of the needed tools and the help of other people at the right times, I think they can follow through on that challenge.

Starkweather approached teaching WRT 305 with the questions he wished to explore as teacher-scholar. In the reflective essay that introduced his teaching portfolio, he proposes answers to those questions and supports those answers by drawing readers' attention to events in the course he taught. As he does so, he represents the complexities of teaching a specific course in a particular learning community. Although Starkweather's reflective inquiry differs from Brown's in content and focus, it shares with Brown's characteristics of the scholarship of teaching under development in the Syracuse Writing Program. Both professional writing instructors' essays look across and beyond the particular teaching experience they explore. Both are retrospective and prospective. Both are purposeful compositions written to explore issues of interest to their readers, offering strategies and insights that colleagues may adapt or adopt into their teaching. Both invite criticism and evaluation. Both contribute to a base of knowledge that is developing not only in the Syracuse Writing Program but also in the field of composition studies.[20]

Publication of the reflective essay that Brown composed to introduce her teaching portfolio led her and her colleagues to re-think how they would revise a course they had co-planned and co-taught, to plan for and teach the sequel to the course, and in close reading of students' writing to gain insights into their teaching and their students' learning. Publication of the reflective essay that Starkweather composed to introduce his teaching portfolio led him and his colleagues to re-think the modes of instruction available to them and their students, to better understand the relationship of introductory and advanced writing courses to one another, and to reconsider the relative usefulness of various modes of instruction to student writers at different levels of maturity and experience. Discrete studies, Brown's and Starkweather's essays are the work of teachers who teach students whose experiences, preparation, learning styles, and rates of development differ, and who do so within the constraints of course boundaries, time lines, and their own and the public's expectations for the quality of students' writing.

In the Syracuse Writing Program, the reflective essays that introduce teaching portfolios not only document, explore, theorize, and problematize teaching that is community property,[21] but they also suggest that the scholarship of teaching is fundamentally a scholarship of discovery. The literature that we find in these portfolios documents scholarly "acts" of literacy teaching; it also advances discoveries about literacy teaching. In so doing, it highlights a line of inquiry that scholars and policymakers might usefully pursue as the academy works to better understand the nature of scholarship that leads to effective teaching and learning.

The Scholarship of Teaching, Composition Studies, and Contingent Faculty

Why, you may ask, do we include an essay about the scholarship of teaching and argue that the scholarship of teaching is a holistic scholarship of discovery, integration, application, and teaching—all at once, altogether—in a collection of essays about the work of contingent faculty in composition studies in higher education? We do so for two integrally related reasons: first, to draw attention to composition studies, a field whose shape and content find their origins in the challenge to teach the most widely required course in higher education; second, to draw attention to the majority of faculty and instructors who have taught introductory composition (Freshman English) since its inception over a century ago—contingent faculty in composition studies.

It has taken several decades for the academy to acknowledge its dependence on contingent faculty to teach not just the majority of composition courses in higher education but also, at the current moment, the majority of general education courses in higher education. Although it remains necessary, it is no longer sufficient to focus discussions of the work of contingent faculty on the personal and academic prices that they and their students pay for the counterproductive conditions in which they teach. The field of composition studies and the work of contingent faculty who teach in the field argue our point: The "making of knowledge in composition"[22]—to borrow Stephen M. North's phrase—may well be viewed as an outstanding, perhaps *the* outstanding, example of the scholarship of teaching in American education.

It is time to extend and complicate discussions of the work of contingent faculty by drawing attention to their scholarship, a scholarship that stands to contribute substantially to two of higher education's pressing problems: the reinvigoration of teaching as scholarship, and fuller, more authentic understanding of the scholarship of teaching.

Notes

For their insightful readings and helpful criticisms of this essay, we thank our colleagues Ann Austin, Catherine Lydia Fleck, Cathy Fleischer, Penny Gardner, Kim Kessler, Jay L. Robinson, and Janet Swenson. For the richness of their talk together, Patti also thanks the generous members of the Scholarship of Teaching seminar with whom she had the privilege to work at the University of California–Santa Barbara during the fall of 1999: Doug Baker, Sheridan Blau, Teri Chavkin, Ralph Cordova, Lydia Cosentino, Judy Garey, Judith Green, Chris Johnston, Joe Little, Jenny Michlson, and Silvia Neves.

We are grateful to Catherine Lydia Fleck and Nevin Leder for drawing Gregory Bateson's conception of metalogue to our attention.

1. In *Scholarship Reconsidered*, Ernest Boyer notes that the categories of scholarship he presents are based upon a conception of faculty roles developed by Eugene Rice, his colleague at the Carnegie Foundation for the Advancement of Teaching. Rice is currently scholar in residence and director of the Forum on Faculty Roles and Rewards at the American Association of Higher Education.

2. We are referring, of course, to reports that range from Charles J. Sykes's indictment of the professoriat, *Profscam* (1989) to Lynne V. Cheney's bit-

ing criticism of academics, *Tyrannical Machines: A Report on Education Practices Gone Wrong and Our Best Hopes of Setting Them Right* (1990) to less biting but nonetheless critical reports like the one issued by the Carnegie Foundation for the Advancement of Teaching, *Campus Life: In Search of Community* (1990).

3. For one well-known description of this work and an introduction to the theory Shulman built upon it, see Lee Shulman, "Knowledge and Teaching: Foundations of the New Reform," *Harvard Education Review* 57(1), February 1987, 1–22.

4. See, for example, Lee Shulman, "Toward a Pedagogy of Substance," in *AAHE Bulletin 41*(10), 8–13, "Teaching as Community Property," *Change,* November/December 1993, 6–7, "Taking Learning Seriously" *Change,* July/August 1999, 11–17, as well as Edgerton, Hutchings, & Quinlan, *The Teaching Portfolio: Capturing the Scholarship in Teaching* (1991), Pat Hutchings, *Making Teaching Community Property* (1996), and Pat Hutchings (ed.), *The Course Portfolio: How Faculty Can Examine Their Teaching to Advance Practice and Improve Student Learning* (1998).

5. See, for example, B. M. Shore et al., *The Teaching Dossier: A Guide to Its Preparation and Use* (revised edition, 1986), and Peter Seldin, *The Teaching Portfolio: A Practical Guide to Improved Performance and Promotion/Tenure Decisions* (1991).

6. Lee Shulman has called for the development of such a literature in a number of his speeches and writings. In some, he has argued for the development of a case literature in teaching. See for example, Lee S. Shulman, "Toward a Pedagogy of Cases," in Judith Shulman (ed.), *Toward a Pedagogy of Cases: Case Methods in Teacher Education* (1991). In publications emerging from her work at the American Association of Higher Education, Patricia Hutchings has documented the value of cases to provoke faculty discussion and to advance the scholarship of teaching. See, for example, *Using Cases to Improve College Teaching: A Guide to More Reflective Practice* (Washington, DC: AAHE, 1993) and "Windows on Practice: Cases about Teaching and Learning" (*Change,* November/December 1993, 14–21).

7. Work that has been conducted by the AAHE and the Carnegie Foundation for the Advancement of Teaching since the publication of *The Teaching Portfolio* in 1991 has documented how teaching portfolios have contributed to the development of a discourse of teaching in various settings. These projects are discussed in a variety of publications— among them, Erin Anderson (ed.), *Campus Use of the Teaching Portfolio: Twenty-five Profiles* (1993) and Pat Hutchings, *Making Teaching*

Community Property (1996). These discussions do not emerge from nor are they focused on communities that have defined themselves from the outset as teaching communities.

8. In her important article "Practical Wisdom and the Geography of Knowledge in Composition" (*College English* 53.8, 863–885), Louise Wetherbee Phelps, the founding director of the Syracuse Writing Program, discusses the ways in which theory and practice discipline one another in the creation of new knowledge and in the teaching of composition.

9. Within its spiral curriculum, instructors in the Writing Program teach four studio writing courses to approximately six thousand undergraduates a years. Studio I (WRT 105), taken by virtually all students during the fall semester of their first year at Syracuse, focuses on the various uses of writing as a means of learning; Studio II (WRT 205), taken by most students during the spring semester of their sophomore year, focuses on writing for various audiences, purposes, and occasions within and outside the academy; Studio III (WRT 305), taken by approximately 20 percent of the student body during their junior or senior year, focuses on issues associated with writing in disciplinary or methodological studies; and Studio IV (WRT 405), taken by approximately 40 percent of the student body in their junior or senior year, focuses on issues associated with writing done in the professions, government, and the marketplace.

10. In a publication about the AAHE Teaching Initiatives Program, *Making Teaching Community Property: A Menu for Peer Collaboration and Peer Review* (1996), Pat Hutchings collects and reflects on various campus reports of cultural practices they have introduced to support a scholarship of teaching (e.g., Kent State University, teaching circles; Temple University, reciprocal visits and observation; Stanford University, mentoring; and so on). In the Syracuse University Writing Program, not one but all of the practices reported in Hutchings's study (with the exception of intercampus collaboration) were put in place simultaneously to construct a culture of teaching.

11. The charter that details the evaluation process is published in the Writing Program's inhouse library and on the Internet (find the program's Web site at http://wrt.syr.edu, go to the "Publications" section and the "Teacher's Sourcebook" subsection, and choose the link marked "Teacher Evaluation").

12. Materials that instructors publish in their portfolios (e.g., reflective essays, syllabi, writing assignments, and so on) are also published separately in classrooms, in the inhouse library, and on the Internet. Often

they are also published in local, regional, and national conference presentations and in locally, regionally, and nationally published journals and books.

13. Instructors' reflective essays are published each year in the Writing Program's inhouse library and on the Internet. Readers turn to these essays not just to evaluate the teaching they represent, but also to mine them for ideas for course designs and teaching practices.

14. As it happens, many portfolios composed in the Syracuse Writing Program take shape in forms that William Cerbin, professor of psychology at the University of Wisconsin–La Crosse, has named *course portfolios*, portfolios that Pat Hutchings calls cousins of the teaching portfolio in her edited volume *The Course Portfolio: How Faculty Can Examine Their Teaching to Advance Practice and Improve Student Learning* (1998). Because the Writing Program teaches a four-course curriculum, many portfolios are also composed to explore the scope, sequence, and relationships of writing studio courses to one another.

15. It is interesting to note that Writing Program portfolios also customarily include discussions of five elements that Lee Shulman has identified as embodiments of teaching: vision, design, interactions, outcomes, and analysis of courses. See Lee S. Shulman, "Course Anatomy: The Dissection and Analysis of Knowledge through Teaching," in *The Course Portfolio* (1998), edited by Pat Hutchings.

16. In "The New Paradigm Wars: Is There Room for Rigorous Practitioner Knowledge in Schools and Universities?" (*Educational Researcher* 28.5, 12–21, 40), Gary L. Anderson and Kathryn Herr argue that new critical constructs are required in order to measure the rigor and value of practitioner research. Among the constructs they propose is outcome validity, which Anderson and Herr define as "the extent to which actions occur which lead to a resolution of the problem that led to the study" (15).

17. The Odyssey Project, designed originally by Stock, was piloted during the 1990–91 academic year and initiated in seventeen classes by twelve Professional Writing Instructors in the fall semester of 1991. Conceiving of literacy teaching, learning, and assessment as research that students and teachers would conduct together, the Odyssey Project regards these as reciprocally informing activities. Over the years, the project has developed and evolved in keeping with the interests of faculty involved and the needs of their students.

18. The contractually required groups in which instructors meet weekly to talk about their teaching are called Coordinating Groups. In them,

instructors talk about their courses and students within the Writing Program's holistic teaching project.

19. John Starkweather, "Interacting with Advanced Student Writers: Modes of Instruction and Intervention," *Reflections in Writing: Advanced Writing/Advanced Writer* 20, Spring 1999, http://www.wrt.syr.edu/wrt/pub/reflections/20/starkweather.html

20. As it happens, both Brown and Starkweather have presented work they included in the portfolio reflections reproduced here at sessions of the annual Conference on College Composition and Communication.

21. We are not the first by far to call teaching community property. Among others, Lee Shulman and Pat Hutchings have done so in print.

22. We allude here to the title of North's important book, *The Making of Knowledge in Composition: Portrait of an Emerging Field* (1987).

Works Cited

Anderson, E. (Ed.). (1993). *Campus use of the teaching portfolio: Twenty-five profiles*. Washington, DC: American Association for Higher Education.

Anderson, G. L., & Herr, K. (1999, June–July). The new paradigm wars: Is there room for rigorous practitioner knowledge in schools and universities? *Educational Researcher, 28(5)*, 12–21, 40.

Bateson, G. (1972). *Steps to an ecology of mind*. New York: Ballantine Books.

Boyer, E. (1990). *Scholarship reconsidered: Priorities of the professoriate*. Princeton, NJ: Carnegie Foundation for the Advancement of Teaching.

Carnegie Foundation for the Advancement of Teaching. (1990). *Campus life: In search of community. A special report*. Princeton, NJ: Author.

Cheney, L. V. (1990). *Tyrannical machines: A report on education practices gone wrong and our best hopes of setting them right*. Washington, DC: National Endowment for the Humanities.

Edgerton, R., Hutchings, P., & Quinlan, K. (1991). *The teaching portfolio: Capturing the scholarship in teaching*. Washington, DC: American Association for Higher Education.

Emerson, R., Fretz, R., & Shaw, L. (1995). *Writing ethnographic fieldnotes*. Chicago: University of Chicago Press.

Fishman, A. (1988). *Amish literacy: What and how it means*. Portsmouth, NH: Heinemann Educational Books.

Grice, H. P. (1975). Logic and conversation. In P. Cole & J. Morgan (Eds.), *Speech acts* (pp. 41–58). *Syntax and semantics III*. New York: Academic Press.

Hutchings, P. (1996). Making teaching community property: A menu for peer collaboration and peer review. Washington, DC: American Association for Higher Education.

Hutchings, P. (Ed.). (1998). The course portfolio: How faculty can examine their teaching to advance practice and improve student learning. Washington, DC: AAHE.

Lipson, C., & Voorheis, M. (2001). The material and the cultural as interconnected texts: Revising material conditions for part-time faculty at Syracuse University. In E. E. Schell & P. L. Stock (Eds.), *Moving a mountain: Transforming the role of contingent faculty in composition studies and higher education*. Urbana, IL: National Council of Teachers of English.

Lytle, S. L. (2000). Teacher research in the contact zone. In M. L. Kamil, R. Barr, P. Mosenthal, & D. Pearson (Eds.), *Handbook of reading research, vol. III*. Mahwah, NJ: L. Erlbaum Associates.

North, S. M. (1987). *The making of knowledge in composition: Portrait of an emerging field*. Upper Montclair, NJ: Boynton/Cook Publishers.

Phelps, L. W. (1991, December). Practical wisdom and the geography of knowledge in composition. *College English, 53(8)*, 863–885.

Rice, R. E. (1996). *Making a place for the new American scholar*. Washington, DC: American Association for Higher Education.

Rorty, R. (1989). *Contingency, irony and solidarity*. Cambridge; New York: Cambridge University Press.

Seldin, P. (1991). *The teaching portfolio: A practical guide to improved performance and promotion/tenure decisions*. Boston, MA: Anker Publishing.

Shore, B. M., et al. (1986). *The teaching dossier: A guide to its preparation and use*. (Revised edition). Montreal: Canadian Association of University Teachers.

Shulman, L. (1989, June). Toward a pedagogy of substance. *AAHE Bulletin, 41(10)*, 8–13.

Shulman, L. (Ed.). (1991). *Toward a pedagogy of cases: Case methods in teacher education*. New York: Teachers College Press.

Starkweather, J. (1999, Spring). Interactings with advance student writers: Modes of instruction and intervention. *Reflections in Writing: Advanced Writing/Advanced Writer, 20.*

Stock, P. L., & Robinson, J. L. (1990). Literacy as conversation: Classroom talk as text-building. In J. L. Robinson (Ed.), *Conversations on the written word: Essays on language and literacy*. Portsmouth, NH: Boynton/Cook.

Sykes, C. (1988). *Profscam: Professors and the demise of higher education*. Washington, DC: Regnery Gateway.

Weir, P. (Director). (1985). *Witness*. [Motion picture]. Hollywood, CA: Paramount Pictures.

Wolf, M. (1992). *A thrice told tale: Feminism, postmodernism and ethnographic responsibility*. Stanford, CA: Stanford University Press.

CHAPTER FOURTEEN

What's the Bottom Line? Literacy and Quality Education in the Twenty-First Century

EILEEN E. SCHELL

Syracuse University

T he Ground is Broken! Become a Part of the Rare Academic Adventure of Establishing a New State University." Advertising the new state university's commitment "to implementing, supporting, and rewarding new and innovative techniques," this caption in the *Chronicle of Higher Education* in spring 1997 represented the advertised institution's faculty as scholars "willing to experiment, assess, change and laugh" (quoted in Chait, 1998, p. 20). In addition to offering these enticing features, the advertised campus boasted a prime location between Fort Myers and Naples, Florida. Like most ads, this one had "fine print": "The State University System Board of Regents authorizes multiyear appointments at Florida Gulf Coast University" (p. 20). Florida Gulf Coast University was to be staffed with contract faculty who had multiyear appointments without the benefit of tenure (p. 20).

Florida Gulf Coast University was built, but who would come? The answer is surprising. Some tenured faculty even left their jobs to take non-tenure-line appointments!

As writers in the *Chronicle of Higher Education, Academe* and this collection warn, there is an increasing turn in our country and abroad toward contingent labor to reduce costs and increase institutional flexibility. Like it or not, faculty and academic administrators know that the growing employment of part-time and non-tenure-track faculty is likely to continue (Leatherman, 1999, A14–16). For academics, one concern is how the use of contingent faculty will affect the tenure system and academic free-dom; another is how employing larger numbers of part-time fac-ulty will affect the quality of undergraduate education. What will it mean to sustain existing academic programs, initiate curricu-lar reform, advise and mentor students (both graduate and un-dergraduate), and participate in faculty governance in an era marked by shrinking numbers of tenure-track faculty? How suc-cessful will a "trifurcated" faculty in a posttenure era be at work-ing across lines of rank and discipline toward common educational goals? How, for example, will English departments and writing programs improve undergraduate education and, more specifi-cally, undergraduate literacy instruction with growing numbers of non-tenure-line faculty? In this essay, I discuss questions such as these from a rhetorical perspective, reflecting on the ways in which discussions of quality education have been framed in de-bates surrounding part-time and non-tenure-track employment. As I discuss these issues, I argue that four conditions—compen-sation, contracts, conditions of work, and coalition building—are needed if we are to provide quality writing instruction in higher education.

Rhetorics of Lack and the Rhetorics of Responsibility: Addressing Issues of Contingent Faculty Employment and Educational Quality

Do part-time faculty spend less time on course preparation and meeting with students because they are compensated inad-equately? Are students, especially under-prepared students, dis-advantaged because their faculty "are not remunerated to provide the out-of-class support that is particularly essential" to them? Do part-time faculty members' purported "lack of collegial in-volvement or professional support make them less knowledge-able about their employers and therefore less able to represent, orient, or respond to their students" ("Statement" 57)? These are crucial questions that theorists, activists, and educational advocates are striving to answer, especially as the numbers of part-time and non-tenure-track faculty increase. Indeed concern over non-tenure-track hiring practices and their effects on educational quality sparked the 1997 Conference on the Growing Use of Part-time/Adjunct Faculty, a meeting where representatives from ten professional associations in the humanities and social sciences gathered to address concerns about educational quality. In the "Statement from the Conference on the Growing Use of Part-Time and Adjunct Faculty" conference, participants identified four areas of "educational quality" that are potentially breached by the overuse and exploitation of part-time faculty: "student access to faculty, cohesive curricular development and implementation, the intellectual community, and faculty governance" ("Statement" 54). As one NCTE delegate who attended the conference, I share the concerns in the "Statement" that emerged from the conference. Unfortunately, concerns about the effects of part-time teaching on quality education often turn into critiques of part-time faculty as individuals or as a class of undifferentiated faculty—a problematic rhetorical move that shifts responsibilities from institutions to individuals who occupy the problematic positions. Focusing on individuals instead of institutions deflects attention from colleges' and universities' policies and practices and in so doing impedes systemic analysis and critique of hiring patterns and working conditions in higher education.

Consider for example, David and Edith Foster's article, "It's a Buyer's Market: 'Disposable Professors,' Grade Inflation, and Other Problems" (1998). In it, Foster and Foster, two faculty working off the tenure track, chronicle the advantages and disadvantages of employing part-time faculty. Overall, they argue that the overuse of temporary faculty "lowers standards, undermines the coherence of curricula, worsens relations between students and faculty, and weakens students' affection for and loyalty to colleges" (p. 35). Claiming that part-time faculty on temporary appointments are particularly prone to inflate grades ("the temporary professor's struggle for survival provides a strong incentive to relax standards in the hopes of getting the good teaching evaluations that might distinguish him or her in a tight job market" (p. 32), Foster and Foster argue that part-time faculty are so busy working and trying to obtain additional or other jobs that they are professionally and materially constrained from giving "themselves wholeheartedly to preparing lectures, discussing ideas, or grading essays" (p. 32). Offering an anecdote about a student who tried to bully and cajole a part-time faculty member into changing his grade as evidence of the problematic working conditions they name, Foster and Foster do not cite qualitative or quantitative studies to support their claims. They also elide significant differences among part-time faculty: differences in terms of employment, differences in working conditions in different disciplines at different institutions. The result is an article that tends to portray part-time faculty as less competent teachers; the result is an article that once again constructs part-time faculty in a problematic light.

Throughout articles about part-time faculty, like the Fosters', scholars equate part-time faculty with transient faculty and tend to characterize them as those who lack understanding of programs, curricula, and students; hence, they are labeled inadequate or poor teachers. While part-time faculty employed on short-term contracts do face extremely challenging working conditions that must be addressed, and while Fosters' article does foreground those significant problems, researchers such as Gappa and Leslie point out that 45 percent of all part-timers "have worked at their current institutions for at least four or more years, 17 percent have worked there for six to ten years, and another 16 percent have worked there for more than ten years. These percentages challenge the myth of a temporary and transient part-time work force" (p. 11). All too often we only hear about "damage" done to programs that employ "transient" part-timers. It is certainly important to address the working conditions of "transient, part-time faculty but what about part-time percent of faculty who have been at their institutions for four or more years? What are the benefits incurred in programs that employ a steady, professionally active group of part-time or full-time non-tenure-track faculty? What can be done to support part-time and full-time, non-tenure-track faculty members in their work with students and their professional development opportunities? How can we work around what I have come to call the "hidden economy" of part-time work, the ways in which institutions often profit from the undercompensated emotional and material investments that non-tenure-line faculty make in their teaching?

These emotional and material investments constitute a not-insignificant, hidden economy of part-time labor. Many part-time faculty members do not complain publicly or organize against problematic working conditions because they fear that doing so may jeopardize their continued employment. Instead, these faculty members persevere, holding uncompensated office hours and commenting on drafts of papers. When they do not have offices, they confer with students in empty classrooms, stairwells, cafeterias, and fast-food restaurants. Often facing limited access to telephones, institutional e-mail access, or duplicating equipment, they may end up providing students with their home telephone numbers, private e-mail addresses, and they may open up copy accounts that they or their students subsidize. These compensatory practices—the stuff of the hidden economy—are not often discussed in what I have come to call the "rhetoric of lack" that constructs the part-time faculty member, a rhetoric that assumes, often incorrectly, that part-time faculty invest in their teaching only in proportion to the institutional compensation they are given.

In particular, women faculty, graduate students, and under-employed Ph.D.'s are those who support this hidden economy of part-time labor. As I argue in *Gypsy Academics and Mother-Teachers: Gender, Contingent Labor, and Writing Instruction*, many part-time faculty in the humanities are women accustomed, it is thought, to working for a "psychic income." Place-bound because of a spouse or partner's job, raising families, caring for elderly parents, women often seek part-time labor for the flexibility it affords. Graduate students or recent postgraduates, male and female, M.A.'s and Ph.D.'s who see part-time teaching as part of an apprenticeship toward full-time employment often invest themselves above and beyond their compensation because they hope their work experience will figure as credit and experience toward full-time employment. As a part-time faculty member in the late eighties, I served in the apprenticeship track at a community college. Earning less than minimum wage, I spent hours preparing to teach, grading papers, conferring with students, and moonlighting at waitressing and tutoring jobs to support my "teaching habit." Working hard for little pay, I believed my part-time position would someday lead to full-time work if not at that institution then at another. After talking to a number of part-time colleagues and a faculty mentor at the college, I realized that this path to a full-time employment was a long shot. I left part-time teaching, earned a doctorate, and was fortunate enough to eventually obtain a tenure-track job in my field. Yet the onward and upward success story is hardly the norm in the profession. As critics and commentators have pointed out (Nelson, 1995), the apprenticeship model can become exploitation when market conditions defer endlessly the possibility of a full-time job (see Curren, 1994).

Given the gendered and classed nature of the hidden economy of part-time labor, the generative question for higher education's policymakers and administrators to ask is not, Why don't part-time faculty provide quality education to their students? Rather it is, Why do institutions hire and then fail to provide part-time faculty with working conditions necessary for the provision of quality education? The bottom-line answer is simple: cost-savings—yet cost-savings at what cost to students, to educational programs, to educational quality? Leslie found that institutions that hire part-time faculty as a cost-saving measure to replace more expensive full-time faculty "became more fragmented, less concerned about quality, and less able to control their own futures. However, institutions that used part-time faculty selectively for clearly articulated reasons were far more likely to preserve the kind of academic community that serves as the foundation for good intellectual work" (1997, p. 7). In other words, the use of part-time faculty must be aligned with institutional and unit missions to serve educational goals for students. To be sure, ensuring the creation, production, and dissemination of new knowledges means a university must have "a critical mass of intellectually immersed and engaged faculty to do these things well" (p. 11)—whether they be full-time, tenure-accruing faculty or part-time or full-time non-tenure-track faculty.

Rather than belaboring the "rhetoric of lack" of part-time and non-tenure-track faculty, we would do well to focus our attention on faculty-student working-learning conditions. We would do well to ask the following questions: What learning conditions do students need? What working conditions do part-time and non-tenure-track faculty need in order to fulfill their obligations to their students? Under what circumstances do effective teaching and learning take place? In other words, we would do well to focus our attention on what is required for part-time and non-tenure-track faculty to be successful in their work. Within a "rhetoric of responsibility"—responsibility of institutions to faculty and students, faculty to students and institutions, students to learning—we must confront generatively issues of compensation, contracts, conditions of work, and coalition building.

Part-Time and Non-Tenure-Track Faculty and Quality Writing Instruction

Robert Connors reminds us that the working conditions in college writing courses have been problematic since their inception in the 1880s (1990). Although improvements have been made, the inconsistency of working conditions—contractual and monetary compensation—among writing faculty nationwide is dramatic. For example, in the regional area of the northeastern university where I work, my husband, who worked as a writing instructor for five years while he followed my career, earned $2,600 teaching first-year writing at a private research university (which offered a merit scale that would have allowed him to eventually make $3,600 per course); he was offered $1,300, to teach the same course twenty miles away at a private liberal arts college. He would have earned $1,800 to teach the course at a community college just miles away from our house had he chosen to do so.

To be sure, specific institutions' past and present administrative and economic histories and levels of funding dictate salary levels and working conditions. Still, the variable rates of pay for teaching a course at the core of the undergraduate curriculum are noteworthy. While influential scholars have drawn our attention to the hazards of curricular inconsistency in the introductory composition course (see for example, Crowley, 1991) few scholars have focused our attention as effectively on how the working conditions of part-time and non-tenure-track determine the quality of composition courses as surely as their content does. The working conditions of so many part-time and non-tenure-track writing faculty stands in sharp contrast to the academy's renewed interest in undergraduate education, to the importance of literacy education for students living in an information economy, and to demographic trends in the country. In *Failing the Future: A Dean Looks at Higher Education in the Twenty-first Century*, Annette Kolodny, former dean of the University of Arizona, argues that between the years 1997 to 2015, we will witness a 20 percent increase in enrollments. Students of the new millennium will increasingly come from racial and ethnic minority groups and from "poor families and even poorer school districts" (p. 34). Arguing against the bottom-line rhetoric of higher-education management policies, Kolodny insists that students will "need more professors, more classrooms, more computers, more foreign language instruction, and better equipped science laboratories if they are to receive a quality education and fulfill the employment needs of the coming century" (p. 34). As a result, more—not less—funding will be needed for "scholarships, loans, counseling, academic tutoring, and remediation programs" (p. 34). Writing programs and writing centers will become increasingly important places in which students will learn "how to analyze . . . information, recognize recurrent patterns or connections, and extract what is truly important" (p. 34). However, focusing on what students need to know without focusing on what working conditions and resources faculty need to teach is problematic.

In an environment of challenged funding for public education, how do we link the quality of education to quality working conditions? What do we mean by the phrase "quality writing instruction," especially since "quality" is an abstraction currently used with wild abandon in higher-education literature. For some, quality instruction in first-year writing courses can only be provided by tenure-line faculty trained in composition. This was the controversial argument made in the CCCC "Statement on Principles and Standards for Postsecondary Writing Instruction." For others, quality means creating working conditions that allow thoughtful and engaged writing instruction to occur no matter who is in the writing classroom. This was the view of those who drafted the "Wyoming Resolution," a labor statement meant to argue for improvements in the working conditions of all writing faculty. From my vantage point, quality writing instruction depends on fair compensation, contracts, working conditions, and—

it has become clear—on coalition building. Experience has taught those of us in composition studies that these conditions are necessary for viable and sustainable teaching cultures, for cultures that enable the growth and development of both teachers and students.

Enacting the Four Cs: Compensation, Contracts, Conditions, and Coalition Building

When salaries range as widely as $900–$3,500 per section for writing courses (AAUP Committee G, 1993, p. 44), how can institutions claim that students are getting the best quality writing instruction? The provision of quality writing instruction becomes especially questionable when we look at how salaries translate into compensation for the actual work completed. Let's break down the wage levels of a part-time writing faculty member who earns $1,800 per section. Writing courses, like most non-lecture humanities courses, are labor-intensive. Each course requires the instructor to undertake ten or more hours of instruction and preparation per week. So let us say, this hypothetical writing instructor spends three or four hours a week teaching an assigned writing class. Let us say she also spends an additional seven hours a week meeting with students, preparing for class sessions, and commenting on student work. If we calculate the average wages for an instructor who spends ten hours a week teaching, preparing, and grading for fifteen weeks, her average wage will be around $12.00 per hour. It should be noted that this is a conservative time estimate at best—the actual time spent on teaching preparations and commenting on and grading papers would likely be much higher.

The $12.00 per hour wage may sound like a respectable one only if it is considered in isolation of other factors. If this writing faculty member wishes to earn the equivalent of a full-time income from teaching writing, he or she would have to teach eight or more courses per year—a labor-intensive enterprise that would leave little or no time for the faculty member to participate in professional conferences or publication, the work most likely to lead to professional recognition and career advancement. Furthermore, because her contract is only semester-to-semester, the instructor may not know if she can count on working at one institution in order to earn a full-time income. She may end up pursuing what Helen O'Grady calls interinstitutional teaching, cobbling together a full course load at multiple institutions, commuting miles between institutions, negotiating different writing curricula, commenting on endlessly accumulating stacks of papers. Even if she could count on a continued academic-year appointment at one institution, compensation and future job security would still be an issue: She would earn only $14,400 for teaching the eight courses. Is a $14,400 a fair salary for teaching a full, academic course load for one year? Does that compensation encourage innovation, continued growth of the faculty member, continued investment in the institution and the students? The answer is a resounding "No." An instructor trying to survive on such a salary would have to teach summer courses and perhaps moonlight at another job. Let me add as well that her employing institution, given its piecework pay rates, would probably be reluctant to offer her the equivalent of a full-time position. If it did so, it would probably have to provide benefits and that would impinge on its use of part-time labor as a cost-saving measure. Even if she had other means of support (a spouse or partner with a better-paying job), the working conditions under which she would labor provide disincentive for the improvement of teaching even as this faculty member may, at the same time, struggle to do the best she can to provide her students with quality writing instruction. Again, the hidden economy of contingent labor must be evoked with its gendered dimensions. Thus, the part-time and non-tenure-track piecework system persists.

To address the problems of this piecework system (low salaries, uncertain contracts, few or no benefits), many colleges and universities have successfully created non-tenure-track positions with salaries, benefits, and renewable or multiyear contracts (see, Brumberger, Lipson and Voorheis, and Maid in this volume). These institutions have come to realize that the quality of instruction across the institution is affected by the ways in which writing faculty are hired, contracted, paid, oriented (or not), mentored (or not), evaluated (or not), and/or offered professional development opportunities (or not). As Eva Brumberger argues, though, these positions must be integrated into departments, not kept at a "separate" and "unequal" status in relation to full-time tenure-track positions. In other words, improvements in working conditions must be linked to the creation and sustenance of a viable teaching culture, a reward system, and an intellectual culture that value teaching-intensive positions. Institutions that have been the most successful at establishing such positions are those that offer instructors the opportunity to participate in the creation of a teaching culture that allows them to inform and reflect on their teaching within a community of others engaged in such practices. Patti Stock and her co-authors in this volume make an important argument for making reflective scholarship of and about teaching a significant component of such communities.

Changing working conditions, however, may prove to be more easily attainable than changing the intellectual culture. Messages about the "proper" and "fitting" academic careers transmitted to generation upon generation of graduate students and beginning faculty members live on despite dramatic changes to the careers of the professoriate. In institutions where the research ideal is held up as the proper aspiration, those who do not attain research-oriented academic jobs are made to feel as if they failed to realize their potential. Those who locate in teaching-intensive positions, many of them non-tenure track, are made to feel as if they failed as well. Those in teaching-intensive positions in composition are often made to feel that their work lacks intellectual rigor, that it is uninteresting drudgery. The result can be a seriously demoralized faculty that does not value or realize its full potential because of the burden of an unrealistic ideal and a set of exploitive working conditions.

In a culture where higher education will play an increasingly important role in creating a literate, informed citizenry, we can ill afford a system that exploits and demoralizes those who hold the primary responsibility for teaching literacy courses such as first-year writing. Yet advocates for improving part-time and non-tenure-track faculty's working conditions often face the accusation that by organizing to improve working conditions they are, in essence, creating a two- or even three-tiered faculty and further eroding tenure. Ironically, the two- and three-tiered faculty system already exists and will be further exploited if faculty do not act now to better working conditions. We cannot afford to make purist arguments about preventing a two-tiered faculty when one already exists. Educating tenure-track faculty about their common cause with part-time and non-tenure-track faculty remains an important but challenging element to successful organizing.

How can such arguments for equitable salaries, contracts, and conditions of work be made? Before attempting any efforts, interested parties would be well advised to inform themselves about the best way to undertake coalition building and collective organizing efforts. An invaluable resource can be found in the organizing kit, "Working for Renewal: A Kit for Organizing on the Issues of Part-Time and Non-Tenure-Track Faculty," available from the American Association of University Professors (K. Thompson, e-mail to author, March 20, 2000). After surveying available options, a group of concerned parties can pursue organizing efforts through a variety of means. One step may be to organize and form a union to bargain collectively for improved working conditions (see Jacobsohn, Kirscht, & Tingle in this volume). At a nonunionized campus, a task force or standing committee on part-time and non-tenure-track issues might be assembled to undertake a three-pronged strategy for addressing compensation and contracts: (1) a local study; (2) a comparison of the local study to regional and national data; (3) a proposal for changing working conditions accompanied by a coalition-building effort.

In such efforts, the first strategy is to issue questionnaires/studies of part-time and non-tenure-track faculty's working conditions, analyzing how much time part-time contingent faculty spend preparing class plans, commenting on drafts, grading, and working with students outside of class. In addition, surveys/questionnaires should ask part-time and non-tenure-track faculty how their working conditions enable and disable them from providing the quality education students need. University, college, and department mission statements or outcomes assessment plans can be used as measures against which teachers can evaluate their ability to provide quality instruction. Conducting such studies can help determine how contingent faculty's work is compensated and how their working conditions may interfere with their ability to provide the sort of instruction and attention students need. It is important to focus attention on working conditions that are necessary if teachers are to provide their students quality learning conditions.

The second strategy is for committees to undertake peer institution surveys, to learn about section rates/salaries, contracts, and professional development opportunities at comparable institutions. This comparative data can be used to make arguments for needed improvements in contracts and compensation. It is worth emphasizing, however, that the best of proposals cannot be implemented without a collective group advocating for change.

The untapped allies that contingent faculty have in the fight for quality working conditions are our students. Elana Peled and her colleagues' article in this volume provides an excellent example of how a coalition of part-time and full-time faculty and students mobilized successfully to defend writing instructors' jobs. Students can be helped to understand that their educational interests are connected to the plight of part-time and non-tenure-track faculty. As Karen Thompson has argued: "They [students] need to see where their money is going, or not going; how their issues are connected to our issues. It's not just tuition versus salaries. Restrictions in course offerings, reductions in enrollment, cuts in student aid are all part of the contraction of higher education, which includes downsizing faculty and rising administrative spending" (p. A23). Thompson has also argued that writing teachers should specifically "devote one class period per term to discussing these issues" (K. Thompson, e-mail to author, 2000).

In addition to students, writing program administrators and department chairs are especially important advocates for professionalizing and stabilizing temporary positions; they cannot, however, do this advocacy work alone. Professional organizations, which have provided statements about part-time and non-tenure-track employment, need to provide specific advice and assistance on how to negotiate recommended professional guidelines given the constraints of local institutions. The recent MLA/CCCC survey on working conditions for part-time and non-tenure-track faculty will provide much-needed national data on the compensation, contracts, and conditions of part-time and non-tenure-track writing teachers. Once this survey is released, it should provoke a profession-wide conversation about what working conditions are needed to ensure quality education. But until that data is released, those seeking immediate data on part-time and non-tenure-track positions would do well to consult the AAUP's "Report On the Status of Non-Tenure-Track Faculty."

Accrediting agencies must also serve as key players in the struggle to improve working conditions. As former AAUP President James Perley puts it: "We can insist that accrediting bodies be more than agents hired to certify that institutions are fiscally sound and do what their mission statements say they intend to do. We can insist that institutions meet minimal standards for certification" (1998, p. 57). In the state of Washington, the regional accrediting association's failure to enforce minimum standards led to a complaint being filed with the U.S. Department of Education in September 1997. Adjunct philosophy and psychology professor Keith Hoeller filed the complaint, and it may serve as a much-needed wake-up call to accrediting associations that faculty are serious about issues of quality and that they will take their grievances to the legal system if necessary (Leatherman, p. A12). Another possible arena of action is through legislation, specifically the use of "funding disincentives or caps to discourage overreliance on part-time faculty for undergraduate instruction" (Perley 1998, p. 58)—an option currently being pursued in the state of California.

Overall, the organizing strategies that will work best must be adaptive and multiple; they must involve coalition building that connects the working conditions of part-time and non-tenure-track faculty to the quality of education available to students. Advocates for improving contingent faculty's working conditions should consider the following broadly conceived activist educational agenda:

♦ improve part-time faculty's working conditions from poorly paid semester-to-semester contracts into year or multiyear contracts with decent pay and benefits;

♦ consolidate excessive temporary part-time positions into permanent part-time ones or full-time non-tenure-track positions with contractual permanence and fair salaries;

- work to create a reward system that values teaching-intensive positions and creates a teaching culture that rewards and recognizes reflective teaching;

- advocate hiring more full-time, tenure-track faculty to strengthen college and university curricula, programs, and the academic governance system;

- examine the growth of administrative positions in light of the shrinking resources available for instructional faculty and make that information widely available to multiple publics;

- advocate for an informed and considered use of distance education when appropriate but avoid its spiraling and unchecked use;

- work with faculty, students, staff, and others to advocate the preservation of public funding for higher education and to keep higher education affordable and accessible.

- find rhetorically effective ways to communicate this broad activist educational agenda to legislators, parents, and taxpayers.

The contributors to this volume have indicated different approaches that demonstrate how this agenda can be realized. Yet our true challenge lies in whether faculty of all ranks can work collectively across lines of difference to address contingent faculty's working conditions in light of issues of educational quality. We must ask: "What's the bottom-line for higher education's consideration of issues of educational quality?" The bottom-line on educational quality is employment equity.

Works Cited

AAUP Committee G Report on Part-Time and Non-Tenure Track Appointments. (1993, July–August). Report: The status of non-tenure track faculty. *Academe, 79(4)*, 39–48.

CCCC Executive Committee. (1989, October). Statement of principles and standards for the postsecondary teaching of writing. *College Composition and Communication, 40(3)*, 329–336.

Chait, R. (1998, September/October). Build it and who will come? *Change: The Magazine of Higher Learning 30(5)*, 20–29.

Connors, R. (1990, Fall). Overwork/underpay: Labor and status of composition teachers since 1880. *Rhetoric Review, 9(1)*, 108–126.

Crowley, S. (1991, Fall/Winter). A personal essay on freshman English. *Pre/Text 12(3–4)*, 156–176.

Curren, E. D. (1994). No openings at this time: Job market collapse and graduate education. *Profession 94*, 57–61.

Foster, D., & Foster, E. (1998, January/February). It's a buyer's market: Disposable professors, grade inflation, and other problems. *Academe, 84(1)*, 28–35.

Gappa, J. M., & Leslie, D. W. (1993). *Two faculties or one?: The conundrum of part-timers in a bifurcated work force.* New Pathways: Faculty Careers and Employment for the 21st Century Working Papers Series. Washington, DC: American Association for Higher Education.

Kolodny, A. (1998). Failing the future: A dean looks at higher education in the twenty-first century. Durham, NC: Duke University Press.

Leatherman, C. (1997, November 7). Do accreditors look the other way when colleges rely on part-timers? *Chronicle of Higher Education*, p. A12.

Leatherman, C. (1999, April 9). Growth in positions off the tenure-track is a trend that's here to stay, study finds. *The Chronicle of Higher Education, 45(31)*, pp. A14–A16.

Leslie, D. (1997, September). *The myths and realities of the 'invisible faculty'.* Presentation at the Conference on the Growing Use of Part-Time and Adjunct Faculty in Higher Education, Washington, DC.

Nelson, C. (1995, Fall/Winter). Lessons from the job wars: Late capitalism arrives on campus. *Social Text, 13(3)*, 119–134.

Perley, J. (1998, November/December). Educational excellence: Presidential address. 1998 American Association of University Professors Annual Meeting. *Academe, 84(6)*, 54–57.

Robertson, L., Crowley, S., & Lentricchia, F. (1987, March). Opinion: The Wyoming Conference Resolution opposing unfair salaries and working conditions for postsecondary teachers of writing. *College English, 49(3)*, 274–280.

Schell, E. E. (1998). *Gypsy academics and mother-teachers: Gender, contingent labor, and writing instruction.* Portsmouth, NH: Boynton/Cook.

Statement from the Conference on the Growing Use of Part-Time and Adjunct Faculty. (1998, January/February). *Academe, 84(1),* 54–60.

Thompson, K. (1998, February). The ultimate working conditions: Knowing whether you have a job or not. *Forum, Newsletter of the Non-Tenure-Track Faculty Special Interest Group. College Composition and Communication, 49(1),* A19–24.

Select Bibliography: Contingent Labor Issues in Composition Studies and Higher Education (Current to 1998)

MARGARET M. CUNNIFFE AND EILEEN E. SCHELL

AAUP Committee A on Academic Freedom and Tenure. (1978, September). On full-time non-tenure track appointments. *AAUP Bulletin, 64(3)*, 267–73.

AAUP Committee A on Academic Freedom and Tenure. (1981, February). The status of part-time faculty. *Academe, 67(1)*, 29–39.

AAUP Committee G on Part-Time and Non-Tenure Track Appointments. (1992, November–December). Report on the status of non-tenure track faculty. *Academe, 78(6)*, 39–48.

AAUP Committee G on Part-Time and Non-Tenure Track Appointments. (1993, July–August). Report: The status of non-tenure track faculty. *Academe, 79.4*, 39–48.

AAUP Committee W on the Status of Women. (1987, July–August). Senior appointments with reduced loads. *Academe, 73(4)*, 50.

AAUP Special Committee on Nontenured Faculty. (1972, Summer). Report of the special committee on nontenured faculty. *AAUP Bulletin, 58(2)*, 156–59.

AAUP Special Committee on Nontenured Faculty. (1973, Summer). 1973 report of the special committee on nontenured faculty. *AAUP Bulletin, 59(2)*, 185–87.

AAUP Subcommittee on Nontenured Faculty. (1986, July–August). On full-time non-tenure track appointments. *Academe, 72(4)*, 14a–19a.

Select Bibliography

Abel, E. (1976). *Invisible and indispensable: Part-time teachers in California community colleges*. (ERIC) ED 132 984. Santa Monica, CA: Santa Monica College, 1–58.

Abel, E. (1984). *Terminal degrees: The job crisis in higher education*. New York: Praeger.

Abel, E. (1985, Spring). Organizing part-time faculty. *Women's Studies Quarterly, 13*, 16–17.

Accrediting standards regarding part-time instructors. (1997, November 7). *Chronicle of Higher Education*, p. A13.

Agee, A. S. (1984). Shadow into sunshine: Integrating part-time faculty. In M. E. Wallace (Ed.), *Part-time academic employment in the humanities* (pp. 63–65). New York: Modern Language Association.

Aisenberg, N., & Harrington, M. (1988). *Women of academe: Outsiders in the sacred grove*. Amherst, MA: University of Massachusetts Press.

Allen, V. (1992, September). A comment on "teaching college English as a woman" [response to Bloom, 1992]. *College English, 55*, 552–556.

Altbach, P. G. (1995, March). Problems and possibilities: The US academic profession. *Studies in Higher Education, 20(1)*, 27–44.

Altbach, P. G. (1995, January 6). The pros and cons of hiring 'taxicab' professors. *Chronicle of Higher Education*, p. B3.

American Historical Association. (1971, May 25). *Final report of the Ad Hoc Committee on the Status of Women in the Historical Profession*. Washington, DC.

Anderson, M. (1895). English at Stanford University. In W. M. Payne, (Ed.), *English in American universities*. Boston: Heath.

Anderson, S. A. (1949, February). School Board policies concerning teachers' part-time employment. *American School Board Journal, 118*, 50.

Applebee, A. (1974). *Tradition and reform in the teaching of English: A history*. Urbana, IL: National Council of Teachers of English.

Arden, E. (1989, May 17). Point of view. *Chronicle of Higher Education*, pp. A48–49.

Arden, E. (1995, July 21). Ending the loneliness and isolation of adjunct professors. *Chronicle of Higher Education*, p. A44.

Ashton-Jones, E. (1995). Collaboration, conversation, and the politics of gender. In L.W. and Janet Emig (Eds.), *Feminine principles and women's experience in American composition and rhetoric* (pp. 5–26). Pittsburgh: University of Pittsburgh Press.

Association of Departments of English. (1993, Spring). ADE policy statement and guidelines. *ADE Bulletin, 105*, 43–48.

Association of Departments of English. (1993, Spring). ADE statement on the use of part-time and full-time adjunct faculty. *ADE Bulletin, 104*, 62.

Association of Departments of English of the Modern Language Association. (1983, Spring). Statement on the use of part-time faculty. *ADE Bulletin, 74*, 65.

Association of Departments of English of the Modern Language Association. (1996, Spring). ADE statement of good practice: Teaching, evaluation, and scholarship. *ADE Bulletin, 113*, 53–58.

Auser, C. P. (1974, November). Part-time employment: '. . . Nothing as desperate . . .' *ADE Bulletin, 43*, 11–12.

Balester, V. (1992, May). Revising the 'Statement': On the work of writing centers. *College Composition and Communication, 43*(2), 167–171.

Bannerji, H. et al. (Eds.). (1992). *Unsettling relations: The university as a site of feminist struggles*. Boston: South End Press.

Bargaining unit status of part-time faculty. (1979, July). *Journal of Law and Education 8(3)*, 361–378.

Barr-Ebest, S. (1995, Spring). Gender differences in writing program administration. *WPA: Writing Program Administration 18(3)*, 53–72.

Basinger, J. (1998, January 23). State judge clears way for U. of Alaska adjuncts to bargain. *Chronicle of Higher Education*, p. A14.

Batson, L. G. (1988, Fall/Winter). Defining ourselves as woman (in the profession). *Pre/Text*, 207–209.

Bauer, W. K. (1979, Winter). Adjunct professors: Appropriate and inappropriate personnel policies and procedures. *Journal of College and University Personnel Association, 30*, 47–53.

Bauer, W. K. (1982, Winter). Adjunct faculty: Collective bargaining and affirmative action policies and procedures. *Journal of College and University Personnel Association, 34(4)*, 1–7.

Bazerman, C. (1995). Response: Curricular responsibilities and professional definition. In J. Petraglia (Ed.), *Reconceiving writing, rethinking writing instruction* (pp. 249–259). Mahwah, NJ: J. L. Erlbaum Associates.

Bedics, R. A., & Smith, C. (1985, January). Part-time instructors: An inservice program to increase teaching effectiveness. *Industrial Education, 74*, 22–23.

Behrendt, R. L., & Parsons, M. H. (1983). Evaluation of part-time faculty. *New Directions for Community Colleges, 11(1)*, 33–43.

Benjet, R. G., & Loweth, M. (1989, February). A perspective on the academic underclass, the part-timers. *Teaching English in the Two-Year College, 16(1)*, 40–42.

Berger, J. (1998, March 8). After her Ph.D., the scavenger's life: Trying to turn a patchwork of part-time jobs into an academic career. *New York Times, 147* (Section 1), 35, 38.

Bergman, B. R. (1983, September–October). Feminism and economics. *Academe, 69(5)*, 22-25.

Bergman, B. R. (1986). *The economic emergence of women*. New York: Basic Books, Inc.

Bergman, B. R. (1991, November–December). Bloated administration, blighted campuses. *Academe, 77(6)*, 12–16.

Berlin, J. (1984). *Writing instruction in nineteenth-century American colleges*. Carbondale, IL.: Southern Illinois University Press.

Berlin, J. (1987). *Rhetoric and reality: Writing instruction in American colleges, 1900–1985*. Carbondale, IL.: Southern Illinois University Press.

Berlin, J., & Vivion, M. J. (Eds.). (1992). *Cultural studies in the English classroom*. Portsmouth, NH: Boynton/Cook Heinemann.

Berlow, L. H., & Collos, A. L. (1974, November). Part-time employment: We teach; therefore, we are. *ADE Bulletin, 43*, 9–11.

Bernard, J. (1974). *Academic women*. University Park, PA: Pennsylvania State University Press.

Bérubé, M., & Nelson, C. (Eds.). (1995). *Higher education under fire: Politics, economics, and the crisis of the humanities*. New York: Routledge.

Berver, K., Kurtz, D., & Orton, E. (1992, November–December). Off the track, but in the fold. *Academe, 78(6)*, 27-29.

Biklen, S. K. (1995). *School work: Gender and the cultural construction of teaching*. New York: Teachers College Press.

Biles, G. E., & Tuckman, H. P. (1986). *Part–time faculty personnel management policies*. New York: American Council on Education: Macmillan Publishing Co.

Billett, R. E. (1957, November). Pros and cons of the half-day teacher. *Ohio Schools, 35*, 23.

Bishop, J. F. (1968, December). College women as part-time workers. *Journal of College Placement, 29*, 113-114.

Bissex, G. L., & Bullock, R. H. (1987). *Seeing for ourselves: Case-study research by teachers of writing*. Portsmouth, NH: Heinemann.

Bizzell, P. (1992, Fall). Opportunities for feminist research in the history of rhetoric. *Rhetoric Review, 11(1)*, 50–58.

Bledstein, B. (1976). *The culture of professionalism: The middle class and the development of higher education in America*. New York: Norton.

Bloom, L. Z. (1992, November). Teaching college as a woman. *College English, 54(7)*, 818–825.

Bloom, L. Z., Daiker, D., & White, E. (Eds.). (1996). *Composition in the twenty-first century: Crisis and change*. Carbondale, IL: Southern Illinois University Press.

Blum, D. E. (1990, February 7). Community college rescinds a faculty pact. *Chronicle of Higher Education*, p. A18.

Bonham, G. W. (1982, April). Part-time faculty: A mixed blessing. *Change, 14(3)*, 10–11.

Bottiani, S. (1994, March 16). *Part-time teaching/full-time parenting/full-time consequences*. (ERIC) ED 371 365. Paper presented at the Conference on College Composition and Communication, Nashville, TN.

Bowen, H. R. (1980, Summer). A nation of educated people. *Liberal Education, 66(2)*, 132–140.

Bowen, H. R., & Schuster, J. H. (1985, September–October). Outlook for the academic profession. *Academe, 71*, 9–15.

Bowen, H. R., & Schuster, J. H. (1986). *American professors: An American resource imperiled*. New York: Oxford University Press.

Boyar, D., & MacKenzie, D. G. (1987, Winter). The evaluation and development of part-time faculty in community colleges. *Community College Review, 15(3)*, 33–40.

Boyer, E. (1990). *Scholarship reconsidered: priorities of the professoriate.* Princeton: Carnegie Foundation for the Advancement of Teaching.

Bramlett, P., & Rodriguez, R. C. (1982–83, December–January). Part-time faculty: Full-time concern. *Community and Junior College Journal 53(4)*, 40–41.

Brannon, L. (1995). (Dis)missing compulsory first-year composition. In J. Petraglia (Ed.), *Reconceiving writing, rethinking writing instruction* (pp. 239–48). Mahwah, NJ: Lawrence Erlbaum Associates, Publishers.

Bridwell-Bowles, L. (1992, October). Discourse and diversity: Experimental writing within the academy. *College Composition and Communication, 43(3)*, 349–368.

Brodie, J. M. (1995, January–February). Whatever happened to the job boom. *Academe*, 81(1), 12–15.

Brodkey, L. (1994). Making a federal case out of difference: The politics of pedagogy, publicity, and postponement. In J. Clifford and J. Schilb (Eds.), *Writing theory and critical theory* (pp. 236–261). New York: Modern Language Association.

Brown, S. L. (1979). Approaching faculty productivity as a mechanism for retrenchment. *Directions for Institutional Research, Planning Rational Retrenchment, No. 24, 6(4)*, 45–54.

Bruffee, K. (1984). Peer tutoring and the 'conversation of mankind.' In G. Olson (Ed.), *Writing centers: Theory and administration* (pp. 3–15). Urbana, IL: National Council of Teachers of English.

Bruffee, K. (1986, December). Social construction, language, and the authority of knowledge: A bibliographic essay. *College English, 48(8)*, 773–790.

Bullock, R., Trimbur, J., & Schuster, C. (Eds.). (1991). *The politics of writing instruction: Postsecondary.* Portsmouth, NH: Boynton/Cook.

Bullough, V. L. (1958, December). Preliminary study on the utilization of part-time teachers. *Association of American Colleges Bulletin, 44,* 611–623.

Burd, S. (1992, September 30). Humanities chief assails politicization of classrooms. *Chronicle of Higher Education*, pp. A21–22.

Burd, S. (1994, June 1). Health coverage seen for part-time college employees. *Chronicle of Higher Education*, p. A30.

Burd, S. (1994, July 20). Academe watchful on health-care program: Health-care proposals satisfy academic leaders but they are anxious about legislative outcome. *Chronicle of Higher Education*, p. A22.

Burns, M. (1992, Spring). Women, part-time faculty, and illusion. *Thought and Action, 8(1)*, 13–28.

Burns, M. (1993, May–June). Service courses: Doing women a disservice. *Academe, 79(3)*, 18–21.

Cage, M.C. (1995, June 23). AAUP seeks ways to improve the image of the professoriate. *Chronicle of Higher Education*, p. A16.

Cain, W. E. (1992, December 16). Different perspectives on part-time faculty [Letter to the editor]. *Chronicle of Higher Education*, p. B6.

Campbell, J. (1992a, December). Controlling voices: The legacy of English A at Radcliffe College, 1883–1917. *College Composition and Communication, 43*, 472–485.

Campbell, J. (1992b). Women's work, worthy work: Composition instruction at Vassar College, 1897–1922. In M. Secor and D. Charney (Eds.), *Constructing rhetorical education* (pp. 26–42). Carbondale, IL: Southern Illinois University Press.

Campbell, J. (1995). Afterword: Revealing the ties that bind? In C. Hobbs (Ed.), *Nineteenth century women learn to write* (pp. 303–309). Charlottesville and London: University of Virginia Press.

Campbell, O. J. (1939). The failure of freshman English. *English Journal, 28*, 177–185.

Caplan, P. (1993). *Lifting a ton of feathers: A woman's guide for surviving in the academic world*. Toronto: University of Toronto Press.

Caplin, S., & Caplin, D. (1981, October). Job sharing helps teachers, administrators, and students. *American School Board Journal, 168(10)*, 33–34.

Carter, D., & McClelland, B. (1992, Fall/Winter). WPAs assess the CCCC's 'Statement of Principles and Standards'. *WPA: Writing Program Administration, 16(1–2)*, 71–87.

Carter, G.F. (1979, January). Part-time staffing: Management dilemma. *Journal of Physical Education and Recreation, 50(1)*, 49.

Carter, S.B. (1981, Summer). Academic women revisited: An empirical study of changing patterns in women's employment as college and university faculty, 1890–1963. *Journal of Social History, 14(4)*, 675–700.

Cassenbaum, A. (1989, October). A comment on 'The Wyoming Conference Resolution.' *College English, 51*, 636–38.

Caterino, B. (1996, January 19). Fair treatment for adjuncts [Letter to the editor]. *Chronicle of Higher Education*, p. B5.

Cayton, M. K. (1991, October). Writing as outsiders: Academic discourse and marginalized faculty. *College English, 53(6)*, 647–660.

Caywood, C. L., & Overing, G. R. (Eds.). (1987). *Teaching writing: Pedagogy, gender, and equity*. Albany: State University of New York Press.

Caywood, C. L., & Overing, G. R. (Eds.). (1987). Introduction. In C. L. Caywood and G. R. Overing (Eds.), *Teaching writing: Pedagogy, gender, and equity* (pp. xi–xvi). Albany: State University of New York Press.

CCCC: Voices in the parlor, and responses. (1988). *Rhetoric Review, 7(1)*, 195–213.

CCCC Committee on Professional Standards for Quality Education. (1989, February). CCCC initiatives on the Wyoming Conference Resolution: A draft report. *College Composition and Communication, 40(1)*, 61–72.

CCCC Committee on Professional Standards for Quality Education. (1991, November 5). *Memorandum to the CCCC Executive Committee*.

CCCC Committee on Professional Standards for Quality Education. (1993, March 20). *Memorandum to the CCCC Executive Committee*.

CCCC Executive Committee. (1989, October). Statement of principles and standards for the post-secondary teaching of writing. *College Composition and Communication, 40(3)*, 329–336.

CCCC Executive Committee. (1991, October). A progress report from the CCCC Committee on Professional Standards. *College Composition and Communication, 42(3)*, 330–344.

Chell, C. (1982, January). Memoirs and confessions of a part-time lecturer. *College English, 44(1)*, 35–40.

Childers, K., Rackin, P., Secor, C., & Tracy, C. (1981). A network of one's own. In G. DeSole and L. Hoffmann (Eds.), *Rocking the boat: Academic women and academic processes* (pp. 117–127). New York: Modern Language Association.

Cinelli, A. E. (1997, May 2). The consequences of relying on low-paid, part-time lecturers [Letter to the editor]. *Chronicle of Higher Education,* p. B3.

Clark, G., & Halloran, S. M. (Eds.). (1993). *Oratorical culture in nineteenth-century America: Transformations in the theory and practice of rhetoric.* Carbondale, IL: Southern Illinois University Press.

Clark, S. M., & Corcoran, M. (1987, Winter). The professoriate: A demographic profile. *National Forum: The Phi Kappa Phi Journal, 67(1),* 28–32.

Clausen, C. (1988, Fall). Part-timers in the English department: Some problems and some solutions. *ADE Bulletin, 90,* 4–6.

Cline, L. (1993, February). Work to school transition: Part-time faculty bring expertise, challenges to colleges. *Vocational Education Journal, 68(2),* 26–27, 49.

Coalition of Women Scholars in the History of Rhetoric and Composition. (1996, March). *Fact-sheet distributed at the 1996 Conference on College Composition and Communication.* Milwaukee, WI.

Connors, R. (1990, Fall). Overwork/underpay: labor and status of composition teachers since 1880. *Rhetoric Review, 9(1),* 108–126.

Connors, R. (1991). Rhetoric in the modern university: The creation of an underclass. In R. Bullock, J. Trimbur, and C. Schuster (Eds.), *The politics of writing instruction: Postsecondary* (pp. 55–84). Portsmouth, NH: Boynton/Cook.

Connors, R. (1995). Women's reclamation of rhetoric in nineteenth-century America. In L. W. Phelps and J. Emig (Eds.), *Feminine principles and women's experience in American composition and rhetoric* (pp. 67–90). Pittsburgh, PA: University of Pittsburgh Press.

Connors, R. (1996a, February). Teaching and learning as a man. *College English, 58(2),* 137–57.

Connors, R. (1996b). The abolition debate in composition: A short history. In L. Z. Bloom., D. Daiker, and E. White (Eds.), *Composition in the twenty-first century: Crisis and change* (pp. 47–63). Carbondale: Southern Illinois University Press.

Cook, A. H. (1972, September). Sex discrimination at universities: An ombudsman's view. *AAUP Bulletin 58(3),* 279–282.

Cooper, E. J. (1995, September 1). *Re: part-time faculty.* [On-line]. Listserv post to WPA-L. Available: <WPA L@asuvm.inre.asu.edu>.

Cooper, M. M., & Holzman, M. (1989). *Writing as social action*. Portsmouth, NH: Boynton/Cook.

Cottingham, W. T., et al. (1981, Summer). Is there practical help for the part-time faculty—our new and neglected majority? *Community College Review, 9(1)*, 12–17.

Crain, J. C. (1988, January). A comment on "The Wyoming Conference Resolution: Opposing Unfair Salaries and Working Conditions for Post-Secondary Teachers of Writing." *College English, 50(1)*, 95–99.

Crain, J. C. (1990, April). A response to Anne Cassebaum's "A Comment on the Wyoming Resolution Opposing Unfair Salaries and Working Conditions for Post-Secondary Teachers of Writing". *College English, 52*, 469–473.

Crissey, M. (1997, October 17). Allegheny College may cut 3 departments to save money. *Chronicle of Higher Education*, p. A14.

Crowley, S. (1988, Fall/Winter). Three heroines: An oral history. *Pre/Text*, 202–206.

Crowley, S. (1990). *The methodical memory: Invention in current-traditional rhetoric*. Carbondale, IL: Southern Illinois University Press.

Crowley, S. (1991, Fall/Winter). A personal essay on freshman English. *Pre/Text, 12(3–4)*, 156–176.

Cruise, R. J., et al. (1980, Summer). A comparison of full-time and part-time instructors at Midwestern Community College. *Community College Review, 8(1)*, 52–56.

Curren, E. D. (1994). No openings at this time: Job market collapse and graduate education. *Profession '94*, 57–61.

Curzon-Brown, D. (1988, October). The gripes of wrath. *Teaching English in the Two-Year College, 15(3)*, 195–98.

Daiker, D. A., & Morenberg, M. (Eds.). (1990). *The writing teacher as researcher: Essays in the theory and practice of class-based research*. Portsmouth, NH: Boynton/Cook.

Dapper, G. (1969, November). Half-time teachers. *The Instructor, 79(3)*, 87–88.

Dapper, G., & Murphy, J. (1969, November). Part-time teachers and how they work. *Education Digest, 35(3)*, 22–25.

Dasenbrock, R.W. (1993, September). Review: What is English anyway? *College English, 55(5)*, 541–547.

Dasenbrock, R. W. (1996, Fall). The crisis in the job market: Beyond scapegoating. *ADE Bulletin, 114*, 39–43.

Daumer, E., and S. Runzo. (1987). Transforming the composition classroom. In C. L. Caywood and G. R. Overing (Eds.), *Teaching writing: Pedagogy, gender, and equity* (pp. 45–62). Albany, NY: State University of New York Press.

Davidson, B. S. (1983–84, Spring). Community college part-time faculty and student services: A working model. *Community College Review, 11*, 30–34.

Davidson, W., & Kline, S. (1977, September). How to get two experienced teachers for the price of one. *American School Board Journal, 164(9)*, 35–36.

Davidson, W., & Kline, S. (1979, January). Job sharing in education. *The Clearing House, 52(5)*, 226–228.

Davis, E. A. (1970, March). Half-day teacher. *The Instructor, 79*, 156.

Davis, L. (1994, September 19). Tenure is the light. *The Nation*, pp. 280–284.

Delehant, J. E. (1989, September 20). Colleges are exploiting their part-time faculty members. *Chronicle of Higher Education*, B2.

Denham, R.D. (1988, Fall). From the editor. *ADE Bulletin, 90*, 1–3.

DeSole, G., & Hoffman, L. (Eds.). (1981). Rocking the boat: Academic women and academic processes. New York: Modern Language Association.

Dickson, M. (1993). Directing without power: Adventures in constructing a model of feminist writing program administration. In S. I. Fontaine and S. Hunter (Eds.), *Writing ourselves into the story: Unheard voices from composition studies* (pp. 154–173). Carbondale, IL: Southern Illinois University Press.

DiGiulio, J. F. (1982, January). Child welfare practitioners as university teachers. *Child Welfare, 61*, 15–23.

Doeg, F. (1956, May). Am I a part-time teacher? *Virginia Journal of Education, 49*, 32.

Douglas, A. (1988). *The feminization of American culture.* New York: Anchor Press.

Douglas, J. M. (Ed.). (1988, March–April). *Newsletter: National Center for the Study of Collective Bargaining in Higher Education and the Professions, 16(2),* 1–8.

Downturn in job information list advertisements continues in 1992–93. (1993, Summer). *Modern Language Association Newsletter 25(2),* 1–2.

Duggan, W. J. (1992, December 16). Different perspectives on part-time faculty [Letter to the editor]. *Chronicle of Higher Education,* p. B6.

Edgerton, R., Hutchings, P., & Quinlan, K. (1991). *The teaching portfolio: Capturing the scholarship in teaching.* Washington, DC: American Association for Higher Education.

Ehrenberg, R.G., Rosenberg, Pamela, & Li, Jeanne. (1988). Part-time employment in the United States. In R. A. Hart (Ed.), *Employment, unemployment, and labor utilization* (pp. 256–281). Boston: Unwin Hyman.

Ehrenreich, B., & Ehrenreich, J. (1979). The professional managerial class. In P. Walker (Ed.), *Between labour and capital* (pp. 5–48). Sussex: The Harvester Press.

Elbow, P. (1990). *What is English?* New York: Modern Language Association.

Eldred, J. C., & Mortensen, P. (1993, Fall). Gender and writing instruction in early America: Lessons from didactic fiction. *Rhetoric Review, 12(1),* 25–53.

Ellis, R. D., et al. (1984, July). The part-time driver education instructor: Bane or boon? *Journal of Traffic Safety Education, 31,* p. 11+.

Employment in Colleges and Universities [Chart]. (1998, March 13). *Chronicle of Higher Education,* p. A15.

Emspak, F. (1996, April 5). Where have all the jobs gone? *Chronicle of Higher Education,* pp. B1–2.

Englebert, H. F. (1961, January). Semi-pros among college teachers. *Educational Record, 42,* 54–56.

English Council of the California State University System. (1991, October). Principles regarding the teaching of college writing. *College Composition and Communication, 42(3),* 365–367.

Enos, T. (1988). Gender and journals, conservers or innovators. *Pre/Text, 9,* 209–14.

Enos, T. (1996). *Gender roles and faculty lives in rhetoric and composition.* Carbondale and Edwardsville, IL: Southern Illinois University Press.

Enterline, C. G. (1946, November). Teacher part-time employment. *Business Education World, 27,* 160.

Fabisinski, N. M. (1994, December). The role of part-time faculty in Alabama community college English departments: Perceptions of administrators and part-time teachers. *DIA, 55,* p. 1481A.

Facts and Figures. (1993). *ADE Bulletin, 106,* 61–63.

Faigley, L. (1996). *A letter to CCCC members.* Conference on College Composition and Communication. Letter to the membership.

Faigley, L. (1997, February). Literacy after the revolution. *College Composition and Communication, 48(1),* 30–43.

Fairweather, J. S. (1996). *Faculty work and public trust: Restoring the value of teaching and public service in American academic life.* Boston: Allyn and Bacon.

Faragher, J. M., & Howe, F. (Eds.). (1988). *Women and higher education in American history: Essays from the Mount Holyoke College Sesquicentennial Symposia.* New York: Norton.

Farley, J. (1990). Women professors in the USA: Where are they? In S. S. Lie and V. E. O'Leary (Eds.), *Storming the tower: Women in the academic world* (pp.194–207). London: Kogan Page.

Farrell, T. J. (1992a, May). The Wyoming Resolution, higher wizardry, and the importance of writing instruction. *College Composition and Communication, 43(2),* 158–164.

Farrell, T. J. (1992b, November–December). How to kill higher education. *Academe, 78(6),* 30–33.

Faye, A., & Pickett, N. A. (1988). Technical writers as part-time teachers in two-year colleges. *Journal of Technical Writing and Communication, 18,* 389–392.

Feldman, S. D. (1974). *Escape from the doll's house: Women in graduate and professional school education.* New Jersey: McGraw Hill.

Fewer English Ph.D.s land on tenure track, MLA survey finds. (1998, April 17). *Chronicle of Higher Education,* p. A12.

Fife, J. D. (1984). Foreword. In J. Gappa (Ed.), *Part-time faculty: Higher education at a crossroads* (pp. xiii–xiv). *ASHE-ERIC Higher Educa-*

tion Research Report No. 3. Washington, DC: Association for the Study of Higher Education.

Figuli, D. (1984). Legal issues in the employment of part-time and term-contract faculty. In M.E. Wallace (Ed.), *Part-time academic employment in the humanities* (pp. 146–153). New York: Modern Language Association.

Finkelstein, M. (1986, January–February). Life on the 'effectively terminal' tenure track. *Academe, 72*(1), 32–36.

Flaningam, R. R., & Taylor, S. V. (1984, Spring). Part-time faculty and gender differences in job duties, support, and satisfaction. *Journal of the National Association of Women Deans, Administrators, and Counselors, 47(3)*, 8–13.

Flynn, E. (1988, December). Composing as a woman. *College Composition and Communication, 39(4)*, 423–435.

Flynn, E. (1991). Composition studies from a feminist perspective. In R. Bullock, J. Trimbur, and C. Schuster (Eds.), *The politics of writing instruction: Postsecondary* (pp. 137–154). Portsmouth, NH: Boynton/Cook.

Flynn, E. A., Flynn. J. F., Grimm, N., & Lockhart, T. (1986, January–February). The part-time problem: Four voices. *Academe, 72(1)*, 12–18.

Fontaine, S. I., & Hunter, S. (Eds.). (1993). *Writing ourselves into the story: Unheard voices from composition studies*. Carbondale, IL: Southern Illinois University Press.

Fontaine, S. I., & Hunter, S. (Eds.). (1993). Introduction: Taking the risk to be heard. In S. I. Fontaine & S. Hunter (Eds.), *Writing ourselves into the story: Unheard voices from composition studies* (pp. 1–17). Carbondale: Southern Illinois University Press.

Franklin, P., Laurence, D., & Denham, R. D. (1988, May–June). When solutions become problems: Taking a stand on part-time employment. *Academe, 74(3)*, 15–19.

Frey, O. (1987). Equity and peace in the new writing class. In C. L. Caywood and G.R. Overing (Eds.), *Teaching writing: Pedagogy, gender, and equity* (pp. 93–105). Albany: State University of New York Press.

Friedlander, J. (1979, Winter). Instructional practices of part-time and full-time faculty. *Community College Review, 6*(3), 65–72.

Friedman, S. S. (1985). Authority in the feminist classroom: A contradiction in terms. In M. Culley and C. Portugues (Eds.), *Gendered subjects: The dynamics of feminist teaching* (pp. 203–208). Boston: Routledge and Kegan Paul.

Fries, M. S. (1986, January–February). Extended probation at research universities. *Academe, 72(1),* 37–40.

Frost, C. (1993). Looking for a gate in the fence. In S. Fontaine and S. Hunter (Eds.), *Writing ourselves into the story: Unheard voices from composition studies* (pp. 59–69). Carbondale: Southern Illinois University Press.

Frost, C., McGrath, C., Overton, R., & Zak, F. (1994, Fall). The struggle for equity: An agreement reached at SUNY–Stony Brook. *Forum, 6(1),* 7.

Fryer, T. W., Jr. (1977, Spring). Designing new personnel policies: The permanent part-time faculty member. *Journal of College and University Personnel Association, 28,* 14–21.

Fryer, T. (1977). New policies for the part-time faculty. In R. Heyns (Ed.), *Leadership for higher education: The campus view.* Washington, DC: American Council on Education.

Furey, J. P., & Heilbronner, R. (1986, Fall). Sharing a job in Schaumburg, Illinois. *Phi Delta Kappa, 67,* 468.

Gappa, J. M. (1984). *Part-time faculty: Higher education at a crossroads.* Washington, DC: Association for the Study of Higher Education.

Gappa, J. M. (1987, Spring). The stress-producing working conditions of part-time faculty. *New Directions for Teaching and Learning, 29,* 33–42.

Gappa, J. M., & Leslie, D. W. (1993). *The invisible faculty: Improving the status of part-timers in higher education.* San Francisco: Jossey-Bass.

Gappa, J. M., & Leslie, D. W. (1997, May 2). The consequences of relying on low-paid, part-time lecturers [Letter to the editor]. *Chronicle of Higher Education,* p. B3.

Gatwood, D. (1989, October 25). Part-time employees exploited by colleges [Letter to the editor]. *Chronicle of Higher Education,* p. B3.

Gaus, P. J. (1981, October 21). Six years for survival for adjunct professors. *Chronicle of Higher Education,* p. 26.

Gere, A. R. (1996). The long revolution in composition. In L. Z. Bloom, D. Daiker, and E. White (Eds.), *Composition in the twenty-first century: Crisis and change* (pp. 133–145). Carbondale: Southern Illinois University Press.

Gillam, A. M. (1992, Spring). Feminism and composition research: Researching as a woman. *Composition Studies/Freshman English News, 20(1)*, 47–54.

Ginsburg, G. (1988, Fall). The value of adjuncts: Recognize and increase it. *American School and University, 60*, 20b–20c.

Giuliano, J. A. (1995, February 3). The professionalism of adjunct professors [Letter to the editor]. *Chronicle of Higher Education*, p. B4.

Goetsch, D. L. (1981, September). Inservice plan for part-time staff. *School Shop, 41*, 35.

Goetsch, D. L. (1982, June). Tips for part-time teachers. *Vocational Education, 57*, 42–43.

Goodell, R. (1984). Half-time with honor. In M.E. Wallace (Ed.), *Part-time academic employment in the humanities* (pp. 129–130). New York: Modern Language Association.

Gordon, L. D. (1990). *Gender and higher education in the progressive era. New Haven and London*: Yale University Press.

Goswami, D., & Stillman, P. (Eds.). (1987). *Reclaiming the classroom: Teacher research as an agency for change*. Upper Montclair, NJ: Boynton/Cook.

Goulston, W. (1987). Women writing. In C. L. Caywood and G. R. Overing (Eds.), *Teaching writing: Pedagogy, gender, and equity* (pp. 19–30). Albany: State University of New York Press.

Graff, G. (1987). *Professing literature: An institutional history*. Chicago: University of Chicago Press.

Graham, P. A. (1978, Summer). Expansion and exclusion: A history of women in American higher education. *Signs, 3(4)*, 759–73.

Greer, W. (1985, August 18). Temporaries also grow. *New York Times, (Education Summer Survey)*, p. 41.

Greive, D. (1984). *A handbook for adjunct and part-time faculty*. Cleveland: Info-Tec.

Groner, A., & Brall, C. (1970, January). Part-time teachers. *Today's Education 59*, 64–65.

Grumet, M. R. (1988). *Bitter milk: Women and teaching*. Amherst: University of Massachusetts Press.

Gunner, J. (1993). The fate of the Wyoming Resolution: A professional seduction. In S. Fontaine and S. Hunter (Eds.), *Writing ourselves into the story: Unheard voices from composition studies* (pp. 107–122). Carbondale, IL: Southern Illinois University Press.

Guthrie-Morse, B. (1979, Spring). The utilization of part-time faculty. *Community College Frontiers, 7(3)*, 8–17.

Guthrie-Morse, B. (1981, Spring). Agenda for the 80s: Community college organizational reform. *Community College Review, 8(4)*, 32–37.

Haag, P. W. (1997, August 1). Class divisions and academe [Letter to the editor]. *Chronicle of Higher Education*, p. B10.

Haddad, M., & Dickens, M. E. (1978, November). Competencies for part-time faculty—The first step. *Community and Junior College Journal, 49(3)*, 22–24.

Hairston, M. (1985, April 17). We're hiring too many temporary instructors. [Point of view]. *Chronicle of Higher Education*, p. 80.

Hairston, M. (1985, October). Breaking our bonds and reaffirming our connections. *College Composition and Communication, 36(3)*, 272–282.

Hairston, M. (1992, May). Diversity, Ideology, and Teaching Writing. *College Composition and Communication, 43(2)*, 179–93.

Hammons, J. (1981, Winter). Adjunct faculty: Another look. *Community College Frontiers, 9(2)*, 46–53.

Hansen, K. (1995). Face to face with part-timers: Ethics and the professionalization of writing faculties. In J. Janangelo and K. Hansen (Eds.), *Resituating writing: Constructing and administering writing programs* (pp. 23–45). Portsmouth, NH: Boynton/Cook.

Harkin, P. (1991). The postdisciplinary politics of lore. In P. Harkin and J. Schilb (Eds.), *Contending with words: Composition and rhetoric in a postmodern age* (pp. 124–138). New York: Modern Language Association.

Hartleb, D., & Vilter, W. (1986, March). Part-time faculty, full-time problems. *New Directions for Community Colleges, 14(1)*, 15–22.

Hawkins, J. W. (1987, June). Part-time status in university teaching: An ambiguous state. *Journal of Nursing Education, 26*, 253–255.

Head, R. B., & Leslie, D. W. (1979, July). Bargaining unit status of part-time faculty. *Journal of Law and Education, 8(3),* 361–78.

Heilig, H. E., & McMahon, E. E. (1965, Winter). Part-time evening college teacher. *Adult Education, 15,* 96–104.

Heinzelman, K. (1986, January–February). The English lecturers at Austin: Our new M.I.A.'s. *Academe, 72(1),* 25–31.

Heller, S. (1986, July 30). Extensive use of temporary teachers is crippling academe, AAUP charges. *Chronicle of Higher Education,* pp. 23, 26.

Heller, S. (1987, January 28). Part-time teachers turn to unions to alter status as 'academic stepchildren'. *Chronicle of Higher Education,* pp. 1, 12.

Helmers, M. H. (1994). *Writing students: Composition testimonials and representations of students.* Albany, NY: State University of New York Press.

Hendrickson, B. (1981). Job sharing: An alternative to full-time teaching. *Learning, 9,* 4–36.

Herbst, M. A. (1994). *The career perspective of dependent part-time faculty.* Unpublished doctoral dissertation. Michigan State University.

Herman, D. (1997, May 2). The consequences of relying on low-paid, part-time lecturers [Letter to the editor]. *Chronicle of Higher Education,* p. B3.

Herzberg, B. (1991). Composition and the politics of the curriculum. In R. Bullock, J. Trimbur, and C. Schuster (Eds.), *The politics of writing instruction: Postsecondary* (pp. 97–118). Portsmouth, NH: Boynton/Cook.

Hillman, L. (1991, March). *Nontenure track positions in writing programs: A narrative of one.* Presentation at the Conference on College Composition and Communication, Boston, MA.

Hine, P. A., & Latack, J. C. (1978, Spring). Paradox of the part-time professional. *Journal of the National Association of Women Deans, Administrators and Counselors, 41(3),* 98–101.

Hobbs, C., (Ed.). (1995). *Nineteenth-century women learn to write.* Charlottesville: University of Virginia Press.

Hoenninger, R., & Black, R. A. (1978, November). Neglect of a species. *Community and Junior College Bulletin, 49(3),* 25–27.

Hoffman, J. R., & Pool, R. A. (1979, April). Part-time faculty: Their own needs assessment. *Lifelong Learning, 2(8)*, 26–27.

Hoffman, N. (Ed.). (1981). *Woman's true profession: Voices from the history of teaching.* Old Westbury, New York: The Feminist Press.

Hoffmann, L., & DeSole, G. (Eds.). (1976). *Careers and couples: An academic question.* New York: Modern Language Association.

Holbrook, S. E. (1991). Women's work: The feminizing of composition. *Rhetoric Review, 9(2)*, 201–229.

Horowitz, H. L. (1984). *Alma mater: Design and experience in the women's colleges from their nineteenth-century beginnings to the 1930s.* New York: Knopf.

Huber, B. (1990, Spring). Women in the modern languages, 1970–1990. *Profession '90, 58–73.*

Huber, B. (1995, Winter). The MLA's 1993–94 survey of PhD placement: The latest English findings and trends through time. *ADE Bulletin, 112,* 40–51.

Huber, B. J., Pinney, D., & Laurence, D. (1991, Fall). Patterns of faculty hiring in four-year English programs: Findings from a 1987–1988 survey of "job information list" advertisers. *ADE Bulletin, 99,* 39–48.

Hult, C.A. (Ed.). (1994). *Evaluating teachers of writing.* Urbana, IL: National Council of Teachers of English.

Hunter, E. (1998, May 15). Pay more attention to part-timers [Letter to the editor]. *Chronicle of Higher Education,* p. B11.

Hurlbert, M. C., & Blitz, M. (Eds.). (1991). *Composition & resistance.* Portsmouth, NH: Boynton/Cook.

Hutchinson, E. (1928, October). Women and the PhD. *Journal of the American Association of University Women, 22,* 19–22.

Ikenberry, D. J. (1978). *A descriptive study of contract provisions affecting part-time faculty included in the bargaining unit at post-secondary institutions.* Unpublished doctoral dissertation, University of Virginia.

Ikenberry, D. J., & Leslie, D. W. (1979, Fall). Collective bargaining and part-time faculty: Contract content. *Journal of College and University Personnel Association, 30,* 18–26.

Instructors end walkout at Mass. 2-year college. (1990, May 16). *Chronicle of Higher Education,* p. A2.

Ivey, N. A. (1960, September). Part-time instructor and effective teaching. *Junior College Journal, 31*, 40–43.

Ivey, N. A. (1991). Feminism and composition: The case for conflict. In P. Harkin and J. Schilb (Eds.), *Contending with words: Composition and rhetoric in a postmodern age* (pp. 103–123). New York: Modern Language Association.

Jaschik, S. (1992, October 21). 1% decline in state support for colleges thought to be first 2-year drop ever. *Chronicle of Higher Education,* pp. A21, A26–28.

Jaschik, S. (1993, September 29). Reform's winners (or losers?). *Chronicle of Higher Education,* A27, 30.

John, W. C. (1935). *Graduate study in universities and colleges in the United States.* Washington, DC: U.S. Government Printing Office.

Johnson, C. (1977, May). Vocational Education without Higher Costs? *Momentum, 8(2)*, 16–17.

Johnson, C. L. (1994, April). Participatory rhetoric and the teacher as racial/gendered subject. *College English, 56(4)*, 409–419.

Johnson, N. (1991). *Nineteenth-century rhetoric in North America.* Carbondale, IL: Southern Illinois University Press.

Johnson, R. (1989, October 11). Mixed message: Shortage of teachers or glut? [Letter to the editor]. *Chronicle of Higher Education,* p. B4.

Kantrowitz, J. S. (1981). Paying your dues, part-time. In G. DeSole and L. Hoffman (Eds.), *Rocking the boat: Academic women and academic processes* (pp. 15–36). New York: Modern Language Association.

Kaye, C., & Williamson, B. (1986, May). When it takes two to teach. *Instructor, 95(9)*, 50–52.

Keller, E. F., & Moglen, H. (1987). Competition: A problem for academic women. In H. E. Longino and V. Miner (Eds.), *Competition: A feminist taboo?* (pp. 21–37). New York: The Feminist Press.

Kennedy, G. (1967, April). Preparation, orientation, utilization and acceptance. *Junior College Journal, 37*, 14–15.

Kerr, W. 1984. Part-time faculty at Wesleyan University. In M. E. Wallace (Ed.), *Part-time academic employment in the humanities* (pp. 143–145). New York: Modern Language Association.

Killingsworth, M. J., Langford, T., & Crider, R. (1989, Winter). Short-term faculty members: A national dilemma and a local solution. *Bulletin of the Association of Departments of English, 94*, 33–39.

Kimmelman, M. I. (1992, April). Quality assurance for part-time faculty. *Business Education Forum, 46(4)*, 5–6.

Kirsch, G. E., & Ritchie, J. S. (1995, February). Beyond the personal: Theorizing a politics of location in composition research. *College Composition and Communication, 46(1)*, 7–29.

Kitzhaber, A. R. (1990). *Rhetoric in American colleges, 1850–1900*. Dallas: Southern Methodist University Press.

Klein, Waldo C., Weisman, Dan, & Smith, Thomas Edward. (1996, Spring/Summer). The use of adjunct faculty: An exploratory study of eight social work programs. *Journal of Social Work Education, 32(2)*, 253–263.

Knoblauch, C. H., & Brannon, L. (1993). *Critical teaching and the idea of literacy*. Portsmouth, NH: Boynton/Cook.

Knutson, P. (1995, January–February). An academic peddler. *Academe, 81(1)*, 16–18.

Koblitz, N. (1993, September 1). Bias and other factors in student ratings. *Chronicle of Higher Education*, p. B3.

Kohlberg, L. (1981). *Essays on moral development: Vol. 1. The Philosophy of Moral Development*. San Francisco: Harper & Row.

Koltai, L. (1977, September). King Solomon and the bowl of spaghetti: Part-time junior college instructors. *Community and Junior College Journal, 48(1)*, 18–20.

Kreinin, M. E. (1982, January 27). For a university in financial trouble, a faculty buy-out plan can save money and face. *Chronicle of Higher Education*, p. 56.

Kroll, K. (1994). A profile and perspective of part-time two-year college English faculty. *Teaching English in the Two-Year College, 21(4)*, 277–287.

Kroll, K. (1994, Winter). A profile of community college English faculty and curriculum. *Community College Review, 22(3)*, 37–54.

Kuhns, E. P. (1963, January). Part-Time Faculty. *Junior College Journal, 33*, 8–12.

Laclau, E., & Mouffe, C. (1985). *Hegemony and socialist strategy: Towards a radical democratic politics*. London: Verso.

Lamb, C. E. (1991, February). Beyond argument in feminist composition. *College Composition and Communication, 42(1)*, 11–24.

Landrus, M. (1996, September 20). The working poor on campus [Letter to the editor]. *Chronicle of Higher Education*, p. B6.

LaSalle U. professor presents plaque honoring adjunct faculty. (1998, February 6). *Chronicle of Higher Education*, p. A10.

Lauter, P. (1979, May 14). Exploitation of part-time professors. *Chronicle of Higher Education*, p. 72.

Lauter, P. (1991). *Canons and contexts*. New York: Oxford University Press.

Lay, H. L. (1985, Summer). The problem of 'teaching a little'. *SLJ, 32*, 49.

Leatherman, C. (1993, February 3). Faculty unions lower their expectations in the recession. *Chronicle of Higher Education*, pp. A16/18.

Leatherman, C. (1993, July 28). Survey finds college officials preoccupied with finances. *Chronicle of Higher Education*, p. A16.

Leatherman, C. (1996, October 25). More faculty members question the value of tenure. *Chronicle of Higher Education*, p. A12–13.

Leatherman, C. (1997, March 28). Heavy reliance on low-paid lecturers said to produce "faceless departments". *Chronicle of Higher Education*, p. A12–13.

Leatherman, C. (1997, October 10). Growing use of part-time professors prompts debate and calls for action. *Chronicle of Higher Education*, p. A14.

Leatherman, C. (1997, November 7). Do accreditors look the other way when colleges rely on part-timers? *Chronicle of Higher Education*, p. A12–14.

Leatherman, C. (1997, November 28). Adjunct professor in Washington State battles regional accreditor. *Chronicle of Higher Education*, p. A14.

Leatherman, C. (1997, December 5). Leaders of scholarly groups outline response to growth in use of part-time faculty. *Chronicle of Higher Education*, p. A18.

Leatherman, C. (1998, February 6). Part-timers at Rutgers U. agree on contract. *Chronicle of Higher Education,* p. A12.

Leatherman, C. (1998, February 13). Part-time instructors vote to unionize at Chicago's Columbia College. *Chronicle of Higher Education,* p. A16.

Leatherman, C. (1998, February 27). Faculty unions move to organize growing ranks of part-time professors. *Chronicle of Higher Education,* p. A12–14.

Leatherman, C. (1998, April 10). Faculty salaries increased 3.4% in 1997–98: Highest raises were at doctoral institutions. *Chronicle of Higher Education,* pp. A14–A15.

Leatherman, C., & Magner, D. K. (1996, November 29). Faculty and graduate-student strife over job issues flares on many campuses. *Chronicle of Higher Education,* p. A12–14.

Lefevre, K. B. (1987). *Invention as a social act.* Carbondale, IL: Southern Illinois University Press.

Lemon, H. S., et al. (1993, March/April). *The permanent temps' lament: Why not tenure status?* Paper presented at the Conference on College Composition and Communication, San Diego, CA.

Lerner, Neal. (1996, Spring–Fall). The institutionalization of required English. *Composition Studies/Freshman English News, 24(1–2),* 44–60.

Lesko, P. D. (1995, January 6). Re-examining the role of the true adjunct [Letter to the editor]. *Chronicle of Higher Education,* p. B4.

Lesko, P. D. (1995, May/June). Adjunct issues in the media during 1994–1995. *the adjunct advocate, 3(5),* p. 16–19.

Lesko, P. D. (1995, December 15). What scholarly groups should do to stop adjuncts' exploitation. *Chronicle of Higher Education,* p. B3.

Leslie, D. W. (Ed.). (1978, Summer). *Employing part-time faculty. [New Directions for Institutional Research, No. 18].* San Francisco: Jossey-Bass.

Leslie, D., & Gappa, J. (1994, Summer). Education's new academic work force. *Planning for Higher Education, 22,* 1–6.

Leslie, D. W., & Head, R. B. (1979, Winter). Part-time faculty rights. *Educational Record 60(1),* p. 46–67.

Leslie, D. W., Kellams, S. E., & Gunne, G. M. (1982). *Part-time faculty in American higher education.* New York: Praeger.

Levenstein, A., et al. (Eds.). (1980, December). Focus on the part-timer. *Newsletter of the National Center for the Study of Collective Bargaining in Higher Education and the Professions, 8(5),* 1–7.

Levine, G. (1993). The real trouble. *Profession '93,* 43–45.

Litt, S., & Margoshes, A. (1966, November). Marginal college teacher. *The Journal of Higher Education, 37,* 451–454.

Lomperis, A.M.T. (1990, November–December). Are women changing the nature of the academic profession? *The Journal of Higher Education, 61(6),* 643–677.

The loneliness of the part-time lecturer. (1980, March 7). *The New York Times Higher Education Supplement,* p. 5.

Lonn, E. (1924, January–March). Academic status of women on university faculties. *Journal of the American Association of University Women, 17,* 5–11.

Looser, D. (1993, Fall). "Composing as an essentialist"? New directions for feminist composition theories. *Rhetoric Review, 12(1),* 54–69.

Lucas, C. J. (1994). *American higher education: A history.* New York: St. Martin's Press.

Lunsford, A. (1990, February). Composing ourselves: Politics, commitment, and the teaching of writing. *College Composition and Communication, 41(1),* 71–82.

Lunsford, A. (1991). The nature of composition studies. In E. Lindemann and G. Tate (Eds.), *Introduction to composition studies* (pp. 3–14). New York: Oxford University Press.

Lunsford, A. (Ed.). (1995). *Reclaiming rhetorica: Women in the rhetorical tradition.* Pittsburgh: University of Pittsburgh Press.

Luskin, B. J. (1980–81, December–January). The need to change and the need to stay the same. *Community and Junior College Journal, 51(4),* 24–28.

Lynn, M. (1995, Spring). Interview with P. D. Lesko, founder of *the adjunct advocate. Forum: Newsletter of the Part-Time Faculty Forum 6(2),* 6–7.

Magarrell, J. (1977, September 6). Increasing use of part-timers condemned by teachers' union. *Chronicle of Higher Education,* p. 4.

Magarrell, J. (1978, January 16). Part-time professors on the increase. *Chronicle of Higher Education,* pp. A1, A6.

Magner, D. K. (1990, February 14). 45 part-timers laid off by mistake at Bridgeport University. *Chronicle of Higher Education,* p. A2.

Magner, D. K. (1994, January 26). Association of university professors challenges the belief that professors are underworked. *Chronicle of Higher Education,* p. A18.

Magner, D. K. (1995, March 31). Tenure re-examined: Association hopes 2-year study will lead to more flexibility in academic careers. *Chronicle of Higher Education,* pp. A17–A18.

Magner, D. K. (1996, September 20). Minnesota regents' proposals would effectively abolish tenure, faculty leaders say. *Chronicle of Higher Education,* p. A11–A12.

Magner, D. K. (1997, June 13). Questions raised about claims in book by 'downsized' academic. *Chronicle of Higher Education,* p. A13.

Maguire, P. (1983–84, Winter). Enhancing the effectiveness of adjunct faculty. *Community College Review, 11(3),* 27–33.

Maitland, C. (1987, January–February). Tales of a freeway flyer, or why I left college teaching after 10 years. *Change, 19(1),* pp. 8–9+.

Mangan, K. S. (1987, March 4). Part-time instructors offered programs to help them become better teachers. *Chronicle of Higher Education,* pp. 13, 16.

Mangan, K. S. (1991a, August 7). Many colleges fill vacancies with part-time professors, citing economy and uncertainty about enrollments. *Chronicle of Higher Education,* pp. A9–A10.

Mangan, K. S. (1991b, November 13). More colleges resort to faculty and staff layoffs in response to sluggish U.S. economy. *Chronicle of Higher Education,* pp. A37–38.

Mannix, C. E. Jr., & Ross, K. A. (1995, August 11). Putting to rest the damaging myths about mathematics. *Chronicle of Higher Education,* p. A40.

Marcuse, A. G. (1997, December 19). Use of part-timers and accreditation [Letter to the editor]. *Chronicle of Higher Education,* p. B12.

Matthaei, J. A. (1982). *An economic history of women in America: Women's work, the sexual division of labor, and the development of capitalism.* New York; Brighton, Sussex: Schocken Books; Harvester Press.

Maul, R. C. (1965, December). Biggest problem: Finding good teachers: Part-time teachers. *Junior College Journal, 36,* 6.

Mayhew, L. B. (1979). *Surviving the eighties.* San Francisco: Jossey-Bass.

McCleary, B. (1988). Two committees to implement Wyoming Resolution begin their work. *Composition Chronicle, 1(2),* 1–3.

McCleary, B. (1989, May). 'Nonregular' faculty members and the Wyoming Resolution. *Composition Chronicle, 2,* 7, 10.

McCleary, B. (1989, November). Four C's issues final draft of standards for fair treatment of college writing teachers, conversion of part-time and temporary jobs to tenure track. *Composition Chronicle, 2,* 1–3.

McClelland, B. W. (1981). Part-time faculty in English composition: A WPA survey. *WPA: Writing Program Administration, 5(1),* 13–20.

McConnel, F. R. (1993). Freeway flyers: The migrant workers of the academy. In S. Fontaine and S. Hunter (Eds.), *Writing ourselves into the story: Unheard voices from composition studies* (pp. 40–58). Carbondale: Southern Illinois University Press.

McDonald, J. C. (1990). Louisiana writing programs and the Wyoming Resolution. *Louisiana English Journal, 27,* 15–28.

McDonald, J. C. (1991, October). The state of Louisiana writing programs. *Composition Chronicle, 4(6),* 4–6.

McDougle, L. G. (1980, Summer). Orientation programs for part-time faculty members. *Community College Review, 8(1),* 20–23.

McGaughey, J. L. (1985, December). Part-time faculty: Integrity and integration. *New Directions for Community Colleges, 13(4),* 37–47.

McGuire, H. L. (1984, April). Opting for part-time, or combining motherhood with teaching. *English Journal, 73(4),* 38–40.

McLeod, D., & Kenney, C. (1980, Winter). ADE debates. *ADE Bulletin, 66,* 34–36.

McLeod, S. H. (1995, October). Pygmalion or golem? Teacher affect and efficacy. *College Composition and Communication, 46(3),* 369–386.

McMillen, L. (1986, May 14). One in two part-time teachers at 2-year colleges would accept full-time position if offered. *Chronicle of Higher Education, 25,* 28.

Mejia, E. K. (1996, September 13). Academe's new class of migrant workers. *Chronicle of Higher Education,* p. B5.

Merrill, R. (1992, May). Against the 'Statement.' *College Composition and Communication, 43(2),* 154–158.

Merrill, R., Farrell, T. J., Schell, E. E., Balester, V., Anson, C. M., & Gaard, G. (1992, May). Symposium on the 1991 'Progress Report from the CCCC Committee on Professional Standards.' *College Composition and Communication, 43(2),* 154–175.

Middle States Association of Colleges and Schools. (1989). *Characteristics of excellence in higher education: Standards for accreditation.* Philadelphia, PA: Commission on Higher Education, Middle States Association of Colleges and Schools.

Mikitka, K. F. (1984, Spring). Job-sharing couples in academia: Administration policies and practices. *Journal of the National Association of Women Deans, Administrators, and Counselors, 47(3),* 21–27.

Milanes, C. R. (1991). Risks, resistance, and rewards: One teacher's story. In C. M. Hurlbert and M. Blitz (Eds.), *Composition & resistance* (pp. 115–124). Portsmouth, NH: Boynton/Cook.

Miller, E. W. (1984). Demotion and displacement: Career paths for women in academe. In M. E. Wallace (Ed.), *Part-time academic employment in the humanities* (pp. 83–85). New York: Modern Language Association.

Miller, S. (1991a). *Textual carnivals: The politics of composition.* Carbondale: Southern Illinois University Press.

Miller, S. (1991b). The feminization of composition. In R. Bullock, J. Trimbur, and C. Schuster (Eds.), *The politics of writing instruction: Postsecondary* (pp. 39–54). Portsmouth, NH: Boynton/Cook.

Millward, J., & Hahn, S. (1995, March 22). *Other choices, other voices: Solutions to gender issues.* Paper presented at CCCC Feminist Workshop, Washington, DC.

Miner, V. (1993). Writing and teaching with class. In M. M. Tokarczyk and E. A. Fay (Eds.), *Working class women in the academy: Laborers in the knowledge factory* (pp. 73–86). Amherst: University of Massachusetts Press.

MLA Executive Council. (1994). Statement on the use of part-time and full-time adjunct faculty. In *A career guide for Ph.D.'s and Ph.D. candidates in English and foreign languages.* (Revised by Elaine Showalter.) New York: Modern Language Association.

Monaghan, P. (1989, April 5). Feeling they are exploited, writing instructors seek better treatment and working conditions. *Chronicle of Higher Education,* pp. A13, A15.

Moodie, C. L. R. (1980, March 10). Overuse of part-time members. *Chronicle of Higher Education,* p. 72.

Moodie, C. L. R. (1980, March 10). Point of view. *Chronicle of Higher Education,* p. 72.

Mooney, C. J. (1992, October 28). Critics within and without academe assail professors at research universities. *Chronicle of Higher Education,* pp. A17–19.

Mooney, C. J. (1992, November 18). AAUP criticizes colleges' reliance on part-time teachers. *Chronicle of Higher Education,* p. A16.

Mooney, C. J. (1993, January 13). Tenured professors spared in latest round of belt tightening. *Chronicle of Higher Education,* p. A17–18.

Moorman, B. (1981, January–February). Job sharing: An administrative view. *Thrust, 10,* 21–23.

Murphy, J. J. (Ed.). (1990). *A short history of writing instruction from ancient Greece to twentieth century America.* Davis, CA: Hermagoras Press.

Mydans, S. (1995, January 4). Part-time college teaching rises, as do worries. *New York Times,* p. A17.

Myers, C. (1979, July 2). Judge barred from teaching job. *Chronicle of Higher Education,* p. 15.

Myers, K. (1996, March 25). Velvel: More adjuncts as profs to keep class size low. *The National Law Journal, 18(30),* p. A16, col. 3.

Nance, G., & Culverhouse, R. (1991–92, Winter). The hidden costs of part-time faculty. *Planning for Higher Education, 20(2),* 30–38.

Naparsteck, M. (1996, September 20). The working poor on campus [Letter to the editor]. *Chronicle of Higher Education,* p. B6.

National Adjunct Faculty Guild. (1995). *Call for proposals and participation: Second Annual NAFG Conference on Adjunct and Part-Time Faculty,* 1–2.

National Committee on Pay Equity. (1994). The wage gap: Myths and facts. In A. M. Jaggar (Ed.), *Living with contradictions: Controversies in feminist social ethics* (pp. 73–79). Boulder: Westview Press.

National Council of Teachers of English. (1996). Pamphlet. *Researching practice: Working conditions*, 1–5.

National Endowment for the Humanities. (1990, November 14). Excerpt from NEH report on education practices. *Chronicle of Higher Education*, pp. A22, A24–26.

Nelson, C. (1995a, Fall/Winter). Lessons from the job wars: Late capitalism arrives on campus. *Social Text, 13(3),* 119–134.

Nelson, C. (1995b, November–December). Lessons from the job wars: What is to be done. *Academe, 81(6),* 18–25.

Nelson, C. (Ed.). (1997). *Will teach for food: Academic labor in crisis.* Minneapolis: University of Minnesota Press.

Nelson, C., & Bérubé, M. (1994, March 23). Graduate education is losing its moral base. *Chronicle of Higher Education*, pp. B1–B3.

Nelson, C., & Bérubé, M. (1995). Introduction: A report from the front. In M. Bérubé and C. Nelson (Eds.), *Higher education under fire: Politics, economics, and the crisis of the humanities* (pp. 1–32). New York and London: Routledge.

New, M. (1988, Spring). Research versus teaching: Once upon a time in Teachalot. *ADE Bulletin, 89,* 56–59.

Newcomer, M. (1959). *A century of higher education for American women.* New York: Harper and Bros.

Newkirk, T. (1991). The politics of composition research: The conspiracy against experience. In R. Bullock, J. Trimbur, and C. Schuster (Eds.), *The politics of writing instruction: Postsecondary* (pp. 119–135). Portsmouth, NH: Boynton/Cook.

Nickerson, M. (1997, May 2). The consequences of relying on low-paid, part-time lecturers [Letter to the editor]. *Chronicle of Higher Education*, p. B3.

Nollen, S. D., et al. (1977). *Permanent part-time employment: The manager's perspective.* Washington, DC: National Technical Information Service.

Normand, D.B. (1995–1996, Fall and Spring). Suggestions to improve the well-being of the not-eligible-for-tenure. *Forum: Newsletter of the Part-Time Faculty Forum, 7(1–2),* 9–10.

North, S. M. (1987). *The making of knowledge in composition: Portrait of an emerging field.* Portsmouth, NH: Boynton/Cook.

Nystrom, J. W. (1964, Winter). Can industrial laboratories supply part-time college teachers? *College and University, 39,* 135–146.

Ohmann, R. (1976). *English in America: A radical view of the profession.* New York: Oxford University Press.

Ohmann, R. (1990, March). Graduate students, professionals, intellectuals. *College English, 52(3),* 247–257.

Ohmann, R. (1991). Foreword. In R. Bullock, J. Trimbur, and C. Schuster (Eds.), *The politics of writing instruction: Postsecondary* (pp. ix–xvi). Portsmouth, NH: Boynton/Cook.

O'Leary, V. E., & Mitchell, J. M. (Eds.). (1990). Women connecting with women: Networks and mentors. In S. S. Lie and V. O'Leary (Eds.), *Storming the tower: Women in the academic world* (pp. 58–73). London: Kogan Page.

Paprock, K. E. (1987, June). Techniques: A model for differentiation of adjunct faculty. *Lifelong Learning: The Adult Years, 10(8),* 28–29.

Parsons, M. H. (Ed.). (1980). Using part-time faculty effectively. [*New Directions for Community Colleges, 8(2).*] San Francisco: Jossey-Bass.

Part-time Faculty in Colleges and Universities [Symposium]. (1981). *Current Issues in Higher Education Annual Series, 4,* 1–17.

Part-time instructors settle with Philadelphia College. (1981, May 11). *Chronicle of Higher Education,* p. 22.

Payne, W. M. (Ed.). (1895). *English in American universities.* Boston: Heath.

Perry, S. (1982, November 3). New union presses its case and finds a whole lot of things you can do. *Chronicle of Higher Education,* 27–28.

Peterson, J.E. (1991). Valuing teaching: Assumptions, problems, and possibilities. *College Composition and Communication, 42(1),* 25–35.

Petraglia, J. (1995). Introduction: General writing skills instruction and its discontents. In J. Petraglia (Ed.), *Reconceiving writing, rethinking writing instruction* (pp. xi–xvii). Mahwah, NJ: Lawrence Erlbaum Associates, Publishers.

Phelps, L. W. (1988). *Composition as a human science: Contributions to the self-understanding of a discipline.* New York: Oxford University Press.

Phelps, L. W. (1991a, December). *A different ideal. . . and its practical results.* Paper presented at the Annual Meeting of the Modern Language Association, San Francisco, CA.

Phelps, L. W. (1991b, December). Practical wisdom and the geography of knowledge in composition. *College English, 53(8),* 863–885.

Phelps, L. W. (1995). Becoming a warrior: Lessons of the feminist workplace. In L. W. Phelps and J. Emig (Eds.), *Feminine principles and women's experience in American composition and rhetoric* 289–339. Pittsburgh: University of Pittsburgh Press.

Phelps, L.W., & Emig, J. (1995a). Editors' reflections: Vision and interpretation. In L. W. Phelps and J. Emig (Eds.), *Feminine principles and women's experience in American composition and rhetoric* (pp. 407–425). Pittsburgh: University of Pittsburgh Press.

Phelps, L.W., & Emig, J. (Eds.). (1995b). *Feminine principles and women's experience in American composition and rhetoric.* Pittsburgh: University of Pittsburgh Press.

Pollack, A., & Breuder, R. L. (1982, Spring). The eighties and part-time faculty. *Community College Review, 9(4),* 58–62.

Pollack, J .S. (1986, January–February). The erosion of tenure in the California state university. *Academe,* 72(1), 19–24.

Popper, A. F. (1997, March). The uneasy integration of adjunct teachers into American legal education. *Journal of Legal Education, 47(1),* 83–91.

Potter, R. H. (1984, Fall). Part-time faculty: Employees or contractors? *Journal of the College and University Personnel Association, 35(3),* 22–27.

Pratt, L. R. (1995). Going public: Political discourse and the faculty voice. In M. Bérubé and C. Nelson (Eds.), *Higher education under fire: Politics, economics, and the crisis of the humanities* (pp. 35–51). New York and London: Routledge.

Prentice, A. L., & Theobald, M. R. (Eds.). (1991). *Women who taught: Perspectives on the history of women and teaching.* Toronto: University of Toronto Press.

Purvis, T. (1995 and 1996, Fall and Spring). Editor's note. *Forum: Newsletter of the Part-Time Faculty Forum, 7(1–2),* 1–3.

Quigley, M. S. (1986, January 22). In defense of the adjunct faculty member. *Chronicle of Higher Education,* p. 40.

Rabalais, M. J., & Perritt, J. E. (1983, Fall). Instructional development for part-time faculty. *Community College Review, 11(2),* 20–22.

Ray, R. E. (1993). *The practice of theory: Teacher research in composition*. Urbana, IL: National Council of Teachers of English.

Reagon, B. J. (1983). Coalition politics: Turning the century. In B. Smith (Ed.), *Home girls: A black feminist anthology* (pp. 356–369). New York: Kitchen Table–Women of Color Press.

Reed, S. (1985, August 18). Part-time instructors proliferate. *New York Times,* (Education Summer Survey), pp. 40–41.

Reichman, H. (1997, May 2). The consequences of relying on low-paid, part-time lecturers [Letter to the editor]. *Chronicle of Higher Education,* B3.

Report of the Special Committee on Academic Personnel Ineligible for Tenure. (1966, September). *AAUP Bulletin, 52,* 280–282.

Reynolds, J.M. (1998, February 20). Jazz professors at new school vote to form union. *Chronicle of Higher Education,* A14.

Rhoades, G. (1996, November–December). Reorganizing the faculty workforce for flexibility: Part-time professional labor. *Journal of Higher Education, 67(6),* 626–659.

Rich resource: Part-time teachers. (1969, Fall). *New York State Education, 56,* 14–17.

Rifkin, J. (1995). *The end of work: The decline of the global labor force and the dawn of the post-market era.* New York: G.P. Putnam's Sons.

Ritchie, J. S. (1990, Fall). Confronting the 'essential' problem: Reconnecting feminist theory and pedagogy. *Journal of Advanced Composition, 10(2),* 249–273.

Robertson, L. R. (1988). Alliances between rhetoric and English: The politics. *Composition Chronicle, 2(4),* 1–3.

Robertson, L. R., Crowley, S., & Lentricchia, F. (1987, March). Opinion: The Wyoming Conference resolution opposing unfair salaries and working conditions for post-secondary teachers of writing. *College English, 49(8),* 274–280.

Robertson, L. R., & Slevin, J. F. (1987, Spring). The status of composition faculty: Resolving reforms. *Rhetoric Review, 5(2),* 190–194.

Robinson, W. S. (1991, October). The CCCC statement of principles and standards: A (partly) dissenting view. *College Composition and Communication, 42(3),* 345–349.

Ronald, A. (1990, Spring). Separate but (sort of) equal: Permanent non-tenure-track faculty members in the composition program. *Bulletin of the Association of Departments of English, 95,* 33–37.

Rose, Mike. (1989). *Lives on the boundary: A moving account of the struggles and achievements of America's educational underclass.* New York: Penguin Books.

Rosenblum, G., & Rosenblum, B. R. (1990, July). Segmented labor markets in institutions of higher learning. *Sociology of Education, 63(3),* 151–164.

Rubin, D. (1993). *Gender influences: Reading student texts.* Carbondale, IL: Southern Illinois University Press.

Russell, S. (1991, Spring). The status of women and minorities in higher education: Findings from the 1988 national survey of postsecondary faculty. *CUPA Journal,* 1–11.

Russell, S., et al. (1988a). *A descriptive report of academic departments in higher education institutions.* National Center for Education Statistics, 90–339.

Russell, S., et al. (1988b). *Faculty in higher education institutions.* [Contractor report]. National Center for Education Statistics, 90–365.

Russell, S., et al. (1988c). *Institutional policies and practices regarding faculty in higher education.* [Contractor report. 1988 National Survey of Postsecondary Faculty. Survey Report]. National Center for Education Statistics, 90–333.

Sandler, B. (1986). *The campus climate revisited: Chilly for women faculty, administrators, and graduate students.* [Final report]. Washington, DC: Association of American Colleges.

Savage, H. J. (1921). Personnel for college composition. *English Journal, 10,* 439–449.

Schell, E. E. (1992, May). Teaching under unusual conditions: Graduate teaching assistants and the CCCC's 'Progress Report.' *College Composition and Communication, 43(2),* 164–167.

Schell, E. E. (1998). Gypsy academics and mother-teachers: Gender, contingent labor, and writing instruction. Portsmouth, NH: Boynton/Cook Publishers.

Schilb, J., & Harkin, P. (Eds.). (1991). *Contending with words: Composition and rhetoric in a postmodern age.* New York: Modern Language Association.

Schmidt, P. (1996, November 1). State support for higher education shows largest percentage increase since 1990. *Chronicle of Higher Education,* pp. A31–34.

Schmiedicke, R. E. (1964, May). Utilize part-time faculty in education for business. *Balance Sheet, 45,* 398–400.

Schneider, A. (1997, November 7). Faculty leader on Southern U. campus says chancellor threatens her job. *Chronicle of Higher Education,* A14.

Schneider, A. (1998, March 13). More professors are working part time, and more teach at 2-year colleges. *Chronicle of Higher Education,* A14–A16.

Schwager, S. (1988). Educating women in America. In E. Minnich, J. F. O'Barr, and R. Rosenfeld (Eds.), *Reconstructing the academy: Women's education and women's studies* (pp. 154–193). Chicago: University of Chicago Press.

Schwalm, D. (1994). Evaluating adjunct faculty. In C. A. Hult (Ed.), *Evaluating teachers of writing* (pp. 123–132). Urbana, IL: National Council of Teachers of English.

Searle, J. (1992). The storm over the university. In P. Berman (Ed.), *Debating P.C.: The controversy over political correctness on college campuses* (pp. 86–124). New York: Dell.

Seldin, P. (1991). *The teaching portfolio: A practical guide to improved performance and promotion/tenure decisions.* Boston, MA: Anker Publishing.

Selingo, J. (1997, December 12). Alabama Supreme Court says law applies to tenure bids at 2-year colleges. *Chronicle of Higher Education,* A14.

Selingo, J. (1998, February 20). Two-year college in Texas to hire 60 full-time professors. *Chronicle of Higher Education,* A14.

Selvadurai, R. H. (1989–90, Fall–Spring). Advantages and disadvantages of hiring part-time faculty in higher education. *Community Review, 10(1–2),* 35–36.

Shaffer, K. L. (1995). *Savior or servant: What is the role of part-time faculty?* Unpublished doctoral dissertation, Michigan State University.

Sherfick, K., & Trimmer, J. F. (1984). Part-time faculty employment at Ball State University. In M. E. Wallace (Ed.), *Part-time academic employment in the humanities* (pp. 95–99). New York: Modern Language Association.

Shulman, C. H. (1973). *Employment of nontenured faculty: Some implications of Roth and Sindermann.* (ERIC/Higher Education Research Report 8). Washington, DC: American Association for Higher Education.

Siegried, J. J. (1996, January 19). Fair treatment for adjuncts [Letter to the editor]. *Chronicle of Higher Education,* B5.

Simeone, A. (1987). *Academic women: Working towards equality.* South Hadley, MA: Bergin & Garvey.

Singleton, D. (1991). The names we resist: Revising institutional perceptions of the nontenured. In C. M. Hurlbert and M. Blitz (Eds.), *Composition & resistance* (pp. 32–41). Portsmouth, NH: Boynton/Cook.

Sledd, J. (1991a). How we apples swim. In C. M. Hurlbert and M. Blitz (Eds.), *Composition & resistance* (pp. 145–149). Portsmouth, NH: Boynton/Cook.

Sledd, J. (1991b, Fall). Why the Wyoming Resolution had to be emasculated: A history and a quixotism. *Journal of Advanced Composition, 11(2),* 269–281.

Slevin, J. F. (1987, Fall). A note on the Wyoming Resolution and ADE. *ADE Bulletin, 87,* 50.

Slevin, J. F. (1991). Depoliticizing and politicizing composition studies. In R. Bullock, J. Trimbur, and C. Schuster (Eds.), *The politics of writing instruction: Postsecondary* (pp. 1–21). Portsmouth, NH: Boynton/Cook.

Solomon, B. M. (1985). *In the company of educated women: A history of women and higher education in America.* New Haven: Yale University Press.

Sommer, B. (1994, Summer). Recognizing academe's other faculty. *Planning for Higher Education, 22(4),* 7–10.

Sound bites from the NCTE Annual Convention in Chicago. (1997, February). *The Council Chronicle, 6(3),* 8.

Spofford, T. (1979, November–December). The field hands of academe. *Change, 11(8),* 14–16.

Stearns, P. (1986). Anger at work: A contemporary approach. In C. Z. Stearns and P. N. Stearns (Eds.), *Anger: The struggle for emotional control in America's history* (pp. 110–156). Chicago: University of Chicago Press.

Strenski, E. (1994). Peer review of writing faculty. In C. A. Hult (Ed.), *Evaluating teachers of writing* (pp. 55–72). Urbana, IL.: National Council of Teachers of English.

Strenski, E. (1995). Recruiting and retraining experienced teachers: Balancing game plans in an entrepreneurial force-field. In J. Janangelo and K. Hansen (Eds.), *Resituating writing: Constructing and administering writing programs* (pp. 82–99). Portsmouth, NH: Boynton/Cook, Heinemann.

Strohm, P. (1986, January–February). Non-tenure-track faculty. [Editorial]. *Academe, 72(1),* 11.

Strosnider, K. (1997, June 6). An aggressive, for-profit university challenges traditional colleges nationwide. *Chronicle of Higher Education,* pp. A32–33.

Styne, M. M. (1997, February). Those unfamiliar names and faces: The hiring, management, and evaluation of part-time faculty. *Teaching English in the Two-Year College, 24(1),* 50–55.

Sugg, R. (1978). *Motherteacher: The feminization of American education.* Charlottesville: University Press of Virginia.

Survey says colleges struggle to bring technology into classes. (1995, August 11). *Chronicle of Higher Education,* pp. A17–18.

Swofford, J. (1982, Winter). Part-time faculty and collective bargaining. *Journal of the Junior College and University Personnel Association, 34(4),* 9–21.

Sykes, C. (1988). *Profscam: Professors and the demise of higher education.* Washington, DC: Regnery Gateway.

Szilak, Dennis. (1977, September). Teachers of composition: A re-niggering. *College English, 39(1),* 25–32.

Tamm, M. (1984). In praise of part-time employment. In M. E. Wallace (Ed.), *Part-time academic employment in the humanities* (pp. 86–88). New York: Modern Language Association.

Taylor, W. (1929). *A national survey of the conditions in freshman English.* Madison: University of Wisconsin Bulletin No. 11.

Thompson, C. H. (1967, May). Faculty development in evening colleges. *Adult Leadership, 16,* 15–16+.

Thompson, K. (1992, Spring). Piecework to parity: Part-timers in action. *Thought and Action 8(1),* 29–37.

Thompson, K. (1992, November–December). Recognizing mutual interests. *Academe, 78(6),* 22–26.

Thompson, K. (1995, Spring). Central contingencies: Part-time faculty and the future of higher education. *Forum: Newsletter of the Part-Time Faculty Forum 6(2),* 1–4.

Thompson, M. O. (1988, October). The part-timer's wish list. *Teaching English in the Two-Year College, 15,* 199.

Thompson, S. (1930). A national survey of freshman English. *English Journal, 19,* 553–557.

Three Canadian universities reach tentative agreements with adjuncts. (1998, March 27). *Chronicle of Higher Education,* A52.

Tinberg, H. B. (1991, February). "An Enlargement of observation": More on theory building in the composition classroom. *College Composition and Communication, 42(1),* 36–44.

Tobias, S., & Rumberger, M. (1974). Full-status part-time faculty. In W. T. Furniss and P. A. Graham (Eds.), *Women in higher education* (pp. 128–137). Washington, DC: American Council on Education.

Torgovnick, M. (1982, December). How to handle an adjunct. *College Composition and Communication, 33,* 454–456.

Townsend, B. K. (1986, May 28). Outsiders inside academe: The plight of temporary teachers. *Chronicle of Higher Education, 72.*

Townsend, B. K. (1986, October). Temporary college teachers: Outsiders inside academe. *Education Digest, 52,* 53–55.

Trimbur, J. (1991). Literacy and the discourse of crisis. In R. Bullock, J. Trimbur, and C. Schuster (Eds.), *The politics of writing instruction: Postsecondary* (pp. 277–296). Portsmouth, NH: Boynton/Cook.

Trimbur, J. (1996). Writing instruction and the politics of professionalization. In L. Z. Bloom, D. Daiker, and E. White (Eds.), *Composition in the twenty-first century: Crisis and change* (pp. 133–145). Carbondale: Southern Illinois University Press.

Trimbur, J., & Cambridge, B. (1988, Fall–Winter). The Wyoming Conference resolution: A beginning. *WPA: Writing Program Administration, 12(1),* 13–18.

Troubled times for tenure. (1990, February 26). *Time,* 72.

Tuckman, B. H., & Tuckman, H. P. (1980, March). Part-timers, sex discrimination, and career choice at two-year institutions: Further findings from the AAUP survey. *Academe, 66(2)*, 71–76.

Tuckman, B. H., & Tuckman, H. P. (1981, March). Women as part-time faculty members. *Higher Education 10(2),* 169–179.

Tuckman, H. P. (1978, December). Who is part-time in academe? *AAUP Bulletin, 64(4),* 305–315.

Tuckman, H. P. (1981, January–February). Part-time faculty: Some suggestions of policy. *Change, 13(1),* 8–10.

Tuckman, H. P., & Belisle, M. (1987, Winter). New doctorates in the job market: Have opportunities declined? *Educational Record, 68(1),* 32–35.

Tuckman, H. P., & Caldwell, J. (1979, November–December). The reward structure for part-timers in academe. *Journal of Higher Education, 50(6),* 745–760.

Tuckman, H. P., Caldwell, J., & Gapinski, J. (1978). *The wage rates of part-timers in higher education: A preliminary inquiry.* Proceedings of the American Statistical Association.

Tuckman, H. P., & Pickerill, K. L. (1988). Part-time faculty and part-time academic careers. In D. W. Breneman and T. I. K. Youn (Eds.), *Academic labor markets and careers* (pp. 98–113). New York: The Falmer Press.

Tuckman, H. P., & Vogler, W. D. (1978, May). The 'part' in part-time wages. *AAUP Bulletin, 64(2),* 70–77.

Tuckman, H. P., Vogler, W. D., & Caldwell, J. (1978). *Part-time faculty series.* Washington, DC: American Association of University Professors.

Tuell, C. (1993). Composition teaching as 'women's work': Daughters, handmaids, whores, and mothers. In S. Fontaine and S. Hunter (Eds.), *Writing ourselves into the story: Unheard voices from composition studies* (pp. 123–139). Carbondale: Southern Illinois University Press.

Tuman, M. C. (1991, October). Unfinished business: Coming to terms with the Wyoming resolution. *College Composition and Communication, 42(3),* 356–364.

Turner, M. A., & Phillips, H. E. (1981). *The care and feeding of part-time faculty.* Gaithersburg, MD: Associated Faculty Press.

Two teachers instead of none. (1967, October). *Michigan Education Journal, 45,* 39.

Unemployment rate drops for new mathematics Ph.D.s. (1998, January 9). *Chronicle of Higher Education,* A14.

Valette, R. M. (1965, October). Young mother in academe. *Liberal Education, 51,* 379–381.

Vaughn, G. B. (1986, March). Part-time faculty: Nemesis or savior? *New Directions for Community Colleges, 14(1),* 23–30.

Veysey, L. (1965). *The emergence of the American university.* Chicago: University of Chicago Press.

Villanueva, V. (1993). *Bootstraps: From an American academic of color.* Urbana, IL: National Council of Teachers of English.

Wallace, M. E. (1982, December). Comments on 'Memoirs and confessions of a part-time lecturer.' *College English, 44(8),* 859–861.

Wallace, M. E. (1982, Winter). New policies for part-time faculty. *ADE Bulletin, 73,* 47–52.

Wallace, M. E. (Ed.). (1984a). *Part-time academic employment in the humanities.* New York: Modern Language Association.

Wallace, M. E. (1984b, October). The richness of language and the poverty of part-timers: Impact and invisibility. *College English, 46(6),* 580–586.

Wallace, M. E. (1991, October). A one-time part-timer's response to the CCCC Statement of Professional Standards. *College Composition and Communication, 42(3),* 350–355.

Watkins, B. T. (1978, May 30). California community colleges brace for cuts in local revenue. *Chronicle of Higher Education,* 10.

Watkins, B. T. (1979, July 16). AFT to press for unionization of part-timers. *Chronicle of Higher Education,* 1.

Watkins, B. T. (1985, April 3). Frustrated part-timer sues U. of Cal. for full-time job. *Chronicle of Higher Education,* pp. 23, 26.

Watkins, B. T. (1989, October 4). Colleges urged to use full-time professors in writing programs. *Chronicle of Higher Education,* pp. A13, A15.

Watkins, E. (1989). *Work time: English departments and the circulation of cultural value.* Stanford, CA: Stanford University Press.

Weis, L. (1987, January–February). Academic women in science 1977–1984. *Academe, 73*(1), 43–47.

Weston, E. (1986, Winter). On part-time college teaching. *Thought and Action, 2,* 149–152.

Whelan, W. L. (1980, May). The legal status of part-time faculty. *Lifelong Learning: The Adult Years, 3(9),* 18–21.

Whichard, N. W., et al. (1992, Spring/Summer). Life in the margin: The hidden agenda in commenting on student writing. *Journal of Teaching Writing, 11(1),* 51–64.

Wiley, M., Gleason, B., & Phelps, L. W. (Eds.). (1996). Composition in four keys: Inquiring into the field: Art, nature, science, politics. Mountain View, CA: Mayfield.

Willett, L. H. (1980, October–December). A comparison of instructional effectiveness of full- and part-time faculty. *Community/Junior College Research Quarterly, 5,* 23–30.

Williams, F. N. (1972, September). The neglected teachers: The part-time faculty. *Adult Leadership, 21(3),* 83–84.

Williams, J. E., & Johansen, E. (1985, March/April). Career disruption in higher education. *Journal of Higher Education, 56(2),* 144–160.

Williams, M. L., & Wiatrek, D. (1987, Winter). Part-time and full-time faculty communications problems in community colleges: Analysis and suggestions. *Journal of Thought, 22,* 20–30.

Williams, R. F. (1969, March). Part-time teachers. *Virginia Journal of Education, 62,* 15–16.

Wilson, R. (1994, November 23). Education department study of faculty members finds most have full-time appointments. *Chronicle of Higher Education,* A16.

Wilson, R. (1995, March 10). Scheduling motherhood. *Chronicle of Higher Education,* A14–A15.

Wilson, R. (1996, June 14). Scholars off the tenure track wonder if they'll ever get on. *Chronicle of Higher Education,* A12–13.

Wilson, R. (1996, September 20). Weary of commuter marriages, more couples in academe make career sacrifices to be together. *Chronicle of Higher Education,* A10–A11.

Wilson, R. (1997, October 31). Career success for some Ph.D.s comes by leaving academe behind. *Chronicle of Higher Education,* pp. A12–13.

Wilson, R. (1998, January 9). Citing 'crisis' in job market, MLA urges changes in graduate education. *Chronicle of Higher Education,* pp. 15–16.

Winkler, K. J. (1979, December 3). Two who share one academic job say the pros outnumber the cons. *Chronicle of Higher Education,* pp. 3–4.

Woody, T. (1974). *A history of women's education in the United States.* (Vols. 1–2). New York: Octagon Books.

Wyche-Smith, S., & Rose, S. K. (1990, October). One hundred ways to make the Wyoming Resolution a reality: A guide to personal and political action. *College Composition and Communication, 41(3),* 318–324.

Yang, S., & Zak, M. W. (1981). *Part-time faculty employment in Ohio: A statewide study.* (ERIC) ED 205 140. Ohio: Kent State University.

Yee, M. (1991). Are you the teacher? In C. M. Hurlbert and M. Blitz (Eds.), *Composition & resistance* (pp. 24–30). Portsmouth, NH: Boynton/Cook.

You can beat the teacher drop-out problem. (1968, September). *School Management, 12,* 72–76.

Ziv, N. (1985, September). Comment on 'The richness of language and the poverty of part-timers.' *College English, 47(5),* 540.

INDEX

Abel, Emily, 3, 12
Adamany, D., 186
Adjunct faculty. *See* Contingent
    faculty
"Adjunct passing," 171
Administrators and policymakers
    adverse publicity and, 226
    dialogue with, 5–6
    distance-education issues and,
        279–81
    distancing of, 70–71
    justification of status quo by,
        186–87
    in labor disputes, 224–29
    missions statements and, 133,
        135–42
    pressure from, 63–69
    responsibility of, 190
Advancement, 114–18
Affirmative action policies, 238
African Americans, 13–14
American Association of
    University Professors
    (AAUP), 17, 18, 22, 26,
    125, 247, 332, 337
Anadolu University (Turkey),
    268
Anderson, Erin, 318n
Anderson, Gary L., 295, 320n
Anson, Chris M., 31, 61, 72, 273
    as director of composition
        program, 61–74
    "Shadows of the Mountain,"
        47–75
Aronowitz, Stanley, 35, 173, 193

Baby boomers, 199–201
Barber, Les, 249
Bateson, Gregory, 296
Benefits, 53–54, 93, 110–11,
    240, 253
Benjamin, Ernst, 4, 5
Benko, Deborah, 37
    "Climbing a Mountain: An
        Adjunct Steering
        Committee Brings Change
        to Bowling Green State
        University's English
        Department," 245–58
Berlin, James, 241
Berlow, Lawrence H., 11, 15–17,
    39
Berry, Ellen, 252, 253, 254
Bérubé, Michael, 21, 22, 25, 177
"Best of Times, The Worst of
    Times: One Version of the
    'Humane' Lectureship,
    The" (Brumberger),
    91–106
Birkert, Sven, 264
Blumentsyk, G., 268
Boettcher, G. T., 263, 274
Bowen, H. R., 5, 10
Bowling Green State University,
    37, 245–57
Boyer, Ernest, 88
    *Scholarship Reconsidered:
        Priorities of the Professor-
        ate,* 287–88, 289, 317n
Brodkey, L., 147
Brown, Amanda, 38

reflective essay of, 297–308
"The Scholarship of Teaching:
Contributions from
Contingent Faculty,"
287–323
Brumberger, Eva, 31, 32, 33, 97,
104, 333, 334
"The Best of Times, the Worst
of Times: One Version of
the 'Humane' Lectureship,"
91–106

Calderonello, Alice, 249, 252,
253, 254
California Faculty Association
(CFA), 233
California Federation of Teachers,
208–9
California Public Employee
Relations Board (PERB),
221
California Teachers Association
(CTA), 208
Carnegie Foundation for the
Advancement of Teaching,
318n
Case studies, need for, 28–29
Cather, Willa, 177
Center for the Study of Education
and Tax Policy, 9
Cerbin, William, 320n
Certified Employees Council
(CEC), 210
Chait, R., 324
Chaplin, Miriam T., 153n
Chell, Cara, 17, 166–67
Cheney, Lynne V., 317–18n
Clifford, John, 133, 146
"Climbing a Mountain: An
Adjunct Steering
Committee Brings Change
to Bowling Green State
University's English
Department" (Benko),
245–58

Coalition building, 20–28, 150–51,
163–66, 191–94, 233–35,
335–38
Coalition on the Academic
Workforce (CAW), 5, 27,
40n
Coley, R. J., 264, 267
Collective bargaining, 335
at local level, 210–13
at state level, 213–16
Collegiality, 192–93
Collos, Alana L., 11, 15–17, 39
Community College Reform Act
(California), 213
Community colleges, 36, 56
use of part-time faculty in,
196–216
Composition studies, 7–8. *See
also* Writing programs
distance-education issues and,
281–83
English departments and, 76,
99–105
historical perspective on,
240–41
impact of technology on, 264–65
as interdisciplinary study, 56
marginalization of, 91
as part of English major, 101
scholarship of teaching and,
316–17
separation from oral rhetoric,
240–41
Conference on College
Composition and
Communication (CCCC),
7, 17, 18, 29, 65, 72
"Statement of Principles and
Standards for Postsecondary
Teaching of Writing," 18,
135–37, 281, 331
Connors, Robert, 8, 240, 241, 330
Consciousness raising, 191–92
Constantinides, J., 93
Contingent faculty
benefits packages of, 53–54,

81–82, 93, 240, 253
capability of, 10–11, 15
coalition building by, 20–28,
    162–66
complicity of, 170
contributions to scholarship of
    teaching by, 295, 297–316
critical literacy discourse and,
    133–35, 143–50
criticism of, 23
demographics of, 3, 8, 13–14,
    197
disempowerment of, 169–73
dissatisfaction of, 169
distance education and, 261–84
diversity among, 11–14, 327
elusiveness of full-time status
    for, 113
ethnic minorities as, 13–14
exploitation of, 159
freeway flyers, 51, 132–53
as gendered class, 132, 150,
    328–29
growth of, 185–86, 284n
handbook for, 248
hiring trends for, 4–5, 185–186
identity problem of, 169–73
increases in, 9–10
invisibility of, 162–66
involvement in contract
    negotiations, 222
lack of politicization of,
    169–173
leadership roles for, 109, 110,
    111
as lobbyists, 224
material conditions of, 107–31
merit tier system and, 109,
    114–18, 129–30
mission statements and, 133,
    135–42
need for discourse on, 5–6
peer evaluation of, 109, 118–20,
    131
pressure to hire, 63–69
program expansion and, 201

quality of teaching and, 133–53,
    325–32
reliance on, 2–8, 159–60,
    186–87
research on, 1–2, 8–39
responsibility of, for problems,
    189, 326
salaries of, 54–55, 57, 58, 81,
    93, 97, 110, 115, 210–16,
    330, 332–33
as second-class citizens, 15–16,
    96, 140–41
self-perceptions of power
    among, 167
status of, 140–41
in steering committees, 245–57
suggestions for, 99–105, 190–95
taxonomies of, 12
teaching of literature and, 96
Course load, 77, 93–94, 96–97,
    161–62, 281–82
    and student-to-teacher ratios,
    136–40
Cradler, J., 264, 267
Creative writing, 102
Critical literacy discourse, 153n
    contradictions in, 133–35,
    143–50
Cross, K. Patricia, 25
Crowley, S., 8, 91, 103, 330
Curren, E. D., 329
Curriculum reform, 108

Daniel, Sir John, 267, 268
Dasenbrock, R. W., 8
Davis, Rebecca Harding, *Life in
    the Iron Mills,* 179–80
Deibert, R. J., 273
DeVoss, Danielle, 37–38, 263
    "Distance Education: Political
    and Professional Agency
    for Adjunct and Part-Time
    Faculty," 261–86
"Discretionary" sections. *See*
    "Release" sections

Distance education, 261–84
  as locus for change, 263,
    274–77
  for departments and
    institutions, 279–81
  for English studies
    profession, 281–83
  for individual teachers,
    277–79
  personal experiences with,
    261–62, 269–74
  problems with, 266–69
  staffing for, 262
  support structures for, 278–79
"Distance Education: Political
    and Professional Agency
    for Adjunct and Part-Time
    Faculty" (DeVoss,
    Hayden, Selfe, and Selfe),
    261–86
Du Bois, W. E. B., 13–14

Edgerton, Russell, *The Teaching
    Portfolio: Capturing the
    Scholarship of Teaching,*
    288–92, 307, 318n
Education Employment Relations
    Act (California), 210
Elder, Amy, 186
Engel, P., 264, 267
English departments, writing
    programs and, 76–77,
    110, 220
Enrollment patterns 1, 2–3, 160,
    162, 265
  forecast for, 331
  local demographics and, 199–201
  overenrollment, 236–37
Ethnic minorities, 13–14, 200–201

"Faculty at the Crossroads:
    Making the Part-Time
    Problem a Full-Time Focus"
    (Thompson), 185–95

"Faculty member as bureaucrat"
    model, 188
Faigley, Lester, 91
Flint, Calvin C., 196
Florida Gulf Coast University, 324
Finner, Steve, 185–86
Fiscal restraints, 1, 11, 110, 150,
    236
  flexibility within, 111–12
Foothill–De Anza Community
    College District, 196–216
Foster, David, 326
Foster, Edith, 326
Foster, John, 174–75
Franke, David, 38
  "The Scholarship of Teaching:
    Contributions from
    Contingent Faculty,"
    287–323
Freeway flyers, 51, 132–53, 208
  mission statements and, 133,
    135–42
  quality of teaching and, 133–35
  radical discourse and, 143–50
Freire, Paolo, 134, 142, 144,
    145, 146, 148, 152, 153n
Frye, S., 103

Gaard, Greta, 72
Gale, Xin Lu, 133, 143, 144–45
Gappa, Judith M., 3, 12, 25, 26,
    29, 40n, 167, 168, 173,
    187, 197, 201, 327
  The Invisible Faculty, 3–4,
    20–21
Giddens, A., 275
Gilman, Charlotte Perkins,
    Herland, 177
  Moving the Mountain, 1
Ginsberg, Bruce, 143
Giroux, Henry, 134, 146–47,
    153n
Gladieux, L. E., 263, 265, 266,
    274
Golden handshakes, 229

Gordon, Margaret, 40n
Grade inflation, 326
Graduate education, 3
Graff, Gerald, 165–66
Graves, Mark, 245
Greene, S., 242
Grice, H. P., 297
Griffin, Susan, 230
Gunne, G. Mary, 11

Handy, Charles, 187–88
Haraway, D., 276
Harris, J., 103
Harvard University, 240
Haught, Julie, 252, 257
Hayden, Dawn, 37–38, 263–64
    "Distance Education: Political
        and Professional Agency
        for Adjunct and Part-Time
        Faculty," 261–86
    personal experiences as
        distance educator, 261–62,
        269–74
Heidegger, Martin, 277
Heilbrun, Carolyn, 194
Herr, Kathryn, 295, 320n
Herzberg, B., 133
Higher education
    accessibility of, 174
    changes in, 1
    corporatization of, 21
    as failing business, 169
    funding cuts in, 1
    hiring trends in, 4–5
    image in media, 182
    market economy in, 172,
        173–76, 220
    need for contingent faculty in,
        2–8
Hines, Diana, 36–37
    "Same Struggle, Same Fight: A
        Case Study of University
        Students and Faculty
        United in Labor Activism,"
        233–44

Hiring trends, 4–5
    in community colleges, 196–216
    fair practices and, 18–19
    forecast for, 185–86
    job searches and, 103–4
    no hire policy and, 250
    shift to part-time faculty, 201–3
    women, 12–13
Hoeller, Keith, 337
Holzman, M., 133, 147, 148
Honan, W. H., 182
"How Did We Get in This Fix? A
        Personal Account of the
        Shift to a Part-Time
        Faculty in a Leading
        Two-Year College
        District" (Lovas), 196–217
Hull, K., 103
"Humane" lectureship. *See* P/ET
        APL position
Hutchings, Patricia, *The Teaching
        Portfolio: Capturing the
        Scholarship of Teaching*,
        288–92, 307, 318n, 319n

Institute for Higher Education
        Policy, 268, 282
Instructional quality, 325–32
    critical literacy theory and,
        133–35, 143–50
    mission statements and, 133,
        135–42
    working conditions and, 150–52
Intellectual rights, 56–57
Invisibility, of contingent faculty,
        162–66
Invisible Faculty, The (Gappa
        and Leslie), 3–4, 20–21

Jacobsohn, Walter, 35, 335
    "The Real Scandal in Higher
        Education," 159–84
Jay, Gregory, 165–66
Jewell, Richard, 31

personal experiences of, 49–60
"Shadows of the Mountain,"
47–75
Job satisfaction, 171
Job searches, 103–4
Johnson, J. W., *Autobiography of an Ex-Coloured Man,* 172

Kellams, Samuel E., 11
King, Peter, 185
Kirscht, Judith, 36, 335
"A Place to Stand: The Role of Unions in the Development of Writing Programs,"
218–32
Klein, R., 248
Knoblauch, Cy H., 133, 143, 144, 145
Kolb, Katherine, 245, 247
Kolodny, Annette, 331

Labor disputes, 225–29. *See also* Collective bargaining; Unions
students united with faculty in, 233–44
Laurence, D., 262
Layoffs, 236
Leatherman, C., 324, 337
Lecture series, 100–101
Lecturers. *See* Contingent faculty
Lentricchia, F., 91, 103
Lesko, P. D., 22, 256
Leslie, David W., 11, 12, 26, 29, 167, 168, 173, 187, 197, 201, 327
The Invisible Faculty, 3–4, 20–21
Lipson, Carol, 31, 32–33, 293, 333
"The Material and the Cultural as Interconnected Texts: Revising Material Conditions for Part-Time Faculty at Syracuse University," 107–31

Literacy discourse. *See* Critical literacy discourse
Lobel, Arnold, 47
Long Island University–Brooklyn, 161–83
Lovas, John, 36
"How Did We Get in This Fix? A Personal Account of the Shift to a Part-Time Faculty in a Leading Two-Year College District," 196–217
Lunsford, A. A., 147

MacDermid, S. M., 25
Macedo, D., 142, 146
Maid, Barry, 31, 32, 33, 333
"Non-Tenure-Track Instructors at UALR: Breaking Rules, Splitting Departments," 76–90
Market economy, 172, 173–76, 220
oversaturation of new Ph.D.'s and, 187
Martin, Michael, 36–37
"Same Struggle, Same Fight: A Case Study of University Students and Faculty United in Labor Activism," 233–44
"Material and the Cultural as Interconnected Texts: Revising Material Conditions for Part-Time Faculty at Syracuse University, The" (Lipson and Voorheis), 107–31
Material conditions. *See* Working conditions
McClelland, Ben W., 95, 98, 99–102, 104
McVay, Chris, 22, 168
Merit tier system, 114–15, 127
problems with, 115–18

sample policy for, 129–30
Michigan Technological University, 261–64, 269–74
Miller, D. Sharon, 197–98, 201–2
Miller, Richard E., 29, 188
Mission statements, contradictions in, 133, 135–42
Modern Language Association (MLA), 17, 18, 51, 281
Moglen, H., 147
Morrison, Toni, 177

National Council of Teachers of English (NCTE), 281
Nelson, Cary, 21–22, 25, 151, 173, 179, 247, 257n
NNTR (non-tenure-track renewable), 51, 74n
Non-tenure-track faculty. *See* Contingent faculty
"Non-Tenure-Track Instructors at UALR: Breaking Rules, Splitting Departments" (Maid) 76–90
North, Stephen M., 317, 320n
Nystrand, Martin, 242

O'Donnell, J., 273
Odyssey Project (Syracuse University), 297–308, 320n
O'Grady, Helen, 33–34, 333
"Trafficking in Freeway Flyers: (Re)Viewing Literacy, Working Conditions, and Quality Instruction," 132–55
Ohmann, Richard, 145–46
Open University (United Kingdom), 267–68
Outsourcing model, 187
Overenrollment, 236–37

Part-time faculty. *See* Contingent faculty
Peer evaluation, 118–20
sample policy for, 131
teaching portfolio and, 289, 293
Peled, Elana, 36–37
"Same Struggle, Same Fight: A Case Study of University Students and Faculty United in Labor Activism," 233–44
Pelias, Michael, unionization efforts of, 162–66, 167, 182
Peralta Decision (California), 207
Perley, James, 26–27, 337
P/ET APL (probationary to extended term academic professional lecturer) position, 32, 91–105
creation of, 93
criteria for, 93–94
improvements accompanying, 94–95
status of, 96–99
Phelps, Louise, 111, 114, 319n
Pinarski, Annmarie, 252
"Place to Stand: The Role of Unions in the Development of Writing Programs" (Tingle and Kirscht), 218–32
Policymakers. *See* Administrators and policymakers
Political identity, of contingent faculty, 169–73
Pratt, Linda Ray, 22, 27, 176–77
Pro rata compensation, 190–91
Professional development, 54, 82, 94–95, 98, 112–13
Proposition 209 (California), 238

Quinlan, Kathleen, *The Teaching Portfolio: Capturing the Scholarship of Teaching,* 288–92, 307, 318n

Radical literacy discourse. *See* Critical literacy discourse
"Real Scandal in Higher Education, The" (Jacobsohn), 159–184
Reflective essay, 293, 294–97, 334
  of Amanda Brown, 297–308
  function of, 296–97
  genres included in, 296
  of John Starkweather, 308–16
"Release" sections, 111–12
Reverand, C., 101
Rhoades, Gary, 149, 151
Rice, R. Eugene, 23–24, 317n
Rich, Adrienne, 256
Robertson, L., 91, 103
Rodrigues, D., 273
Ronald, Ann, 95, 103, 105
Rorty, Richard, 296
Royster, Jacqueline Jones, 13–14
Rumberger, Margaret, 11–12
Rutgers University, 192–93
Rutz, C., 61

Sabbaticals, 97
Salary, 54–55, 57, 58, 81, 93, 110, 115, 330, 332–33
  bargaining for, 204–6, 210–16
"Same Struggle, Same Fight: A Case Study of University Students and Faculty United in Labor Activism" (Peled, Hines, Martin, Stafford, Strang, Winegarden, and Wise), 233–44
San Francisco State University, 36–37, 233–44

San Jose State University, 198
Santa Clara County, demographics of, 199–201
Schell, Eileen E., 7, 38–39, 40n, 145, 150, 152n
  "What's the Bottom Line? Literacy and Quality Education in the Twenty-First Century," 324–40
  "Working Contingent Faculty In[to] Higher Education," 1–44
Scholarship of teaching, 287–321
  contingent faculty contribution to, 297–317
  redefining, 287–88
  reflective essays, 294–316
  teaching portfolio as evidence of, 289–92
"Scholarship of Teaching: Contributions from Contingent Faculty, The" (Stock, Brown, Franke, and Starkweather), 287–323
Scholarship Reconsidered: Priorities of the Professoriate (Boyer), 287–88, 289
Schuster, J. H., 2, 4, 5, 10, 197
Search committees, 110
Seldin, Peter, 289
Selfe, Cynthia L., 37–38, 264
  "Distance Education: Political and Professional Agency for Adjunct and Part-Time Faculty," 261–86
Selfe, Richard J., Jr., 37–38, 263, 264, 265, 266, 267, 268
  "Distance Education: Political and Professional Agency for Adjunct and Part-Time Faculty," 261–86
Self-terminating contracts, 221
75–25 law (California), 213–14
"Shadows of the Mountain"(Anson and Jewell), 47–75

"Shamrock" model, 187–88
Sherron, G. T., 263, 274
Shor, I., 133, 134, 153n
Shore, B. M., 318n
Shulman, Lee, 288–89, 294, 307, 318n, 320n
Shumar, Wesley, 170–71, 172, 173
Slevin, James F., 102, 135, 147
Snyder, T. D., 265
Social Darwinism, 66
Staffing, 20, 249–50
    in community colleges, 197–98
    for distance education courses, 262
    flexibility in, 2–4
    trends in, 4
Stafford, Anne, 36–37
    "Same Struggle, Same Fight: A Case Study of University Students and Faculty United in Labor Activism," 233–44
Stanford University, 198
Starkweather, John, 38
    reflective essay of, 308–16
    "The Scholarship of Teaching: Contributions from Contingent Faculty," 287–323
"Statement from the Conference on the Growing Use of Part-Time and Adjunct Faculty," 72–73
"Statement of Principles and Standards for Postsecondary Teaching of Writing" (CCCC), 18, 135–37, 281, 331
St. Cloud State University, 48, 49–56
Steering committees, 245–58
    accomplishments of, 250–53, 254–55
    as ad hoc union, 245
    barriers to, 247–48

goals of, 248, 253
membership of, 246
need for, 247
recognition of, 252
Stock, Patricia Lambert, 7, 38, 118, 262, 263, 334
    "The Scholarship of Teaching: Contributions from Contingent Faculty," 287–323
    "Working Contingent Faculty In[to] Higher Education," 1–44
Strang, Brian, 36–37
    "Same Struggle, Same Fight: A Case Study of University Students and Faculty United in Labor Activism," 233–44
Strikes, 175, 177, 185
Stuckey, J. Elspeth, 147, 148, 153n
Students
    contextualizing experiences of, 143–50
    demographics on, 265
    involvement in labor disputes, 233–44
Student-to teacher ratios, 136–40, 281–82
Subcontracting. *See* Outsourcing model
Supply and demand, 187
Swail, W. S., 263, 265, 266, 274
Sykes, Charles, 23, 317n
Syracuse University, 32–33, 107–31, 292–316

Teaching culture, 120–26
    improving, 120–22
    problems with, 122–26
    resistance to change in, 123–25
Teaching load. *See* Course load
Teaching portfolio, 289–92
    composition of, 293–94

as document of discovery, 291
focus of, 290
public access to, 294
reflective essays in, 293, 294–316
as requirement for review, 289,
    293
unfulfilled potential of, 291–92
Team-teaching, 100
Technical writing, 86, 94, 95
Technology
    impact on composition studies,
        264–65
    inequitable distribution of
        resources, 266–67
Tenure, erosion of, 6, 18
Tenure-track faculty
    as bureaucrats, 188
    collegiality with contingent
        faculty, 192–93
    crisis in higher education and,
        176–80
    declines in, 2
    dissatisfaction of, 108
    as endangered species, 186
    graduate education and, 3
    hiring trends for, 4–5
    responsibility of, 189–90
Thompson, Karen, 22, 27, 35–36,
    335, 336
    "Faculty at the Crossroads:
        Making the Part-Time
        Problem a Full-Time
        Focus," 185–95
Tingle, Nick, 36, 335
    "A Place to Stand: The Role of
        Unions in the Development
        of Writing Programs,"
        218–32
Tobias, Sheila, 11–12
Total Quality Management
    (TQM), 188
"Trafficking in Freeway Flyers:
    (Re)Viewing Literacy,
    Working Conditions, and
    Quality Instruction"
    (O'Grady), 132–55

Traub, James, 188
Trimbur, J., 8, 133, 147
Tuckman, Barbara, 12–13
Tuckman, Howard P., 9, 10,
    12–13
Tyner, Tom, 214

Unions, 162–66, 199. *See also*
    Coalition building
    call for, 247
    collective bargaining and,
        210–16
    determining number of
        members, 162–63
    establishing, 108, 163–66,
        208–9
    lessons learned from, 220
    local executive boards, 218–31
    obstacles to, 164–65
    role of, 165–66, 218–31
University Council of the
    American Federation of
    Teachers (UC-AFT) (Santa
    Barbara), 218–31
University of Arkansas at Little
    Rock, 32, 76–90
University of California at Santa
    Barbara, 36, 218–31
University of Minnesota, 48, 49,
    59–74
University of Phoenix, 187, 188
University of Santa Clara, 198
University of Wyoming, 32,
    91–105
UPS Teamsters, 185, 191–92,
    193, 194

Van Vorhis, Andrea, 251, 255
Vietnamese American students,
    200–1
Virtual universities, 266
Vogler, William D., 9, 10
Voorheis, Molly, 31, 32–33, 293,
    333

"The Material and the Cultural as Interconnected Texts: Revising Material Conditions for Part-Time Faculty at Syracuse University," 107–31
Voting privileges, 97

Wallace, M. Elizabeth, 14, 30
Weber, Max, 223
"What's the Bottom Line? Literacy and Quality Education in the Twenty-First Century" (Schell), 324–40
Wiemelt, J., 242
Williams, Jean C., 13–14
Wilson, John K., 13
Winegarden, Mary, 36–37
    "Same Struggle, Same Fight: A Case Study of University Students and Faculty United in Labor Activism," 233–44
Winton Act (California), 210
Wise, Melanie, 36–37
    "Same Struggle, Same Fight: A Case Study of University Students and Faculty United in Labor Activism," 233–44
Women, 12–13, 168, 328
    as majority of contingent faculty, 166–67
    psychic reward myth and, 145, 328
Woolfson, Charles, 174–75
Working conditions, 3–5, 159–60, 334–35. *See also* Benefits; Course load; Professional development; Salary
    critical literacy theory and, 146–50

external evaluation of, 108–9
historical perspective on, 330
improvements in, 94–95, 107–31
    impetus for, 108–10
    leadership roles, 110–11
    merit tier system, 114–18
    peer evaluation, 118–20
    representation, 112–13
opinions about, 48
origins of, 240
quality of instruction and, 131–53
teaching culture and, 120–26
"Working Contingent Faculty In[to] Higher Education" (Schell and Stock), 1–44
Writing programs. *See also* Composition studies
    autonomy of, 227–28
    creation of, as separate unit, 84–90, 107
    distance education and, 274–83
    English departments and, 76–77, 99–105, 110, 225
    external evaluations of, 108–9
    politics of teaching in, 239–44
    resistance to change in, 123–25
    role of unions in, 218–31
    scholarship of teaching and, 287–321
    teaching culture in, 120–26
    teaching of literature and, 96
    teaching portfolios and, 292
Wyoming Conference Resolution, 18, 19, 91, 108, 331

Yale University, 245, 247, 257n
Yang, Shu, 12

Zak, Michele W., 12

EDITORS

Eileen E. Schell is assistant professor of writing and rhetoric at Syracuse University, where she teaches first-year composition, advanced composition, and graduate courses in composition and the history of rhetoric. She was formerly co-director of the first-year composition program at Virginia Tech and adjunct instructor of writing at North Seattle Community College. Her first book was *Gypsy Academics and Mother-Teachers: Gender, Contingent Labor, and Writing Instruction*. She is co-chair of the CCCC's Taskforce on Part-Time and Adjunct Faculty.

Patricia Lambert Stock is professor of English and director of the writing center at Michigan State University. She served as the first associate executive director of the National Council of Teachers of English with special responsibilities for issues in higher education and has written articles on the scholarship of teaching, teacher research, inquiry-based literacy instruction, writing center theory and practice, and the politics of literacy instruction and assessment. Her books include *fforum: Essays on Theory and Practice in the Teaching of Writing* (1983) and *The Dialogic Curriculum* (1995), which received the Richard A. Meade Award.

CONTRIBUTORS

Chris M. Anson was previously professor of English and Morse-Alumni Distinguished Teaching Professor at the University of Minnesota, where he directed the composition program from 1988 to 1996. He is now professor and director of the Campus Writing and Speaking Program at North Carolina State University. A former co-chair of the CCCC Committee on Professional Standards for the Teaching of Writing, he is a strong advocate of improved working conditions for all composition teachers.

Debra A. Benko was a full-time instructor at Bowling Green State University (Ohio) during the 1998–99 academic year. She is completing her dissertation on the critical reception of regional writers Alice Cary, Sarah Orne Jewett, Alice Dunbar-Nelson, and Willa Cather. She hopes one day to see adjuncts organize all across the country.

Amanda Brown is a senior part-time instructor at Syracuse University. She teaches a variety of undergraduate writing studios and is currently focusing on teaching composition to nontraditional undergraduate students. She completed a doctoral degree in May 1999. Her dissertation was entitled "Practitioners' Understanding of Teaching College Composition."

Eva Brumberger is an academic professional lecturer (APL) in the University of Wyoming's English department, where she teaches writing courses. Her previous experience includes adjunct teaching at three institutions and working as a technical writer. She is currently on a leave of absence in order to pursue a doctorate in rhetoric and professional communication at New Mexico State University.

Margaret M. Cunniffe is lecturer in American thought and language at Michigan State University. She is completing a doctoral dissertation on Joyce Marshall the feminist Canadian writer of novels, short stories, and works of nonfiction.

Danielle DeVoss is a doctoral student in the rhetoric and technical communication program at Michigan Technological University. Her work has most recently appeared in the *Writing Center Journal*. Her research interests include women's interactions with and resistances to computer technologies, computer-related literacies, and the performance of gender in online realms.

David Franke earned his Ph.D. in composition and cultural rhetoric in June 1999 from Syracuse University, where he worked as a non-tenure-track composition teacher for a number of years. His dissertation "The Practice of Genre: Writing (in) a Reflective Community" studies the teacher-researcher community of non-tenure-track teachers at Syracuse. His areas of research include the scholarship of teaching, genre studies, and rhetorical theory. In fall 1999, he began work as assistant professor of English at the State University of New York, Cortland.

Dawn Hayden has worked as an adjunct English instructor since 1995. She has taught computer-assisted developmental writing courses, literature, advanced composition, and most recently, advanced composition via distant education. Last year she served as the assistant Web editor for a joint endeavor between NASA Technological Briefs and Michigan Technological University, where she is currently a graduate student working on her Ph.D.

Walter Jacobsohn has taught in a variety of universities in the New York metropolitan area. He is currently an independent scholar and writer who lives and works in New Jersey.

Richard Jewell is a full-time writing specialist at the University of Minnesota, Twin Cities, where he teaches upper-division writing and is the composition Web master. He has three master's degrees and has taught in adjunct positions in two- and four-year colleges and at St. Cloud State University.

Judy Kirscht (MA, MFA, University of Michigan) taught composition at the University of Michigan English Composition Board from 1979 to 1986, when she moved to University of California, Santa Barbara; she held several positions on the local and state UC-AFT Boards, including local president and UC-Council southern vice president and bargaining team member. She has published articles in composition journals and is currently director of the UCSB Writing Program.

Carol Lipson is associate professor of writing and English at Syracuse University, with considerable administrative experience in both the English department and the writing program. Her research interests currently involve study of the rhetoric of Ancient Egypt and also study of the rhetoric of sixteenth- and seventh-century anatomical writing.

John C. Lovas has taught composition and literature for thirty-four years, the first twelve at Foothill College and the last twenty-two at De Anza College. He has been active in campus governance through both the faculty union and the faculty senate, as well as serving as dean of language arts for nine years. In 1998, he served as chair of the Two-Year College English Association of the National Council of Teachers of English.

Barry M. Maid was professor of rhetoric and writing at the University of Arkansas at Little Rock (UALR) and is now professor and head faculty of technical communication at Arizona State University East in Mesa. In addition to teaching, he has been director of freshman composition and chair of the Department of English at UALR. His current professional interests are technical communication, program administration, personality theory, and computer-mediated communication.

Helen O'Grady is a Ph.D. candidate in rhetoric and composition at the University of Rhode Island. This chapter draws on her dissertation, titled "Part-timers: Deliberating the Contradictions." Her interests focus on critical literacy, portfolio evaluation, and rhetorical/literary theory intersections. She also teaches writing part time at various colleges and universities in Rhode Island.

Elana Peled, Diana Hines, Michael John Martin, Anne Stafford, Brian Strang, Mary Winegarden, and **Melanie Wise** were colleagues together at San Francisco State University in the fall of 1996. All have Masters degrees in English and formal training in teaching composition. Together, they weathered a frontal assault on their discipline, which, since the victory described in their article, has not been repeated at this university. In their current work, each maintains a commitment to the ideals expressed in this article: access to affordable higher education for all students, adequate provision of courses that meet the needs of students accepted into institutions of higher education, and fair employment practices including equitable pay, benefits and working conditions for all those committed to providing quality education in American schools and colleges.

Cynthia L. Selfe is professor of humanities at Michigan Technological University, and founder (with Kathleen Kiefer) and co-editor (with Gail Hawisher) of *Computers and Composition: An International Journal for Teachers of Writing.* Selfe has served as the Chair of the CCCC, Chair of the College Section of the NCTE, and Chair of NCTE's Assembly of Computers in English and Instructional Technology Committee. In 1995, Selfe was awarded the EDUCOM Medal for innovative computer use in higher education—the first woman and the first English teacher ever to receive this award. Selfe has authored and edited books, journal articles, and book chapters on computer use in composition classrooms.

Richard J. Selfe directs the Center for Computer-Assisted Language Instruction, a communication-oriented computer facility at Michigan Technological University. He teaches computer-intensive first-year English, technical communication, and graduate computer studies courses. His interests lie in communication pedagogy as well as the social/institutional influences of electronic media on our culture and that pedagogy.

John Starkweather is assistant professor of English at the Onondaga Community College in Syracuse, New York, where he teaches literature and writing. He is also a long-term professional writing instructor at Syracuse University. He teaches a wide variety of courses and specializes in working with basic writers, adult learners, and those with learning disabilities.

Karen Thompson teaches in the English Department's Writing Program at Rutgers University. During her 20 years there, she has helped to organize an independent union of part-time lecturers affiliated with the AAUP and to lead the negotiation of two collective bargaining agreements for the PTL unit. She also currently chairs the national AAUP's Committee G on Part-Time and Non-Tenure-Track Appointments and co-chairs the CCCC's Taskforce on Part-Time and Adjunct Faculty.

Nicholas Tingle has taught in the University of California–Santa Barbara Writing Program since 1980. He was founding member of Local 2141 and has been a dues paying member of the UC/AFT Unit 18 since 1985.

Molly Voorheis has been a professional writing instructor at Syracuse University since 1983. She teaches workplace and technical writing courses, and team-teaches in a writing-across-the-curriculum Gateway course in Syracuse University's Maxwell School. She also directs the Writers' Guild, a group for at-risk students who want to develop their writing skills.

This book was typeset in Adobe Sabon by Electronic Imaging.
Typefaces used on the cover were Futura, ITC Fenice, and Optima.
The book was printed on 50-lb. Husky Offset
by IPC Communication Services.